THE PERGAMON ENGLISH LIBRARY

EDITORIAL DIRECTORS: GEORGE ALLEN AND BORIS FORD
EXECUTIVE EDITOR: ESMOR JONES

HUMAN HOPE
AND THE
DEATH INSTINCT

By the same author

POETRY

Imaginings	Putnam, 1961
Against the Cruel Frost	Putnam, 1963
Object Relations	Methuen, 1967
Old World, New World	Rapp & Whiting, 1969

FICTION

Lights in the Sky Country	Putnam, 1962
Flesh Wounds	Methuen, 1966

CRITICISM

Llareggub Revisited	Bowes & Bowes, 1962
The Quest for Love	Methuen, 1965
The Masks of Hate	Pergamon Press, 1971

ON EDUCATION

English for Maturity	Cambridge, 1961
English for the Rejected	Cambridge, 1964
The Secret Places	Methuen, 1964
The Exploring Word	Cambridge, 1967
Children's Writing	Cambridge, 1967

HUMAN HOPE
AND THE
DEATH INSTINCT

AN EXPLORATION OF PSYCHOANALYTICAL THEORIES
OF HUMAN NATURE
AND THEIR IMPLICATIONS FOR
CULTURE AND EDUCATION

DAVID HOLBROOK, M.A.

Sometime Fellow of King's College, Cambridge

PERGAMON PRESS

OXFORD · NEW YORK · TORONTO
SYDNEY · BRAUNSCHWEIG

PERGAMON PRESS LTD.

OXFORD   NEW YORK

TORONTO   SYDNEY   BRAUNSCHWEIG

First edition 1971

Library of Congress Catalog Card No. 72–130367

Printed in Great Britain by A. Wheaton & Co., Exeter

008 015798 X 471

Contents

Part V Psychoanalysis and Existentialism

Part VI   Conclusions

For
Cambridge

Ce qu'on peut dire, c'est que tout se passe dans notre vie comme si nous y entrions avec le faix d'obligations contractées dans une vie antérieure; il n'y a aucune raison dans nos conditions de vie sur cette terre pour que nous nous croyions obligés à faire le bien, à être délicats, même à être polis, ni pour l'artiste athée à ce qu'il croie obligé de recommencer vingt fois un morceau dont l'admiration qu'il excitera importera peu à son corps mangé par les vers, comme le pan de mur jaune que peignit avec tant de science et de raffinement un artiste à jamais inconnu, à peine identifié sous le nom de Ver Meer. Toutes ces obligations, qui n'ont pas leur sanction dans la vie présente, semblent appartenir à un monde différent, fondé sur la bonté, le scrupule, le sacrifice, un monde entièrement différent de celui-ci, et dont nous sortons pour naître à cette terre, avant peut-être d'y retourner revivre sous l'empire de ces lois inconnues auxquelles nous avons obéi parce que nous en portions l'enseignement en nous, sans savoir qui les y avait tracées ces lois dont tout travail profond de l'intelligence nous rapproche et qui sont invisibles seulement et encore! pour les sots.

(PROUST, *La Prisonnière*)

The preliminary investigations which led to this book were made possible by the grant to the author of a Leverhulme Senior Research Fellowship in 1964–5.

Excerpts have already been published as follows: 'Non-psychological Psychology' in *The Cambridge Review*; 'Society and Our Instincts', in *Universities Quarterly*; 'Education, Culture and Moral Growth' in *The Journal of Moral Education*; and 'Is R. D. Laing an Existentialist?' in *Encounter* and *Twentieth Century*.

I am grateful to Mr. Tom Deveson for help with the final editing of this work.

Acknowledgements

For permission to use copyright material acknowledgement is made to the following: Associated Book Publishers (International) Ltd. for quotations from D. W. Winnicott, *Collected Papers*, published by Tavistock Publications Ltd.; Baillière, Tindall and Cassell Ltd. and the *International Journal of Psychoanalysis* for quotations from *The Manic Depressive Problem in the light of the Schizoid Process* by H. Guntrip and from *On the Nature and Aims of Psychoanalytical Treatment* by W. R. D. Fairbairn; Basil Blackwell for quotations from *Philosophy and Psychoanalysis* by John Wisdom; The *British Journal of Medical Psychology* for quotations from *A Study of Fairbairn's Theory of Schizoid Reactions* by H. Guntrip; Cambridge University Press and Open Court Illinois for quotations from *The Philosophy of Martin Buber* (edited Paul Arthur Schillp and Maurice Friedman); Constable and Co. Ltd. and Coward McCann for an extract from a contribution by Peter Lomas from *Psychoanalysis Observed* edited by C. Rycroft; Constable and Co. Ltd. and Basic Books Inc. for quotations from *The Ways of the Will* by L. H. Farber; The Garnstone Press for quotations from *Naked Ape and Homo Sapiens* by B. Towers and J. Lewis; William Heinemann Medical Books Ltd. for quotations from *Introduction to the Work of Melanie Klein* by H. Segal and from *Our Adult Society and Its Roots in Infancy* by M. Klein; The Hogarth Press Ltd. for quotations from *Personality Structure and Human Interaction*; The Hogarth Press and Basic Books Inc. for quotations from *Schizoid Phenomena, Object-Relations and the Self* by H. Guntrip; The Melanie Klein Trustees and the Hogarth Press Ltd. for quotations from *Love, Hate and Reparation* by M. Klein; The literary estate of Dr. D. W. Winnicott, the Hogarth Press Ltd., and the International Universities Press of New York for quotations from *The Maturational Process and the Facilitating Environment*; Laurence Pollinger Ltd. and the estate of the late Mrs. Frieda Lawrence (also reprinted by permission of the Viking Press Inc.) for a quotation from *Manifesto* from the *Complete Poems of D. H. Lawrence* edited by Vivian de Sola Pinto and F. Warren Roberts, copyright 1923, renewed 1951 by Frieda Lawrence and published by William Heinemann and the Viking Press Inc.; Penguin Books Ltd. for quotations from R. D. Laing, *The Politics of Experience*, copyright © R. D. Laing, 1967; Routledge and Kegan Paul Ltd. and Basic Books Inc. for quotations from *The Origins of Love and Hate* (1935) by Ian D. Suttie (also acknowledged Penguin Books) and *Psychoanalytical Studies of the Personality* by W. R. D. Fairbairn.

Every effort has been made to trace owners of copyright material but in some cases this has not proved possible. The publishers would be glad to hear from further owners of copyright material reproduced in *Human Hope and the Death Instinct*.

Introduction

A WRITER must make his mind up about human nature. The question I explore in this book is whether I believe that human life can have a future. Perhaps all I arrive at in the end is a way of looking at this problem But in the course of my explorations I hope to introduce the reader to some fresh sources of insight into the nature of human nature, coming to us from psychotherapy.

Implicit in these theories there seems to me an emerging hope that man can survive, however timidly one is bound to make this assertion nowadays.

The belief that we may be able to escape from our own destructiveness, which I believe can be found in the interpersonal psychology of the object-relations 'school', is grounded in concepts of the nature of human nature very different from psychological notions prevalent in popular thought, as will appear. What emerges from this 'philosophical anthropology' is radically different from the attitudes to man in traditional Freudian theory. But I found in object-relations theories a realism which as poet and educationist I was looking for. In my work with children as a teacher I developed a belief in individual capacities to develop towards integration and maturity. I recognised these energies as 'human facts' because I knew from experience that such positive dynamics emerge in children where they were given the right kind of opportunity to grow through creativity. They did grow, as human beings, with astonishing vitality. Yet what I learned from them seemed irreconcilable with popular, and even 'serious', attitudes to human nature around me – until I came upon the writers discussed in this book.

From my experience of children's creativity I not only derived great satisfactions myself of a kind that enriched my own life, but I was also fascinated by the qualities of humanness I found, not least in the most immature and handicapped child. I took this feeling back with me to my desk, and tried to let it guide both my criticism and my creative writing in that more isolated work. In my creative writing I sought to capture the problems of finding a sense of meaning in the small and undramatic moments of my own normal 'peace-time' life. Meanwhile in a novel about war I sought to delineate my own first-hand experience of the worst that hate could do, meaning this as a contribution to those insights which may help us survive. In all this work I felt that it was urgent to try to contribute to the possibility of human survival, and to the capacity in us to discriminate between true and false solutions to the problems of identity, and to the problem of finding a meaning in life. When I wrote about these things I found myself saying that what we must do above all is to accept that we were human with human needs. But what did this mean?

Inevitably this raised questions of what one believed about the structure of human make-up. I was assuming, for one thing, that the emotions could be educated and that there was a value in this. Was I right? Are there innate elements in human nature which can never be modified and are thus inaccessible to education? A hopelessness about human betterment seemed to be growing among 'progressive' people. Was my belief in education naïve and foolish in the face of the 'grim realities' of human make-up offered by pessimistic commentators whose views have become so influential in the sixties?

Those who are dealing with children daily, in school, in child-care work, or family case-work, psychotherapy or counselling, imply by their efforts that it is worth trying to contribute to human development. In such work they assume that we are contributing to individual goodness and thus, indirectly, to the good of society. Then, perhaps, after a day's work at a clinic or school, the teacher or social worker goes to the theatre and sees an *avant-garde* play, reads the *International Times*, or Desmond Morris's *Naked Ape*. In these he finds implicit views of human nature which are not only totally at odds with his own – but which may imply that all his day-time effort is futile and meaningless. How much is he aware of this? How much have we examined this dichotomy?

The strange thing is that more often than not we do not seem to be aware of it. Even if we do see that what we do and what we think are irreconcilable, we will often in theory take recourse to the theories of Freud or the animal behaviourists, believing that, by contrast with our views, these are based on 'objective realism'. 'Science' seems to tell us that what is 'real' about us are our 'instincts', or some impersonal drive like the 'id'. Yet, of course, we have not escaped our dilemma, because although the attitudes of Morris or Freud seem to bear out the implications of the *avant-garde* dramatist, neither seems to confirm what we feel and know to be true from our knowledge of children, our inward life, or our own relational and social experience. Yet perhaps we do not know where else to turn for truth, or even how to begin to pursue the question further.

We may feel that we have nothing in common with Freud's social attitudes, such as his remarks, for instance, that 'masses are lazy and unintelligent: they have no love for instinctual renunciation . . . the individuals composing them support one another in giving free rein to their indiscipline' (*The Future of an Illusion*, Freud [34]*).

Yet we may feel bound to endorse the prevalent attitude of enlightened commentators in the world of, say, film reviewing or popular journalism on sex and morality, who believe with Freud that there is a need 'to lessen the burden of the instinctual sacrifices imposed on men'. 'Release' may seem to us the only way to save us from repression and from hypocrisy. Indeed, we may feel such 'freedom' alone can liberate us from 'bourgeois morality'.

We may, however, have doubts about R. D. Laing's point of view that, in consequence of the inimical effects of a 'senescent capitalism', art must be 'insurrection' (Laing [53]). Is what our children do in school, when they create, 'insurrection' – or something more integrative and constructive? If art is 'insurrection', how justified are we in promoting creativity in education, or therapy, as a means to personal growth, so that individuals may 'contribute in' to society? Is this work perhaps merely promoting the 'adaptation' of individuals to society? If so, is this to 'sacrifice' them to 'alienation'? How many of us have really examined these questions?

I certainly felt happier when I came upon the work of the paediatrician D. W. Winnicott, who immediately struck me as being on my own wavelength, perhaps because I am dealing with children too. Here, for instance, Winnicott is writing for mothers:

* Numbers in square brackets given after authors' names refer to the bibliography on p. 303.

Devotion to one child is the greatest strain of all, and it is a good job it only lasts for a while. . . . So here you are with all your eggs in one basket. What are you going to do about it? Well, enjoy yourself! Enjoy being thought important. Enjoy letting other people look after the world while you are producing a new one of its members. Enjoy being turned-in and almost in love with yourself, the baby is so nearly part of you. Enjoy the way in which your man feels responsible for the welfare of you and your baby. Enjoy finding out new things about yourself. (Winnicott [95], p. 26.)

I do not have to emphasise that Winnicott's tone here shows that he belongs to a world in which I feel at home. I could link his approach with what I am trying to do in my own work. It is a passage which one could usefully discuss with students alongside passages in D. H. Lawrence's *The Rainbow* or Tolstoy's *War and Peace* in order to promote discussions of the origins of identity in mother–child relationship. Yet Winnicott is a Freudian psychoanalyst, however far his tone seems from the severe and sometimes negative tone of Freud's clinical and theoretical writings.

His tone is even further from the prevalent tone of our fashionable literary culture (compare *Last Exit to Brooklyn, The Beard*, Genet, Sartre, Violette le Duc, *Fucknam*, Montherlant, *The Naked Ape*). The prevalent emphasis in this culture is on disgust, violence, hatred, hatred of woman especially, and conviction of our 'animality'. It is different again from that of the theorists of 'enlightenment'. Who, then, speaks best for man and his realisation? In his *The Politics of Experience* Laing pays tribute to Winnicott among others. But Laing takes a very different view when he says himself: 'The Family's function is to suppress Eros. . . . Long before a thermonuclear war can come about, we have had to lay waste our own sanity. We begin with the children. It is imperative to catch them in time. Without the most thorough brain-washing their dirty minds would see through our dirty tricks.' Laing quotes Sartre, in a passage we can compare with that of Winnicott above: 'Take a living child, sew him up in a dead man's skin, and he will stifle in such senile childhood with no occupation save to reproduce the avuncular gestures, with no hope but to poison future childhoods after his own death' (Sartre, Foreword to *The Traitor* by André Gorz, quoted by Laing [53], p. 56).

This brief quotation alone is sufficient to indicate a whole school of attitudes utterly at odds with ours in education. The book from which this excerpt comes was published by John Calder, the publisher of *Last Exit to Brooklyn*. Calder believes that we need to read more about violence in order to become able to understand and 'control' violence. His view would be endorsed by Susan Sontag, who is one of the proselytes of a 'new sensibility'. She urges, for the sake of the world, 'more violence' in expression, to 'release' man's 'sensuality' – because his sensuality has been crushed by the dominance of intellectual deadness and 'bourgeois' morality, to the 'devastation' of his powers. Calder believes we must know more about violence, etc., in order to learn to control it. This is only to indicate some of the assumptions of the world of fashionable *avant-garde* culture – the world of the Anti-university, the 'underground', the P.E.N. conference, and the way-out theatre, from the National Theatre in England to the 'happenings' invented by Alan Kaprow in America. To this we must add the ethos of the journalistic world which has so enthusiastically endorsed the work of Desmond Morris, Robert Ardrey, and Konrad Lorenz and which endorses 'frankness' about the 'human zoo'. Perhaps most people now quite seriously believe with Freud that 'men are not gentle kindly creatures', but brutes, and that there is 'scientific' evidence for this view.

There would seem to be no reconciliation between Winnicott's attitude to the role of the mother and the family and the growth of human qualities in the child, with all its cultural implications, and, say, the rejection of a belief in human goodness and 'idealism' in a playwright such as Harold Pinter. The teacher concerned with the humanities may enjoy a culture which rejects both the family and society, as instruments of 'violence' and 'absurdity'. Our imaginary teacher, leaving his classroom for the theatre, passes from one world of thought to another which is irreconcilable with it. Does he see 'adult' sex in the cinema as the expression of a new realism? Or does he say to himself, with Viktor E. Frankl, 'Sexual libido most often becomes rampant in an existential vacuum'? Ought we not to make up our minds which attitude to human nature – the family, the individual and society, is more true to experience – and which is more real and relevant to the problems of human survival?

PART I

What is Man?

CHAPTER 1

What is Real?

THE purpose of the present work is to introduce those concerned with education and social work, culture, symbolism, and other subjective disciplines to some recent psycho-analytical theories. It is obvious that some regard this concern of mine as 'inadequate', or suspect on some such grounds as that these theories must be based on 'abnormalities'. Others, like social scientists, may feel that they are based on nothing better than con-jecture, 'playing with words', 'vagueness', or 'verbosity'.* If the reader goes to a library he may find the books I refer to under the label of 'abnormal psychology'. Or they may not be there at all. Indeed, at the time of writing I am trying to find whether my students can obtain the books I would like them to read from the Psychology Library of the University of Cambridge. There is a separate part of this library (the MacCurdy Library) devoted to abnormal and developmental psychology and psychiatry: most of the facilities are devoted to experimental and physiological psychology. This library contains a few books by Freud, Melanie Klein, and Ernest Jones. On its shelves is Ian D. Suttie's *The Origins of Love and Hate* but not Freud's *Collected Papers*. There are no books by John Bowlby, Erik Erikson, Harry Guntrip, R. D. Laing, J. D. Sutherland, or D. W. Winnicott. There was not even a copy of *Philosophy and Psychoanalysis*, even though this was written by the Professor of Philosophy in the same university. The librarian cannot understand why I think the work of Martin Buber or Soren Kierkegaard should be in the Psychology Library. (Some faculty libraries did not reply to my inquiry at all.)

Obviously, in the background here are assumptions about *what is real* and *by what methods an account of reality may be given*. These questions will be re-opened with the inten-tion of trying to give those concerned with subjective disciplines a new confidence. As will be explained in the next chapter, I am seeking to foster recognition of psycho-analytical psychology as a form of 'philosophical anthropology'. A corollary to this is an implication (taken from Guntrip, who takes it in turn from a Behaviourist Scientist, C. Taylor) that the kind of psychology for which most of the material in such a psychological library as that at Cambridge provides is 'non-psychological psychology'.

In this book I shall try to interest the reader in that psychology which tries to answer the philosophical question What is man? I believe that there are valuable answers coming from psychoanalysis because those therapists who contribute to its theories are now accepting psychotic patients – patients who have no human identity. These must

---

* Guntrip says: 'Many scientifically trained people seem reluctant to recognise psychic reality as a fact. . . . Mayer-Gross, Slater and Roth say that, "psychiatric literature . . . owes its existence to the possi-bility of playing with words and concepts and the scientific worker in psychiatry must continually bear in mind the risks of vagueness and verbosity" ' (*Clinical Psychiatry*, Guntrip [38], p. 371).

find their humanness or perish. Confronted with such individuals, the therapist must needs find real answers. In such a situation there can be no place for insincerity, and so, from psychotherapy, as I believe, there is emerging a new and profound awareness of what man really is – and a method of exploring this reality. To my satisfaction, this method is essentially a poetic, intuitive, 'female' one (the significance of the last term will become evident as we go on).

Certainly it helps us to take the first step in examining our prevalent present-day assumptions about what is real about man. Here I am, of course, referring to the assumption that what is most real about man is his aggression. This assumption appears in many forms, as we shall see, and it is the cause of our argument – for it raises the problem of the degree to which we are responsible for our hate and destructiveness. Shall we attribute these to a 'death instinct' – and so no longer bear the burden of them?

Hate and destructiveness are undeniable realities of human life, not least of our era. Our diagnosis of the origins of these is surely bound up with the problem of whether we can believe that man has a future. Those who believe that hate and aggression arise from primary realities in human make-up must obviously feel hopeless about our future or, at most, resigned. If, as Freud thought, our hate is the expression of a death instinct, then attempts to improve civilisation and foster the healthy socialisation of man are doomed to frustration. If man's aggression is the essential brutish reality of his nature as it evolved, then we are only deluding ourselves if we base our hopes for the future on seeking to modify these or find ways of lessening them. The most we can hope for is to educate 'reason' to some extent, so that these blind impersonal forces in us can be controlled – while perhaps finding ways of 'releasing' 'inhibitions' so that these volcanic forces in us do not break out and cause havoc in the world.

Such assumptions about human make-up seem nowadays to the popular mind 'realistic' and scientific. Because of this science has lost a great deal of popularity, while 'idealism' in the realm of the creative arts and subjective disciplines has come under suspicion as but a romantic delusion. The present work is an attempt to suggest that what takes itself for 'realism' here is neither 'scientific' nor, in the light of philosophical anthropology, an adequate account of human make-up, experience, and behaviour. It is rather itself based on a crude kind of subjective speculation, whether one takes Freud's concept of the 'death instinct' or the 'naked apery' of those who base their theories of human nature on analogies with certain facts of animal behaviour. Moreover, I shall try to show that there are much more satisfying theories to account for hate and destructiveness – at once more complex, more perplexing, and more hopeful.

Let me take first an example of thought in the realm of fashionable *avant-garde* culture about the reality of being human. Compare the attitudes to human nature implicit in the work of a teacher in the classroom or a child-care worker, with the attitudes implicit in the following note on an *avant-garde* playwright:

> One way of looking at Pinter's work is to say that it is a constant stratagem to uncover nakedness. The behaviour of his characters is so seldom a reflection of the way people normally behave and so often a reflection of the way they would like to, if they weren't afraid to, or a refraction of fears and anxieties in the form of actions. Violence occurs because animality is unleashed and, unlike the Greeks who took a high view of human dignity and kept the violence off-stage, Pinter peers in through the glass wall with no reverence for humanity, no belief in our lives being mapped out by divine powers and a keen eye for the cracks in the surface of normal conversation and normal behaviour. He is always on the alert for the moments when his characters betray what is underneath and then he simply records what he sees and what he hears, not in order to evolve theories and not in order to warn us against ourselves. His vision and his hearing are both highly tuned instruments, invaluable in his one-

man forays into the inarticulate and irrational no-man's-land inside the modern Everyman. (*Harold Pinter* by Ronald Hayman [39], p. 79.)

Here two assumptions are evident, assumptions which are commonly found in *avant-garde* literature today and in its critical vindications. The playwright is not concerned to 'evolve theories' or to 'warn us against ourselves'. There is no moral purpose in his work. He is only concerned with 'truth'. He 'records what he sees', it is implied, with 'vision' and honesty. This implies that there is a reality which Pinter simply reports – he merely peers 'through the cracks' at it. There is here no recognition of the processes of 'as-if' symbolism involved in any work of art. It is assumed that Pinter simply 'looks into the heart of things' and tells us what he sees 'betrayed' beneath the 'surface'. This, of course, is to fail to see the nature of creative symbolism and its processes of relevant selection. But the writer also assumes that what is 'there' to be seen is an unalterable 'animality', a primary reality. The truth is not that of the Greeks, that man has 'dignity': the truth is that man has an 'animality' which can become 'unleashed' – if man gives way to it. If man really became what he would like to become, he would be a violent animal. This is human reality and it even excuses the artist from responsibility, for there is no need for the writer to concern himself to warn us because (it is implied) man's fundamental nature cannot be altered by any form of education or moral influence. Any alternative view of man is dismissed as idealism: Pinter has 'no belief in our lives being mapped out by divine powers' and no 'reverence for humanity'.

Pinter's point of view is endorsed by an earlier reference in the same book to animal aggression. The implications are that man is simply an animal, and his aggression is to be explained by behaviourist accounts of animal activity. These confirm 'scientifically' that Pinter is right:

> Reading Konrad Lorenz's book *On Aggression*, I was struck again and again by the similarities between the animal behaviour he describes and the behaviour of Pinter's characters. There are so many battles for territory and battles for possession of the female. Lorenz tells us how an aquarium six feet long wasn't big enough for two young coral fish, scarcely an inch long. One had to live in a corner behind the bubbles of an air-generator while the other patrolled the rest of the space. The main reason coral fish are coloured so brightly is that this has the effect of making them fight fish who wear the same colours – not fighting to death, but driving the rivals away so that they don't compete for the same food in the same water. The animal's readiness to fight depends partly on the distance he is from the centre of the territory he 'owns'. Often, when one animal is chasing another away from its home territory, the fugitive, arriving on home ground, turns to attack the pursuer vigorously and unexpectedly, driving him away and pursuing, and the process repeats itself until the combatants achieve a point of balance where they threaten each other without fighting. Julian Huxley has compared the animal territories with air balloons pressing against each other in a glass container and expanding or contracting in accordance with the variations in internal pressure.
>
> Most animals become vicious and more territorially greedy when they have paired but, looking at *The Homecoming* in these terms, Teddy has the disadvantage of being away from what is now his home and coming into the lair of a particularly aggressive family who mob together against him, as they have against Sam.
>
> It is no accident that the motif of hunting occurs so often in Pinter's work, as it does in Beckett's. (Hayman [39], p. 78.)

With no sense of the confusion of dimensions, the critic slips naturally backwards and forwards between the animal kingdom and human reality and between subjective and objective disciplines. He is also implicitly confusing experience and behaviour, while ignoring the subjective elements in perception itself: 'Pinter's own position, as an observer, outside things, is not unlike that of the naturalist, inspecting humanity through the glass wall of an aquarium tank' (Hayman [39], p. 79).

Here it is necessary to raise the question of what happens as a naturalist looks through the glass wall of an acquarium – and how this compares with a playwright looking at human experience. Firstly, perhaps we need to emphasise that genuine science nowadays has to take into account all those problems which arise from the recognition that the scientist is a 'participant observer'. The work of individuals such as Lorenz who study animal behaviour is fascinating in itself as painstaking ethology. But Lorenz slips into subjectivity when he makes deductions about man from goose. In their study of the work of Desmond Morris, Konrad Lorenz, and Robert Ardrey, *Naked Ape – Or Homo Sapiens?*, Dr. Bernard Towers and John Lewis say:

> The anatomy, structure and corresponding mode of life of both fish and birds differ fundamentally from those of the mammal, and there can be no possible justification for transferring the instinctual patterns of geese to man, especially when it is remembered that the basic brain structure is so radically different as to be quite incapable of the neural processes of even the most primitive mammal let alone of man. When the mode of life, the instinct patterns and behaviour are so different, it is difficult to concede that geese are likely to provide relevant clues to human behaviour. Lorenz explains this parallel between geese and man as due to *convergent evolution*. But the evolution of small-brained and highly instinctive animals like birds, with very limited means of manipulation and no possibility of becoming tool-using in the human sense, reveals no convergence, but extreme divergence. (Bernard Towers and John Lewis [83], p. 28.)

Lorenz is scientific in his observations of animals. His theoretical anthropological deductions are invalid because human structure is so different anatomically that his analogies are unacceptable scientifically. They are to be judged on the same plane as fiction. From another point of view, of the philosopher and sociologist,* his deductions are not only subjective, but also degrading:

> Man adjusts to his neighbour by intelligent appreciation of means and ends, and by attaining the mental and spiritual level of recognising and striving for values. We know of nothing approaching this in birds or fish. It does really seem to be a gratuitous degradation of the human species to imagine that the key to its behaviour is to be found by discussing it in the crude terms of fighting fish and geese! (Towers and Lewis [83], p. 28.)

These writers reject the extrapolation of ethology to man: 'This is the kind of argument from analogy that invariably leads to error if the alleged parallel cannot be subjected to crucial test to verify its validity.'

From our point of view we have to ask, why do such writers prefer a subjective theory which *degrades man*? Yet this kind of 'philosophical anthropology', which has no scientific validity and is very dubious philosophically, is taken as the basis of the prevalent 'realism' in contemporary culture at the level of popular thought.

Towers and Lewis also deal with the work of Robert Ardrey, the successful dramatist who turned to anthropology and ethology as a hobby. This writer's theories are based on the observation that birds and many other animals stake out an individual patch of territory and in the mating season defend this against all comers. The robin thus does not sing for joy, or to please us, but to proclaim his ownership and to warn other robins to keep their distance – a view which squares very well with Lorenz's ideas. Ardrey 'sees the instinctive and hereditary instinct for possession' as handed down through his ape ancestors to man, and, since 'our infant species is not yet divorced from evolutionary process, nations, human as well as animal, will continue to obey the laws of the territorial imperative' (Ardrey [1]).

Here, then, Ardrey concludes, 'is the cause of modern war'.

As Towers and Lewis point out, Ardrey's deductions about the fundamental intra-

* Bernard Towers is an embryologist and lecturer in anatomy at Cambridge. John Lewis teaches philosophy and sociology at Morley College, London.

specific antagonism based on this struggle for territory are based on a few scraps of information from anthropology. His conclusion that man is by his inherited and unalterable nature 'a predator whose natural instinct is to kill with a weapon' is based on no careful scientific procedure at all:

> These expressions do not merely tell us that man now eats not only vegetables and fruit but also flesh. They are intended to show us (*without any evidence except a few pebble tools and animal bones*) that the first men were ferocious, combative, cruel, and instinctive aggressors. . . . The purpose of the theory is to prove that modern man is instinctively aggressive and that this is the cause of his incessant war-making. (Towers and Lewis [83], p. 32.)

His theories lead Ardrey to pessimistic conclusions about the future of man, and he finds Freud's point of view inevitably congenial. He quotes Freud from *Civilisation and Its Discontents*:

> In all that follows I take up the standpoint that the tendency to aggression is an innate, independent, instinctual disposition in man. . . . The natural instinct of aggressiveness in man, the hostility of each one against all and of all against one, opposes the programme of civilisation. This instinct of aggression is the derivative and main representative of the death instinct we have found alongside Eros, sharing his rule on the earth. (Ardrey wrongly attributes this quotation to *Beyond the Pleasure Principle*: it is from *Civilisation and Its Discontents*, p. 102; see Towers and Lewis [83].)

Ardrey describes this as 'the last fresh breeze of common sense to reach that dark, many-chambered nautilus, modern psychology'. He believes that Freud's view has received further support from the theory that 'aggression grows greater if it does not draw retaliation'. As we shall see, Freud regarded this basic instinct of aggression and destruction as the greatest obstacle to civilisation. Robert Ardrey and Desmond Morris accept without hesitation the transfer of these aggressive instincts from animal to man. Ardrey says: 'I can discover no qualitative break between the moral nature of the animal and the moral nature of man . . . we have here an innate behaviour pattern, an open instinct, an inward biological demand placed in our nature by our evolutionary history . . . we deal with the changeless' (Ardrey [1], pp. 78, 279, 280, 103).

Such deductions are grim – and, in someone with a genuine concern for truth, to justify their ominousness would surely demand the most meticulous scientific concern for objective fact and the most responsible philosophical discipline. Yet, as Towers and Lewis indicate, they are based on neither.

> In these two books [*African Genesis* and *The Territorial Imperative*] there is rarely any attempt to pass beyond the purely speculative hypothesis. But guesses are not scientific fact unless proven; and matters that have been disproved, as so many of his statements are, cannot be asserted as facts. . . . One cannot but question his competence to deal with material demanding extreme caution, discriminating, and accurate statements of comparative anatomical and geological fact – but here Mr. Ardrey is not in a position to help us. As he himself tells us, he 'blundered into the field, brandishing ignorance like a coat of arms, not knowing a humerus from a tibia'. These are hardly the qualifications we require to reveal the true nature of those ancestors whose predatory and aggressive instincts we are supposed to inherit. (Towers and Lewis [83], p. 32.)

These authors of popular 'scientific' books on the nature of man are popularly commended for their 'realism': yet from a scientific point of view they completely misuse objective facts and the methods by which it can be accounted for:

> Morris and Ardrey have buttressed their works with a huge apparatus of references. But very few authorities actually appear in the text or are directly quoted by way of support, and the majority of them do not share the author's opinions. In fact whatever qualifications Desmond Morris and Robert Ardrey have, these do not extend to any familiarity with modern theories of evolution, or to genetics, on which their whole case rests, or to the study of comparative psychology. (Towers and Lewis [83], p. 32.)

The authors do not question Desmond Morris's competence to discuss captive apes, or Lorenz's to describe fighting fish, geese, or other animals. But of the three popular exponents (Morris, Ardrey, and Lorenz) whose 'nothing-but-an-animal' view of man is so widespread today in popular thought, they say:

> (while they 'tend to destroy all real faith in the future' and state that 'man has no future at all'), in fact, whatever qualifications Desmond Morris and Robert Ardrey have, these do not extend to familiarity with modern theories of evolution, or to genetics, on which their whole case rests, or to the fossil history of early man and his precursors – a highly specialised study – or to the study of comparative psychology . . . . competence in one sphere, however great, does not extend to totally different disciplines. It seems highly problematical that recognised experts in the field of neurology, human evolution and comparative psychology would endorse the theories so gaily set before us in these books. (Towers and Lewis [83], p. 33.)

From the point of view of the empirical concern with *what is real*, these books do not stand the test of scientific examination. From our point of view, we must examine them as a form of imaginative speculation, poetry, or symbolism. As will appear, I believe their symbolism can be seen as forms of expression of a particularly *schizoid* attitude to experience. Certainly what is characteristic of them is the inculcation of a certain kind of *relief* at finding 'really' that we are unalterably 'bad':

> The effect of the theories of Desmond Morris and his associates on public opinion has been unfortunate; it has deepened the pessimism concerning the human condition, which had already reached depressing levels, and gives little hope for human betterment. This is reflected in many reviews and comments on their books. Anthony Storr in *The Sunday Times* argues that when regarded, as we must be if these arguments are accepted, 'in the same light as the other animals', then we are indeed 'inescapably hostile and competitive'. (Towers and Lewis [83], p. 23.)

The writers then quote a number of typical journalists on this topic. Katherine White-horn, they point out, finds herself 'accepting the position, not without some satisfaction': 'The desire to have and to hold, to screech at the neighbours and say, "Mine, all mine" is in our nature too. Ardrey and his allies have let us off perfection and I for one feel a lot better for it' (*The Observer*, 29th October, 1967).

In *The New Statesman*, Atticus (Nicholas Tomalin), they point out, wrote that our ancestors were: 'Hairy neo-fascists, wenching, warring and damning the wogs': their creed 'patriotism is enough', 'fight for every inch of territory you need for yourself', 'hate thy neighbour' – we are descended, Tomalin declares, on the basis of these books, from 'jingoistic brutes with the meanness of bourgeois property instincts'. It follows, if the principles of these animal behaviourists are correct, that 'any idea of progress in politics which ignores these ape-like qualities is doomed . . . we are fooling ourselves if we think our aggressive impulses have been squashed.'

Such attitudes are endorsed by psychological writers such as Anthony Storr who pronounces that 'we are the cruellest and most ruthless species that ever walked the earth' (Storr [76], p. ix).

Lewis and Towers appropriately link the implicit attitude to man in this prevalent 'realism' to the underlying *laissez-faire* attitude to man which found in Darwinian Evolution a vindication of convenient economic policies: '[Darwin's original idea that man was "nothing but" an improved ape] fitted in very well with the *laissez-faire* theories of a period which saw, as a result of the economic struggle for existence, the emergence of the "fittest", by which was meant the more efficient and the elimination of the less efficient.'

For similar reasons, the press of the commercial–industrial world has given immense publicity to the 'naked ape' theorist:

> Thousands of books, plays, newspaper articles, radio and television programmes, have sought to make such things respectable and even to extol them as being more honest. We are encouraged unceasingly to think ourselves excused, so far as anything reprehensible is concerned, on the grounds that we are only acting 'according to our nature', which is bestial. Our 'nature' is defined by reducing man to a plaything of whatever violent elements may be seen in some areas of the evolutionary process. With this kind of thinking men and women can deceive themselves into thinking they have a right to give way to any kind of violent passion they may feel, and even feel themselves to be justified and virtuous in doing so. (Towers and Lewis [83], p. xix.)

How is it that theories which have no scientific validity can be so enthusiastically taken up in popular thought and believed to be 'real'? From what follows I believe we can see this itself as a psychological problem: in our general undisciplined thinking about man in a subjective way we need to believe that he is 'bad'. Though it is in a sense depressing and hopeless, it is also comforting to think that what is 'real' about us is our ineradicable animal badness. It is too frightening and painful to recognise that what is most real about us is our weakness, our vulnerability, our mixed and ambivalent emotional nature, our dependence on others, and the inaccessibility of our not-easily-changed *human* psychic or inner reality. The 'changeless animal' in us is a symbol disguising from ourselves our intractable inward humanness, and the problem of our existence.

Whatever the objections to such theories of human make-up from the scientific point of view, from the point of view of a concern with creativity and culture, they seem a poor form of philosophical anthropology, or even bad poetry. Their 'scientific' dress merely disguises their crudity as such. Another reason for turning to psychoanalytical theory is that one finds in it a growing objection to the reductionist implications of pseudo-scientific thought of this kind, from a discipline that seeks human truth in all gravity.

The present author came across the important work of Viktor E. Frankl too late to discuss his work fully in this volume. Frankl survived Auschwitz, and his remarkable book *From Death Camp to Existentialism* is an attempt to establish what aspect of himself as a man it was that enabled him to survive this dreadful ordeal. His conclusions forced him to completely revise his theory as a psychoanalyst. He came to discard the views that it was the will-to-pleasure that dominates man, or the will-to-power: he came to conclude that what is primary in human make-up is the will-to-meaning. A man will not die for his instinctual life, nor even to fulfil his aggressive impulses: but he will die if the meaning of his life is threatened. Frankl finds that the predominant problem in our world is 'existential frustration'. He knew, in the concentration camp,

> acute states of existential frustration – evanescence of any meaning to one's existence. . . . In concentration camps the age-old adage *primum vivere deinde philosophare* was no longer applicable. In these extreme situations the ultimate question was to find a meaning in life and to account for the meaning of death. . . . What really mattered was *primum philosophare deinde mori*. . . . the question which beset me was, 'Has all this suffering, this dying around us, a meaning? For if not then ultimately there is no meaning to survival; for a life whose meaning stands and falls on whether one escapes or not . . . ultimately would not be worth living at all.' (*From Death-camp to Existentialism* by Viktor E. Frankl, Beacon Press, Boston, 1959, p. 104.)

Frankl's meaning is to be found in reparative acts, in love, and even in suffering: 'We have not only the potentiality of giving meaning to our lives by creative acts and by the experience of nature and culture or through the experience of love . . . but also by suffering: by the way and the manner in which we face our fate, in which we take our suffering upon ourselves.'

Meaning, which is the primary human need, is thus found in that realm of personal existence which reductionist views of man implicitly deny. These views, which are predominant in so many spheres of thought, from academic psychology to sociology, and in concepts of human need abroad in the world, from commerce to administration, are seen by Frankl as a monstrous form of nihilism. He sees the dehumanisation of the concentration camp as arising inevitably out of the dehumanised concepts which man holds of himself at large. Today, says Frankl:

> man is threatened by existential frustration, by frustration of his will-to-meaning, by his unfulfilled claim to a meaning for his existence, by his existential vacuum, by his 'living' nihilism. For nihilism is not a philosophy which contends that there is only nothing and therefore no being: nihilism says that being has no meaning; a nihilist is a man who considers being (and, above all, his own existence) meaningless. But apart from this academic and theoretical nihilism there is also a practical, as it were, 'living' nihilism: there are people who consider their own lives meaningless, who can see no meaning in their personal existence and therefore think it valueless.
>
> Nihilism has held a distorting mirror with a distorted image in front of their eyes, according to which they seemed to be either an automaton of reflexes, a bundle of drives, a psychic mechanism, a plaything of external circumstances or internal conditions, or simply a product of economic environment. I call this sort of nihilism *homunculism*; for it misinterprets and misunderstands man as being a mere product. No one should be surprised today that young people so often behave as if they did not know anything about responsibility, option, choice, sacrifice, self-devotion, dedication to a higher goal in life, and the like. Parents and teachers, scientists and philosophers, have taught them all too long a time that man is 'nothing but' the resultant of a parallelogram of inner drives and outer forces. Again and again I am reminded of the Psalter, for there we find a verse running like this: The Idolizers became like the Idols they were worshipping. In actual fact, man becomes more and more like the image of the man he has been taught about. Man grows according to his interpretations of himself. And let us not forget, homunculism can make history – has already done so. We have only to remember how in recent history the concept of man as 'nothing but' the product of heredity and environment – or, as it was then termed, 'blood and soil' – pushed us all into enormous disasters. I believe it to be a straight path from that homunculist image of man to the gas chambers of Auschwitz, Treblinka, and Maidanek. (Frankl, *op. cit.*, pp. 108–9.)

Such evils arise from the wish that we were not as we are, not human.

CHAPTER 2

Non-psychological Psychology

THE charge of 'homunculism' may be levelled at a good deal of psychology. As an example I will briefly refer to a popular article in a journal for mothers on 'Monkeys and their mothers' by Laurie Taylor. In his article this psychologist says:

> Delinquency . . . maladjustment . . . neurosis . . . wherever any of these topics come up for discussion one can be fairly certain that someone will mention the importance of the early relationship between the mother and the child. Unfortunately, *there is not much evidence* upon which to base any assertions. This is a pity, for it means that we have no way of distinguishing between the many theories of child development which are described in popular literature . . . psychologists like myself who are irritated by the way in which such theories proliferate in the absence of *hard facts* can do little to change the position; for it is almost impossible to conduct any experiments in this area without arousing the humanitarian feelings of the rest of society. . . .
>
> One of the things we clearly need to know is: how much does a child need a mother . . .? (Taylor [126]; my italics.)

To say we have no 'hard facts' or 'evidence' about how much a child needs its mother is outrageous to anyone with any experience of children, or indeed to anyone who has grown up as a human being. To common sense such a view seems ridiculous – and to some perhaps almost psychopathological. The approach to the subject here reveals an astonishing narrow-mindedness: 'hard facts' are those derived exclusively from external observation:

> If we were to separate a child from his mother in the first few days of life and bring the child up separately, would we notice any differences in the way that he developed compared with a similar child who had remained with his mother? To do our experiment properly we would have to keep him away not just from his mother but from any other social contact in case this affected the issue. We would have to bring him up in isolation. It is not difficult to envisage the reaction to such a proposal. (Taylor [126].)

The psychologist's irritation at maddening 'humanitarian feelings' seems to obscure his capacity to take into account other rich sources of insight into the experience of being mothered. Observation of what happened to a baby who was brought up in isolation might tell us something about how his functions were affected. When experiments were conducted with monkeys, as Mr. Taylor reports, they formed a relationship with the cloth which had been substituted for a mother monkey and 'whenever they were frightened . . . they would run . . . to the cloth mother and cling to it'. These experiments did not prove that 'the mother was dispensable' (Mr. Taylor reports almost with disappointment) – when the motherless monkeys grew up they showed serious difficulties in 'adjustment'. They did not play, they were aggressive, and they had great difficulties over mating. When they became mothers themselves they failed to look after their

15

offspring in the normal way. 'These maternally deprived monkeys would sit in their cages all day, often rocking to and fro and sucking their fingers in a fashion which has reminded some psychologists of children they have studied in institutions.' (Taylor [126].)

Perhaps these monkeys also reminded the psychologists of other sources of human fact which seem strangely absent here. There are in the world some 2000 million human beings all of whom could speak of how much a child needs his mother from 'inside' experience. There are also many works of art, including millions of depictions of the Virgin and Child, symbolising the human experience of the need for a mother.

In what sense do the 'hard facts' of empirical experimentation seem preferable to the kind of human fact we all know from the inside about our need for a mother or mother substitute? Why not study the wretched children in institutions anyway? Do not they provide 'hard facts' enough?

There are, too, many orphans in the world already: we hardly need to make more in the name of 'science'. To reduce a child to the existential anguish of the children who sit rocking and sucking their fingers in institutions would not only be barbaric – prohibited as properly as the Nazi 'experiments' on 'racial sub-species' and mentally ill children would have been in a civilised society. Such 'psychology' is an assertion of the reductive power of the I–It, over the unique realm of the I–Thou, to such an extent that any findings derived from such an inhuman experiment would surely themselves be distorted by the intellectual hate involved. By which I mean that, as in sexology, such a schizoid separation of the organism from its human wholeness in existence would vitiate any application of the 'scientific' findings, since the dehumanisation necessary would inevitably colour, in a subjective way, the kind of 'hard fact' that was deduced and the way in which it could be received by the world.

For generations men have looked at babies from the 'outside': yet they have been unable to see certain 'facts'. D. W. Winnicott came along, and was able to say 'There is no such thing as a baby' to the British Psychoanalytical Society. This was not a 'scientific' hard fact, but an intuitive insight of great significance. No one had previously been able to see that what we took for granted – a baby with a separate identity – does not exist at the beginning. A baby cannot be said to exist until its separate existence has been established by the mother's creative reflection. Here we are indicating a human truth which has been reached by imaginative projection, so that the baby's experience has been experienced 'from the inside'.

It is this kind of truth which I believe we need to recognise as real. Psychoanalysis is in the throes of trying to win recognition of the 'hard facts' which can be apprehended by learning from individuals of their deepest personal experiences, subjectively. Where we are dealing with such problems as to whether a child needs its mother, this kind of inward human fact needs to be the subject of scientific investigation, and is more valid as data that 'facts' which might be obtained from experimentation. It is certainly more valid than 'generalisation from animal to human behaviour', such as is implicit in the work of the Wisconsin Primate Laboratory (or in the work of Lorenz). As in sexology, most of what such 'scientific objectivity' does merely confirms what every human being knows already, while still remaining blind to primary truths. To a psychologist such as Laurie Taylor such animal work 'provides some cause for enthusiasm after several centuries of speculation'. Yet it only confirms partially and in a general way what has been observed as human fact, in a much more profound and relevant way, by observers like Winnicott who work not in the laboratory, but with living human beings in need.

We may, for instance, compare the bare behavioural facts of the monkey's relationship with the 'cloth mother' with the highly complex theory developed by Winnicott from his exploration of the *signs* and *meanings* of the child's relationship with his 'cloth mother' – the cuddly rag a child clings to, which Winnicott calls a transitional object, symbolising his internal possession of the mother. This insight, so illuminating for culture, is based on the subjective experience of man as a living subject. To isolate a child as Taylor suggests would be to reduce it or even destroy it as a human being – and in his irritable urge to do such a thing we perhaps have the manifestation, often found in psychology, to reduce man to a dead object of investigation the implications of which we shall later examine. On the other hand 'transitional object' phenomena could never have been investigated by 'objective modes' merely because *meaning* is involved.

'Psychological psychology' is the study of man as a living subject, and here I believe it is appropriate to pay a tribute to one outstanding figure in contemporary British psychology without whose work the present volume could never have been written. My survey could never have been made without the immense work of clarification and insight achieved by Harry Guntrip in his two books, *Personality Structure and Human Interaction* (1961) and *Schizoid Phenomena, Object-relations, and the Self* (1968).

Guntrip's work is beginning to appear as an important English contribution to an international trend of thought, in the investigation of man's nature. There are now a number of spheres of thought from which the assumptions of 'objective' psychology and the 'hard fact' models of human nature underlying 'social science' are being challenged. These include the philosophy of Martin Buber and Existentialist thought in America; Existentialist psychiatry (Leslie H. Farber in America; R. D. Laing in England); the neo-Kantian philosophy of those concerned with man as symbolising animal such as Ernst Cassirer; and the object-relations school of psychoanalytical theory – of which Guntrip is the most thorough chronicler and exponent.

Guntrip's work is of especial significance because he works in one of the few departments of psychiatry in a British university (at Leeds). He is also a practising psycho-therapist, and so can learn from his patients by way of that intuitive kind of knowledge, subjective and empathetic, that is so important in education, medicine, and the arts. Yet in his thinking and lecturing he has been able to bring into play a philosophical training – and so is able to challenge the assumptions of traditional 'scientific' approaches to man and the concept science holds of itself and its scope in the realm of the study of man. By his first work, *Personality Structure*, Guntrip offered a challenge, which was never taken up as it should have been, by his meticulous reconsideration of Freud, his thorough 'placing' of Melanie Klein, and his interpretation of Fairbairn and others. With *Schizoid Phenomena, Object-relations, and the Self* he brought the exploration into deeply disturbing territory of theoretical analysis of the 'very start of the human identity', from which many deep problems arise both for psychotherapy and for the theoretical study of man. In the cultural sphere the implications of the work that has been done in this area are profound – and they cast doubt on many of the assumptions on which our attitudes are based.

The traditional 'model' of human make-up, as endorsed by such works as Arthur Koestler's *The Ghost in the Machine*, Desmond Morris's *Naked Ape*, or C. P. Snow's *The Sleep of Reason*, implies a dualism of 'mind' or 'reason', on the one hand, and 'flesh' (or

D. H. Lawrence's 'blood'), on the other. With a glance back at Nietzsche, some believe that it is necessary to release the instincts in a Dionysiac way (*Hair!*): others prefer the 'sanity' of 'control' by reason. The fundamental model, as we shall see, remains the same, with Plato, St. Paul, Freud, and with 'material' or natural science. All the forms of 'philosophical anthropology' referred to above tend to react against the traditional model of man as being marked off from the other animals by his reason. Without in any way disparaging reason, they will not accept it as the determinative factor in establishing what man essentially is: 'even man's hunger is not an animal's hunger' (Buber). And they seek for a different model to find man's 'totality' existentially.

The psychodynamic theory emerging from Fairbairn, Winnicott, and Guntrip essentially renounces the dualistic model, and seeks to employ a radically different one which is truly personal and psychodynamic. In upholding the model of human nature in which there is a dualism between mind and 'flesh', 'blood', or 'body', Guntrip believes, we have all been guilty of a kind of collusion to preserve myth on which a certain false sense of inward strength depends:

> We have all been in unconscious collusion, suffering individuals, religious, philosophical and educational thinkers, and now psychodynamic researchers, to keep attention diverted from the deepest and ultimate causal factors and concentrated on a middle region of defensive endopsychic activity mistakenly regarded as causal and ultimate. . . . The tremendous resistance to its recognition is based on mankind's universal preference for feeling bad but strong rather than weak and afraid. The 'depressive' diagnosis fixes our attention on our badness, the 'schizoid' diagnosis fixes it on our weakness in a frightening change of emphasis and the more we explore it, the more far-reaching it appears to be. (Guntrip [38], p. 134.)

Schizoid Phenomena, Object-relations, and the Self follows that development in psychoanalytical thought of which Guntrip says: 'This shift in the centre of gravity in psychodynamic theory will enforce a radical reassessment of all philosophical, moral, educational and religious views of human nature' (Guntrip [38], p. 126).

This shift in psychodynamic theory, as we shall see parallels a development in philosophical thought – as for instance, in the impulse of Martin Buber to bring about a development which leads to 'an increasing insight into the problematic nature of human existence'.

Guntrip's kind of investigation of man belongs to this exploration of man's existence from the 'inside'. As a commentator on Buber says, it was originally Kant's 'critical revolution' in philosophy that 'threw the inquiring individual back with a new urgency' on the question What am I? (Wheelright in Buber [10]). As therapists like Winnicott and Guntrip find, it is this question which patients in psychotherapy need to answer before they can go on living. Psychotherapy thus belongs to those existentialist subjective disciplines, which explore man according to the principles of a tradition descending from Kierkegaard. As well as finding thought 'rooted in existence', it draws our attention to the foundations of intellectual structures in kinds of personality, and also implies that there are blindnesses in some accounts of human make-up that exclude 'psychic reality' altogether. Alongside Buber's philosophy, psychoanalytical thought is drawing attention to certain human ways of experiencing and dealing with the world that many present forms of anthropology, psychology, and social science have either taken for granted or have simply not been able to take into account as they should.

Psychoanalysis also follows a path parallel to that of philosophers such as Suzanne Langer and Ernst Cassirer who see as important categories in man's grasp of his world the correlatives *sign* and *meaning*. It shares Buber's preoccupation with such elements in our experience as *betweenness, thouhood, relationship,* and *self-hood* – the whole world of I–Thou experience as opposed to I–It experience. Along with the recognition of such areas of 'human fact' *only* approachable through 'subjective disciplines', object-relations theory rejects a great deal of our present-day thinking about man as too objective, too likely to reduce man to the status of a dead thing – a dehumanised object of study in terms of its externally observed functions. In reducing I–Thou to I–It, this kind of thinking loses sight of all that makes *being human* valid. In any case, as Guntrip points out, many 'hard fact' approaches to human reality are based on fallacies and speculative leaps – and should no longer be given the respect we assume to be due to 'scientific objectivity' since their assumptions are based on logical and epistemological confusions.

Buber, of course, is having a salutary effect here. In the same volume of essays on his work already mentioned there is a short discussion of *I–Thou and I–It in The Natural Sciences* which ought to have a revolutionary effect on thought in this realm. Carl F. von Weizsäcker of the Philosophisches Seminar at Hamburg points out that the assumption that 'science is objective and knows objects only' is an intellectual position which has been increasingly revealed as inadequate since the beginning of the century. Many, he says, like Hume and Mach have pointed out that objects are always objects for a certain subject, while the data of science is now essentially seen as 'modes of description which relate to possible experiments', i.e. 'to possible acts of perception voluntarily produced'. 'They describe phenomena and not things in themselves. To contemporary physics all qualities concerning which it speaks are of the same category as the colour red . . . geometric and mechanical qualities are not placed on a plane which is not essentially different from the quality of colour' (Buber [10], p. 606).

In science, as von Weizsäcker points out, the realm of I–Thou now becomes increasingly significant in physics: the influence of the persona of the experimenter and the theoretician needs analysis as much as the descriptions they concoct. So he concludes: 'It will not be the task of physics to see the Thou in its fullness. But it will certainly be its task to make clear to itself that its methodological procedure excludes this fullness, and that *it is not a truism that what it does not see does not exist*' (Buber [10], p. 607; my italics).

What shall we say of that psychology which is based on the same approach to man as physics, and is content to put forward descriptions of experiments – 'possible acts of perception voluntarily perceived' – and then makes deductions from these observations of *behaviour* to apply to the realm of experience?

Guntrip answers this virtually when he analyses the behaviourist approach:

> In a letter to the editor of the *Quarterly Bulletin of the British Psychological Society* (April 1952) Eysenck compared 'papers devoted to scientific (experimental and statistical) studies in abnormal psychology' with 'papers dealing with ideographic, psychoanalytical and other 'dynamic' topics'. The first he called 'factual' and the second 'speculative', and he has consistently maintained that point of view in subsequent publications. The fallacy of refusing the status of 'fact' to what one's own favourite method is incapable of taking account of, should be obvious. But this dangerous, narrow-mindedness of the exclusively 'scientifically' moulded mind is . . . widespread still. (Guntrip [38], p. 329.)

Guntrip devotes a fascinating appendix to 'psychodynamic science' in which he attempts to expose several of the fallacies of those who cling to a definition of 'scientific fact' in psychology which excludes quite evident facts of human experience. He quotes C. Taylor, *The Exploration of Behaviour*: 'To assume from the superiority of Galileo's principles in the sciences of inanimate nature, that they *must* provide the model for the scenes of animate behaviour, is to make a speculative leap, not to enunciate a necessary conclusion' (Taylor, quoted by Guntrip [38], p. 372).

It is here that Taylor concludes that behaviourism is 'non-psychological psychology.'

This raises the question of how far the study of man can be scientific, or how far science is capable of giving an account of man. As Guntrip says:

> Science is the emotionally detached study of the properties of 'Objects' which are held to be accounted for when they can be classified according to their species and genus . . . science seeks to establish what phenomena have in common so that the isolated individual object or event can be grouped with its fellows and 'understood' according to what science means by understanding. This scientific approach is easily applicable to the human body as to any other body, and the medical sciences, beginning with anatomy, physiology, and biochemistry, find no difficulty in adopting it. (Guntrip [37], p. 16.)

This 'understanding' which belongs to the approach to objects, was automatically and unthinkingly transferred to the consideration of persons. 'When science turned to the study of "mental life", as it was traditionally called, the same approach was automatically made. . . . Physiological psychology grew up on the basis of neurological reflexes, simple and conditioned. Pavlov and J. B. Watson made the "scientific approach" ' (Guntrip [37], p. 16).

But such a 'scientific' psychology takes little or no account of the truth that 'personal events are experiential'. Can the concept of 'science' be extended to include experience? How can a science of man take account of man's primary need (as Frankl sees it) for meaning – for this is a human fact?

Guntrip is concerned to emphasise that psychotherapy can be seen as a valid form of research:

> Psychotherapy is a practical procedure involving the art of sustaining an actual kind of personal relationship. It can be studied scientifically but not by methods which fail to take into account the all-important personal facts of motivation, understanding, and emotional relating. At this point the very concept of science must be broadened beyond the scope of the purely objective study of the 'facts' of the material universe. (Guntrip [38], p. 330.)

If we extend the concept of science in this way and take subjective human facts into account we may certainly come to see the problem of *What is real about man* in a very different light from the predominant fashionable theories of human nature.

To anyone who gives assent to vindications of the realism and 'honesty' of those who see men as 'mere animals', it must come as something of a shock to find a psychoanalyst such as Winnicott saying categorically that 'we cannot satisfactorily describe human beings in terms of what they share with animals' (Winnicott [93], p. 16.)

When Winnicott looks into the tank he obviously sees something very different from what Pinter, Ardrey, or Lorenz see, and accepts responsibility for it in a way they do not. Since Winnicott, from his own calculation, has dealt with many thousands of cases in person as a paediatrician and psychotherapist, we can perhaps legitimately compare his observations with theirs. On the subject of aggression he writes like this:

> Put in a nutshell, aggression has two meanings. By one meaning it is directly or indirectly a reaction to frustration. By the other meaning it is one of the two main sources of an individual's energy. Immensely complex problems arise out of further consideration of this simple statement. . . .
> . . . first I must make a general observation. It is wise to assume that fundamentally all individuals are essentially alike, and this in spite of the hereditary factors which make us what we are and make us individually distinct. I mean, there are some features in human nature *that can be found in all infants,* and in all children and in all people of whatever age, and a comprehensive statement of the development of the human personality from earliest infancy to adult independence would be applicable to all conscious and unconscious destructive ideas and reactions to such ideas, appear in the child's dreaming

and playing, and also in aggression that is directed against that which is accepted in the child's immediate environment as worthy of destruction. (Winnicott [95], p. 239.)

Winnicott is obviously discussing something human, something familiar, something universal – having a symbolism we recognise from poetry, fiction, and other traditional accounts of the nature of human nature.

Winnicott's achievement in the essay from which I quote above, as elsewhere throughout his work, is to give our interpretation of aggression a human *meaning*, not in terms of an inward animality which has to be 'controlled' or suppressed, but as a manifestation of positive human striving towards feeling alive and real and significant, from which there are, inevitably, at times, departures into destructive channels. These forms of destructiveness we know to be there, too, of course, in human life.

> If time is allowed for maturational processes [i.e. 'allowed' by the mother – D. H.] then the infant becomes able to be destructive and becomes able to hate and kick and scream instead of magically annihilating that world. In this way actual aggression is seen to be an achievement. As compared with magical destructiveness, aggressive ideas and behaviour take on a positive value, and hate becomes a sign of civilization, when we keep in mind the whole process of the emotional development of the individual, and especially the earliest stages. . . .
>
> . . . I have tried to give an account of just those subtle stages by which, when there is good enough mothering and good enough parentage, the majority of infants do achieve health and a capacity to leave magical control and destruction aside, and *to enjoy the aggression* that is in them alongside the gratifications, and alongside all the tender relationships and the inner personal riches that go to make up the life of childhood. (Winnicott [95], p. 239; my italics.)

Aggression, then, can be seen as a manifestation of living energy and a sign of civilisation, of the need to feel that one is human and up against something, or someone, in a contact which confirms one's existence. If this is so, then aggression belongs to the realm of human identity, not to an 'animality' or a biological urge towards death at all. It can thus, under normal circumstances, be enjoyed as a life-energy and contribution to one's richness.

As we shall see, Winnicott's view is that the roots of our aggression are in the need of certain regressed weak areas of our ego to feel real, alive, and meaningful. Once accepted, this origin of our hate can be embraced as a potential source of richness. This attitude is very different from the hopeless assumption behind the 'naked ape' view, which sees an unchangeable brutishness beneath the 'surface' – the surface being a mere 'conformity' by 'adaptation'. It is also very different from the view of Freud that 'men are not gentle friendly creatures wishing for love'. (As G. H. Bantock says, '*Homo homini lupus* sums up his assessment of the situation'; Bantock [3], p. 46).

Professor Bantock is concerned to reject the Freudian view that what is real about man is his *badness* from the point of view of one of those working in education for whom I am writing:

> Freud . . . sometimes speaks as if the 'real' personality is manifested only in the cruder instinctual strivings. For example, in his *Introductory Lectures* he tells of a young man's relation to his father – one of outward piety, involving tender ministrations during his father's protracted illness, but, if a dream analysis is to be believed, masking an unconscious antagonism. Freud comments on the latter state of affairs:
>> I have no doubt that this was, *in reality*, his attitude towards his father during the protracted illness and that his ostentatious assertions of filial piety were designed to divert his mind from any recollections of the sort. (Bantock [3], p. 60; italics supplied.)

As Bantock says, the implication of this is that, as Freud himself asserted, 'The Unconscious is the true psychical reality'. The young man's goodness, his piety, can hardly be allowed to exist:

The psychically 'real' tends to be equated with those primitive strivings, those crude instinctual urges it is the function of civilisation to control and repress. I believe that this tendency to equate the true psychic 'reality' with the primitive rather than the 'moral' self has been profoundly influential in our era, especially in its literature. It has induced a whole new school of 'realist' writers, especially in America, to prefer passion and the exploitation of crude behaviour to the examination of moral sensibility. (Bantock [3], p. 50.)

Bantock speaks of how, with the above young man patient of Freud's 'The piety, after all, is as "real" as the antagonism, for it constitutes the civilising "form" which *controls* the primitive urges, (Bantock [3], p. 50; my italics).

Here we enter upon further problems, indicated by the word 'controls', involving many assumptions about the relationship between the individual, his culture, and society. Consider some of Professor Bantock's phrases and their implications:

The development of most children can be encompassed by a greater attention to the arts and crafts, which mingle the emotional and intellectual proportionately as means to the *control of the self* . . . the effort of thought concentration can be a *great emotional calmer* . . . one (attitude) regards it (emotion) as a disorder, because we appreciate calmness and rationality . . . all people have emotions . . . and . . . the question of *coping with them*. (Bantock [3], *passim*; my italics.)

D. W. Winnicott also uses the word 'control' above in the phrase 'states that denote hate and control of hate'. But Winnicott also speaks of the infant as achieving 'health and a capacity to *leave* magical control and destruction *aside*, and to enjoy aggression' (my italics). To leave an aggressive impulse aside is significantly different from 'controlling it': 'putting away childish things' different from 'learning to cope'. Winnicott's phrases suggest an emerging positive maturity rather than a strengthening of authority over unruly impulses.

The contrast would seem to suggest that to Professor Bantock 'control' (together with 'calming' and 'rationality', in 'coping') is a 'good' thing, while to Winnicott 'control' and the intellectual effort to calm emotion would imply the diversion of energy from more positive directions, and sometimes an attempt to manipulate or deny reality in an unreal, or 'magical' way. Professor Bantock is putting the problem in a more negative way than Winnicott. Bantock sees us as learning to use reins: Winnicott sees us as developing a delight in riding, so that we seem to be at one with the horse – that wants not to run away but to enjoy the ride and being ridden.

My explorations below will, I hope, help us to clarify some of these issues. Is there inevitably a conflict between 'emotion' and 'reason', between 'the emotional' and the 'intellectual'? And is our problem of emotional growth one of learning to 'cope' and 'control of *the self*'? Do we seek 'emotional calmness'? In so far as he uses such phrases, Professor Bantock has perhaps implicitly and indirectly taken over aspects of Freud's diagnosis of the problem of human make-up – that these are caused by an aggressive animal lurking under the reasonable surface which needs 'taming' or at least 'refining' by intelligence.

As will appear, I believe recent diagnoses of human make-up in terms of *problems of identity* are yielding a more profitable approach to such problems as that of aggression, and leading us out of the dilemma. The implicit model of a reined beast has almost disappeared from Winnicott's account.

Aggression can be looked at as a 'main source of an individual's energy' and a 'reaction to frustration'. Although aggression can be terribly destructive, its roots are in the need to assert a human identity. What we have to do is to distinguish between true and false assertions.

In such a view there is no need for the concept of the 'death instinct', and the pessimistic assumption that there is a brutal 'real' underlying force in us. Hate is not an innate and unalterable 'animality' which is insoluble, which can only be coerced or hidden, but which can never be wholly turned towards positive directions. Moreover, since the origins of hate and aggression are in the problem of feeling real and alive, it would seem possible that if we do everything we can to contribute, at every stage of the individual's development, to ways in which it is possible for him to feel 'confirmed' in his identity, we could actually reduce the amount of hate abroad. It is possible to contribute at large to potentialities for the 'integration' to which Professor Bantock refers, and which he sees as a problem of balance between the emotional and intellectual life. The implications of Winnicott's view are that culture and social living are not mere means to coerce an animal or even to 'control' it into being civilised against its 'real' id impulses, but a primary need of man, in the provision for which he finds his greatest satisfaction – because it is in these activities that he finds a sense of the point of life, and confirmation of the sense of being human. It is civilisation that is most 'real' about us.

CHAPTER 3

Psychology as a Form of Philosophical Anthropology

THE present comparative lack of interest in psychoanalytical ideas is particularly to be regretted because, although it is not an 'exact science' (a concept about which science itself is fortunately having doubts), psychoanalysis is an important discipline from which fresh ways of thinking about human nature and experience are emerging. As Leslie Farber says, psychoanalysis is a 'kind of cross-breed between medical science and something very different from science'. It was Freud who devised the essence of this discipline – the specific practice of working through interpersonal contact between doctor and patient:

> His introduction of a close, prolonged, and intense relationship with a patient for several hours a week – and extending over a period of years – meant a novelty so unprecedented in the medical sciences as virtually to remove psychotherapy from the field of science altogether. Since the kind of interpersonal relation which developed out of this is without parallel in medicine, even in the closest friendship with a family doctor, psychiatrists have had to look for parallels outside the sciences; in the general field of education, including moral and religious instruction. (Farber [20], p. 156.)

What emerges from this process of deductions from 'meeting' in therapy we shall call here 'philosophical anthropology', devoted to the question What is man? This kind of inquiry which Martin Buber has pursued with psychoanalysts and others in America has greatly stimulated existentialist psychiatry and philosophy there. One major concept which has emerged is our need to be 'reflected', as a means to discover and realise ourselves: 'the wish of every man to be confirmed as what he is, even as what he might become, by men; and the innate capacity in man to confirm his fellow-men in this way' (Buber [101], p. 102, quoted by Farber [20], p. 156).

This process of confirmation, of course, is part of daily life. But it is a process which is especially exemplified in the psychotherapeutic relationship, especially where the patient is a psychotic, whose desperate problem is that of asking 'What am I?' As Winnicott puts it: 'Psychotic patients who are all the time hovering between living and not living force us to look at this problem, one which really belongs not to psychonuerotics but to all human beings . . . the question, *what life is about*' (Winnicott [130], p. 370).

Answers to such questions, What is man? What is the point of life? What is life about? cannot be given by science. But by this 'cross-breed between medical science and something very different' they have to be found if therapy is to succeed with severely ill patients. Of course, for them it would be ridiculous to give answers to such questions in terms of what is real in the material world. They can only be valid in terms of 'inner reality', and so from psychoanalysis is arising something that accepts rationally, and in a disciplined way, the fact of man's need for a sense of meaning. It can thus claim to be a valid form of 'considered study of man', of which science needs to take account. To do so, science must needs expand its conception of what is 'scientific'.

This way of knowing 'what it is to be human' is thus not only very different from the approach to man as a phenomenon belonging to natural history, of nineteenth-century biology – it is also deeply opposed to that kind of approach to man as an object. This approach to man in the subjective way relates psychoanalysis to existentialism. As Sartre says, of his own brand of existentialism, this theory alone is compatible with the

> ... dignity of man, it is the only one which does not make man into an object. All kinds of materialism lead one to treat every man including oneself as an object – that is as a set of pre-determined reactions, in no way different from the patterns of qualities and phenomena which constitute a table, or a chair, or a stone. Our aim is precisely to establish the human kingdom as a pattern of values in distinction from the material world. But the subjectivity which we thus postulate as the standard of truth is no narrowly individual subjectivism, for . . . it is not only one's own self that one discovers in the *cogito*, but those of others too. . . . The man who discovers himself directly in the *cogito* also discovers all the others, and discovers them as the condition of his own existence. He discovers that he cannot be any-thing (in the sense that one says one is spiritual, or that one is wicked or jealous) unless others recognise him as such. . . . The other is indispensable to my existence . . . we find ourselves in a world . . . of 'inter-subjectivity'. (Sartre [73], p. 303.)

In this intersubjectivity *human facts* can be validly established, as we shall see.

Here, however, we may at once note a crucial problem, even in the terms used by Sartre. Is the nature of man to be expressed in terms of *cogito*? What is it that we know of ourselves? And is this knowledge merely the kind which belongs to thinking? Does Sartre's *cogito* include imagination? As we shall see, there is a bodily way of knowing, a feminine way of knowing, and an inner creative reparative urge, all of which are often excluded from accounts of how we know, and from accounts of man.

However, we may leave these problems for the time being, and merely note that Sartre is drawing our attention to the dangers of that kind of cognition that reifies. Farber says of Freud: 'Freud himself may be held responsible for one of the chief im-modesties of this psychoanalytical age: namely for the presumption that one can, instead of imagining, actually know the other in his essence' (Farber [20], p. 157).

Freud's rationalism, as we have seen, involves a number of fallacies. As Farber says:

> While this may be called 'rationalism' it nevertheless represents an irrational elevation – almost a divinisation – of the outer world as the only reliable source of knowledge. Fortunately, however, such a through going exaltation of the outer or visible world at the expense of inner truth is almost impossible to put into practice. In practice, subjectivity, common sense – imagination itself – were all smuggled into the Freudian therapy under some rather conflicting terms of natural science. And although this had the welcome effect of bestowing on subjectivity a little of that intellectual prestige previously enjoyed only by scientific 'objectivity' other results were less fortunate. In particular I should class it as a misfortune that so many intellectual processes and values, so many aesthetic or philosophical or religious meanings, had now to be translated into vague romantic terms of natural 'feeling' or else into vague but equally romantic terms of natural 'instinct'. (Farber [20], p. 159.)

As Farber says, the result in the modern world has been in 'intellectual impoverish-ment' which was at the same time a narrowing of experience. The existentialist move-ment represents an attempt to break out of this limitation on our approaches to experience, and this is why it is felt to have something especially relevant to offer us today. But obviously everything depends upon what kinds of knowledge and experience existentialism is willing to recognise.

This is in part a semantic problem, to do with the definition of man. As Farber says,

'A violent separation or abstraction from the whole has . . . been accomplished through language— through the increasing application of a medical or scientific terminology to describe the whole of man's existence.' (p. 151). The source of many of our difficulties here derive from the language of Freud's psychotherapy— 'the terms he chose for defining his science'. (p. 162).

Just as in science there has grown an increasing sense of doubt as to the possibility of making a 'complete and coherent' account of the physical universe, and an increasing awareness of the problems of perception raised by relativity, so the 'omniscient observer' has given way to the 'participant observer', not least in the field of psychology. But there is a further problem, to which Farber points, of the relevance of any form of account of experience:

> The question for philosophical anthropology is not whether such imagined viewpoints are omniscient, but whether they are relevant: whether they are true in the sense of being appropriate to man's existence, conducive to a 'human' way of life. And this comes down to a question of language, for man can see himself, in terms of the natural or physical sciences, or in some other terms. He *sees* himself by means of the language that defines him as a man, and, of course, *he behaves accordingly*. (Farber [20], p. 161; my italics.)

While psychotherapists have leaned over backwards to avoid omniscience, Farber believes that they have 'never . . . discriminated between one kind of omniscience and another, nor between the kind of language appropriate to each . . . we, as psychotherapists, have not sufficiently questioned the appropriateness of using scientific terms to define our work, our patients, and ourselves. . . .'

Thus, when we approach Freud, we need to '[disentangle] his valuable insights into human nature from all those naturalistic and romantic theories about nature itself in which they are embedded' (Faber [20], p. 162).

This impulse itself may be seen as part of the existentialist movement in its attention to the subjective. The problem which arises at once is that if we cease to regard man as an object which can be a proper subject of 'scientific' investigation (as in academic psychology), and if we are to give up believing in his struggle with 'instinct' – whatever do we have left, on which to rely as 'fact'?

Here we may go back to Kierkegaard. Paul Roubiczek says Kierkegaard was concerned with 'thinking existentially – that is . . . regarding inner experience as valid evidence of what is real . . . and testing his thought in its light' (Roubiczek [120]).

Here perhaps it will help if I define the term 'philosophical anthropology' a little more fully. Fortunately, to help us here we now have available the most valuable symposium *The Philosophy of Martin Buber*, recently published by Cambridge University Press (Buber, [10]).

The essays in this book help to define the fresh perspective which Buber demanded on the problem, What is it to be human? For instance, an essay by Philip Wheelwright on 'Buber's philosophical anthropology' makes it plain that Buber's influence belongs to a development of philosophy itself, which helps to 'bring the anthropological problem to maturity'. As Philip Wheelwright points out, this has in part to do with a reaction against 'the traditional over-emphasis upon the rational character of man, whereby, even though the force of his non-rational impulses was, of course, admitted, it was nevertheless his ability and activity as a reasoner, both contemplative and practical, that were said to mark him off from other animals' (Buber [10], p. 71).

We may associate this traditional approach with the persisting dualistic attitude to the 'conflict' between 'reason', on the one hand, and 'animal' or 'instinctual drives', on the other, which underlies so many assumptions about human nature today. Buber sought to draw attention to other factors:

> Now while Buber does not ever disparage man's rational faculty, and indeed there is plenty of evidence that he prizes it highly, he is unwilling to accept it as the determinative factor in establishing what man essentially is. For, he holds, it is not by his reasoning alone that man differs from his animal cousins: 'even man's hunger is not an animal's hunger.' Problems of human reason must be seen not simply as contrasted with man's animal nature, but as growing out of it and still bearing a vital relation to it. Consequently the problem of philosophical anthropology is not primarily that of man as rational, in contrast to other beings and to non-rational parts of himself; it is rather the problem of a specific totality and of its specific structure. (Buber [10], pp. 71–72.)

As we shall see, this matter of 'seeing man in his totality' involves a different kind of knowledge from the ratiocinative, empirical, and 'objective'. It involves the recognition of certain human realities which are not to be found by empiricism, such as the observation (in psychology) of *behaviour*: they are the facts of *experience*, of the *inner* world. They recognise the mind's existence in a body which has a history and in which a person lives with his unique experiential history and his personal culture. What is most real about man is his psychic reality, with its signs and meanings, from phantasy to creative art and symbolism in living.

These realities can be validly established by the collocation of imaginative and intuitive perceptions and the comparing of insights in the 'common pursuit of true judgement'. The essential process here, however, our capacity to perform this imaginative 'throwing' of ourselves into the very identity of another person is uncanny, and is so far beyond the scope of 'objective' science that some scientists tend to deny its existence altogether. Yet, as we shall see, identification is itself the very basis of human identity: and belongs to certain modes of perception and communication that belong especially to what we shall here call (from Winnicott: see below, p. 173) the *female element* in human nature. To this realm also belongs our capacity to be in touch with ourselves. So it is the recognition of this *female way of knowing* that seems to be emerging from such philosophies as that of Buber. As Farber says:

> When Buber describes those early or primitive experiences of the *Thou*, he is not looking at the behaviour of the infant or his mother. Nor is he imagining any abstract relation which may exist between the two. He is rather imagining the experience of the mother towards her child, and of the child towards his mother. And he is imagining this to be a mutual experience of reciprocity – of shared relation. Buber therefore believes that human experience begins, both in the race and in the child, with *relation* . . . what he means by relation . . . [is] imagined from the inside, as a mutal experience . . . not the same thing as an abstract concept of relationship . . . 'seen' or imagined from the outside, as an event occurring between human objects. (Farber [20], p. 583.)

This approach to human 'fact' by 'imagining from the *inside*' requires a radical reconsideration of our concepts of man's reality, and this in return requires a revolution in our attitude to human culture.

This 'philosophical anthropology' in no way seeks to devalue man's powers of reason, but seeks rather to draw attention to major realms of experience and knowledge which we too easily take for granted, even though our human identity depends upon them. Indeed, we often seek to impose on these forms of ideation, as Emmanuel Levinas says:

> The I–Thou relation consists in confronting a being external to oneself, i.e. one which is radically other, and to recognise it as such. The recognition of otherness, however, is not to be confused with the *idea* of otherness. To have an idea of something is appropriate to the I–It relation. What is important is not thinking *about* the other, even *as* an other, but of directly confronting it and of saying Thou to it . . . the movement which relates the Thou is not like one that sets any theme of discourse. The being who is invoked in this relation is ineffable because the I speaks *to* him rather than *of* him, and because

in the latter case all contact is broken off with the Thou. To speak *to* him is to let him realize his own otherness. (Buber [10], p. 138.)

The reductive elements in our culture and intellectual traditions that threaten the I–Thou relation, and so tend to reduce the capacity to 'realise one's otherness', are but part of a whole tendency towards dehumanisation which Martin Buber was especially concerned to resist. The nature of this dehumanisation is part of the theme of the present work in which it is hoped to explore some of its psychic origins. Buber believed that the traditional approach to the nature of man itself dehumanised us because it leaves out of account the essential element of relation: if, for instance, we believe a scientific approach to man to mean that 'man is to be understood as constituting a species of potentially insolable individuals, coming together merely for emotional warmth and common utility', then for Buber 'no science of man can exist'. Yet this kind of 'science' dominates much of the psychology and sociology of culture and education.

To Buber, the notion of man as in the first instance

as a solitary ego . . . which by multiplication and induction is expanded into a general notion of mankind . . . looks not to the fulfilment but rather, in Buber's view, to the virtual nullification of man. In practice as a man moves towards essential isolation Buber holds that he does so at the cost of abdicating from his essentially human status, hence of becoming something less than man; and consequently that theory which sets up some conception of the isolated man, whether primarily as doer or primarily as knower, as its starting point, is resting upon an unreal abstraction. (Wheelwright, in Buber [10], p. 69.)

This instance on the dimension of relation in which identity is created and confirmed is parallel to Winnicott's point of view from which 'there is no such thing as a baby'.

In the face of nihilistic homunculism in our thought today we urgently need a view of man which is capable of embodying his essential human status, his unique existence, and his inner life. From many directions we are being threatened by the 'unreal abstraction' of a hominoid, as in sociology and 'hard fact' psychology, popular 'naked ape' pseudo-science, behaviourism, sexology, – and the worlds of business economics, political planning and the exploitation of symbolism in advertising and the mass media. Everywhere concepts of human life are being nullified, subjected to nihilism and 'the idolizers become like the idols they worship'. What is needed is a more whole approach concerned with subjective human experience, and with meaning. As Frankl says, 'Nihilism must be fought by humanism' – which gives attention to the 'noetic' – and, I would add, the poetic. It needs to be emphasised here, however, that the tradition running from Kierkegaard to Buber, and into existentialist psychology in America, is one, as will be seen, very different from that of the line of thought influenced by Sartre in England and Europe.

In *What is Man?* Buber says: 'Only in our time has the anthropological problem reached maturity, that is, come to be recognised and treated as an independent philosophical problem.' The reasons why Buber felt this to be so are explored by Philip Wheelwright. His first reason was sociological:

It is founded on the 'increasing decay of the old organic forms of the direct life of man with man'. Communities have become 'too big to allow the men who are connected by them to be brought together ever anew and set in a direct relationship . . . with one another'. There has been a relentless decay of such social forms as the family, the village community . . . while such forms as the club, the political party, and the trade union . . . have increasingly taken over. Like the older forms these newer ones kindle men's feelings of collective security and thereby give them a sense of larger scope and significance in their lives, but they have not been able to re-establish the sense of permanence and security which was given by the older forms. They operate by dulling man's sense of solitude by immersing him in bustling activities, instead of providing him with the stillness in which 'confronted with the problem of his existence' he might learn to 'experience the depth of the human problematic as the ennobling centre of his life'. (Wheelwright, in Buber [10], p. 70–71.)

The relationship of this approach to that of D. H. Lawrence's *Rainbow* and to that of *Culture and Environment* by F. R. Leavis and Denys Thompson will be obvious. Later it will be seen that the world 'bustling' used above has a particular significance. There is a kind of activity in unsatisfactory child nurture by which the inadequate mother makes up, by 'doing for' what she cannot supply by 'being' for the child, while on his part, unable to make use of her in terms of 'being', he substitutes an intense nervous activity and intellectual 'bustling' for genuine growth in security. If we set this failure of 'being' alongside Buber's emphasis on the I–Thou experience as against I–It ideation, I believe we can see that his criticism of modern society is a criticism of a failure in human life in our time *to be able to be*. The bustling activity of our world is itself a form of false solution in 'doing' to the problem of life. Since 'doing follows from being' this means less efficient 'doing', too. By its capacity to 'dull', this 'false-solution' bustling tends to carry man further and further from that stillness in which he can be 'confronted with the problem of existence'. Below we shall also examine some reasons why man prefers not to be 'confronted' with this problem.

The attitude to man which seems prevalent in our culture complements appropriately a world in which 'communities have become too big' and organisations have 'not been able to give security'. To this reason for his emphasis on philosophical anthropology Buber adds a second 'reason', *seelengeschichtlich*, having to do with the soul's history: 'This shows itself in man's tendency to "lag behind his works"; to his increasing inability to master the world which he himself has brought into being' (Buber [10], p. 71).

The above philosophical reasons for the emergence and clarification of the idea of 'philosophical anthropology' Philip Wheelwright classifies as negative. A more positive explanation can be found by tracing the lineage of the idea to Kant. Buber refers to Kant's earlier *Handbook to his Lectures on Logic*, where 'philosophy in the universal sense . . . is taken as asking four fundamental questions: (1) What can I know? (2) What ought I to do? (3) What can I hope? (4) What is man?' 'Kant declares that these four questions find their answers respectively in metaphysics (what is later to be designated epistemology), ethics, religion, and anthropology . . . in the earlier version Kant declares that the anthropological question is the most fundamental of them all, since the first three questions may be regarded as phrases of it' (Wheelwright, in Buber [10], p. 72).

Kant did not elaborate this germinal idea. It was rather Kierkegaard who later, as Buber said, 'indicated that thought cannot authorise itself, but is authorised only out of the existence of the thinking man'. But it was Kant, as we have seen, who brought back the question, What am I?: 'Generalised, the question becomes: What is the nature of the subjects who are the points of transcendental activity, making all this common phenomenal world possible?' (Wheelwright, in Buber [10], p. 72).

As Wheelwright points out, in Kant's later writings there is no longer any problem corresponding to the fourth question, What is man? – which he 'takes for granted as presupposed, or tacitly involved in all the others'. So, in academic philosophy Kant's philosophical heritage tended to lack explicit formulation of this fourth question.

The anthropological question was always implicit when the other three questions were asked, but there was the danger that 'it would reach, instead of the subject's genuine wholeness, which can become visible only by the contemplation of all its manifold nature, a false unity which has no reality' [Buber,

> *Between Man and Man*] . . . a legitimate philosophical anthropology must know that there is not merely
> a human species but also peoples, not merely a human soul, but also types and characters, nor merely
> human life but also stages in life. (Wheelwright, in Buber [10], p. 73.)

Here, I believe, we have an indication of how, as it becomes a subjective discipline in the exploration of man's wholeness, psychoanalysis has overcome those objections which have for decades been made to it, on the grounds that it is reductive.

G. H. Bantock's doubts, expressed in his two essays on psychoanalytical ideas and education (Bantock [3])' provide a useful reference point here, because his doubts focus on the ambivalence in Freud's approach to culture and morality. It is here that the most significant developments have taken place in psychoanalysis itself. Many of us concerned with creativity and education have felt that psychoanalysis involved an implicit reduction to secondary status or to 'delusion' of those activities we regarded as most valuable, and thus was a threat to the very meaning of our work.

As Bantock says, Freud had a curiously ambivalent attitude to art and literature:

> For all his admiration and respect for the artist, in the last analysis Freud thought of him as the
> provider of substitute gratifications. Art provides compensation – or at most therapy – rather than a
> means of apprehending features of the 'real' world . . . art becomes a matter of relaxation rather than
> an incredibly difficult 'form' of apprehension leading to a profounder appreciation of the external
> world and to some enjoyment of it. (Bantock [3], p. 56.)

Below I pursue the development of post-Freudian thought, through its tortuous rejection of this attitude of Freud, towards a concern with creativity as something more primary. To Winnicott, for instance, personal culture is bound up with the whole question of the point of life, while to such a writer as Marion Milner even our objective perception derives from our capacity to discover integration in the inner world.

So far has psychoanalytical thought moved from Freud, that this discipline has come to see creativity as something even more fundamental than Professor Bantock allows it to be. Art is no mere 'form' of apprehension, leading to an appreciation of the external world and 'some enjoyment of it'. Creativity is nothing less than the very basis of identity and the essence of being human, in the pursuit of meaning. Bantock quotes Freud as saying 'Art does not seek to be anything else but an illusion': Winnicott has turned the problem round, and shows us how illusion is the basis of everything meaningful in our existence.

The concepts of human nature embodied in object-relations psychology contain, as Winnicott says, a 'belief in human nature', and recognition of the truth of love in human existence, with all its creative power. As Winnicott says:

> The early management of an infant is a matter beyond conscious thought and deliberate intention. It
> is something that becomes possible only through *love*. We sometimes say that infant needs love, but we
> mean that only someone who loves the infant can make the necessary adaptation to need, and only
> someone who loves the infant can graduate a failure of adaptation to follow the growth of the individual
> child's capacity and make positive use of failure. (Winnicott [95], p. 183.)

Winnicott has been courageous enough in his thought to be able to insist that the growth of every human identity depends upon the intractable delusion called love and on such strange processes as the gradual 'disillusionment' of the growing child. (By contrast I believe we can say our *avant-garde* playwright or pseudo-scientific 'realist' is simply not brave enough to see that man is weak rather than strong – so, he seeks to endorse the 'taboo on weakness'.)

Love is, of course, a delusion: but we must live with the recognition that on such delusions universal sanity depends. Here we can learn much from those who have suffered from severe mental illnesses, in which normal perception has broken down. An example here is the account written by a woman who recovered from schizophrenia, Morag Coate, in her book *Beyond All Reason* (Coate [14]). In discussing delusion she points out that falling in love and parental care are both common delusory experiences:

> If falling in love were not such a common experience, and if doctors in their private lives were not also subject to it, it might already have become a text-book subject for psychiatrists to study. For it is the one universally prevalent form that delusional disturbance takes . . . I can say with assurance that the delusional content in the state known as falling in love rises and falls in the same way as it does in an acute psychotic episode. Anyone who has tried to reason with a person who is in love can confirm that one of the most obvious features of the condition is a lack of insight. . . . Falling in love is a healthy, normal, process and it has a vital and constructive purpose in human life. That it is highly irrational does not detract from its real and realistic purpose. It is not always wise or healthy for people to be too sane. This is not the only violently irrational condition that is rightly taken for granted as a part of normal life. Parental love of all sorts, and maternal love especially, is in its first awakening highly delusional, too. To the new parents their first child is something quite different and quite special and much more important than all the other children in the world. This useful delusion tides them over the first difficult adjustments and distracts their attention from the fact that a young baby is a relatively unattractive, most time-consuming and often very tiresome intruder into their life. (Coate, [14], pp. 203–5.)

It is the world of these delusions which Winnicott and others have explored, with the result that Winnicott himself believes that during parturition the mother extends her personality in such a way as to suffer what would be a schizoid illness were it not for the baby (if the baby dies her condition shows up as such). Thus in his writing to mothers he is concerned to help them find insight into the strange processes, some of them seemingly telepathic, which take place between mother and infant:

> If you wait you will sooner or later discover that the baby, lying over there in the cot, finds a way of letting you know that a motion has been passed; and soon you will even get a inkling that there is going to be a motion. You are now at the beginning of a new relationship with the baby, who cannot communicate with you in an ordinary grown-up way, but who has found a way of talking without words. It is as if he said, 'I think I am going to want to pass a motion; are you interested?', and you (without actually saying so) answer 'yes', and you let him know that if you are interested this is not because you are frightened that he will make a mess, and not because you feel you ought to be teaching him how to be clean. If you are interested it is because you love your baby the way mothers do, so that whatever is important to the baby is also important to you. (Winnicott [95], p. 42.)

Winnicott here is stressing the importance of the delusional aspects of what seems to be a merely functional process. The passing of a motion is 'a little orgy that enriches the life of the infant, makes life worth living, and the body worth living in'.

The philosophical and poetic importance of these insights will appear later. For, as individuals like Winnicott penetrate to the origins of identity, they discover the primitive origins of such problems as those developed into a philosophical system by Bishop Berkeley. In the relationship between mother and infant there is 'the beginning of a relationship with the world'. At first the infant is virtually 'merged' with the mother. She is taken into him as 'subjective object', and he has no knowledge that he has not created her, and while we would speak as if he felt that she was a creature of his imagination, he cannot know this, but implicitly feels that she *is* him, and can, as it were, be made and unmade by him (though he cannot think in such terms – how he does think, of course, we can apprehend only by thinking of magic and delusion).

Even those things which he finds in the world, to which he attaches significance, such as his first cultural symbols (like Linus's blanket in *Peanuts*) the infant believes (in so far as he can) he has made. As Winnicott says:

If we go back to the first object, which may perhaps be a Harrington square, or a special woollen scarf, or the mother's handkerchief, we must admit, I believe, that from the infant's point of view it would be inappropriate for us to ask for the word 'ta' and the acknowledgement that the object came from the world. From the infant's point of view this first object was indeed created out of his or her imagination. It was the beginning of the infant's creation of the world, and it seems that we have to admit that in the case of every infant the world has to be created anew. The world as it presents itself is of no meaning to the newly-developed human being unless it is created as well as discovered. (Winnicott [95], p. 169.)

The implications of this are that we cannot perceive the world until we are able to bring our own imagination to it: indeed, *make* it, first. Here we may find Winnicott's insights confirmed by the insights of many others. Keats spoke of how some aspects of experience required a 'greeting of the spirit to make them seem real'. Discussing George Santayana, Marion Milner says: 'Without our own contribution we see nothing.' It seems that those who are cured of blindness, after having being blind from birth, cannot invest their world with meaning through the impressions they now receive through their eyes, and suffer grave psychic problems. Not only do they have to learn to see, but they find they have not learnt to 'make' their world employing this powerful sense. Such individuals may 'lose all their peace and self-respect' (Gregory [36]. This study, incidentally, is an example of the limitations of experimental psychology. It ignores disastrously the subjective and imaginative realities behind perception by sticking to 'fact' defined as what can be measured in exclusively external terms). As Morag Coate says: 'For each of us there is ultimately no universe except our own' – and, to use Harry Stack Sullivan's phrase, we are all 'participant observers'. If the subjective capacities to experience are disturbed in any way, physical or psychical, 'the integration and co-ordination of our personal universe has become unsound':

We take for granted the knowledge of the spaciousness and distinctness of our surroundings. But, at first, all we knew of space was what our limbs could reach. Sense data from our moving limbs received and co-ordinated in the brain, gave us a three-dimensional map of our immediate environment; to this was added information interpreted with growing skill from a pattern of sense-impressions received on the small curved surface of each retina. It is, when we think of it, a pretty fabulous mental feat, that we can interpret the tiny patterns received through the lenses of our eyes, enlarge them and project them outwards in imagination so thay they correspond with our three-dimensional environment. (Coate [14], p. 146.)

It is, in fact, even more fabulous than Morag Coate says, because our interpretation of the data is not merely a 'mental feat', for it is conditioned by the whole body–mind relationship between external and internal reality, begun with the mother, developed by our culture, and inherent in both the psychic and physical tissue of our being.

If our perception of the world depends thus upon our subjective capacities and our imagination, to select, make sense, and then project our interpretation outwards over reality, obviously there can be no such thing as merely 'seeing' 'what there is' in the outer world or 'inside' human nature and recording it. The mind is simply not like a camera, and what a camera does is only a shadow of the recording process performed by the material eye. The interpretation of data between the retina and the mind, and the projection of interpretations back on the world is all that belongs to our culture and spiritual existence as men – who are not cameras nor to be found analogous with cameras.

This transformation of psychoanalytical thought towards the acceptance of phantasy as primary means that we must re-examine Freud's devoted attachment to reason, combined with his distrust of imagination and everything he called 'illusion', which included philosophy. Leslie H. Farber quotes Will Herberg, who said; 'Reason is Freud's

God, and truth – which he identifies with scientific truth – the only epiphany he recognises' (Freud, religion and social reality, in *Commentary*, **23** (March 1957), quoted in Farber [20], p. 158).

This adulation of reason on Freud's part can be linked to his theory of human make-up. As Farber says:

> [Religion, art and philosophy provided man with comforting 'illusions' that] compensated man for the instinctual sacrifices exacted upon him by a repressive civilisation.
> Now such a view of natural instinct as war with human civilisation is, of course pure romanticism. For, like most of the great naturalists of the nineteenth century, Freud combined a romantic and almost mystical celebration of instinct with an equal reverence for its logical opposite: that is, reason, defined as scientific truth. And here the definition was as candidly naturalistic as a camera: truth was the 'correspondence (of scientific thought) with the real external world'. (Farber [20], p. 158.)

We find the same fallacies, of course, in the assumptions underlying Lorenz's deductions about man from geese and coral fish, or the psychologists preference for 'hard facts' over his own subjective experience of his needs for mothering. A parallel confusion lies behind the domination of educational psychology by the experimental psychologists who oblige teachers with many years of experience of children to study films of pigeons playing table tennis.

Linked with the problem of 'scientific truth' and the belief in reason are many difficulties over Freud's confusion of moral ideals. Freud was driven by his own model of human nature to place his belief in 'strengthening the ego for rational control', and 'education to reality'.

MacIntyre said of him:

> Freud's whole recognition of unconscious purposes is a discovery that men are more, and not less, rational than we thought they were. His whole method of treatment rests on an assertion that men can face and cope with their situation rationally, if only they are given the opportunity. Freud himself helps to conceal this from us by his disavowal of any moralistic purpose in his work. Nevertheless he promotes a moral ideal for which rationality is central. (A. C. MacIntyre, *The Unconscious*, quoted by Bantock [3], p. 56.)

At the same time, as Bantock points out, there was an ambiguity in the therapeutic role. Freud claimed that 'You are quite misinformed if you imagine that advice and guidance concerning conduct in life forms an integral part of the analytic method . . . we want nothing better than that the patient should find his own solutions for himself', and 'We are not reformers . . . we are merely observers'. Yet, as Bantock says: 'however permissive the analytic situation may seem to be, the very meeting of doctor and patient implies an inequality of roles, and an orientation of the patient to the analyst of a qualitatively different nature from that of analyst to the patient.'

Freud on one occasion called psychoanalysis a 'kind of re-education'.

As Bantock points out, we know that the rationalist assumption is false:

> Behind all this emphasis on the acquiring of insight lies the rationalist assumption that if only the world knew its own mind a little better, it would automatically prefer the good to the bad – 'insight' is supposed to lead to morally superior behaviour. Advocates of this point of view forget, for instance, the action of the 'hidden persuaders', those who attempt to make a good commercial proposition out of insights gained from a knowledge of depth psychology. (Bantock [3], p. 37.)

It is indeed deeply shocking to find a person using the knowledge gained from psychology for purposes of 'depth' advertising for his own commercial gain. But such moral lapses indicate that the concept of psychoanalysis as a 'scientific education' as some theorists still seek to define it will not do. Psychoanalysis has come to see the doctor–patient relationship as one in which it may become possible for an individual to complete

c

certain processes of psychic growth, by a form of regression into a 'mothering' relation-ship, in which rational awareness is only one factor, and the predominant factors are cultural and relational ones, involving symbolism and phantasy. Thus if a patient continues to behave in ways which examined rationally seem anti-social or immoral, then this can be seen as a manifestation of forms of immaturity or incompleteness in the personality. Implicit in this is a concept of maturity and completeness, and the growth of a 'healthy moral sense', but these are never fully realisable in any actual living individual. Some aspects of a person may simply be incapable of growth or change, faults in the psychic tissue which he has to live with: you can't make a silk purse out of a sow's ear even by psychoanalysis.

In coming to accept such truths psychoanalysis has simply come to accept the great complexities of the texture of human nature, and the inevitable faultiness and intract-ability of human personality. On our part, we need to see that insight itself is not going to solve human problems which require a much deeper cure, while science itself has delusions here.

The romantic concept of a complete and ideally perfect individual often lurks in the background of rationalist attitudes. The mind can spin, in a schizoid way, a perfect intellectual system, and by intellectual hate (as Marion Milner indicates) it is possible for us to try to impose such systems on non-perfect life, and on the intractable areas of psychic reality (as in sexology). Freud's impulse to be 'scientific' itself can be suspected of being impelled by a schizoid pursuit of perfectibility and omniscence. In consequence, psychoanalysis still suffers from the romantic fallacies of rationalist assumptions. As Farber says, in the 'scientific' impulse of psychoanalysis itself there is this implicit pursuit of omniscience:

> Freud's . . . chief fire was reserved for any system of meanings which dared to set itself up in competi-tion with science. Science alone was able to produce a complete and coherent picture of the universe, from which to deduce – in more or less identical terms – a complete and coherent science of man. Now this may be called positivism, or it may be called the omniscient approach to man. (Farber [20], p. 160.)

This omniscience belongs to a period of confidence in science and its capacity to know which came to an end with relativity, while notions derived from post-relativity physics have found their way into psychology, such as that of the 'participant observer' (an uncertainty which now even extends to astronomy*).

The confidence of scientific omniscience, as we shall see, led to many abuses in Freud, associated with that 'chief immodesty' as Farber calls it, that 'one can, instead of imagin-ing, actually know the other in his essence'. This presumption in psychology has always been that which has frightened off many who are concerned with imagination and creativity, because implicitly it denied the subjective, unique, and intractable realm of the I–Thou.

Here, there is a crisis in knowledge itself in which psychoanalysis is involved. Psycho-analysis as philosophical anthropology is not scientific in the Galilean–Newtonian way. But the existence of the human facts it explores suggests that science itself needs to extend its terms and scope. To cling to 'scientific omniscience', however, is to cling to that pursuit of perfectibility which Farber characterises as a heresy, because it so much resembles

---

* 'Cosmology has become entwined with theological, philosophical and indeed emotional difficulties – and perhaps these might, in the end, be part of the solution we are seeking' (Sir Bernard Lovell, *Our Present Knowledge of the Universe* [59]).

those religious heresies which sought to believe in earthly perfection. 'Stripped of its usual scientific qualifications, it might be expressed in this manner: however rarely the goal of perfection may be achieved, man is a creature who is, nonetheless, psychologically perfectible, by virtue of either the early and happy accident of childhood or the later and unhappy necessity of psychoanalysis' (Farber [20], p. 210).

One often finds in scientists, and in non-scientists, the hope that 'one day we will be able to control our emotional life, just as we control disease nowadays'. There is perhaps the same impulse behind some forms of reliance on the efficacy of drugs and electric shocks in psychiatry. Drugs, as Guntrip points out, really only suspend the human problem of growth and development by a 'drugged condition', however much they relieve the immediate agony of mind, and solve the problem of mass treatment.

But another consequence of the heresy of perfectibility, as part of the essential romanticism of this kind of science of man, was that there grew up a concept of being human which failed to accept the inevitable agonies and anguishes of being mortal – including the important experience of despair, or 'tragic awareness'. Through psychology there began the pursuit of a perfectibility conceived in terms of the 'absence of defect' – and at the same time there developed a neglect of other sources of information about the nature of man, while the significance of culture was not seen.

To expose this development is not to deny the possibilities of becoming 'whole': but, as Farber says, the pursuit of perfectibility may well defeat our potentiality for wholeness, and estrange us from other sources of knowledge of ourselves. His remarkable paragraph on this subject makes it plain why so many remained so suspicious of psychoanalysis for so long:

> With the development of psycho-analysis at the turn of the century, a whole new body of psychological evidence and hypothesis, all proceeding exclusively from attention to psychological disorder or pathology, invigorated the perennial issue of what is human. In the sheer excitement of these discoveries and inventions, analysts tended to forget older sources of wisdom pertaining to the same question. Instead, as though they were the first citizens to arrive on this planet, they attempted to derive an entire way of life from their theories of pathology. The examples are legion. If authoritarian fathers produce neurotic children, children should be raised in cooperative nurseries away from parental pressures. (Farber [20], p. 218.)

Farber lists many examples ('If repressed hostility accounts for certain types of misery, then free expression of anger is evidence of maturity'). The theme is always 'complete absence of all defects means complete virtue, or – perfection'.

It was this that the Nazis sought by the extermination of the Jews and mentally deficient patients: seen as an aspect of the collective insanity of schizoid ('final') solutions, we see this quest for 'purity' through an idealised intellectual system at its most menacing. It lives on in communism, in its various forms. But it also underlies the fallacies of permissiveness. From the point of view of those concerned with what Bantock calls 'moral sensibility' the impulse looks as it does to Farber:

> Virtues which are the absence of defects have very little relevance to any knowledge of virtue we may have that has come to us, not from psychology, but from other sources of information about what is human: history, philosophy, religion, or our own experience – all of which have not only always recognised human imperfectibility, but have constantly warned man against the grave dangers of believing himself perfectible. The theories of psycho-analysis seem to tempt us to forget, or even ignore, these warnings, offering us a promise and a plan for our own perfection. Nevertheless, we must remind ourselves that, though imperfect, we may still become whole. And should we succumb to the heresy of perfectibility, our tragedy will be that we defeat our potentiality for wholeness. Such heresy, however, does not rise inevitably from our doctrines, but captures us only when we use those doctrines to estrange us from all other knowledge of ourselves. (Farber [20], p. 219.)

Any attempt to use psychological theory to impose a 'pure' pattern on life could obviously be disastrous, and, in so far as it becomes philosophical anthropology, psychology should become able to recognise how futile such an impulse would be – while increasingly recognising the validity of other sources of knowledge of ourselves. Psychoanalysis thus comes closer to the arts and humanities.

At the same time it reveals much about our capacity to perceive reality. Bantock says: 'the view of "reality" we consciously or unconsciously accept subtly interpenetrates our vision of the world, which is itself in part the creation of the assumptions *in terms of which we interpret what we see*' (Bantock [3], p. 58; my italics).

Professor Bantock's last phrase is eminently endorsed by recent psychoanalytical writers of the 'object-relations' school. From their point of view, as we have seen, there is, furthermore, a sense in which we have to create the world before we can perceive it, which takes the problem of perception still deeper. Our capacity to perceive is at one with the 'psychic tissue' of our subjective life. For we do not only interpret the world in terms of certain 'assumptions' by which we 'interpret what we see'. It is rather that our capacity to see a world at all derives from the earliest processes by which, in relationship with the mother as the first object, we 'made' her, while also making or discovering ourselves.

This primary basis of 'being' underlies every capacity for vision and intellectual power – as we know from schizophrenics, in whom these primary processes have not been completed adequately. For them there may be neither relationship, perception, intellectual life, nor meaning. As Farber says:

> If schizophrenia can be thought of as an extreme withering of the *Thou* capacity (i.e. the capacity for relationship) with corresponding impairment in the world of *It* (i.e. the perception of things), it is not surprising that it should be accompanied by a crippling of the intellect. I mean intellect here not in the narrow sense of a measureable reason or intelligence, but in a larger sense – experience informed with imagination ordered by knowledge and judgement. (Farber [20], p. 148.)

The latter concept surely corresponds to Bantock's 'moral sensibility'. Farber refers to a Rorschach study of schizophrenia made by Margaret Rioch which found that the prospects for recovery were poorest whenever the patient's intellectual and imaginative powers were most severely limited. Farber implies that the intellectual dissociation of the schizophrenic is as 'fearfully impoverished' as his capacities for relationship with others.

What we have emerging from psychoanalytical thought is, then, a growing recognition that our powers of ego-maintenance in the inner world are at one with our capacity to perceive the outer world. Bantock indicates something of this when he quotes Freud from *The Claims of Psychoanalysis to Scientific Interest*: 'Psychoanalysis unhesitatingly ascribes the primacy in mental life to affective processes, and it reveals an unexpected amount of affective disturbance and blinding of the intellect in normal no less than in sick people' (Bantock [3], p. 47).

In this area of insight I believe we have an indication of a possible meeting point between science and art, between the objective and subjective exploration of the truths of existence. Both are ways of describing and acting on experience, one experience in 'outer space', the other experience in 'inner space': and they are in complex in everyone.

While science requires a certain kind of exactness of mensuration to achieve which it seeks to exclude subjective factors as far as possible, art is concerned which the realm of man's experience of himself as subject. This inward reality can only be explored through imagination, and facts here can only be established by the collocation of descriptions. What is of great significance today is the growing recognition that both science and the subjective disciplines are both but ways of *describing,* while in both intuitive capacities and imagination are pre-eminent – they are both human activities.*

Of his calling Farber says it suffers from two fallacies: 'this illusion is twofold: first that psychology is, or ought to be, an exact science, and, second, that exact sciences are those which do not require imagination' (Farber [20], p. 157).

Of Freud's work Farber says:

> Because scientists have imagined that no valid source of knowledge could be found in imagination, psychoanalysts, beginning with Freud, have made heroic efforts to deny the sources of much of their own knowledge with the result that imagination has had to be smuggled into the halls of science through the janitor's entrance. . . .
>
> Freud's insistent claim to be a man of science, offering only the most empirical facts about the human psyche, has misled nearly everyone, beginning with himself. And yet in 1900 he wrote with a surprising frankness; ' . . . I am not really a man of science, not an observer, not an experimenter, and not a thinker. I am nothing but by temperament a *conquisiator* – an adventurer . . . with the curiosity, the boldness, and the tenacity that belongs to that type of being.' . . . He had none of that scholar's caution, that timidity of the scientist or historian or lawyer, that sticks to the rules of evidence, no matter the cost. He, Freud, without knowing what it, was a poet. He put no real trust in the fallible laws and man-made facts of evidence. What he was after was the pure ideal, the pure imagined ideal: the truth itself. (Farber, [20], p. 163.)

Therefore, while in consequence it is not really appropriate to acclaim Freud as a great scientist,† it is necessary now to urge that science itself must become able to include that kind of knowledge gained by imagination and projective identification, if it is to take satisfactory account of human truth. This point is also made by R. D. Laing and the American existentialist writers, and throughout his work by Guntrip. Guntrip says that one of our problems of the knowledge of man is that 'when science begins to treat man as an object of investigation, it somehow loses sight of him as a person' (Guntrip [37], p. 16).

He insists that: 'A human being can only be known as a living and highly individual, unique "person". Aspects of his total being can be reduced by analysis and abstraction to the level of classified phenomena, and that has its uses; but what he really is, is then missed. Psychoanalysis is, or should be, the special custodian of this truth in the field of science' (Guntrip [37], p. 16).

This means, however, that psychoanalysis must 'question the traditional exclusion by science of the fact of individuality, the one fact that is ultimately inescapable in any realistic attempt to study and understand human beings' (Guntrip [37], p. 17).

Some forms of existentialist thought, and the psychoanalysis influenced by these, are seeking to restore to authenticity the subjective disciplines of exploring individuality. So whereas we in the humanities have previously felt that we must champion the unique inner reality of man as a living being against homunculism, we can now recognise that there has developed a crisis in psychoanalysis itself over this very problem. We find that psychoanalysis seeks to 'outgrow its origins in a neurophysical and psychobiological philosophy of man, using the instinct concept as a basis of theory, into a truly psychodynamic theory of the personality implying a philosophy of man that takes account of his reality as an individual person' (Guntrip [37], p. 17).

Moreover, psychoanalysis puts an urgent emphasis on those cultural and relational needs with which the humanities have always been concerned. Here, for instance, we may

---

* See Wiesäcker above and also *The Art of Scientific Investigation* by A. Beveridge, which has chapters on Intuition and Imagination. Also Polanyi and Marjorie Grene.

† Professor Bantock 'places him among the supreme scientific geniuses of all time, the equivalent of Copernicus, Newton, Darwin and Einstein' (Bantock [3], p. 60).

take the concepts of meeting and confirmation. The capacity for confirming and being confirmed between individuals, says Farber, 'depends, according to Buber, on what he calls "imagining the real" ' – as we would say in literary criticism, 'realisation'. Farber speaks of man's 'need to be confirmed "even as what he can become".' This is exactly what imaginative creativity and education are concerned with. 'Applied to intercourse between men, "imagining" the real means that I imagine to myself what another man is at this very moment wishing, feeling, perceiving, thinking, and not a detached context but in his very reality, that is, as a living process in this man' (Buber [101], p. 103).

Farber adds: 'The need to be confirmed as what one is, "even as what he can become" – this need would seem indisputable in one's ordinary existence, but in the extra-ordinary existence that is psychotherapy, the therapist is concerned only with the patient's need for confirmation, often at the expense of his own.' (Farber [20], p. 157).

It is this process of creative confirmation which is common to the experiences of (a) rearing a baby, (b) symbolic creativity in art, (c) psychotherapy, (d) creative teaching. If we look at psychotherapy in this sense we can see that it is very different indeed from what tends to be implied by the name 'psychoanalysis' itself, and from concepts of this process as merely seeking for and exposing suppressed memories, or sources of guilt, or bringing about a reaction, or giving 'scientific education', or promoting 'rational strengthening of the ego'. It is rather surely a process of love and imagination, belonging to those creative cultural activities and experiences of 'meeting' which create a sense of 'the point of life', as Winnicott sees them. Frankl sees psychotherapy as needing a 'concept of man that is directed . . . in steady search for meaning' – a process he calls 'logotherapy'.

In Farber's discussion in his chapter 'The Therapeutic Despair' his observation that therapy provides 'confirmation', leads him to examine radically the origins of psycho-analysis in Freud, and that 'presumption that one can, instead of imagining, actually know the other in his essence'. In his case histories Freud was led to a 'rather comical kind of omniscience': 'an omniscience akin to that assumed by the historian':

> For the author tells us (of 'Dora') that he has been able to trace the 'whole origin and development' of this case 'with complete certainty and almost without a gap'. The comedy broadens as the many gaps in this case history become so apparent, event to the historian, that he now has to justify his 'meagre information'. This he does on at least four grounds, three of which must surely be superfluous. The alibis range, with a refreshing absence of logic, from 'medical discretion' and premature termina-tion of analysis, to the suggestion that all homosexuals are liars anyhow! (Farber [20], p. 165.)

Yet a whole theory of homosexuality was built on this case!

If we insist that psychology must be an exact science, then exposures of Freud's lack of logic could be taken as evidence that psychoanalysis is disreputable. However, if we accept that Freud was exploring human experience poetically, but nonetheless authentically for that, then his case history and his theoretical insights derived from it become perfectly acceptable and valid. As Farber says: 'Freud's imagination came brilliantly to the rescue [at this moment of his greatest scientific defeat, which was to fail to give a complete account of a case with "complete certainty and almost without a gap"] offering to his intellect many ingenious insights and a few profound truths' (Farber [20], p. 165).

These 'truths' were what I would call poetic truths, but through them Freud

> offered many profoundly useful insights into that kind of history which has nothing to do with medical or natural history, and into the human kind of nature that has nothing to do with the 'real external world' and may, perhaps be entirely false to that nonhuman world. Insofar as these insights must be called true, I should like to call them facts: facts that are no less real or imagined than those which

science has defined as facts, but which obey different laws and concern quite another subject than do the facts of nature. (Farber [20], p. 165.)

The crisis in psychoanalysis, then, centres round the definition of human 'facts', and how we are to give an account of them.

One of our difficulties in turning from the world of culture to psychoanalysis has always been that when psychoanalysis turned to works of art there often seemed to be an implicit reductiveness in its attempt to explain away the creativity of man in terms of more primary impulses belonging to some reality other than the reality of meaning. Yet elsewhere in psychoanalysis there are insights which seem profoundly relevant to creativity. This dichotomy has already been noted by Lionel Trilling, as Farber points out:

> As Lionel Trilling put it: 'Freud . . . has much to tell us about art, but whatever is suggestive in him is not likely to be found in those of his works in which he deals expressly with art itself.' Nevertheless, 'It was left for Freud to discover how, in a scientific age, we still feel and think in figurative formations, and to create, what psychoanalysis is, a science of tropes, or metaphor, and its variants.' (Trilling [84], p. 42, quoted in Farber [20], p. 162.)

'In other words,' adds Farber, 'when Freud is approached, not as a scientist investigating the nature of the organism, but rather as a critic investigating the nature of language and imagination, then, ironically enough, his great value as an imaginative, and even poetic, genius, becomes apparent.' Such an observation would, of course, have made Freud himself very uneasy.

In psychoanalysis Freud's point of view meant that subjectivity, common sense, and imagination had to be smuggled into Freudian therapy under some rather conflicting terms of natural science, while aesthetic, philosophical, and religious meaning had to be translated into vague romantic terms of natural 'feeling', or else into the less vague but equally romantic terms of natural 'instinct'. While this may have elevated some subjective aspects of experience to intellectual prestige by scientific 'objectivity', it also caused much intellectual impoverishment, a point which Professor Bantock is also much concerned about.

Works of art, as Farber suggests here, were explained in terms of their 'origins': on *Hamlet* Freud wrote: 'I have followed the literature of psychoanalysis closely, and I accept its claim that it was not until the material of the tragedy had been traced back to the Oedipus theme that the mystery of its effect was at last explained' (*The Moses of Michaelangelo*, quoted in Farber [20], p. 159).

As Farber says: 'Here, in such reductive "explanations" of a work of art, is a good example of that genetic fallacy which always explains the nature of a hen by calling her an egg. . . . Freud's genetic explanations had necessarily to reduce all intellectual or aesthetic values to the level of a non-verbal wish or preintellectual condition' (Farber [20], p. 159).

This impulse is more insidious than that which seeks to claim that art is 'nothing but' a childish motive or that man is nothing but an animal or child. 'What it does is more insidious. It first explains an intellectual pursuit entirely in nonintellectual terms of motive; and, secondly, explains the motive entirely in terms of animal "instinct" or of infantile "feeling" ' (Farber [20], p. 160).

Later we shall try to analyse some of Freud's unconscious motives in this. But here, this implicit denial of certain primary human needs may be associated with another problem we have had, in involving psychoanalysis, which is the frequent dehumanisation of its terms. As Farber points out, the norms and standards which derive from psycho-analytical theory tend to be expressed in singularly inhuman language. Farber quotes Fairbairn:

> Mature dependence is characterized neither by a one-sided attitude of incorporation nor by an attitude of primary emotional identification. On the contrary, it is characterised by a capacity on the part of a differentiated individual for co-operative relationships with differentiated objects. So far as the appropriate biological object is concerned, the relationship involving evenly matched giving and taking between two differentiated individuals who are mutually dependent, and between whom there is no disparity of dependence. (Fairbairn [19], quoted by Farber [20], p. 132.)

This quotation is from a psychoanalytical writer who sought himself to resist the claim of his own discipline to be a science. Below I endorse Fairbairn's view of mutual depend-ence in independence between individuals. But one cannot but agree with Farber's comment on the language:

> Without examining these normative statements in detail, the reader can see why psychiatry is so often charged with being reductive. For, though the creatures described above may bear some resem-blance to animals or steam engines or robots, or electronic brains, they do not sound like people. They are, in fact, constructs of theory, more hominoid than human; and, whether they are based on the libido theory or on one of the new interpersonal theories of relationships, it is just those qualities most distinctively human that seem to have been omitted. It is a matter of some irony, if one turns from psychology to one of Dostoevsky's novels, to find that, no matter how wretched, how puerile, or how dilapidated his characters may be, they all possess more humanity than the ideal man who lives in the pages of psychiatry. (Farber [20], p. 133.)

One is always liable, as an 'arts' man, to feel cowed by 'scientific accuracy' and its terminology, and perhaps there is something of this in our recourse to the language of, say, object-relations psychology, to seek to vindicate even our preoccupation with phantasy. But through the crisis in psychoanalysis itself we can now perhaps come to see that where we find attempts to reduce human experience to the components of a hominoid construct we may see them as forms of compensation for the weakness and fear of being human. Strength in the confrontation of human truth lies with those who are willing to experience the explorations made by the poetic in the recognition of the intractability of 'inner reality'. Here is the importance of Buber. As Farber says of him: 'Buber avoids the romantic attitude toward feeling that is peculiar to current philosophy. The romantic regards feeling as a spontaneous impulse arising either from above or from below: either as divine or poetic inspiration, or else as some daemonic force or instinct – as represented, for example, by the id' (Farber [20], p. 139).

As in object-relations psychology, Buber explores feeling as a manifestation of our needs to find ourselves confirmed in relationship:

> Buber's emphasis upon the relation between selves, rather than upon the individual self in its relations with the world, constitutes an obvious difference from Freudian psychology. His difference from Sullivanian psychology [which tends to see every problem in terms of communications – D. H.] will become evident as a difference in meaning assigned to the word relation. For example, when Buber spoke of the *I–Thou* as it may occur either in the young infant or among primitive races, it is clear that he was relying on his own imagination to give him knowledge of these unknowable states of subjectivity. He was thus able to avoid the genetic fallacy that is common to all nineteenth-century psychology. This fallacy springs, like behaviourism, from a natural-science view of objects that is then applied to such invisible phenomena as human subjectivity or human experience. For example, when the nineteenth-century psychologist 'looked at' an imaginary child or primitive, he was not imagining their experience, but quite literally visualising an object: a bodily object, in its bodily behaviour. Seen through the spectacles of natural-science theory this bodily object would appear as a 'natural object'; a 'human animal' or 'organism'. And, since he supposed the origins of man's experience to lie in his bodily behaviour, the psychologist could then suppose that the behaviour of children, or primi-tives, and even of animals, would give him the 'real' origins – and thence the 'real' truth – about the

whole of human experience. But the most striking fact about human experience, of course, is that so much of it is invisible. (Farber [20], p. 140.)

For 'invisible' we can read, again, 'impossible to apprehend except by projective identification and imagination'. If we do so, then we can see how limited is that approach to psychology which is confined to experimental 'hard facts' or sees the mind as an 'information processing' or 'communications' system.

The 'nothing but' attitude, that all natural phenomena can be now satisfactorily explained as forms of 'machine', was promoted at large by the Reith Lectures given by Dr. Edmund Leach in 1968. As Professor W. H. Thorpe, F.R.S., Professor of Animal Ethology at Cambridge University, pointed out in an article criticising Leach, this view represents a misuse of certain scientific tools. Science, he pointed out, involves the construction of theories conceived in some degree in mechanistic terms. 'Scientists make these assumptions as a working hypothesis; deliberately, for practical purposes, leaving out of the picture the mind, the perception and the personal devotion of the scientist making the study. This approach can be called "mechanistic monism".'

The trouble is that misinterpretation of this working assumption leads many to 'assume that the method of science based on the assumption that a significant understanding of natural events can be reached primarily – if not entirely – by regarding the world as an inter-locking series of mechanisms can be a *basis of a general philosophy*' (*The Times*, 25 January, 1969; my italics).

The scientific view of the world, as Professor Thorpe emphasises, is a partial view 'a deliberate restriction to certain areas of our total experience – a technique for understanding certain parts of that experience and achieving mastery over nature.'

Another such significant technique is that of attempting to explain the mechanisms of life in terms of components: 'It is right and proper that scientists should do as they are continually doing – attempt to explain the complex in terms of the simple, to explain physical and biological mechanisms in terms of the behaviour of electrons, atoms and molecules. This is known as the method of "reductionism".'

The trouble arises when such techniques of science are extended in the fallacious and irresponsible assumption that these are exclusive ways, the only valid ways, of exploring and accounting for our total experience: 'It is the duty of all those who write for the public on such topics to make sure they have really understood, and have taken account of, all the relevant considerations, so that they do not lead others into a morass of their own making. Reductionism – like mechanistic monism – is, of course, an essential tool for science; but as a general philosophy it can have no validity whatever.'

A willingness to admit the regions of 'inner reality', and the dimension of our psychic being seems to urge many to make this mistake of attempting to erect such scientific tools into 'general philosophies'. In this we must include Freud himself, the pseudo-scientists of animal behaviourism, no less than Dr. Leach.

Freud shared the attitude of the 'nothing but' behaviourist:

When he looked at the child's behaviour Freud saw megalomania, narcissism – libidinal drives operating in isolation, abstracted from the human experience. With his behaviourist view of motives he sees 'parental love' too, as something that is 'touching' but is 'at bottom . . . childish'. Indeed, Freud defines 'parental love' as '*nothing but* parental narcissism born again'.

Here is an example of the genetic fallacy according to which the supposed origins of parental love are more real or important than the experience of love, so that love becomes *nothing but* the narcissism of the child. . . . This springs from the behaviourist fallacy which claims that what cannot be seen or observed [or, one might add, measured – D. H.] in a man's behaviour, cannot be known to man. (Farber [20], p. 140.)

This reductiveness in psychoanalytical thought has been one of those elements in this approach which have tended to alienate thinkers in the field of culture and education. In his chapter 'Freud and Education' G. H. Bantock refers to some of Freud's main formulations:

> The assumption of natural goodness was dismissed as one of those 'unfortunate illusions' which 'bring only disaster'. Freud, indeed, would have no truck with the notion of human beings as 'gentle friendly creatures wishing for love'. . . . Until contact with reality necessitates 'reaction formations' of instinctual strivings, children comprise simply bundles of ego-centric, satisfaction-seeking impulses; they 'assert their animal nature naively enough and demonstrate persistently that they have yet to learn their purity'. (Bantock [3], p. 46.)

This attitude to children is still obviously endorsed by the author of *Lord of the Flies*. Moreover, as Freud's attitude implies, if the primary 'reality' is man's essential id impulses civilisation can only exist under the most severe restraints. Golding's children, removed from civilisation, revert to the id. (*Id* is also the name of the house magazine of A. S. Neill's 'free' school, Summerhill.) Professor Bantock pronounces this view of human nature 'sombre' – but yet points out that, extraordinary as the implications are, it is cheerfully absorbed into the theories of 'progressive' education:

> In contradistinction to [the] view of the enlightenment, Freud posited the egocentric, instinctual strivings of the primitive being. His 'state of nature' is Hobbesian rather than physiocratic. And yet 'progressive' thinking in education so profoundly influenced by notions of natural goodness and theories of free inner development untrammelled by obtrusive adult or pedagogic influence, assimilates without difficulty so sombrely based a theory of human development. (Bantock [3], p. 46.)

There is in fact an ambiguity here, first recognised by Guntrip. It is not strictly possible to reconcile the dualistic model of 'reason' versus impersonal 'id instincts', on the one hand, with the more dynamic concepts of inner conflict represented by Freud's theory of ego-splitting, which we shall examine below.

Instinct theory is a negative way of explaining civilisation. 'The uninhibited indulgence of the id's instinctual strivings would make social life an impossibility; there are two restraining factors, aspects of the developing psyche, which serve as checks on these instinctual demands. These are the ego and the super-ego' (Bantock [3], p. 47).

As we shall see, this essential attitude to the relationship between the 'natural' id impulses, the ego as an 'instrument of adaptation', and the super-ego as an internalised authority, is still the basis of the social and cultural theory of such a radical modern psychologist as R. D. Laing. At the same time, while we may seek to reject the theory of id, ego, and super-ego as it is based on instinct theory, we shall also find it to be the basis of all later psychodynamic theory which yet needs no id, impersonal savage force or death instinct to explain hate.

Bantock quotes Freud from *The Ego and the Id*: 'As the child was once compelled to obey its parents, so the ego submits to the categorical imperative pronounced by its super-ego' (Freud [30]).

And from *Civilization and its Discontents*: 'Civilization therefore obtains the mastery over the dangerous love of aggression in individuals by enfeebling it and disarming it and setting up an institution within their minds to keep watch over it, like a garrison in a conquered city' (Freud [31]).

Pain arises from the excessive zeal of the super-ego according to Freud because it 'troubles too little about the happiness of the ego, and it fails to take into account the . . . strength of instinctual cravings in the id and the hardships of external environment'. Guilt arises as a consequence of the sacrifices necessary for the survival of social life.

As Bantock says, such an attitude to human make-up has meant a 'moral coarsening', which we find now pervading our present-day literature, our cultural life at large, and many prevalent attitudes to ethical questions of censorship, tolerance, and personal behaviour. Fundamentally reductive of human quality, Freud's attitude to the moral agency in man is also, as Bantock points out, equivocal:

> He admits that the 'strengthening of the super-ego' is a highly valuable psychological 'possession for culture'. But at the same time, as a result of his clinical experience, he urges that 'in our therapy we often find ourselves obliged to do battle with the super-ego and to moderate its demands'. Renunciation itself may stimulate the super-ego, because though renunciation of gratification has taken place, the wish persists and cannot be hidden from the super-ego: 'every renunciation becomes a dynamic fount of conscience'. (Bantock [3], p. 49.)

Associated with many of Freud's reductive attitudes to human make-up, then, we may detect ambivalences, and these correspond, as we shall see, with the difference between Freud's therapy and his theory. In his theory he believes in lifting moral restraint, while in his private life he is impeccably moral, in a strict bourgeois manner. Despite his own genuine interest in and admiration for culture, he seeks to reduce the artist in his theory as 'one who is urged by instinctual needs . . . ' – a view which Professor Bantock appropriately pronounces as 'vulgar'. Freud sees the instinctual life as the most real aspect of man's experience, yet believes that civilisation needs to be preserved, as by 'mastery over the dangerous love of aggression'. He seeks in therapy to enable patients to be free to realise themselves: but yet at the heart of his theory there lies the evident belief in this 'dangerous love of aggression' which is unchangeable, innate – and a manifestation of the death instinct. Yet in such a phrase as the 'dynamic fount of conscience' we have the seeds of object-relations psychology and its recognition of the 'healthy moral sense'. Yet Freud in theory urged less morality: '. . . we have found it impossible to give our support to conventional sexual morality or to approve highly of the means by which society attempts to arrange the practical problems of sexuality in life' *Introductory Lectures*, quoted by Bantock [3], p. 52) – a lead which is enthusiastically followed by theorists such as Theodore Reich, Wayland Young, and 'sexual revolutionaries'. But at the same time Freud says: 'It need not be said that a culture which leaves unsatisfied and drives to rebelliousness such a number of its members neither has the prospect of continued existence, nor deserves it' (Freud [34], quoted by Bantock [3], p. 52).

Freud believed in a powerful degree of coercion of the masses by an élite: the 'masses' having no inclination for 'instinctual renunciation'. Yet he had a great respect for the achievements of human culture.

With this equivocal attitude one can also associate what Bantock calls 'the equivocal part played by Freud's hedonism' – a hedonism which makes his attitude to human nature most acceptable to the ethos of a commercial-acquistive society in which the ingestion of quantities of satisfaction has been fostered as the basis of the pursuit of a sense of identity and of meaning in life. Freud's hedonism, as Bantock points out: 'expresses itself in an absence of stimulation rather than a positive state of euphoria, as an itch to be got rid of rather than a creative thing . . . fullness of life has a quantitative – Freud would have called it an 'economic' – not a qualitative connotation' (Bantock [3], p. 53).

As we shall see, our beliefs here have profound implications for culture and education. The development of psychoanalytical theory since Freud has in fact completely reversed his attitude to the quality of life and its aims. Freud reduced 'what it is to be human' to a problem of the economics of stimulation, the discharge of tension, and the elimination of pent-up 'itches' or hungers. By contrast, in a recent paper on culture, Winnicott says:

> Instintual gratifications start off as part-functions, and they become *seductioas* unless based on a well-established capacity in the individual person for total experience. . . . When one speaks of a man one speaks of him along with the summation of his cultural experience. . . . It is these cultural experiences that provide the continuity in the human race which transcends personal existence. (Winnicott [130], p. 370.)

Here we have psychoanalysis talking as Professor Bantock would himself talk – as he implies when he says: 'much of the experience of, say, Eliot's *Four Quartets*, would seem strange to him [Freud] despite the austerity of his own life.'

By contrast, Winnicott's attitude to man such as we have explored above profoundly illuminates Eliot's poetry and is at the same time illuminated by it:

> Caught in the form of limitation
> Between un-being and being. . . .

We are at last, that is, cultural workers and psychologists, beginning to talk the same kind of language, because psychoanalytical thought has gradually relinquished those ways of describing man which belong to Freud's way of reducing man, by the 'natural science' approach, to something less than human. Once again, today, as we find in the remarkable writings of Leslie Farber, Viktor E. Frankl, Guntrip, and Winnicott, psychoanalysts are beginning to face up to primary problems of meaning and existence, and to use the same terms as a philosopher such as Buber who was also 'moralist, theologian, poet, historian, critic, and above all a religious man'. In this psycholanalysis would seem to be recovering from its 'estrangement' from 'other sources of information about what is human'.

As a further example of reductive fallacies Farber quotes Sullivan's view of tenderness between mother and child:

> My theorem is this: the observed activity of the infant arising from the tension of needs induces tension in the mothering one, which tension is experienced as tenderness and as an impulsion to activities towards the relief of the infant's needs. [From *The Interpersonal Theory of Psychiatry*, 1959.]

Farber comments:

> This is a way of defining love as *nothing but* anxiety. And an anxiety that needs to be relieved is not very different from an instinctual or libidinal drive that needs to be discharged. Thus, through these reductive views of man, current philosophy has arrived at a biological and a steam-engine psychology of motives. Love is nothing but a physiological drive that needs relief. (Farber [20], p. 151.)

By contrast, says Farber, Buber makes the kind of approach to the primary I–Thou relationship such as is now gaining grounds, as we shall see, in recent psychoanalytical thought, by imagining the mutual experience of shared relation between mother and child, 'from the inside'.

Psychoanalytical thought has come to preoccupy itself with underlying problems whose origins are in this primary relationship with the mother. Such problems of identity and being require such imaginative penetration to the inside of 'the experience of the child towards its mother and the experience of the mother towards her child'. To the imaginative activity of the psychoanalyst here, however, we can add his experience of children and adults in regression, who can communicate to him not only their present experience of dissociation, but can also illuminate childhood experience far more than any observation of children. As Winnicott says: 'My experiences have led me to recognise that dependent or deeply regressed patients can teach the analyst more about early infancy than can be learned from direct observation of infants, and more than can be learned from contact with mothers who are involved with infants' (Winnicott [94], p. 141).

One of the problems in our thinking about man, obviously, is to accept the truth of what is learned about the earliest stages of formation of identity, from patients under psychotherapy, and to allow this experience to illuminate what we observe of children's behaviour by direct experience. Are we to take Winnicott's point of view, over such issues as nudity in the family, or corporal punishment, or that of sociologists or psychologists who rely exclusively on external observation?

Of course we can find such truth in poetry and other sources of knowledge of human experience. But psychoanalysis offers a more disciplined and conscious approach to problems arising which require profound poetical and philosophical effort – such as, for example, the need to investigate those stages in the child's experience of the mother, which we can imagine only with difficulty, since the child is not yet aware that his mother is distinct from himself. We have no terms as yet to express such unexplored states. How can we speak of the experience of an individual who is not sure that he exists at all in his own right? Or of that of one who needs (as did a patient of Laing's) to preserve chaos within the self as a defence measure?

Such explorations of human identity are beyond the scope of the prevalent methods of empirical science, and the realities in question are not to be found in external manifestations in men or animals. Yet to the poet and philosopher they are bread and butter, and thus those concerned with psychotherapy, and its philosophical anthropology, and those concerned with culture, education, and the humanities, find themselves closer than ever before: or so I believe. The effect could be that all of us in these spheres could gain confidence from one another's disciplines.

PART II

The Reaction Against Freudian Theory

CHAPTER 4

The Origins of Love and Hate

COMMON sense alone prompts one to question Freud's theories in some respects – such as his strange blindness to the mother's role. Ian D. Suttie, of course, did not base his work entirely on common sense – he was a psychiatrist of long experience. But he boldly declared that, from the commonsense point of view, it was mistaken of Freud to fail to see love as a primary reality, since evidence of the truth of its influence was everywhere visible.

Suttie's book *The Origins of Love and Hate* [78] provides a useful starting point for our discussion of psychoanalytical theory in relation to culture and social life – because it was Suttie's concern to 'reintroduce common sense into the science of psychology' (Suttie [78], p. 208).

Suttie was able to point out a radical ambivalence in Freud's work: in his therapy Freud implied a positive attitude to human make-up, while in his 'free' theory he was extremely negative. In this Suttie anticipated many psychoanalytical writers who were to modify Freud, and to confirm his impression that Freudian theory was 'based on hate – a denial of love' (p. 194).

Suttie's book was first published in 1935. Significantly, it contains references to Melanie Klein and to Sandor Ferenczi ('The physician's love heals the patient', p. 199). It was too early for Suttie to produce a complete methodology that both emerged from Freud and yet revolutionised him. His book now looks sketchy in such areas as have since been 'filled in' by the work of Melanie Klein and Winnicott. But Suttie's emphases in many places, based on his knowledge of patients, were significant. They anticipated the work of such writers as Fairbairn who came to re-emphasise aspects of identity, and pointed forward to the work of Melanie Klein and Winnicott, who were to explore the origins of identity in the interplay between mother and child. Suttie's main emphasis was to reject Freud's sexual theory and to insist that man's primary needs are relational.

What seems strange in the light of this is the degree to which Suttie's book is now so seldom referred to by many psychoanalytical writers. It is possible that his approach to Freud itself was felt to be such an offence to an established orthodoxy that his existence had to be denied? His criticisms are surely crucial. It is perhaps by contrast significant how much Suttie is still used and referred to by people working in education because they feel that his work fits their experience of culture and human relationship so much more convincingly than orthodox Freudian theory.

Suttie tackles the whole problem of the moral contradiction within Freudianism which so troubles Professor Bantock. What, he asks, to Freud, was 'cure'? In this we should surely be able to discover Freud's positives – his view of what is an integrated or sane individual, his norm. Discussing *Beyond the Pleasure Principle*, Suttie says that in that book:

> The idea still holds him . . . of the evacuation of a pent-up emotional complex . . . appearing as the 'economic' or 'detensioning' principle of psychic functioning. Needless to say this is an entirely egoistic principle of cure. On this conception, so far as inhibitions are socially established and sanctioned, cure is attained by the *demoralisation* of the individual. (Suttie [78], p. 197; my italics.)

Earlier Suttie has discussed this concept thus:

> 'Cure' is the idea that we must increase the patient's *tolerance* or diminish his censorship of the evil sexual impulses which were at one time imagined to be the main content of the unconcious system. The neurotic was held to be morally hyper-aesthetic, and contact with the broad-minded analysts de-sensitized, or, as many disapproving lay writers held, *demoralized* him to the required extent. (Suttie [78], p. 164; my italics.)

Suttie concludes: 'Needless to say such a theory of therapy was never approved by serious analysts, though it was popular with rebel temperaments who embraced analysis for anti-social reasons – conscious and unconscious' (Suttie [78], p. 164).

The last sentence, 30 years later, can still be applied to many recent approaches to cultural and ethical issues. In the application of psychoanalysis it has led to that 'debility' of which Professor Bantock complains. The views Suttie characterises here as 'egoistic' and 'anti-social' are still believed to be those of psychoanalysis in the popular mind – and in the minds of some practitioners.

Indeed, 'demoralisation' is the basis of prevalent thinking on moral questions, which remains essentially based on Freudian theory and its implicit view of man and its 'coarse' hedonism. As Suttie says, continuing:

> There is enough truth in the idea, however, to warrant closer examination, for the reduction of the patient's intolerance could be construed in either of two ways. Firstly the aim of cathartic treatment might be expressed by this imaginary verbal assurance by the physician to patient: 'These evil thoughts and wishes are not really bad after all. Sex is only bad *for children*; that is why it is hidden by adults from them. Now you are grown up and permitted to wish these things.' We might name this type of therapy, initiation. (Suttie [78], p. 164.)

On the other hand, we might call it *Disillusionment Therapy*: 'Of course you [patient] are bad – if you call sex bad; we *all are* bad in this sense. We are merely hypocrites; and goodness is an illusion' (Suttie [78], p. 164).

This 'demoralisation' approach, says Suttie, is implicit in Freud's metapsychology. Its pessimism and its implicit negative attitude to moral sensibility continue to haunt our culture. Suttie quotes a Dr. Eder, whose motto would be taken to endorse the nihilism of many *avant-garde* works today, and the 'amoral' position of 'realism' about man's brutishness which we have examined: 'We are born mad. We acquire morality and become stupid and unhappy. Then we die.' Suttie [78] adds: 'This Freudian pessimism and aggressiveness has its roots in the author's pre-oedipal separation-anxiety . . . and has no real relationship to his clinical work' (p. 164).

What Suttie is drawing attention to is that ambivalence in Freud, which is associated with the whole ambivalence in our intellectual life – as between a theory of human nature which sees our essential reality as 'animal', while we continue in practice to demonstrate (both in culture and living) that in fact the primary reality in our lives is that which is expressed in human civilisation. Suttie claims that it was evident from the commonsense view that Freud's theory of psychoanalysis simply did not accord with what went on in the consulting room.

Suttie indicates the irreconcilable split between the Freudian general theory of mind and clinical practice: 'Psychoanalytical theory and practice are so far divorced from one another that not only does theory not influence therapy but is even unable to explain it.'

Elsewhere Suttie says of Freud:

> The consistency of Freud's attitudes in these matters is never disturbed by its inconsistency with fact. Where Freud's imagination is free, or where his acquaintance with fact is unsystematic, his pessimistic philosophy of life finds free play. Where, however, he is in close contact with human nature – even with the seamy or latent content sought and displayed in clinical analysis – Freud shows a totally different side of himself. In practice he abandons theory as promptly as the physiological psychiatrist abandons his idea that brain pathology determines thought whenever he comes to reason with patients or opponents. (Suttie [78], p. 191.)

Suttie diagnosed that this division of Freud's work and its effects on ethical attitudes could be explained in terms of the great pioneer's own unconscious motivation. Where Freud dealt with real people, 'particularly in the childlike role of dependent helpless sufferers who trust their physician with their inmost secrets and display emotion without reserve', his 'bitterness' was overcome, and 'parental love' was evoked in him: 'In the free fantasy of the metapsychology, however, his own childish rage and despair find expression in anti-feminism, the subjection of love to sex, the acclamation of aggression and hate as universal – a complete social pessimism' (Suttie [78], 191).

From this diagnosis Suttie proceeds to tackle the death wish and its origins in Freud's own make-up. Freud's death wish, Suttie suggests, is a projection of his desire to dissolve the boundaries separating him from the mother.

> The thwarted purpose too is [covertly] revealed in the theory of the Death Wish, for the dissolution desired is psychic – in fact nothing but a loss of the boundaries which delimit the self from the mother. [His personal horror of death is manifestly related to this.] Freud's theory is the work of a thwarted infant revenging itself on mother. His practice is that of the ambitious parent who would teach the whole world to grow up – his way. (Suttie [78], p. 199.)

According to Suttie, childlike Freud, the theorist, spends every effort in *denying* love, while Freud the practitioner (who is essentially dealing with adults regressed to childlike selves who are suffering and evoke pity) spends every moment in the 'exhibition' of love. One syndrome belongs to contact, love, and whole experience: the other belongs to isolation, hate, and what D. H. Lawrence called 'mind-will'. This diagnosis of the way in which the mind can be an enemy to the whole being leads on to the work of Fairbairn, Winnicott, Farber, and Marion Milner, each of whom have explored the falsifying power of 'intellectual hate' and will.

Suttie condemns the negative attitude of Freud to love as unreal: 'Freud conceives all motive (a) as a "letting off of steam", an evacuation or detensioning, and (b) as a quest for gratification.'

By contrast, Suttie argues that 'the need to give love and to have it accepted is as real in its way as the need to have our bodily wants satisfied [p. 53]. . . . We must, in fact, for peace of mind, either feel ourselves loved or in a position to be loved' (Suttie [78], p. 39).

Suttie could not yet arrive at the picture given by Bowlby, Melanie Klein, Winnicott, and Fairbairn of the child's need for love in the beginning in order to form an identity at all and as the basis of his whole reality sense. But he goes some way towards seeing this, speaking of 'an innate need-for-companionship which is the infant's only way of self-preservation'. 'This need, giving rise to parental and fellowship "love", I put in the place of the Freudian libido, and regard it as *generally independent of genital appetite*' (this last phrase we shall examine in a moment).

Moreover, in culture and society; as in personal relationships: 'The Freudian conception of self-expression as a "detensioning" process or emotional evacuation now seemed to me false and in its place I imagined expression as an offering or stimulus directed to the other person, designed to elicit a response while love itself was essentially a state of active harmonious interplay' (Suttie [78], p. 58).

The gist of Suttie's objections to Freudian theory of 'detensioning' is given in a footnote: 'It would be as absurd to regard the sex act as having a selfish "detensioning" evacuatory motive as to say that a woman desires maternity for the drainage of her mammary glands. . . . It is a failure in the love-response-factor in coitus which produces anxiety, not a failure of sensual satisfactions' (Suttie [78], p. 58).

Suttie was the first writer working in psychotherapy to seek to reject the economic or steam-engine theory of 'impulse' by his insistence on the 'love-response-factor' as primary.

Subsequent explorations along object-relations lines have come to see 'active harmonious interplay' not only as primary in personal relationships, but as the basis of human identity itself as between mother and infant at the very earliest stages. As Susan Isaacs said, 'Play begins at the mother's breast' and it is in this primal interplay, part instinctive, part symbolic play, that human being begins. The roots of identity are in this give and take of love, while the quest for meaning begins to emerge as more primary in man than instinctual drive.

The difficulty in recognising this lies in that very intellectual hate which Suttie recognised. It is painful for us to accept the ego-weakness within us, so it is painful to accept our dependence – not least the fact that we were once totally dependent on a woman. It is especially disturbing for us to accept that our identity and sense of meaning themselves depend upon anything as evanescent and delusory as love. To recognise this is especially painful to the schizoid person who fears love.

It is deeply disturbing for us to contemplate the truth that what happened to us in early infancy when we were helpless and totally dependent, and involved in maturational processes which cannot be 'willed' but only lived with, affects us all our lives.

All our intellectual energies tend to deny the truth as Bowlby has put it, referring to the psychic analogy with the consequences of organic damage sometimes cause in pregnancy: 'There is also plenty of reason to think that in just the same way emotional experiences at certain very early and special stages of mental life may have very vital and long-lasting effects' (Bowlby [6], p. 17).

The grim truth seems to be that early damage or neglect has an effect which may be permanent, or at best only eradicable by immense efforts: 'The evidence is fairly clear that if the first phase of development – that of establishing a relation with one particular person recognised as such – is not satisfactorily completed during the first twelve months or so, there is the greatest difficulty in making good: *the character of the psychic tissue has become fixed*' (Bowlby [6], pp. 61–62; my italics).

Damage in the primary interpersonal relationship may cause many problems, from anti-social behaviour to the incapacity to learn, from the inability to feel real to the inability to form adequate personal relationships. The ability to enrich one's life by cultural and symbolic play (Suttie implied) may itself be damaged by deprivation in early childhood: 'the brief intimate games which mother and baby invent to amuse themselves as accompaniments to washing, dressing, feeding, bathing and returning to sleep – they are all missing. In these conditions, a child has no opportunity of learning and practising functions which are as basic to living as walking and talking.' (Bowlby [6], p. 68).

This primary psychic matrix in the subtle relationship between mother and infant escaped Freud's attention altogether – a blindness perhaps to be associated with the traditional attitudes to woman in Freud's social background* – though it also must have had strong unconscious motives.

Significantly, what emerges predominantly from Freud is the archetypal myth of killing the father and possessing the mother. The earliest problems of the need for the child to form his identity by taking the mother into himself, and being reflected by her as if by a creative mirror, escape him. The depth of Freud's failure to be able to imagine experience of early infancy is shown by the fact that at one point he even implies that the only difference to the child between father and mother is that the mother does not have a penis! The whole world that the mother is to the child, and the whole infant experience of her face and her voice and her breast, the smell of milk, her 'handling', and the warmth of her body, seem to have escaped him. Suttie strove to find the mother and her love again.

From his preoccupation with primary love, Suttie later comes to raise the question which, as we have seen, is now very much to the fore – that of in what sense psychoanalysis can be called a science. He points out that love is the 'affair of poets, romancers and the religious – not of science': there is an impulse in science to deny love altogether, and with it the *I–Thou* experience as Buber was to call it.

> We can compare, identify, and name our colour experiences by pointing to the same object and agreeing upon a word to denote out optical sensations. But this simple procedure will not detect colour-blindness – a qualitative difference in sensation. It is infinitely more difficult to compare love emotions and thus to be sure that we attach the same meanings to the words supposed to denote them. (Suttie. [78], p. 52.)

To 'love emotions' we could add 'all feelings to do with the inner world'. Suttie says, of the impulse to compare 'love emotions';

> An *experimentally devised* situation would excite interest not love, unless it took the subject by surprise. In the second place people's character and disposition react so differently to the same situation. The exact observation and experimental study of love therefore is impossible, and this is a bar to the conception of *'love' as distinct from the relatively definite appetites* being accepted and employed by science. Science has, therefore, an all but unavoidable tendency to equate love with the organic appetites subserving and expressing it. (Suttie [78], p. 52.)

Suttie perceives that this denial of love is somehow associated with 'bitterness': 'The disposition of love is the centre of all the bitterness of human nature and this leads directly to the denial of the existence of love.'

Suttie's next point leads on to Melanie Klein and Fairbairn: 'I have said that the need to give love and have it accepted is as real in its way as the need to have our bodily wants satisfied, though certainly privation in the former case does not lead to bodily death' (Suttie [78], p. 53).

This reveals how far psychoanalytical theory has come since, for it can even be said that it now recognises that frustration of the need for love by the mother *does* lead, if not to bodily death, certainly to death of the personality, and possibly, in some infants,

---

* As Erikson says, when the German father comes home 'even the very walls seem to draw themselves closer together' (Erikson [18]).

where the facilitating environment is utterly absent, to actual inanition. Where the capacity to relate in infancy has not been developed we have neither a human intellect nor the capacity for human relations, as in schizophrenia.

On the other hand, when he comes to discuss the origins of hate we can see how impossible it was to produce a satisfactory account before Melanie Klein's emphasis on the roles of aggression and phantasy in primitive development, as when Suttie says:

> We can reject therefore once and for all the notion of the infant mind being a bundle of co-operating or competing instincts, and suppose instead that it is dominated from the beginning by the need to retain the mother – a need which, if thwarted, must produce the utmost extreme of terror and rage, since the loss of the mother is, under natural conditions, but the precursor of death itself. (Suttie [78], p. 12.)

This position of Suttie's was valuable in countering the 'bundle of instincts' psychology (though he sees that obviously instincts such as suckling are from the beginning there to be taken into account, albeit complicated from the beginning by aspects of conscious-ness). Suttie's importance is in turning an emphasis, from common sense, away from Freud's instinct theory, towards a recognition of the primary nature of the mother–child relationship, of our ultimate need for relationship (rather than for release in 'detension-ing') and of love. 'We now have to consider whether this attachment to mother is merely the sum of the infantile bodily needs and satisfactions which refer to her, or whether *the need for a mother is primarily presented to the child mind as a need for company and as a discomfort in isolation*' (Suttie [78], p. 13).

Suttie made further valuable insistences on this primary relationship as a source of culture and social capacities ('I think play, co-operation . . . and culture-interests generally are substitutes for the mutually caressing relationship of child and mother'). He emphasised the origins at this stage of the capacity for 'tenderness' and love in the adult, and interpreted the contraries of love and tenderness – anger, fear, and hate – as *consequences of frustrated love*. But what Suttie failed to see were the dynamic elements of phantasy – of internalised objects – involved, and the full force of these elements in 'inner' reality to which Melanie Klein was to draw attention so profitably later.

Suttie did, however, see that love is the gateway to the formation of an identity and the capacity to deal with reality. The first need in infancy is for the child to be convinced (as Fairbairn puts it) that he is loved for his own sake. Without this, his hopes to become a person virtually perish. There is an even earlier stage at which the mother's love (or 'primary maternal preoccupation') is the only possible guarantee for the beginnings of a whole separate identity at all. Without her love to provide a facilitating environment the emerging creature is doomed to not-living.

The object-relations theory of the origins of human identity is, as we shall see, now complex and subtle. Suttie was writing decades before it was possible for such theories to develop. But from his commonsense point of view he could not accept the theory that the origins of hate must be in an impersonal primary destructive force or a death instinct. He could only see hate as a consequence of separation anxieties – the child fearing that the mother would abandon it and it would die. Later insights have raised the problem of how an infant could have separation anxiety before he could conceive of being separate. But Suttie was surely correct in seeing the origins of hate in *protest against being deprived of love*. He says: "Earth hath no hate but love to hatred turned, and hell no fury but a baby scorned." Hatred, I consider, is just a standing reproach to the hated person, and owed all its meaning to a demand for love' (Suttie [78], p. 19).

The word 'just' here seems a doubtful qualification when one contemplates all that man's hate is capable of. But what is important is that Suttie's emphasis here is on seeing the origins of hate not in a death instinct, but in the impulse to live and to be:

> Hate, I regard not as a primal independent instinct . . . but as a development or intensification of separation-anxiety which in turn is roused by a threat against love. It is the maximal ultimate appeal in the child's power. . . . Its purpose is not death-seeking or death-dealing, but the preservation of the self from the isolation which is death, and the restoration of a love-relationship. (Suttie [78], p. 25.)

A few pages before this Suttie speaks of a time before the infant is aware of the difference between the self and the not-self, and also of the inability of the infant to distinguish between actuality and phantasy. How can 'separation fear' apply at such a time? Yet it would seem that at such a time hate is born. Later writers have sought to solve this problem and I believe they confirm Suttie in his insistence that the origin of hate is not in a specific 'instinct', but in the inevitable discoveries of one's separate existence, in an inevitably not-quite-good-enough environment, and the consequent hunger to live.

As we saw above, Winnicott approaches the whole problem of aggression as a manifestation of the sense of being alive. But here again Suttie seems unwilling to accept the more extreme truths of human nature: thwarted love can be terribly death-dealing, whether or not this is its purpose, and nothing is to be served by simply regarding it as an 'appeal' or 'just a standing reproach', for surely hate can reach a state when it is far beyond being 'just' an 'appeal' or a 'reproach'.

But though hate is terrifying and seems to have its own volition and energy, it does not square with clinical practice (Suttie urged), and does not help with theory to attribute it to a 'death instinct'.

> . . . love can *turn into* hatred, which is merely its negative or frustration aspect. From this it follows that 'cure' of psychosocial ills (into which hate always enters) is theoretically easier than could be believed from the Freudian standpoint, which regards hate as proceeding from a 'Primal, independent, instinct of destruction', and hence as ineradicable. (Suttie [78], p. 207.)

Suttie thus anticipated in 1935 modes of thinking later developed by the object-relations school of psychoanalytical writers who have also come to believe that there are no grounds for believing that the origins of human hate are 'ineradicable'.

Suttie was also anticipating later developments when he placed the emphasis on our need to accept 'dependence' in love, and our need to find ourselves confirmed in the recognition and 'meeting' of another person.

> At the same time we will have to bring this conception of love into relation with sex, since we deny that the latter is its origin. It seems to me that the complete passion of love integrates genital appetite with that 'love' or tenderness which is the descendant or derivative of infantile need. It utilises it, as it were, as a means of restoring the lost sense of union with the mother; for sexual intercourse and suckling are alike and unique in this respect, that in neither should there be any difference or conflict-of-interest between the partners. It is absurd to consider who gives and who gets, or who gains and who loses, in the sex act as it would be to propound these questions in regard to suckling. The act, or rather its culmination, is totally reciprocal, otherwise it becomes associated with anxiety. It restores the free give-and-take of infancy, where there is as yet no doubt of 'welcome' or 'acceptance'. Hence its extreme value in allaying morbid anxiety (a value which helped to mislead Freud himself as to the relationship of sex and anxiety); but hence also the ease with which anxiety in turn hinders its consummation. Here again we are able to explain our admitted Freudian error, namely, the mistaking of anxiety ('morbid') for unsatisfied libido. It is of course unsatisfied *love*. (Suttie [78], p. 58.)

In this Suttie represents the kind of commonsense attitude which those concerned with culture and education have found cogenial because it interprets the goals of human libido in such a very different way from Freud. Suttie anticipates Fairbairn's theory that 'the individual in his libidinal capacity is not pleasure-seeking but object-seeking'.

From his capacity to report on his experience of human beings in therapy without being blinkered by Freudian theory, Suttie was able to insist on the reality of altruism, and indeed on all those manifestations of 'natural goodness' which Freud denied in favour of the 'more real' instinctual drives for gratification. Suttie virtually places the incapacity to give, receive, and recognise love as a disease itself, while he sees hedonism and cynicism as unreal and 'neurotic' (now, perhaps we would rather say 'schizoid'):

> Cynicism and asceticism appear to be the twin offspring of this temperament which demands a love from others which shall afford the givers no pleasure and which is undeniably unselfish and 'genuine'. The cynic observes that amiable behaviour brings pleasure and concludes that it is done for this reason. For him this is merely an inverted form of selfishness and hence worthless. The sole motive he can see is the pursuit of pleasure in accordance with the demands of one's own nature. This view finds philosophical expression in Psychological Hedonism. . . . The ascetic, like the cynic, feels that love is not *real* if it is pleasurable. Self-sacrifice and self-denial for him are also the measures of goodness. (Suttie [78], p. 53.)

So while cynic and ascetic are at logger-heads, both miss the essential point: 'Cynic and Ascetic alike prove the biological truism that it is not possible to love without pleasure. Their error lies in their original neurotic demand for this impossibility' (Suttie [78,] p. 54).

From his recognition of the reality of human altruism Suttie could insist that:

> Psychoanalytical Theory is recognising more clearly the social nature of man, and is no longer presenting his psychology as that of a self-contained entity independent of his fellows except insofar as his bodily appetites and gratifications demand their services. Psycho-analysis in fact is losing much that made it obnoxious to European philosophy, good sense, and good feeling.

Suttie's importance was that he was able to accuse psychoanalysis of 'not taking a wide enough view of its subject matter'. To Suttie man was naturally a social creature, while civilisation was the expression of positive impulses in man, and art and science were *primary* aspects of consciousness, not mere 'sublimation'. He also insisted that the 'need-for-companionship' was primary, too. Suttie's demand for a 'reorientation' thus appealed to many in education and culture. He says of his own work:

> Fundamentally, the tentative theory I have formed belongs to the group of psychologies that originates from the work of Freud. It differs fundamentally from psycho-analysis in introducing the conception for an innate need-for-companionship which is the infant's only way of self-preservation. This need, giving rise to parental and fellowship 'love', I put in the place of the Freudian libido, and regard it *as generally independent of genital appetite.*
> The application of this conception seems to re-orient the whole psycho-analytic dynamics. It attributes to the mother the significance in rearing that Freud formerly attached to the father. It lessens the importance attached to *individual sense-gratification* as a motive and increases the significance of *social* desires and interests (i.e. it represents 'expression' as an offering or stimulus applied to others not merely as a pleasant exercise of function). It denies the sexual basis of culture-sublimation and it relegates the Oedipus Wish and Sexual Jealousy to third place in primacy and importance as disturbers of social development and harmony. (Suttie [78], p. 5; my italics.)

Suttie hinted at possibilities of psychoanalytic theory coming to preoccupy itself more and more with the primacy of inner resources: 'Cultural interests do ultimately form a powerful antidote to loneliness even where there is no participator present in person; that is to say, cultural pursuits have a social value even where 'the other person' is imagined or left unspecified' (Suttie [78], p. 15).

This anticipates Winnicott's theory of culture as 'transitional object' phenomenon. (See below, p. 236 ff.)

As we shall see, however, profound questions are raised between Suttie's phrase 'independent of genital appetite', 'social desires', 'loneliness', and 'social value'. He sought to insist on the social and cultural nature of man and his capacities to overcome his destructiveness which emerged from frustrated love. But in a way, to suppose as Suttie did that amelioration could come through activities on an adult social plane seems now unrealistic. We can perhaps approach this problem by pondering further Suttie's phrase 'the taboo on tenderness'. Our reaction to this is to feel that we should perhaps promote more tenderness: but at once the futility of this becomes evident. The point is rather that the tenderness is urgently necessary in the first year of a human being's life, and an adult incapacity for tenderness springs from those primary months. In adult life the person who has not experienced tender care in infancy now needs something more radical than mere adult tenderness. Moreover, there is a deeper problem than tenderness.

We are forced to say that, while he seems 'right' in terms of cultural attitudes and the realism of love, Suttie's aetiology of psychic states *does not go back far enough*. And while the insistence on the need for companionship and 'tenderness' are right, in that they imply norms, the origins of the 'taboo on tenderness' are too deep to be affected by cultural influences or altered by explicit awareness. A lack of tenderness can only be made worse by moralising about the need for tenderness. You cannot *make* anybody tender: you cannot export tenderness. Whether or not a person is capable of love or tenderness is determined by deep processes of the formation of consciousness in the first year of life – even the first four months – in the context of the process of 'primary material preoccupation'. While we need to believe in the possibilities of overcoming hate, and fostering love, since these originate in such primary processes, there is obviously little possibility of breaking the 'taboo on tenderness' by any direct social policy.

While confirming his rejection of Freud's negative view of human nature, later psychoanalytical writing has essentially cast doubt on Suttie's optimism here. The 'taboo on tenderness' is undeniably apparent in our culture and civilisation: but Suttie attributed its origins to what now seems quite a late stage in infant development – to the mother's capacity to caress her child and to such influences as toilet training.

While in psychoanalysis there has grown an increasing acceptance of culture as primary, and of the need for relationship rather than mere 'individual sense-gratification', there has also been an even deeper investigation of 'genital appetite' and the problems of identity bound up with the body. For since our capacity for object-relationships is developed in our most primitive months, our senses of identity and of reality are inevitably bound up with bodily feelings, and with phantasies and feelings based on ingestion and evacuation. Psychoanalysis, however, has learnt to discuss appetite and impulse not in terms of 'detensioning', and the satisfaction of hunger, but rather in terms of symbolism of *poetic-philosophical exploration of the boundaries of the self*. The origins of cultural symbolism are in this giving and taking, of exploring and possessing, of eating and meeting. Here are the dim origins of metaphorical activities which range from the impulse to annihilate, to the desire to make the whole world.*

The increasing positive insistence in psychoanalysis on the pre-eminence of culture

---

* While I cannot accept that the basis of all metaphor is 'sphincter control' (as she suggests) it may be that the basis of metaphor is in primary functions of the body and their philosophical meaning (in terms of 'carrying across' from one world to the other) to the emerging consciousness. (See Ella Sharpe, [122].) This paper is mostly on patients' metaphors in clinical work. Metaphor is undeniably 'woven in the weakness of the changing body', and associated with the kind of bodily meanings which Freud began to interpret as symbolic.

in the development of personality has thus been derived from a preoccupation with phantasies first experienced in relationship with the mother as 'first object' at the breast, and experienced largely in anal, oral, and genital terms. Here the capacity to be 'tender' or not is shown to have very deep origins, and to be related to the capacity to feel the I AM feeling.

It was perhaps these origins of the capacity for object-relations that Suttie failed to take into account when he sought to find love 'independent of genital appetites'. Melanie Klein's work suggests that all human problems of one's relationship with oneself and others can never be separated from the earliest infantile genital anxieties. A recognition of these alters our whole approach to adult sexual relationships, for these can now be seen not as being in pursuit of instinctual 'release' but as having many symbolic elements which are inevitably involved in the primary need to find confirmation and fulfilment by finding oneself in the deepest sense of body and mind in a relationship. We can see how early experiences affect adult relationship in the following case history:

> This brought him face to face with his terror of real women, whom he regarded as predatory and persecuting, and of their genitals, and of the babies which they might conceive, which would rob him of their affection which he still needed desperately and exclusively like a very young child. At this stage the only satisfactory intercourse he could imagine for himself would be with the corpse of a woman he himself had murdered. That would be his revenge – his triumph in place of theirs. He imagined it with his mother. She would be dead, like a mackintosh, and so could not laugh at him or abandon him; the act would give her no pleasure (that was essential): he would use his penis like a sword to gouge her inside out; above all there would be no baby to rival and displace him. (Dugmore Hunter [119], p. 303.)

Here the failure to be able to embrace adult sexuality in relationship goes with the failure of the patient to outgrow infantile love-needs and infantile dependence: the patient dare not accept 'dependence in mature independence'. Suttie was correct to point to the need to love and be loved as the fundamental need: but there are genital complications with their origins in the first body-life and body-contact. Suttie, in reaction against Freud's 'detensioning' theory of sex, would seem to have played down these elements excessively, and to have failed to take sufficiently into account the phantasy elements in internal psychic conflict.

Even though we may agree that hate originates in frustrated love rather than in a 'death instinct' it will not do to regard hate (with Suttie) as 'just a standing reproach'. This patient under discussion often took his hate phantasies into the realm of action, with serious consequences, as when he tried to strangle his wife. Relational problems cannot be 'separated from genital appetite', even though we may give primary place to the problems of identity, and fears that love and relationship are too threatening. (Perhaps here we recall Dostoevsky, whose wedding was followed immediately by an epileptic fit): 'His marriage was still premature and neurotic in character. . . . The wedding ceremony would represent, as he said, "a formal and legal break from my mother". When they married on 1st April, he proved impotent. The "April fools" included the patient, his wife, his parents, and his analyst' (Dugmore Hunter (119), p. 305).

The adult woman partner here – once she became a wife – became too much like the mother. The patient (a mackintosh fetishist) brought his wife a mackintosh on honeymoon. But even that made no difference:* 'She had the effect of neutralising it, just like my mother . . . getting into bed with her was just creeping into bed with Mum. . . .'

---

* According to the theories of the behaviourist Professor Eysenck it should have done everything, since he claims that a patient was cured of impotence by having his wall paper changed.

So, the morbid fears are revealed (in this case history of a Freudian analysis nearly twenty years after Suttie's book) as being part of a syndrome whose essence is a need for love and 'tenderness', but which needed more 'genital theory' to unravel than Suttie was prepared to accept (or perhaps to be aware of):

> His fears of intercourse emerged in great profusion and at all levels. In genital terms: no drop of fluid from his penis must go anywhere near Hilda – it would produce a son who would inevitably destroy him. In phallic terms, he was afraid of his penis touching a baby inside and of what it might do to the baby ('he feared to penetrate deeply and wanted to get out as soon as possible'). In anal terms: Hilda's inside was a horrible place – a mess of shit (a projection of his own rottenness and a product of his own attacks). In oral terms: the vagina was a hungry mouth with teeth and would bite his penis off (a projection of his own biting impulses). But the more he avoided intercourse the more did his wife become identified with the feared, attacked genital mother. (Dugmore Hunter [119], p. 305.)

Such an account of a case, with all its complications of a growth struggle, through depression, to the final 'weaning' stage, in fact exposes not only Freud's sexual theory as inadequate, but also shows that Suttie's criticism of Freud was not thorough enough. The constructive triumphs recorded in such a case history, whereby the patient overcame his inability to enter into new social activities, and to love, physically and emotionally, belong to the realm of the civilised, altruistic side of man on which Suttie felt he must insist. But the fundamental problems dealt with turn out not to be those of appetite or 'release' but of identity and relationship. The end of this case history is given in terms of which Suttie would approve. 'In the last hour [of analysis] he said: "You are a human being and I've grown fond of you. . . . Now I can feel tenderness, even these aloof women become human; and if I can sustain this tender feeling, what remains of the mac will do." ' (Dugmore Hunter (119), p. 305.)

The route to this achievement of 'tenderness', however, demanded a deep investigation of the forces of hate, fears of disintegration, and 'genital' problems of primary origin, which could only be engaged with in a close dependent relationship with the analyst, since they were so infantile and bound up with 'genitality'.

Of course, we can see from such a case history the difference between Freudian practice and theory, and it confirms Suttie's conclusion: 'The Freudian conception of self-expression as a "dentensioning" process or emotional evacuation now seems to me false' (Suttie [78], p. 3).

Helping his fetishist patient 'find the other person' – to become capable of object-relationships – was what the analyst in this case history was concerned with. In such an analysis, as in education or creativity, we witness 'self-expression' as 'an offering or stimulus directed to the other person'. This 'offering', however, included a great deal of hate-offering, and genital, phallic, anal, and oral phantasy directed at the analyst – all of which was part of the psychosynthesis, through symbolic exploration of problems derived from earliest stages of development.

Suttie's importance was that he was one of the first to challenge the destructive influence of the schizoid elements in Freud's theory, which he saw as manifestations of hate themselves, and to endorse from a realistic psychoanalytical point of view our common-sense belief in the values of love. His insistence on the positive social and personal impulses in human nature was valuable: and he was able to confound his Freudian opponents because he pointed out that these impulses – altruism, love, and a belief in humanity – were, as they always have been, the driving force of Freudian psychotherapy in practice itself. As Winnicott emphasises, the essence of psychoanalysis is that the patient and doctor share a fundamental belief in human nature. '*A belief in human nature and the developmental process exists in the analyst* if work is to be done at all, and this is quickly sensed by the patient' (Winnicott [90], p. 292).

This belief in human nature, which expresses a much more positive confidence in man than one finds in Freud, has come to pervade object-relations psychology since Suttie.

Thus, despite the fact that his work has been in many ways superseded by deeper investigations of the nature of the child's earliest environment, Suttie's emphasis on love and the need for relationship may have contributed to the change in atmosphere in England, towards a greater receptivity for the more positive psychoanalytical ideas now emerging. As Guntrip says:

> It would take a major cultural revolution to create an atmosphere in which patients might find it easier to accept psychotherapy; a cultural atmosphere from which not only Suttie's 'taboo on tenderness' had disappeared, but also its deeper implications, the 'taboo on weakness'. Then, perhaps, illness of the mind could be treated with the same acceptance of the need for 'healing in a state of passive recuperation' as is already accorded to illness of the body. (Guntrip [114], p. 286.)

We may extend this consideration into the realm of culture in general and attitudes to life. It may be ridiculous and even harmful to campaign for 'tenderness'. But when we see the deeper implications, it may be valuable to campaign for recognition of our human weakness. Such insights could enable us to avoid false solutions which seek to demonstrate that we are strong, in compensation for fear of weakness.

As we shall see, we can also perhaps link the need to accept our weakness with our need to accept the 'female element of being'. D. H. Lawrence would have understood this problem, since it was one he explored in his work. Recent insights give it a new meaning, and they focus on the rediscovery of the central and primary role of the mother. It was Suttie's remarkable achievement to restore attention to the mother and the feminine elements in human nature when Freudian theory had been so grossly blind to these.

CHAPTER 5

Exorcising the Death Instinct

WHILE the concept of the death instinct is *beginning* to disappear from some psycho-analytical theory, it would seem that many psychoanalytical writers are unhappy without it. For instance, Bruno Bettelheim, writing on 'Violence' in *Peace News*, 15 September 1967, says:

> Even among psycho-analysts Freud's death instinct is not quite respectable, because we decree what is supposed not to exist cannot and does not exist; all evidence to the contrary is simply disregarded as non-existent. . . . What I believe is needed instead, is an intelligent recognition of the nature of the beast. We shall not be able to deal intelligently with violence unless we are first ready to see it as part of human nature.

Bettelheim seems to want to attribute violence to an innate death instinct, though he does not say so, as if the horrible things men do cannot be explained in any other way – so we have to turn to a death instinct to explain it, in despair. He finds it difficult to explain human impulses towards death and destructiveness without attributing their origins to 'the nature of the beast', which sounds like some ineradicable animality. As we have seen, something like the death instinct persists behind such implicit assumptions of man's 'real' brutishness. The persistence of this ghost may be associated with what Suttie called Freud's 'theoretical assurance that there is no love apart from genital desire and its derivatives' (Suttie [78], p. 93).

That is, the denial of love and of the need for relationship is assumed to have a scienti-fically realistic justification which centres in the concept of the death instinct as a primary biological force. Here the problem of our belief in a future for man is bound up with Freud's hedonism, his belief that instinct is more 'real' than 'goodness', and the tradition of natural science in so far as it has 'divinised' the external world as the only reliable source of knowledge.

Is Freud's 'death instinct' in the world at all? Though some have recognised that this concept has no empirical basis, they seem to feel this is not to be held against it. Suttie was one of the first to point out how much it does matter. He said: 'all this elaborate theory has not either clinical application or utility, so that Dr. Melanie Klein remarked, when I attacked the validity of the theory, "What does it matter?" A theory whose truth *does not matter empirically* has another very significant resemblance to pure fantasy.'

It matters very much what we believe here. Freudian social and moral attitudes are based on the pain–pleasure principle with the death instinct in the background. The survival of the organism depends upon avoiding 'excessive stimulation', while the primary urge is to seek egocentric fulfilment independently of all other considerations according to a 'pleasure principle'. When life began, according to Freud, it disturbed matter out of its normal (inanimate) state, so living substances have a built-in 'economic' urge to return to that inanimate state. The death instinct is the urge to escape from the disturbance caused by 'stimulation', to a state of equilibrium, and eventually to death as ultimate 'detensioning'. The continuance of life is only a going on in which the organism moves on towards death by mere compulsive repetition of the normal life functions.

The pleasure principle and the death instinct are modified only by the ego (which to Freud has an adaptive function) and such influence as it can exert on the super-ego. This internal conscience frustrates the id instincts by taking into itself the ideals and restrictions of the social world. The effect of modification is the development of a reality principle, but only under protest, and at a loss, involving some devastation of our powers.

The primary urges of the organism are thus pleasure, and libidinal release towards detensioning – peace in inanition as sought ultimately by the death instinct. Thus not only libidinal sex urges but even violent aggressive ones can be seen as natural impulses which we have to suppress, but only because of the necessity to accept, albeit unwillingly, the 'reality principle', the price of survival being a forfeiture of certain potentialities.

The concept of the death instinct, and the denial of love in favour of sex as a 'detensioning' biological function, are both features of the same pessimistic attitude to human nature which Freud expressed in his 'free' theory. As Suttie pointed out, Freud begins by denying that the 'infant loves anything but itself':

> The child does not love his parents, but depends upon them for its gratifications and necessities. It is therefore concerned to maintain good relation with them only for this purpose. Their pleasure and displeasure arouse its fears and affect its happiness only so far as they promise continuance or threaten withdrawal of their nurtural care and/or the infliction of bodily injury. (Suttie [78], p. 190.)

In fact, as Suttie says, Freud's whole philosophy of life is summed up in the line 'Oh! I care for nobody and nobody cares for me'. So, in cultural and political comment, Freud becomes utterly nihilistic: 'The independent "instinct" status he denies to *love* he gives to *hate*, while his pessimism is seen not only in accepting death as the purpose of life, but throughout *The Future of an Illusion*, and in his letter upon war, which declares this to be "inevitable and indeed biologically useful" ' (Suttie [78], p. 186).

In culture 'he starts from the sound assumption that satisfied impulses do not require to seek alternative outlets. Sex is unsatisfied in modern European culture, ergo it is probably the energy source thereof . . . savages are 'free' sexually [an assumption now shown to be false – D. H.] and their culture is *therefore* primitive.'

These connections Suttie says are made only in a very general way, and Freud '*does not consider any alternative interpretations which imply a non-sexual but social interest* [i.e. love] of one individual for another'. Culture, according to Freud, is merely a series of symbolic substitute sexual gratifications.

As Winnicott says, Freud never found a place for culture despite his respect for art, its concerns are essentially 'unreal' and merely disguised a 'real' underlying sexual problem, just as goodness hides a 'real' hatred under the mask:

> Freud tends to dismiss manifest content as *merely a cover* for latent content, a position that is manifestly impossible. For the *unreal interests could never serve to disguise the real* – the meaningless could never hide meaning. . . . The manifest content of mind is real and indeed manifestly the dominant factor in life. Its dismissal as a *mere* disguise to the repressed is manifestly ridiculous. (Suttie [78], p. 187.)

Freud strove to reduce culture to a 'sublimation' activity, in the same way that he seeks to reduce love to sex, and the whole impulse of the organism to the dominating instinct to return to an inanimate state, before life came to 'disturb' matter.

The negative force of Freud's theory is so intense that Suttie calls Freudian theory a *disease*. We can, I believe, see this confirmed from the 'schizoid diagnosis'. As Suttie points out, Freud's whole theoretical impulse is strangely indifferent to the evidence of 'human facts', such as Freud himself knew in his clinic: 'His position is consistent subjectively but not objectively. Therefore it is an expression of temperament not a conclusion based on empirical study' (Suttie [78], p. 189).

Röheim called the death instinct 'the Pillar of the Metapsychology': Dr. Marjorie Brierley saw it as a key or turning point in psychoanalytical theory. Suttie sees it as a supreme expression of hatred:

> Elevating [hate] . . . to the status of a primal, independent, purpose in life – a separate appetite which like hunger requires no external provocation and is an end-in-itself. The conception therefore supplies good evidence, *unless objectively justified*, that it is an expression of subjective antipathy in line with Freud's systematic denial of love. Indeed I hold that the theory is not only as I say an expression of unconscious rage, but what empirical evidence can be adduced in its support *can only be so interpreted* by shutting our eyes to the existence of love. It is therefore doubly perverse since it is scientifically unjustified. (Suttie [78], p. 183.)

Where pragmatic utilitarianism persists it is convenient to see aggression is no more than a principle of the universe and to believe that the organism is inherently ruthlessly egocentric. A process of 'survival of the fittest' is (as even Bruno Bettelheim seems to want to believe) the natural order of things to a 'free' commercial society.

Here certain connections are made plain by Suttie. The concept of the death instinct is at one with the denial of altruism and 'goodwill':

> Where Freud does not attribute culture-civilisation to substitute-sexuality he still finds its motivation in the desire for material gratification. Perhaps his most complete denial of goodwill is contained in *The Future of an Illusion* pp. 10–13 where he regards all civilisation as built upon the selfish coercion of the many by the few for purely material objectives. (Suttie [78], p. 187.)

By this approach, our society's concern with 'material objectives' and with 'doing' instead of 'being' is ordained by the nature of things, and by the nature of man and it is necessary that this should be so. Freud was a 'realist' and he justified 'material gratification' as a principle of life. Thus, as Suttie put it, from Freud:

> 'One gets the impression that culture is something which was imposed on a resisting majority by a minority that understood how to possess itself of power and coercion. If we could abandon coercion and the suppression of the instincts – men might devote themselves to the acquisition of natural resources and to the enjoyment of the same. That would be the golden age.' (Suttie [78], p. 187.)

This view justifies the hedonism of a society which has attached identity to 'doing'. Yet this preoccupation with externals, in Buber's eyes, only serves by its 'bustle' to prevent us from 'confronting the problem of existence'.

The essential demoralisation which pervades culture, under the influence of such attitudes to life as those of Freud, was exposed by Suttie, who sees it correctly as anti-human. Freud lacks faith in human nature: and so he despaired of a golden age ever being attained:

> 'It seems more probable that every culture *must be* built up on coercion and instinctual renunciation' [my italics]. 'All men are destructive' and so anti-social tendencies predominate in any society. . . . The three problems of politics appear to Freud to be (1) how to diminish 'the burden of instinctual sacrifice imposed on men', (2) in 'reconciling' them to these 'inevitable sacrifices' and (3) in 'compensating' them for these'. '*It is just as impossible to do without government of the masses by a minority as it is to*

dispense with coercion in the work of civilization.' Leaders should be independent of the masses by having at their disposal *means of enforcing their authority.* (Suttie [78], p. 188.)

As Suttie pointed out (in 1935!), this means guns, planes, and gas: and it bears a close resemblance to some of the arguments advanced by Hitler.

The only justification for such pessimistic attitudes to human nature, social organisation, and culture could be that they were based on 'scientific realism'. Here it is worth exploring the links assumed to be valid between Freud's 'realistic' theory and biology.

As Suttie says, the central position in his work is reductive, is a way of explaining away 'organic sympathy and love'. 'The social tie which binds men together is . . . a common fear of and subservience to the Superman-patriarch, whose sexual jealousy denies them any natural outlets for genital love.' 'He alone is perfect and natural; he alone has not been deprived by coercion.'

> In this central position Freud's philosophy is perfectly consistent. His evasions, his selection rejection and distortion of evidence, all occur in the attempt to apply this preconception universally . . . the central position (1) ignores the mother for the father; (2) denies tenderness – filial or parental – and universalizes sex; (3) interprets socialization in man as *merely* the overcoming of *sex* jealousy by coercion and fear; (4) regards hate as a spontaneous, ineradicable, appetite and all motive as egoistic; (5) regards all cultural interest as substitute sex gratification and all else as materialistic utilitarian interest. His position is consistent subjectively but not objectively. (Suttie [78], p. 189.)

The consequence is a theory which is inconsistent with fact however consistent in itself, irreconcilable with therapeutic practice, untenable together with a belief in democracy, and destructive of all positive approaches to human identity, emotion, relationship, and culture.

> One can say broadly that Freud sees no positive drives whatever in life. Indeed, he regards it as forced to go on by environmental compulsion against its will to death, and all the complications and elaborations we find in biology, ethnology, and psychology he regards as due to conflicts and unbalances within the vital urge itself. For him the species is absolutely broken up into individuals each seeking its own ends exclusively. Even sexual union with another in the last resort is understood as a lowering of instinctual tension, a step on the road to inertia and dissolution. 'Expression', for Freud, is merely an evacuation, and does not imply 'getting it across' to others or their response.
> All social activities are thus defence-reactions, substitute gratifications, guilt expiations, or aggressions. Guilt is an apprehension of personal loss; grief is its realization; pity is inconceivable; love is unreal. (Suttie [78], p. 191.)

Moreover, as we shall see, whatever the consistency within Freud's system, his own arguments are often more inconsistent: he often contradicts himself, and when a matter becomes a 'potential mare's nest' he quietly (and most unscientifically) avoids drawing attention to it.*

Indeed, a close analysis of Freud's 'scientific' arguments reveals how correct Leslie Farber is when he says: 'He had none of that scholar's caution, that timidity of the scientist or historian or lawyer, that sticks to the rules of evidence, no matter what the cost. . . . He put no real trust in the fallible laws and man-made facts of evidence' (Farber [20], p. 163).

---

* See the appendices to *The Ego and the Id*, 1962 edition: 'It seems likely that on reflection he realized that Ferenczi's discovery was a mare's nest, for the passage was never altered in the later editions of the book' (p. 52). Ferenczi had in fact pointed to incompatible statements which Freud chose to leave incompatible.

CHAPTER 6

Is Life at Home in the Universe?

SUTTIE believed that the death instinct was a manifestation of Freud's 'hate theory' and essentially a symbolic projection of his own inward fears. But what scientific validity has it? In truth, the concept was a highly speculative one, set forth in notably nervous terms by Freud, uncertainly based on biological concepts of his time. It extends concepts developed from the behaviour of small organisms, by dubious analogies, not only to the human organism but to the totally different dimension of the human personality.

Scientific writing today would surely shrink from anything like Freud's confidence in making direct links between biological processes. Biology is humbly tentative in trying to account for the ever-increasing complexity of life, the limitless possible combinations of function, trend, and development in organic processes. The kind of analogies made in the last century about the effect of one process on another would be unthinkable to a biologist of today.

The relevant tone of scientific writing today is perhaps best suggested by the following passage on connections between various levels of structure and function in organisms.

> It may well be, however, that there is a greater gap than we suspect between the intricacies of sub-microscopic structure, and the properties of macromolecules as we know them at present.
> . . . Comparative morphology and behaviour are the chemistry and physics that the biochemist and biophysicist cannot as yet interpret and must for long reject as fields of study, because *concepts are as yet too limited for systems of this complexity to be embraced from the physico-chemical side.* (Picken [68], p. 100; my italics.)

The attitude here to the interpretation of data in order to discuss theories of evolution, selection, and development is ruthlessly empirical and, where hypotheses are concerned, delicately cautious. The first necessity is to discover 'what exactly happens'; 'we need more facts', before the most tentative deductions about the 'directions' of life's development can be made. The available data does not lead itself to simple deductions and correlations, even between biologies. Even in the field of one simple organism the genuine scientist is hesitant in making large deductions about growth and evolution.

Kacser suggests that it may even be that such links can only be explored in a dimension of thought which has yet to be developed. We need mental capacities capable of going beyond normal logical thought in order to begin to make sense of what has been observed:

> It is well known that organisms consist of molecules. It should, therefore, be possible to account for biological behaviour in terms of molecular behaviour. Yet it is evident that the complete enumeration, even were it possible, of all the molecules within an organism would not account for any but its most trivial aspects. The reason for this is, of course, that an organism is not simply a mixture but a system of interacting molecules. It is therefore to these interactions that we must look for an elucidation of biological behaviour. (Kacser [43]).

As with the crisis in astrophysics, the data accumulated by biologists is now so complex that new modes of interpretation will prove necessary, and these may require a complete departure from the cause-and-effect mechanical approaches to phenomena that belong to the ways of thinking of nineteenth-century biology. How much greater, therefore, if the need to relinquish all forms of interpretation of human nature in terms of quantitative processes, economic 'impulse' theory, and all the ambitions that go with the 'nothing but' impulse, in interpreting the origins and nature of human behaviour.

Surely the very complexity of data, combined with enormous developments in its collection, must daunt the impulses of natural science to make simple deductions about human nature from 'scientific' observation of functions. Surely, here, a great uncertainty must inhibit confidence. A writer such as Butler [33], for instance, will speak of how 'The essential feature of [certain] organisms is that all their cells originate from a single fertilised germ cell *by the hardly understood process of development*' (Butler [11], p. 135).

Of his brief sketch of the stages of biological investigation this writer says that only in the first stage of biology (of simplest organisms)

> can we be regarded as having reached (or are in sight of reaching) an adequate knowledge of the mechanisms involved. . . . .
> More is known about the processes utilised in the third stage (i.e. rats, rabbits and humans); *but of the second and the fourth we know practically nothing.* We know neither how organisms are developed from a single fertilised cell, nor do we have any knowledge of the mechanisms involved in perception in the phenomenon of consciousness. (My italics.)

I quote these phrases from recent biological essays, to indicate that the reductive ambition to 'explain' human personality in biological or metapsychological terms is scarcely compatible with the genuine scientific approach to biological problems. Apart from the fact that the crucial truths about man here are in any case subjective, we can see from biology itself that factors in the processes of life involve such complex quantities and relationships that no true scientist would be prepared to make deductions about the processes that go on in one stage or dimension from a knowledge of what goes on in another. Analogies between what happens when, say, a bacteriophage penetrates a bacterium, or when an insect's substance is invaded and environmental impingements on human beings, human consciousness, thinking, or sensation would seem to any modern biologist quite invalid. Nor would a biologist today think of deriving from his empirical work such an anthropomorphic concept as the death instinct, though it is, of course, acceptable to make philosophical speculations from biological data about the origins and nature of the universe of living things.

We can, for instance, try to come to conclusions about whether the cosmos is benign or not. Here, far from confirming the existence of any death instinct or universal enmity to life, the picture is of a continuing energy of development of forms by continual variation and elaboration, caused by 'accidental' modifications which are 'selected' according to whether they survive or not on being 'tested' against the environment. One writer calls it 'seemingly aimless diversification'.* Diversifications are caused largely by mutations which are the result of physical agencies such as ionising radiations, ultraviolet light, bacteriophage invasion, all causing changes in chemical substances which, by

---

* 'As for the evolutionary outlook – supposing that Man, in spite of his ever-increasing power over Nature, allows her lugworm beaches to stay more or less as they are – the available evidence suggests that she will continue awhile with her game of *seemingly aimless diversification*. But aimlessness is not necessarily unprogressive' (Wells [87], p. 000).

combining with some part of the DNA code, make parts of it incapable of giving a 'correct' replica. The human brain emerged out of the potentialities in this process:

> As seen from the present day the course of evolution seems an unbroken succession of more effective and more complex organisms. Whenever a new faculty was needed or could be used, the cell types required seem to have been forthcoming . . . [even] the necessary properties for the conscious brain must have been present in the primitive nerves, as an ability waiting to be exploited. Possibly the primordial mass contained cells of many kinds, perhaps all the principal cellular types were already present, and primitive organisms were produced by the union of DNA's of several types by a process of transduction (i.e. by the operation of bacteriophages in penetrating cells and carrying heritage characters by injecting substances into them). (Butler [11], p. 147.)

There is, however, no place in such an account for the kind of subjective postulation made by Freud, of primal malevolent forces, or of matter having been 'disturbed by the appearance of life'. Rather, life is felt to be the expression of properties always inherent in matter. Even 'aggressive' or destructive behaviour may be a manifestation of the impulse of forms of life to survive and develop (as the function of the seemingly destructive bacteriophage has been to bring about changes by transduction).

In the biological picture of life, there seems to be no single way of reacting to impingement, attack, or competition for place in the world. Some organisms live side by side; some viruses, having taken hold in a host, keep others out; some organisms seem 'designed' to attack others – but their function may be to cause valuable modifications and better changes of renewal and development.

> . . . organisms build themselves because there is, in the total structure, a place for everything, and thermal agitation insures that everything finds its proper place. The forms of living things are a *more or less remotely extrapolated* expression of the properties of matter as we know them in structures of less complexity. What we see as the Pageant of Animal Form is the extrapolated consequence of differences in specific chemical pattern in large molecules. The diversity of the Pageant is primarily due, we believe, to change in the serial order of nucleotides in the nucleic acids of the genetic system. It is the change which is primary, not 'evolution'; and the appearance of manifold complexity in temporal sequences is due to the time required for change to exploit itself. (Kacser [43]).

This sense of biological time is missing, as Towers and Lewis point out, from the pseudo-science behind popular theories of aggression and their pessimism. But the passage demonstrates the difficulties and dangers of philosophical interpretation.

To return to Freud, however, there seems no evidence from biology whatever that destructiveness or the urge to return to a state of minimum stimulus, is a predominant feature of all organic life, or that all life is governed by an impulse to seek the ultimate 'detensioning' by returning to the inanimate state. There is, of course, a tendency for species to survive in a way which seems to us to symbolise a concern for continuity at the expense of the individual: but to look at it thus is subjective, since if we think like this we are reading into biological fact feelings and attitudes appropriate to the dimension of human personality – and its uniqueness which to us makes human life valid.

Life would seem to be a natural development of quantities inherent in the matter of the universe – i.e. the results of potentialities 'built in', in terms of codes in the atoms that exist throughout the universe, brought to flourish under certain favourable conditions. Since those conditions probably exist in 2,000 million stars in our galaxy alone, we can accept that it is possible that life is common throughout the universe and that life is 'at home' in the universe – a natural product of it, not an 'accident' or a manifestation which is always on the defensive among hostile forces. That is, our universe is a marvellously benign environment and man belongs in it, as one of its most remarkable products. There does not seem to be any essential conflict between modern biology and the view of

Teilhard de Chardin, the Catholic philosopher, that: 'Man is not the centre of the universe as once we thought in our simplicity, but something more wonderful – the arrow pointing the way to the final unification of the world in terms of life. Man alone constitutes the last-born, the freshest, the most complicated, the most subtle of all the successive layers of life' (Teilhard de Chardin [80], p. 22).

In some ways recent biology requires considerable readjustment of our ways of thinking about the origins of life For instance, Butler says:

> By whatever means it was achieved, the assembling of 10,000,000,000 nucleotides of the human chromosome in a precisely significant order is the supreme achievement of what Bernard Shaw called the 'life force'. But it has taken . . . at least a million years . . . if we consider that the final assembly was achieved at a rate of addition . . . at an average rate of only ten nucleotides a year, it does not seem a very rapid progress. (Butler [11], p. 148.)

While it would seem that living organisms are the product of the characteristics of molecules, even such a connection cannot be explored with any confidence of direct links being established in terms of causation.

Links between processes in simple organisms are not yet possible: nor can they be pursued according to 'conventional logic': it seems to some writers such as Kacser, that new ways of thinking are involved – and acts of imagination – for biologists even to begin to understand the 'bewildering array of metabolic consequences'. Links between processes in organisms and intra-psychic processes of human personality *even if they were in the same dimension,* could never be made except in any comprehensible form – comprehensible, that is, to conventional thought and behaviour. So much for the metapsychological ambition altogether, and much 'empirical' psychology. The organic basis of our conflicts of love and hate can never be 'explained' in terms of mechanical causation: this is not to say that we cannot learn a great deal from the natural sciences (as, for instance, in considering the organic origin of some psychic disorders).

Freud confuses knowledge of persons with the descriptive intellectual systems by which we account for the data of biology. This confusion arises from the heresy of his presumption 'that one can, instead of imagining, actually know the other in his essence'. One glance at modern biology shows how hopelessly absurd this ambition was. Even supposing it possible to make connections between these spheres, it would be impossible to make deductions in the way in which Freud makes them, or aspired to make them, *especially* where he seeks to vindicate his *essential pessimism about human nature from biological 'fact'.* What I suggest he was doing was to use scientific 'data' (and selected data at that) to *symbolise* his attitudes to human beings poetically, while seeking to give highly subjective speculations (of a philosophical–anthropological kind) a scientific dress of objectivity. This apparent scientific basis of the death instinct is chimerical, while his argument to 'prove' it is anything but deductive, logical, or objective, as we shall see.

CHAPTER 7

An Inescapable Speculation

Ungebändigt immer vorwärts dringt*

FREUD opens his first account of the death instinct with admissions of uncertainty that look strange if we return to them with the knowledge that this concept is still unquestioned dogma for some. What begins as 'curious' invention becomes a structure of arguments from which Freud later comes to the conclusion that he 'could not escape the view . . . ' (Freud [30], p. 5). At the opening of Chapter IV of *Beyond the Pleasure Principle* he writes: 'What follows is speculation, often far-fetched speculation, which the reader will consider or dismiss according to his individual predeliction. It is further an attempt to follow out an idea consistently, out of curiosity to see where it will lead.' (Freud (29), p. 18.)

Freud then seeks to devise by this speculation ('Psychoanalytical speculation takes as its point of departure') a theory of consciousness as a 'function of a particular system' and relates it to 'the views on localisation held by cerebral anatomy'. There seems little point in examining the anatomical analogy now, since, though the modern biologist admits we know nothing about such processes, biology almost certainly knows enough to discount any such view as that quoted by Freud that the 'seat' of consciousness is located in the 'cerebral cortex – the outermost, enveloping layer of the central organ'. It may be that interference with the outer physical layer can disturb the functioning of consciousness, but this does not prove (as some seem to suppose) that consciousness is 'located' there.† Consciousness is the product of a myriad of complex aspects of bodily life whose sum cannot be meaningfully discussed in mechanical terms because the variants and combinations are so astronomically complex – infinitely more complex than those data about molecules and cells about which, as we have seen, the biologist can no longer make connections and deductions to link stages and levels of living process.

Consciousness and personality as we discuss them are more complex functions than is implied by any exploration of the brain and nervous systems as a system of signals, or an information processing system. We are concerned with structures and dynamics, a complete account of which can never be given in terms of impulses, messages, tensions, and other concepts belonging to communications and steam-engine thinking. This 'communications' view of human make-up is still, however, upheld by followers of Harry Stack Sullivan. As Farber says: 'Underlying his theory . . . is a norm or goal having to do

* The repressed instinct 'presses ever forward unsubdued'.
† That mind is located in the head is also a delusion according to Winnicott, who speaks of the 'mental patient's false localisation of the mind in the head' (Winnicott [104], p. 253). As Melanie Klein showed (p. 108) consciousness is at one from the first with *bodily* feelings.

with the capacity for communication, whether verbal or non-verbal. Thus it is no accident that many communications engineers or cyberneticists should, like many social scientists, find support in Sullivan's theories.' (Farber [20], p. 144.)

Farber quotes as a warning here Maurice S. Friedman on 'social communication or sociality':

> It is important . . . not to lose sight of the fact that though the world of the *It* is a social world which is derived from the world of the *Thou*, it often sets itself up as the *final reality*. Its sociality, as a result, becomes largely 'technical dialogue' . . . the mere communication and interaction between human beings who may in fact largely relate to each other as *Its*. (Buber [102], quoted by Farber [20], p. 144.)

As Farber says: 'While Sullivan felt that subjective relations could be studied from the objective viewpoints of a scientist – moreover, of a physical scientist – and that experience could be adequately described in the terminology of the sciences, Buber knew that language may not only determine our concepts but radically change our experiences as well.' We are back to the problem raised by R. D. Laing when he says:

> The theoretical and descriptive idiom of much research in social science adopts a stance of apparent 'objective' neutrality. But . . . the choice of syntax and vocabulary . . . define(s) and circumscribe(s) the manner in which the 'facts' are to be studied. Indeed, in a sense they go further and even create the facts that are studied. (Laing [53], p. 53.)

This is the danger of the implicit reification in metapsychology, which is an attempt to explain these processes of whole being in terms of schemes which can be formulated intellectually, in terms of cause and effect, as quantitative facts. In the light of the fallacies inherent in such economic and quantitative accounts of mind we can examine Freud's theory of the death instinct.

Freud seeks to make his 'speculation' respectable – but only makes it *sound* like science – by pursuing these quantitative mechanical analogies. This leads him to speak of 'excitatory processes' in so far as they affect consciousness as if they were of the same kind as stimuli physically impinging on an organism, like an amoeba being tickled with a probe. Consider his discussion of 'Systems': 'System Cs is characterised by the peculiarity that in it (in contrast to what happens in the other psychical systems) excitatory processes do not leave behind any permanent change in its elements but expire, as it were in the phenomenon of becoming conscious' (Freud [29], p. 19).

What 'consciousness' yields, according to Freud, 'consists essentially of perceptions of excitations coming from the external world and of feelings of pleasure and unpleasure which can only arise from within the mental apparatus; it is therefore possible to assign to the system *Pcpt. Cs* a position in space'. What was a speculation is becoming an anatomical account: what is cultural (or symbolic) 'input' is confused with *physical stimuli*.

It is astonishing to discover, in his accounts of the death instinct, how false are certain uses of argument in Freud. Here, for instance, he seeks to strengthen his use of Fechner's hypothesis by matching it with a hypothesis of his own which he claims is built on *facts*, whereas he means subjective observations of patients by projective identification, which is a different form of truth from biological fact:

> The facts which have caused us to believe in the dominance of the pleasure principle in mental life also find expression in the hypothesis that the mental apparatus endeavours to keep the quantity of excitation present in it as low as possible or at least to keep it constant. The latter hypothesis is only another way of stating the pleasure principle; for if the work of the mental apparatus is directed towards keeping the quantity of excitation low, than anything that is calculated to increase that quantity is bound to be felt as adverse to the functioning of the apparatus, that is as unpleasureable. (Freud [29], p. 3.)

Brewer spoke earlier (*Studies on Hysteria*, Brewer and Freud, 1895) of 'the tendency to keep intracerebral excitation constant'. Freud also spoke of 'neuronic inertia'.

As Guntrip points out, this principle is a physiological not a psychological concept:

> Though it is put forward to explain *mental* events and related to the quantity of excitation that it held to be present in *mind,* this 'mind' is in fact regarded as a mechanical model, an apparatus (as E. Jones emphasized) in which events are automatically regulated – not for the fulfilment of *meaningful aims*, which would be a psychological concept, but for the *reduction of quantity of excitation* to a constant level. (Guntrip [37], p. 126.)

This neurological, physiological psychology Freud was supposed to have dropped in 1885: but it is the basis of his paper of 1920, and remains a basis of the dogma of death instinct in Kleinian theory 80 years after he is supposed to have relinquished it.

When is an increase of 'excitation' unpleasant? It may be (as Guntrip says) if sexual activity is interrupted or checked. But surely the excitation of perception, and of bodily metabolism, whether by love or a spring day or by excited thought or even disaster (as in battle) can be intensely pleasurable. By contrast, the dullness of the mind and perceptions in fatigue or illness can be unpleasurable. As soon as we being to examine the hypothesis, however, its irrelevance is exposed: it is not possible to argue for or against the hypothesis as the factors involved are not accessible to economic analysis. It is perfectly legitimate to discuss relative *feelings* of happiness and unhappiness, as between persons, or inwardly, poetically, subjectively as I–Thou experience, or even in terms of interpersonal psychology of individual experience. What is not valid is an hypothesis which relates pleasure and unpleasure to a physiological model quantitatively conceived in terms of pressures or amounts of impulse. One glance at any general statement of the nature of organisms in biology reveals that these quantitative entities *are not really there to discuss*: they could never be found.

Later (p. 29) we return to the (also invalid) comparison between mental life and the life of a simple organism, pursued yet further: 'Let us picture a living organism in its most simplified possible form as an undifferentiated vesicle of a substance that is susceptible to stimulation.' There are scientific objections here to Freud's account of how organisms react to their environment. But what is of major significance here is the subjectivity of Freud's terms:

> But we have more to say of the living vesicle with its receptive cortical layer. This *little fragment of living substance* is suspended in the middle of *an external world charged with the most powerful energies*; and *it would be killed by the stimulation emating from these if it were not provided with a protective shield against stimuli*. It acquires the shield in this way; its outermost surface ceased to have the structure proper to living matter, becomes to some degree inorganic and thenceforward functions as a special envelope or membrane resistant to stimuli. . . . By its death, the *outer layer has saved all the deeper ones from a similar fate* – unless, that is to say, stimuli reach it which are so strong that they break through the protective shield. *Protection against stimuli is an almost more important function for the living organism than reception of stimuli* . . . against the effects threatened by *the enormous energies at work in the external world* – effects which tend towards a levelling out of them and hence towards destruction. (Freud [29], p. 30, my italics.)

In what sense is Freud talking about a 'little fragment of living substance'? The passage is, I think, so far from scientific argument and so subjective in style ('little fragment', 'charged with the most powerful energies', 'threatened by the enormous energies') that one can take as a symbolic *poetic* projection of Freud's feelings about his own make-up. We can, I believe, even interpret the model as being a picture of the regressed libidinal ego, the True Self, being protected at the core of being, by the 'pseudo-male' doing of the False Self which deals with the world, at a cost: 'By its death, the outer layer has saved all the deeper ones . . . ' – a poetic symbol, surely, of the heroism of False Self Solutions?

Fairbairn believes that the origin of Freud's postulation of the death instinct lay in his experience of psychotherapeutic stalemate, and of the defences a patient will put up to the breaking down of his neurotic construction, a False Self organisation. But it also seems likely that the orign of the concept may be even nearer home – the concept could be a symbol of Freud's own defence of his own 'death circuit', so that his 'scientific theory' can be seen as a vindication of an intellectual or 'hate theory' way of coping with life itself. The 'little fragment' is surely Freud's own core of ego-weakness. By preserving a *deadening construction* 'the outer layer has saved all the deeper ones'. The 'will' of 'hate' has preserved the inner life, the True Self. What Freud is writing is a poem about the strategies of the False Self to protect the unborn self at the core of a schizoid personality – his own!

But Freud is not only writing poetry. He is constructing a perversely destructive rationalisation, and it is this that his 'scientific' dress disguises. He grants at one point, for instance, that there may be other instincts which 'push forward towards progress and the production of new forms' (a point of view which modern biology virtually sees as the principle of life in the universe!). 'This argument must certainly not be overlooked, and it will be taken into account at a later stage.' But it is hardly ever taken into account in Freud's work, because his temperament was utterly against such a positive view:

> . . . For the moment it is tempting to pursue to its logical conclusion the hypothesis that all instincts tend towards the restoration of an earlier state of things. The outcome may give an impression of mysticism or of sham profundity; but we can feel quite innocent of having had any such purpose in view . . . we have no wish to find in those results any quantity other than *certainty*. (Freud [29], p. 31; my italics.)

What kind of 'certainty' was Freud seeking for? It can hardly be scientific certainty. In 1925 he added a footnote: 'The reader should not overlook the fact that what follows is the development of an extreme line of thought. Later on, when account is taken of the sexual instincts, it will be found that the necessary limitations and corrections are applied to it. (Freud [29], p. 31.) As Suttie shows, they are not.

The search for 'certainty' hardly justifies the way Freud begins each stage of his argument with 'Let us suppose' while following this by slipping increasingly into dogmatic assertion. How can 'extreme lines of thought', 'hints', and 'far-fetched speculation' be reconciled with the implications that the method is strictly scientific? 'We seek only for the *sober results of research or of reflection based on it.* Let us suppose, then . . .' (Freud [29], p. 31; my italics).

Having noticed the inconsistency, we need to go on to ask what are the origins of the self-deception. Why is it that, following a nod to 'sober results of research' we have this baseless speculation that follows to account for why Freud wishes to reverse the impression that instincts are life-seeking?

In *The Ego and the Id* what was purely speculative in *Beyond the Pleasure Principle* becomes a system, and a kind of dogmatic diagrammation of the personality as a mechanical structure. It was bad enough trying to follow Freud's model of the System *Pcpt-Cs*, and how it was situated on the 'outside' of the organism like a protective skin, enclosing the other systems. Now we find ourselves deeper in conjecture about spatial aspects of the systems: 'the ego does not completely envelope the id, but only does so to the extent to which the system *Pcpt Cs* forms its [the ego's] surface, *more or less as the germinal disc rests upon the ovum*' (Freud [30], p. 14; my italics).

This is even accompanied by a diagram: 'The state of things which we have been describing can be represented diagrammatically . . . though it must be remarked that the form chosen has no pretensions to any special applicability, but is merely intended to serve for purposes of exposition.'

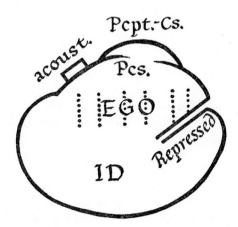

The diagram, I suggest, has no function except to make Freud's system *seem* one of real objective validity and to lend colour to his attempts to explain states and processes of personality in terms of organic function and structure. Wherever *are* the entities labelled in this figure?

I do not propose to analyse this work in detail. We may note that it is generated by the same destructive and negative attitude to human creative potentialities, as is the depressing chapter on ego-ideals. Freud seems under an urgent pressure to explain away human love and idealism: in the end he attributes it to consequences of the Oedipus conflict, which is solved by our taking both parents into ourselves, to form the super-ego. As with the other phenomena Freud seeks to explain, the super-ego is not seen biologically or historically as a means by which human personality is developed, in any positive sense, but rather as the sum of negative impingements: the lengthy duration of man's childish helplessness and dependence, and the fact of his Oedipus complex, the repression of '*which we have shown to be connected with the interruption of libidinal development by the latency period*, and so with the diphastic onset of man's sexual life'. This latter is attributed (from Ferenczi) to 'a heritage of the cultural development necessitated by the glacial epoch' (!) All formative episodes are seen by him as defensive reactions to impingement of one kind or another.

Freud sees no positive value in the long period of nurture, within which by a number of dynamic processes in the individual in the family situation the complex and marvellous human personality is created. All we have is a negative reaction to 'strong forces' which impinge. And so all culture and religion are by this reductive view but substitutes and negatives, too.

> It is easy to show that the ego ideal answers to everything that is expected of the higher nature of man. As a *substitute* for a longing for the father, it contains the germ from which all religions have evolved. The self-judgement which declares that the ego falls short of its ideal produces the religious sense of humility to which the believer appeals in his longing. As a child grows up, the role of father

is carried on by teachers and others in authority; their injunctions and prohibitions remain powerful in the ego ideal and continue, in the form of conscience, to exercise the moral censorship. (Freud [30]).

Here we may note the deceptive trick of argument ('It is easy to show'): the denial of the mother implicit in 'longing for the father' (what of religions that worship godesses?); and the assumption that the father and teachers in authority are solely concerned with injunctions and prohibitions, a view significantly altered by Klein and Winnicott.

In Freud's point of view we are always confined by the chains of being human: 'The tension between the demands of conscience and the actual performances of the ego is experienced as a sense of guilt' (Freud [30], p. 27).

This negative view of guilt and conscience is surely in complex with Freud's blindness to the mother's role, as first object, by whose intuitive care each individual grows to sanity by 'taking into himself' the goodness and richness of his experience of her, with the consequent development of inner creative resources, and capacities to deal creatively with the world as 'object'.

It needs to be said, of course, that as soon as Freud turns thus to talking about conflict within the self, as between the ego and guilt, we find the seminal element in his work – insights into the way the self can become divided against itself. In the essay under discussion, however, Freud is less concerned to pursue this subject than he is to fortify his conjectural instinct theory: 'I have lately developed a view of the instincts which I shall here hold to.'

One set of instincts is Eros, or the life instincts: vaguely those that protected the germ cells, as we have seen (though Freud is elusive about how they remain both conservative and progressive, innocent and modified). The others are the death instinct: 'and sadism its representative'.

This latter extension is startling, as we last saw the theory in a state of supposing that it was in cells and such small particles that instincts tended to retreat to inanimation, or to bring the organism to death from within. It comes as shock to find that this theory has now been transferred by direct analogy to explain wholesale *manifestations of human pesonality* such as sadism. Meanwhile, speculation is no longer left to sound like speculation, while the theory marches on to see the aim of life in death:

> On the basis of theoretical considerations, *supported by biology*, we put forward the hypothesis of a death instinct, the task of which is to lead organic life back into the inanimate state; on the other hand we supposed that Eros, by bringing about a more and more far-reaching combination of the particles into which living substance is disposed, aims at complicating life and at the same time, of course, preserving it . . . both would be endeavouring to re-establish *a state of things that was disturbed by the emergence of life*. (Freud [30]).

Freud's contemplation of the nature of things has, however, now obliged him to postulate a *life instinct*: 'The emergence of life would thus be the cause of the continuance of life and also at the same time of the striving towards death; and life itself would be a conflict and compromise between these two trends' (Freud [30], p. 000).

These dual kinds of instinct are found 'in every particle of living substance'. Here, certainly, we can find no justification in biology, neither old nor new. Even at the end he cannot sound convinced himself, for aspects of reality must break in: 'Over and over again we find, when we are able to trace instinctual impulses back, that they reveal themselves as derivatives of Eros.'

Why then do we go on believing in the death instinct? *Because we have said it exists,* Freud answers! 'If it were not for the considerations put forward in *Beyond the Pleasure*

Principle, and ultimately for the sadistic constituents, which have attached themselves to Eros [which could have other explanations Freud doesn't examine], we should have difficulty in holding to our fundamental dualistic point of view' (Freud [30]).

Why not give it up, then? All Freud can say is: '*But since we cannot escape this view* we are driven to conclude that the death instincts are by their nature mute' (my italics).

There can be no evidence because the death instinct, though it is there, never shows itself in anything that can be taken down in evidence against it. It never speaks, but this only confirms our interpretation of what it says. 'Since we cannot escape this view' does not mean 'we cannot escape the evidence' but 'I cannot give it up'. We also believe 'that the clamour of life proceeds for the most part from Eros' (Freud [30], p. 36).

The word 'clamour' is surely strangely wry, as if life were a troublesome and unwanted child!

Why Freud 'cannot escape this view' subjectively, is perhaps indicated on the next page:

> The ejection of the sexual substances in the sexual act corresponds in a sense to the separation of soma and germ-plasm. This accounts for the likeness of the condition that follows complete sexual satisfaction to dying, and for the fact that death coincides with the act of copulation in some of the lower animals. These creatures die in the act of reproduction because, after Eros has been eliminated through the process of satisfaction, the death instinct has a *free hand for accomplishing its purposes*. (Freud [30], p. 37; my italics.)

Implicit here is an analogy between organism and human identity which we can only see as symbolic.

The fulfilment of libidinal urges inevitably brings about a situation in which an active instinct towards death can achieve its purpose. As Freud realised, this was surprisingly negative:

> We have unwittingly steered our course into the harbour of Schopenhauer's philosophy. For him death is the 'true result and to that extent the purpose of life', while the sex instinct is the embodiment of the will to live. (Freud [30], p. 44.)
> Yet he must also prove that death is 'not natural', it is not founded on any primal characteristic of living substance (Weisemann, 1884, 84) and cannot be regarded as an absolute necessity with its basis in the very nature of life. (Weisemann, 1882, 33). Death is rather a matter of expediency, a manifestation of adaptation to the external conditions of life; for, when once the cells of the body have been divided into soma and germ-plasm, an unlimited duration of individual life would become a quite pointless luxury. (Freud [30], p. 40.)

By analogy, after 'the ejection of sexual substances' the realm in which the individual finds himself feels to Freud like a 'pointless luxury' too. The point of life is only in 'contest with the external conditions of life': ultimate adaptation to these is to die. (Freud saw King Lear's predicament as the need to accept the 'necessity of dying'.)

Here I believe we may link a number of elements in Freud's attitude to experience with his theory. There was his morbid fear of death. There is his anti-feminism and his denial of woman's role. And there is his need to erect a theory on the death instinct and on sexual instinct. In these, I believe, we may see a man tormented by the schizoid fear of loss of identity. Death in the external world seemed an objective correlative of the 'dead' regressed infantile ego within him. This unborn true self, like the baby in a steel drawer of which Guntrip's schizoid patient dreamt, was associated with the vulnerable female element at the core of being. The concept of the death instinct, together with the whole hate-theory built on it, were a form of pseudo-male doing ('bad thinking') on which Freud himself needed to base his identity.

Of course, without such existential agony in the man Freud we would never have had psychoanalysis as an existential discipline, nor its 'uncanny insights'. But it means we must try to discriminate against the schizoid elements in Freudian psychoanalysis itself.

In the light of Winnicott's distinction between 'female element being' and 'male element doing', Guntrip distinguishes between essentially female and male sexual modes. In so far as an individual is schizoid, he tends to fear female element being and love in the sexual sphere, and to take refuge in 'male doing'. Moreover, his 'male doing' may take the form of a 'bustling' false self-activity, or even a form of intellectual 'bad thinking' about sex. In the light of this perhaps we can interpret Freud's position to mean that what he finds most threatening is the realm of 'female element being' in love and giving, confronting the problem of existence from the central stillness of the self. He feels that the identity must be forever engaged in hate activity; thus the sex instinct is the embodiment of the 'will to live' and the sexual theory, an intellectual construct, is the *raison d'être* of his whole philosophy. This alone sustains the organism against a malignant universe, whose whole urge is to return to the dead state of inanition from which the emergence of life disturbed it.

This latter feeling about the cosmos can, I believe, be seen as a rationalisation into a symbolic philosophy of a deep schizoid condition in Freud himself. If the pseudo-male activity of the sex instinct, and of constructing a sexual theory, were to cease, Freud felt he would be confronted by the area of female element being. At the heart of being he felt there was a deadness. Yet, as Guntrip shows, there is also a deep desire in schizoid individual for this dead inmost self to be born again – and this desire emerges in the symbolism of schizoid suicide. Freud's sympathy with the philosophy of Schopenhauer is a sympathy with the (delusory) belief of the schizoid individual who sees the 'true result and to that extent the purpose of life' in a death which is to be the opportunity for the rebirth of the True Self.

We can trace to this schizoid delusion, I believe, Freud's intolerant insistence on his sexual theory, his concept of the death instinct, and his whole negative approach to the nature of the cosmos, and man, and the point of his life. The moment when the germ plasm parts from the soma represented for him the moment of 'implosion' (to use a term from Laing). Once the vigilance of pseudo-male doing and thinking became relaxed, the malignant universe would extinguish the self: this is surely a rationalisation of early experience of threatening 'impingement'. If the sustaining activity of the False Self were relaxed, then there could be found nothing to give point to life. It is as if Freud could find no other source of confirmation of identity, or of a sense of the point of life, except in hate. His perplexity was that if the will to live was expressed in emptying, as by the 'ejection of the sexual substances', then the period of detensioning or 'flop' threatened inanition.

This schizoid fear of utter emptiness and futility has been much explored by recent psychoanalytical writers, and my summary of these has already introduced the reader to the schizoid problem of hollowness at the core. In a paper on 'Communicating and not communicating' Winnicott says:

> Although persons communicate and enjoy communicating, the other fact is equally true, that each individual is an isolate, permanently non-communicating, permanently unknown, in fact unfound. . . . At the centre of each person is an incommunicado element. . . . The violation of the self's core, the alteration of the self's central elements by communication seeping through the defences, for me this would be the sin against the self. (Winnicott [94], p. 187.)

This core 'belongs to being alive', and we may see it symbolised in Freud's 'little fragment of life-stuff' that is threatened with impingement. Guntrip sees this 'central core of the personality' as 'the uncontaminated female element that leads us to BEING', derived from sympathetic experience of the mother. Its incommunicado nature belongs to the world of 'thoughts that do often lie too deep for tears' – and certainly too deep for words – 'an experience', says Guntrip, 'common enough in earliest motherhood, profound friendship and true marital love'. It is this kind of experience that Freud feared above all.

But since 'individuality and separate ego identity, however strongly achieved, are always precariously held against threats from the external world', where this core of being, derived from the mother, is weak, there is obviously a profound fear that this core of the self will be invaded and destroyed. As Guntrip says:

> We cannot stand what Winnicott calls 'the violation of the self's core by communication seeping through our defences'. We must feel able to shut out the external world and maintain our right to an inviolable privacy within ourselves at need if we are to remain healthy persons. We cannot tolerate being psychologically flooded by alien invading experiences, or again, as Winnicott puts it, suffering in reality 'the frightening phantasy of being infinitely exploited'. (Guntrip [38], p. 268.)

What we have expressed in the poetry of Freud's two books in which he develops the concept of the death instinct is a fear of the core of the self being invaded, despite all his defences.

Since the area of female element being is derived from the mother, we can associate his fear of it with Freud's own denial of the mother's role, and his blindness to this, and his consequent inability to believe in a benign universe, and a creative principle in the universe. As Winnicott says: 'The risks inherent in conflict with the mother are great indeed, for with the idea of mother (in unconscious phantasy) is associated the idea of loving care, good food, the stability of the earth, and the world in general; and a conflict with mother necessarily involves a feeling of insecurity, and dreaming of the ground opening, or worse' (Winnicott [95], p. 150).

We can even, I believe, attribute a talion element to Freud's denial of being. Unconsciously, Freud must have been tormented by the recognition that in denying the mother and hating woman as he did he was in a sense making an attack on the castrating mother, the impulse to do so emerging itself from the awareness of his own female element vulnerability and inner weakness. This again can be related to his preference for science and reason – thought as 'male element doing' – over poetry and imagination, the female faculties. In return for this attack on the female element, he fears an attack which will disturb the very stability of his world – the ground threatens to open, and so his universe cannot be benign. While he has deep down the need to love and to be loved, as is manifest in his concern for humanity and his clinical therapy, what he fears most is love, because it reminds him of the fact that he was once totally dependent upon a woman, and was himself no more than weak and human.

His theory must therefore deny love, deny our need to love, to be loved, and our fundamental ego weakness and 'feminine' vulnerability. To counteract this fear of being, hate must be everywhere put in the place of love, even in every particle of living matter. Impingement must be all! Thus to him every particle of life must be seen as urging towards the destruction of the world: Freud is a true child of his age.

CHAPTER 8

Metapsychology and Negation

Um die Schwere des Daseins zu ertragen*

THE problem in rejecting Freud's metapsychology in which the death instinct emerges is thus not one of unravelling a biological argument but of resisting a highly subjective schizoid intellectual denial of our humanness. Freud's theory is a defence against insight and self-awareness – a way of *not* seeing the implications of his own discoveries.† In clinical observation he sees one thing, – the process of the development of object-love, e.g. as in *Beyond the Pleasure Principle* (Freud [29], pp. 47–48): '. . . object love itself presents us with a second example of . . . polarity – that between love (or affection) and hate (or aggressiveness) . . . the familiar ambivalence. . . . If only we could succeed in relating these two polarities to each other. . . .'

There could be a number of possible explanations for this process, one of which would certainly lead to the discovery of the mother's primary role, the dynamic role of phantasy and symbolism, and the creative sphere of relation. But this path Freud could not follow: he must find the death instinct instead.

To Freud, in this perverse poetry of his postulation of a death instinct, that experience which most seems to confirm that we are alive seems to him like a death. He speaks of 'the likeness of the condition that follows complete sexual satisfaction to dying', and links this with the 'fact that death coincides with the act of copulation in some of the lower animals'. This seems less 'science' than a symbolic speculative expression of a schizoid fear of giving in love, which we can associate with Freud's fear of woman. The death instinct for him has a 'purpose', which it becomes free to achieve at the moment of giving in love: the satisfaction of id instinct tension leaves us nothing to live for.

There could never be a more negative and depressive picture of the processes of life, and of the sexual potentialities: uncreative, joyless, haunted, doomed, and loveless. Yet this picture still underlies much psychoanalytical theory, attitudes to man, and approaches to ethical and cultural issues. Believed to be a kind of 'realism' based on 'scientific' thought, it is really nothing of the kind, but is rather a form of dogmatic philosophical anthropology whose origins are most subjective. The schizoid inversions in this hate theory are, morover, by no means confirmed by our experience of human beings in the realm of the I–Thou.

---

* 'To bear the burden of existence.'

† One of Freud's errors was to regard himself as normal. Cf. *The Interpretation of Dreams* [28]: 'Thus it comes about that I am led to my own dreams, which offers a copious and convenient material, derived from an approximately normal person.' Yet he also refuses to reveal everything behind his dreams in the light of which his normality or otherwise could be judged.

It will be obvious from my analysis of the origins of Freud's death instinct that there is great significance in the debate as to whether or not this concept bears any relationship to reality. It could even be that in so far as we accept this concept we are involved in a dangerous psychopathological delusion.

Winnicott, writing about classification in 1959, says: 'The concept of the death instinct seems to disappear simply through being unnecessary. . . . Aggression is seen more as evidence of life' (Winnicott [94], p. 127.)

Winnicott is characteristically concerned with 'the mother's wish to be imaginatively eaten'. There is a need for the emerging infant to 'take the mother into himself' both as food, and in phantasy as a person ('both good and bad' as Melanie Klein said, 'Come into his mind from her'). An aspect of this positive growing process is that oral sadism which can become (if frustrated) consumingly aggressive. It was this kind of incorporating aggression which earlier psychoanalysts could only explain in terms of a death instinct.

Winnicott's very different point of view by which he sees 'aggression . . . more as evidence of life' is closer to how modern biology would see the nature of the energy – even the *destructive* energy – of organisms. There is in modern biology no natural impulse towards death, but only a life-seeking impulse towards survival, continuity, and proliferation. There is no impulse towards 'detensioning' or destruction from within, only towards survival, variety, and the exertion of vitality.

Even those who regard psychoanalysis as a science and who seek to relate its findings directly to biology are not able to uphold Freud's concept. A psychoanalytical study of the psychobiology of instincts by Thomas S. Szasz ('On the psychoanalytic theory of instincts') – was summarised thus by the *International Journal of Psychoanalysis*:

> This paper examines some of the basic concepts underlying Freud's theory of the Life and Death instincts. It is pointed out that Freud based his hypothesis of a Death instinct on the assumption that Fechner's principle, a special case of the second law of thermodynamics (the principle of increasing entropy), was applicable to living organisms. In fact it is valid only for closed systems, whereas living matter is an open system characterized and, indeed, definable by its ability to take energy (negative entropy) from its environment. The hypothesis is therefore suggested that there is but one primary instinct, a Life instinct, the aim of which is to maintain the life processes of any given system in continued operation.
> Carrel's tissue culture experiments are cited as consistent with this hypothesis. Under optimal metabolic conditions, such as probably no longer ever occur in nature, tissues grow indefinitely and are potentially immortal, ageing and death apparently only occurring as a response to environmental interference with the life instinct. Carrel's experiments show further that when the life instinct operates unopposed there is only growth and no development of new structures or functions. Adaptation is therefore the result of frustration. Two kinds of adaptation alone are possible, progressive with increasing differentiation and regressive with loss of differentiation. Among the factors affecting the choice of mode of adaptation the degree of complexity of the organism is of paramount importance, primitive systems tending to adapt progressively, complex ones regressively. (Szasz [125]).

Even leaving aside the question of the validity of analogies between the human personality and biological organisms, Freud's concept is found questionable on the grounds of such physiology. Why does it then persist?

In rejecting the death instinct, of course, we are not seeking to pretend that impulses of a most terrible destructive and self-destructive kind are not found in human nature. The human death impulse and its consequences are obvious realities. What we are concerned with here is explanations of the origins of these. Thinkers like Winnicott have reversed the whole picture, so that forms of behaviour once attributed to the death instinct are now to be seen as the inevitable consequences of the relationship between relational and psychodynamic processes in the earliest stages of development and the early environment. As Winnicott says, before there is a 'whole person', things may go wrong, and produce hate, but even this hate is an attempt to live: 'Failure of fusion, or loss of fusion that has been achieved, produces a potential element of pure destructiveness (i.e. without guilt sense) in the individual, but even this *destructiveness remains a life-line in the sense of its being the basis of object relationships that feel real to the patient*' (Winnicott [94], p. 127; my italics).

That is, even where hate has been completely substituted for love, this itself is an attempt to form and maintain an identity. Later we shall see how Fairbairn's explanation of schizoid problems leads him to regard the death instinct as already indicated as a name for a particular kind of false or negative pattern of solution within the patient under analysis (see p. 284).

Elsewhere Winnicott says ('On communication', 1963):

> If I take the idea of liveliness, I have to allow for at least two other opposites, one being deadness, as in manic defence, and the other being a simple absence of liveliness. It is here that silence is equated with communication and stillness with movement. By using this idea I can get behind my rooted objection to the theory of the Life and Death Instincts. I see that what I cannot accept is that Life has Death on its opposite except clinically in the manic-depressive swing, and in the concept of the manic defence in which depression is rejected and negatived. In the development of the individual infant living arises and establishes itself out of not-living, as communication arises out of silence. Death only becomes meaningful in the infant's living processes when hate has arrived, *that is at a late date, far removed from the phenomena which we can use to build a theory of the roots of aggression.*
>
> For me therefore it is not valuable to join the word death with the word Instinct, and less still is it valuable to refer to hate and anger by use of the words death instinct.
>
> It is difficult to get at the roots of aggression, but we are not helped by the use of opposites such as life and death that do not mean anything at the stage of immaturity that is under consideration. (Winnicott [94], p. 191; my italics.)

But while Winnicott has discarded the concept, we have to note that many followers of Melanie Klein, such as Hannah Segal, who interprets her work for students, still cling to it as the basis of their theory. Their inconsistencies in this respect are pointed out by Guntrip, reviewing Hannah Segal's *Introduction to the Work of Melanie Klein*, 1964, in the *British Journal of Medical Psychology.*

> [Melanie Klein's] work on phantasy calls for a theory of *ego-development by environmental object relations* . . . Kleinians have moved definitely . . . on two fundamental points (a) There is a real ego at birth . . . (b) 'Instincts are by definition object-seeking. . . .' However she overlooks the fact that this cannot be true of the death instinct, which by definition does not seek a proper relationship but the destruction of the object. Clinical experience is pushing the Kleinians towards a type of theory from which the 'death instinct' concept holds them back. If there be a death instinct there cannot be a properly whole ego at birth, nor can object-seeking be the basis nature of our instinctive endowment. (Guntrip, [113], p. 239.)

Thus the death instinct becomes the crucial issue of Kleinian theory, as of much else. 'Kleinian "metapsychology" is an inverted pyramid resting on an unsubstantial apex, the concept of a "death instinct" ' the most speculative and subjectively determined of all Freud's ideas' (Guntrip [113], p. 259.)

The death instinct is for the Kleinians a 'theoretical concept imposed on the data', which has 'become dogma' – to what degree is obvious from Hannah Segal's book. Interestingly enough the term is not defined in her glossary. But it takes a central part in the text. She says:

> To begin with, the early ego is largely unorganized, though, in keeping with the whole trend of physiological and psychological growth, it has from the beginning a tendency towards integration. At times, under the impact of the death instinct and intolerable anxiety, this tendency is swept away and defensive disintegration occurs . . . when faced with the anxiety produced by the death instinct, the

ego deflects it. This deflection of the death instinct, described by Freud, in Melanie Klein's view consists partly of a projection, partly of the conversion of the death instinct into aggression. The ego splits itself and projects that part of itself which contains the death instinct outwards into the original external object – the breast. Thus, the breast, which is felt to contain a great part of the infant's death instinct, is felt to be bad and threatening to the ego, giving rise to a feeling of persecution. In that way, the original fear of the death instinct is changed into fear of a persecutor. The intrusion of the death instinct into the breast is often felt as splitting it into many bits, so that the ego is confronted with a multitude of persecutors. Part of the death instinct remaining in the self is converted into aggression and directed against the persecutors. (Segal [75], p. 12.)

As Guntrip says, this is pure unproven dogma, and 'the only kind of proof implied is the circular argument: the death instinct produces such-and-such a phenomenon, therefore this phenomenon proves the death-instinct'. Yet this notion controls the entire build-up of the Kleinian scheme '. . . everything begins with the ego's fear of its own death instinct . . . the result is a dogma of "original evil" . . . parallel . . . to the theologian's dogma of "original sin".'

If it is true, says Guntrip, the ego is 'split from the start, not by bad object relation experience in real life' but by 'biological inheritance': 'the inborn polarity of instincts – the immediate conflict between the life instinct and the death instinct' (Segal [5], p. 12).

'Since this split is there before the infant has any experience of objects', Guntrip comments, 'all his experience of objects becomes inevitably split . . . not because of what the objects are, but because of what the infant's nature is . . . the whole Kleinian psychopathology, so clinically penetrating, could be built up with an external world that was no more than a blank projection screen.'

Kleinian theory has put forward concepts of the relationship between dynamic phantasy and the real world which begins to explain much of the origins of the patterns of consciousness. As we shall see, such theory helps us to understand the value of that continual activity between the subjective and objective worlds that guarantees sanity and *is* symbolic culture.

Yet Hannah Segal's account attempts to fix the origins of this dynamic in the death instinct! Seeking to avoid the implication of the 'blank projection screen' picture of the external world (as Guntrip points out) she writes: 'If unconscious phantasy is constantly influencing and altering the perception or interpretation of reality, the converse also holds true: reality impinges on unconscious phantasy' (Segal [75], p. 4).

Guntrip asks 'Which comes first?' – unconscious phantasy or the experience of outer reality? For Kleinians (he says) 'unconscious phantasy rests plainly on an inborn faculty, not an experience of outer reality': 'The importance of the environmental factor can only be correctly evalued in relation to what it means in terms of the infant's *own instincts* and phantasies. . . . Actual bad experience . . . *confirms* [Guntrip's italics], not only his feeling that the external world is bad, but also the sense of his own badness' (Segal [75], p. 4).)

I have put *instincts* in italics, to show that here Hannah Segal is clinging to the Freudian dogma of the life and death instincts as the *source* of good and bad phantasies. Guntrip italicises 'confirms' to show that the Kleinian inclination is to see the process of 'bad' phantasy as originating in 'original sin': their word is, he notes, 'confirms' not 'originates': 'Good and bad object phantasy life exists independently of experience of outer reality, which only *confirms* it. Clinical data support rather the view that the good and bad object phantasy life arises *out of the* infant's difficulties in coping with his real outer world.' (Guntrip [37], p. 260; my italics.)

Hannah Segal writes: 'It is not true that without a bad environment, no aggressive and persecutory phantasies and anxieties would exist' ([75], p. 4). This, says Guntrip, grossly oversimplifies the problem. 'No environment can ever be perfect . . . ', and what is not really 'bad' can seem so to a weak and helpless infant because he is so vulnerable. Even with the best of mothers fear and anger will arise, as Winnicott shows out of the very need to feel alive and real. Guntrip concludes: 'There is no clinical warranty for assigning the whole origin of infantile phantasy to an unproven concept of an innate factor like a "death instinct".' Guntrip adds that there is also evidence from experimental animal psychology that destructiveness is a 'learned' not an 'innate' response.

Guntrip then draws attention to the implications of therapy that if this Kleinian dogma is true, 'we are up against fixed and final limits to what can be achieved' because 'one cannot analyse the death instinct'. By implication, all psychotherapy can do is to make superficial adjustments and improvements. If the concept of a death instinct is valid, then 'Marie Bonaparte drew the correct inference when she wrote: "So far as the aggressions are concerned, there seems to be little prospect of man's ever achieving equal happiness and goodness".' But our exploration of the origins of the concept suggests that it is by no means valid, and, indeed, a very dubious one.

PART III

A New View of Human Nature

The Development of Object-relations Psychology

CHAPTER 9

Psychology, Poetry and Science

OUR approach to recent developments in psychoanalysis as I have indicated requires a revision of our concepts of what kind of discipline it is. As we have seen, in discussing Freud and Suttie's criticisms of Freud, psychoanalytical theory has been coloured since its origins by Freud's own personality. As Guntrip says: 'Psychoanalysis itself implies that different types of theoretical orientation will be developed by different types of personality' (Guntrip [37], p. 246).

He quotes Marjorie Brierley from *Trends in Psychoanalysis*, 1951: 'The form of any hypothesis is always influenced by unconscious determinants, since we can only apprehend things in ways permitted by the specific structure of our individual minds' (Brierley [8], p. 96).

The particular structure of Freud's mind has generated the ambivalent impulses in psychoanalysis itself which Suttie and Bantock have noted – much of the theory being 'hate', while contradicted by therapeutic practice, which was a form of 'love'. It is possible that where theorists seek to establish that psychoanalysis can still be a meta-psychology or an exact science we have the persistence of a schizoid element in Freud's thought. Such an insistence lays this discipline open to dismissal since psychologists such as Professor Eysenck can easily demonstrate that, in terms of scientific logic, psycho-analytical arguments are untenable. In trying to see what kind of discipline psycho-analysis is, we need to go back to the duality between theory and practice in Freud.

This duality in Freud's mind is observed by Professor Bantock, and it can be seen as culminating in the concept of the death instinct. It is as if, in the works we have been discussing, Freud was seeking to find a scientific reason for believing that man's 'natural goodness' and his capacities to love are determined or, rather, undermined and brought to nothing, by primary forces of the universe. All manifestations of living are threatened by a primal mechanical force by which the 'disturbances' caused by the arrival of life seek to relax into the equilibrium of inanition. This utter negation of all the point of life marks the most profound reduction of man to a thing – his ultimate dehumanisation.

Yet, at the same time, as Lomas says, Freud was the man who 'more than any other, has enabled us to see the mentally sick patient as more of a person and less of a thing than had hitherto been possible'. And in the consulting room what goes on, it seems, is practice in terms of 'love' at variance in such a way with theory as to make for a strange dissociation within psychoanalysis itself. As Lomas says:

> [Psychoanalysis] is (in America at least) a social force, it has a well-tried technique (psychoanalysts may adhere to a mechanistic theory, but fortunately they do not practise what they preach, as a perusal

of their case-histories will show), and they have a vast clinical literature. Moreover, even confined by a
theory that is basically askew, they have produced formulations about mental disharmony which no
psychotherapist could ignore without the utmost peril. What must be retained and what scrapped?
(Lomas, in Rycroft).

In the world of popular thought, culture, education, and creativity, as I have suggested, we have a dichotomy which matches the dichotomy between theory and therapy in
psychoanalysis itself.

Perhaps in the crisis existentialism offers the beginnings of solution. It offers, as Peter
Lomas says, 'the basic . . . tenet' that 'a person is more than a thing' and 'views the
person as a whole being, the agent of his actions'. In many ways existential psychoanalysis offers positive ways of looking at problems of identity. Yet in existentialist
psychoanalysis, in England at least, underlying implications remain over from Freud's
essentially negative approach. Laing, for instance, sees manifestations of splitting and
anxiety in the schizoid individual as a way of 'struggling to maintain a sense of identity in
the face of a total life-experience designed to destroy it'. This contains both a positive
approach to the struggle as a 'strategy of survival': but it also implies a hostile rather than
a benign environment. Further problems emerge, as we shall see, from the intention to
'provide a thoroughly self-conscious and self-critical account of man' as Laing puts it,
in so far as this becomes itself a intellectualisation of experience. As Lomas says:

> In *The Self and Others* Laing uses the terminology of 'person perception psychology', a phenomeno-
> logical approach, developed by Heider and others, to describe human relationships, in which the
> implicit attributions people make about each other are carefully analysed. The usefulness of this
> language, however, remains in doubt; it shows signs of becoming lost in mathematical formulae. . . .
>   There is a dilemma that in all descriptions of human behaviour that depart from ordinary language
> are in danger of leading us into the very kind of arid, atomistic, mechanistic world which the existen-
> tialists are so anxious to avoid. The need for a satisfactory language with which to discuss relationships
> in a scientific way is a pressing one and has not yet been met. (Lomas, in Rycroft [72], p. 147)

The problem of language, of course, cannot be divorced from the problem of modes of
thinking.

So it will be as well to look at other strands of thought in psychoanalysis, from which
possible solutions might come to the problem of finding a language and a discipline by
which the nature of human nature can be discussed without dehumanisation and 'atom-
isation'. This will lead us towards other influences which embrace subjective disciplines
gladly.

The existentialist psychoanalysts in American are important here. Farber, as we have
seen, has no qualms about calling Freud a 'poet'. Frankl emphasises the 'noetic' and his
logotherapy is concerned with meaning. This recognition of the imaginative element in
psychoanalytical insights is gaining increasing and more confident recognition in
England too. Lomas quotes a paper by Home, which was read to the British Psychoanalytical Society in 1964:

> Psychoanalysis began as a study of neurosis and as a hypothesis explaining its origin and develop-
> ment. As an hypothesis about neurosis it might have made little enough stir, in spite of its delineation
> of an aetiology linking nervous with sexual frustration, had Freud not invoked a totally new principle
> of explanation. This principle of explanation, which ran counter to the tenor of thought prevalent in
> medicine at the time, and which eventually led him on to formulate his revolutionary ideas about the
> unconscious mind, was that the symptom could have a *meaning*.
>   That the symptom has meaning, if it is neurotic, is Freud's basic discovery, the basic insight which
> opened up the way to an understanding of functional illness and the principles of psychoanalytic
> treatment. It is not surprising that, in the excitement of so great a discovery, and one that opened up
> such vast new territories, Freud should have overlooked the logical implications for theory of the step

he had taken. Those implications are, however, very great, for in the mechanistic medicine of Freud's time, as in all organic medicine of our own day, the symptom is logically regarded as a fact and a fact is regarded as the product of causes. In this, medicine simply follows the practice of chemico-physical science and the canons of thought which are exemplified with special clarity in physics. In discovering that the symptom had meaning and basing his treatment on this hypothesis, *Freud took the psychoanalytical study of neurosis out of the world of science into the world of the humanities, because a meaning is not the product of causes but the creation of a subject.* This is a major difference; for the logic and method of the humanities is radically different from that of science, though no less respectable and of course much longer established. (Home, in Rycroft [72], pp. 120–121.)

The solution of our problem of attitudes to the nature of man, then, lies in accepting that the essential disciplines of psychoanalysis, such as its investigation of the meaning of symptoms, belong to the humanities and to their method and logic – though this does not mean they are to be dismissed as beyond the serious consideration of science.

We have seen above how illogical Freud's 'scientific' argument tends to be. But to say only this about him would be to discredit him unfairly: when he turns to actual case histories we encounter his true gifts. As we have seen, Farber points out that Freud's realm was that of 'insights into that human kind of history that has nothing to do with medical or natural history, and into the human kind of nature that has nothing to do with the "real external world" . . . 'facts that are no less real or imagined, but which obey different laws and concern quite another subject than do the facts of nature'.

Freud, however, had a scientist's horror of fancy and imagination, and his training impelled him to reject his best insights as they stood. As Farber says: 'the truths were unacceptable to his intellect or training until he had reshaped them into the clumsy "facts" of medical history.' As though suspecting the role played by imagination in all mental processes, he explicitly denies it as follows: 'The network of causes and effects that I shall now proceed to lay bare is not a product of my gift for combination; it is based on such trustworthy and analytic evidence that I can claim objective validity for it'. (Freud, quoted by Farber [20], p. 166).

As Farber insists, there is an objective validity for Freud's important insights, but it is not in that 'network of cause and effect' – since, as Home reminds us, the logic of human meaning belongs to another dimension from that of scientific logic. This is a valuable insight itself, where our concern with poetry meets the disciplines of psychoanalysis.

Psychoanalysis seems to be undergoing a discovery of humility – though perhaps not fast enough for Dr. Lomas, who complains that 'most psychoanalysts do not even recognise the pressing need for such a radical reformulation' as Mr. Home's. This humility perhaps parallels that in astrophysics, and involves a relinquishment of the urge towards scientific omniscience, and its hidden belief in perfectibility. It is perhaps these which have so far been too much implicit in the 'scientific' language and assumptions. Farber says:

> We have abandoned most of the goals of positivist science, although we cling to many of the positivist assumptions. Although we still hope to trace the whole origin and development of a case, as though plotting the course of a disease, we no longer hope to know everything with 'complete certainty' [Freud's phrase – D. H.] and without a single gap. . . . We no longer hope to be omniscient, although omniscience is the unattainable goal of intellect or knowledge, just as perfect goodness is the absolute ideal of morality or religion. (Farber [20], p. 166.)

'Blasphemy' here is in forgetting the impossibility of the goals of omniscience.

No analyst would agree with the doctrine of perfectibility as explicitly stated: but it lurks, Farber alleges, behind psychoanalytical theory and assumptions, and accounts for many professional miseries, not least among those training for psychotherapy. What seems to be returning to psychoanalysis itself, however, is the capacity for despair, and the recognition of the value of despair. A genuine despair can arise out of the experience of that close relationship between psychotherapist and patient, in which the patient seeks confirmation of his humanness. This despair is the recognition that we are only human, weak, and mortal, and that the attainment of a sense of meaning in our life is only ever going to be partially and temporarily achieved. It would seem that we may be inclined to avoid this creative despair by the delusions of 'certainty' and 'omniscience'. Hence those prevalent tendencies in the modern world to place too heavy a burden on psychology as the source of ethical values, aims, and our sense of what it is to be human – at the expense of other traditional sources of such preoccupations. As Farber says:

> It is for this reason – because everything uniquely human has been translated into medical terms of illness – that the psychoanalyst is now carrying such a heavy burden of responsibility. He no longer deals merely with problems of medical ethics, or with the moral problems arising from his craft. Morality itself has been turned over to him, along with philosophy and religion. It is not only his patients who ask him to solve their moral and religious problems, to tell them that is human. Nor is it only the artist, the philosopher, the teacher who turns to him: moralists and priests and theologians are now turning to the psychoanalyst for their definitions of man. Needless to say, we never asked for a burden of power such as this, which amount to our taking over the sole responsibility for the human fate. Yet it is the scientist, not the layman who must be blamed for this astonishing situation. For it is the medical man's delusion that psychiatry deals not with moral errors, sins, and weakness – not with intellectual failures and with spiritual states of grace or vanity or despair – but only with a special pocket of ailments whose cure and cause lie far outside the realm of moral values. (Farber [20], pp. 153–4.)

So we encounter a number of problems as we turn to what psychoanalysis has to tell us. One is that, as Lomas says, 'Psychotherapy constitutes the only real challenge and alternative to the barren, organic school of psychiatry that holds sway in our country' (Lomas, in Rycroft [72], p. 148).

Another is that 'the language of science . . . is far removed from human history', while psychotherapy itself is only now learning, through the influence of Buber and the existentialists, to 'describe a human meeting in the language appropriate to such meetings' which is 'not the same as . . . describing the interrelatedness of organisms' (Farber).

Here, as we shall see, we encounter, even in the best psychoanalytical writers, a language which tends to perpetuate the very objectifying of human experience from which its spirit is emerging. Peter Lomas even objects to the term 'object-relations' and would prefer to substitute for it 'interpersonal relations': yet, as we shall see, the use of the word 'object' does enable us to keep in mind the philosophical view, of a subject's capacity to relate to an object, who is at first the mother and later the whole world, and the problem of internal 'objects'. But any such objectification tends to contain the fallacies of omniscience and perfectibility, however minutely, so that the implicit norms seem larger than life. As Farber says: 'it is virtually impossible for the psychiatrist *not* to derive his norms and standards from his own theories – thus creating definitions of man out of his fragments of psychopathology.'

This obviously has great significance when the whole problem of the definition of what is human has been turned over to him!

While it is important for us in education and culture to make ourselves acquainted with the theories of human nature emerging from psychotherapy, we must therefore try to avoid the snares of erecting yet another form of humunculism. Farber quotes Kierkegaard, who says: 'In relation to their systems, most systematisers are like a man who builds an enormous castle and lives in a shack beside it; they do not live in their own enormous buildings.' 'We live', says Farber, 'much of our lives in Kierkegaard's shack, or, rather, we live according to that loose repository of wisdom . . . that is known as "common sense".'

Fortunately there are many within psychoanalysis itself who seek the restoration to this discipline itself of human touch and scale. Guntrip, for instance, complains:

> Academic psychology has developed, in its modern methods of personality testing, for diagnostic purposes, a skilfully impersonal way, by means of which, once more, human beings can be classified and categorized without anyone ever coming into intimate personal human rapport with the patient as a meaningful individual in his own right. In the field of psychoanalysis, the conception of 'meta-psychology' and the classic analytic technique in so far as it tended to impersonality belong to the same orientation. (Guntrip [37], p. 17.)

Meanwhile, at large many 'explanations' of human behaviour are still reductive and based essentially in neuro-physiological and psychobiological philosophies and disciplines, with the concept of instinct as the basis of theory. Guntrip argues that

> the struggle to equate 'scientific explanation' with the 'elimination of individuality' goes on, aiming to produce theories which are materialistic and mechanistic. . . . The traditional scientific approach tends always towards an impersonal type of theory, and this is not often honestly admitted to be an expression of a certain philosophical view of man, that *the mind is the brain*.* A great deal of the drive in psychiatry for the discovery of physical treatments, and also the drive to work out a theory of therapy on the basis of 'reconditioning' is motivated as much by this underlying 'philosophy of man' as by the practical need to find methods of quick relief of symptoms. (Guntrip [37], pp. 16–17; my italics.)

In psychiatry, such 'physical' approaches can be a denial of a painful area of complexity:† as Guntrip indicates: 'such treatments also have the advantage of being less disturbing to the psychiatrist . . . than the attempt to treat the patient on a personal level, entering deeply and in a fully personal way into the heart of the disturbed personality.' The parallel with the situation in education will be evident to the reader.

Psychoanalytical theory, however, is as we have seen, moving towards something more poetical and is vindicating once more the natural processes of 'civilisation beginning anew in each child' by creative intuitive dynamics, the basis of which is that symbolism which Suzanne Langer pronounces a primary need in man.‡ The study of these processes and their symbolism belongs to the humanities, and here objective study of the nature of man meets creativity and the arts in such a way as to give these authority and disciplines of their own, enabling them to make a claim to be as significant in the modern world as science.

Attention to psychodynamic theory should also help us to take a step further forward in our exploration of the relationship between the individual and society. Here much social science seems still to lack an adequate psychology. This is perhaps inevitable, while views within psychology have become divided so that while some assume too direct a relationship between the environment and psychic growth, others ignore the environment too much altogether. As Fenichel pointed out: 'Certain authors in their biologistic thinking have entirely overlooked the role of outwardly determined frustrations in the genesis of neuroses and character traits, and are of the opinion that neuroses and character

* See also *Mind and Its Relation to the Psyche-Soma* (1949) in *Collected Papers* by D. W. Winnicott, 1958, p. 243: 'There is no localization of a mind self, and there is no thing that can be called mind' (p. 254).

† This is not to deny that some mental disorders have an organic origin: Guntrip does not, of course, deny this.

‡ Langer [55], see below, pp. 225 ff.

traits might be rooted in conflicts between contradictory biological needs in an entirely endogenous manner. . . .'

There are also certain authors 'who reproach psychoanalysis with being too biologically oriented, and who are of the opinion that the high valuation of the instinctual impulses means that cultural influences are denied or neglected' (Fenichel [21], p. 6; quoted by Guntrip [37], p. 192).

Fenichel's point of view emphasised the environment: 'The character of men is socially determined. The environment enforces specific frustrations, blocks certain modes of reaction to these frustrations, and facilitates others . . . it suggests ways of dealing with the conflicts between instinctual demands and fears of further frustrations; it even creates desires by setting up and forming specific ideals. . . .'

A good deal of such mechanical thinking about the relationship between man and society still underlies the attitudes of those concerned with literature and culture. Meanwhile such critics tend to disregard psychoanalysis, supposing that it is too much concerned with endogenous origins of psychic problems. But, as Guntrip points out, 'The environment is here (in Fenichel) however, still seen only as something external which facilitates, obstructs, deflects and distorts instinctive drives. There is no recognition of the all-important fact of *the internalization of the environment as an inner world*' (Guntrip, [37], pp. 193–4; my italics).

As soon as we begin to use such a concept as that of an internal 'world', however, we meet many tremendous difficulties. One is that even recognition of the very concept of an 'inner world' meets great resistance in us all. Another is that the structure and growth of this inner world is not only extremely complex, but that each psychoanalytical writer has a different view of its processes. This is no more than we should expect for that human make-up is so complex that it can obviously never be pinned down to a simple scheme.

However, if we are to explore the nature of man in his environment more realistically we in culture and education must take cognisance of these theories. For even where we reject much of them, they will also be found to yield valuable insights into our needs and the nature of human nature, and the place of culture in human life. As Guntrip says: 'A psychodynamic theory is now emerging which takes into account the fact that man lives in two worlds as the same time, inner and outer, psychic and material, and has relationships with two kinds of objects, internal and external. Here "depth psychology" and the sociological orientation merge in a synthesis.' (Guntrip [37], p. 194.)

The problem is that to many people Freud's model of the structure and working of the human mind was 'alarmingly complex': yet the picture has since become even more complex: '. . . all forms of pure instinct theory give a picture of mental development in infancy and childhood which is simple compared with the complexities revealed by the investigation of 'internal objects' and the unconscious as an inner world' (Guntrip [37], p. 194).

Guntrip here quotes Melanie Klein who spoke of 'the bewildering complexity of the processes which operate, to a large extent simultaneously, in the early stages of development' (Klein, quoted by Guntrip [37], p. 198).

Yet as we begin to explore these processes the reward is a deep fund of insight into the poetic and symbolic processes which are the foundations of all human thought and culture. We already know these to be 'frighteningly complex', so why should we (as Guntrip says) 'expect to find mental phenomena simple and easy to understand?'

We may begin to explore the new psychodynamic theories, then, with a recognition that they are to be extremely complex, and never exhaustive - the emphasis is in any case being on the primacy of living experience: that is, on accepting that in psychic growth, mothering, child care, education and therapy the creative processes work naturally towards integration and fulfilment, in ways which theory will never fully explain, and which intellect can never fully control. In the end the theory does little for us except to yield small insights into the complex business of living: the important things being that we go on living, actively engaged with our inward perplexities as by the energies of symbolism in creativity – knowing the natural capacities of being in life to be fundamental. Intellectual knowledge is most valuable in human affairs when it recognises the primacy of intuitive being and avoids erecting castles which become the subject of worship, but in which it is impossible for anyone to live.

Yet another approach to the reassessment of the nature and aims of psychoanalysis has come from W. R. D. Fairbairn. Fairbairn has already been mentioned, and we have seen Leslie Farber questioning the 'objective' language in which he expresses his normative concepts of man. For all that, Fairbairn commands great respect in the world of psychotherapy: Lomas, for instance, refers to his 'success' in developing a theory of interpersonal relationships – and implies that he achieved here what Melanie Klein failed to achieve. The work of these two practitioners, however, is radical, and we need to be acquainted with their main theories.

Fairbairn is important because he was one of the first to question in a significant way the scientific assumptions of psychoanalysis.

Fairbairn was a psychoanalyst who lived, studied and practised in Edinburgh from 1926 until his death in 1962, and so was much apart from the main psychoanalytical movement which is, of course, in London. His own training was in philosophy, in Greek and in religious and psychological subjects, as well as in medicine. Some of his most important work has been on the aetiology of sexual deviations and the treatment of sexual offenders, on the war neuroses, and as consultant neuropsychiatrist to the Ministry of Pensions since 1941. His major book was published in 1952, and his first psychoanalytical paper was published in 1940.

His writing is extremely taxing to read because of the density and close discipline of his thought and the complexity of the emerging model of the structure of the psyche which he postulates. Yet this very complexity is itself an indication of Fairbairn's disciplined humanity, for what he records in his book *Psycho-analytical Studies of the Personality* [19] is the emergence of progressive stages of his theory as it was revised in the light of clinical experience, under continual re-examination in the light of further experience of people. He shows himself in this consistently dissatisfied with anything which is too mechanical, and despite Farber's criticisms of his language, he was deeply opposed in his theory of reification. His complexity itself comes about because he essentially respects man as an awesomely complex being, so that generalisations about the processes of his inner world, and their bearing on his conduct, must in themselves be complex. He seeks to develop a model of complex dynamic intrapsychic processes, whose interaction in actual beings is limitless and rich with creative and spontaneous energy. Indeed, it is in his concern with inward processes as 'energies' rather than 'impulses' that makes Fairbairn's work such a revolutionary departure from that of Freud, and so relevant both to recent developments in science, and to the creative concern with man as a being, of the imaginative arts.

Fairbairn's most important contribution, as we shall see, was to explore schizoid characteristics, and to lead attention to the origins of consciousness at the earliest stages of all – to those problems of identity which underlie all psychic problems. In doing this Fairbairn both pursued Freudian lines of thought, but also contributed to the culmination of a complete reconsideration of Freudian theory.

Fairbairn's theory of personality develops out of his concern with problems whose origins are in the earliest stages of growth, and later we shall explore the way in which he reached these by taking object-relations theory beyond Melanie Klein. But here we are concerned with the ways in which Fairbairn differs from Freud. Here I follow closely the exposition of Fairbairn's work by Guntrip. Guntrip is the foremost exponent of Fairbairn for whose work he has a great admiration, and from whose work his own on schizoid problems derives. Indeed, as we follow Guntrip's explanation of the differences with Freud, we find ourselves following a critique of what are felt by Guntrip to be schizoid elements in Freud's theory. Their view confirms Suttie, and by following their development of thought here we can also begin to follow the new directions taken by object-relations psychology.

First, says Fairbairn, while Freud was human enough in his family and private life, 'in his work the human being was absorbed into the Scientist', and 'in his work he evolved a distinctly impersonal type of theory'. By contrast analysts such as Fairbairn (and also Melanie Klein and Winnicott) are each primarily 'a human being using scientific inquiry to further his understanding of other human beings in their struggle to live'.

Freud was primarily the scientist: 'anatomist, physiologist, and neurologist who would have preferred a life devoted to laboratory research.' Because of these preferences he came to underestimate (as Suttie insists) the truth expressed by Ferenczi: 'The analyst's love heals the patient.' Freud 'had to be pushed by events into the field of psychological investigation' – albeit in which he then 'proved to possess powers amounting to genius'. But the same fear of 'dangerous contact' which he expresses unconsciously in his theoretical writings tended also to dominate his therapeutic technique: 'Freud said that he employed the couch technique because he could not stand being looked at by his patients for eight hours a day, and he seems to have disliked "regressed" patients who cannot easily be treated by impersonal methods. . . . He showed fairly clear signs of a resistance against the "human closeness" involved.' (Fairbairn [19], p. 250.)

As we have seen, 'for Freud Science was Truth with a captial T', while religion was nothing but superstition and infantile phantasy. Guntrip, following Fairbairn, finds in Freud's reductionism a specifically schizoid need to separate a pure detached intellectual scheme from whole living. Indeed, Guntrip implies, wherever we have the scientific impulse to omniscience and perfectibility, we have a schizoid phenomenon. Guntrip quotes Fairbairn at this point:

> Intellectual pursuits as such, whether literary, artistic, scientific or otherwise, appear to exercise a special attraction for individuals possessing schizoid characteristics to one degree or another. Where scientific pursuits are concerned, the attraction would appear to depend upon the schizoid individual's attitude of detachment, no less than upon his overvaluation of the thought processes: for these are both characteristics which readily lend themselves to capitalization within the field of Science, based as this is upon the presence of a compulsive need for orderly arrangement and meticulous accuracy, has, of course, long been recognized; but the schizoid appeal is no less definite. (Fairbairn [19], p. 6.)

To be aware of the schizoid elements in intellectual pursuits is not to seek to devalue these, for such unemotional detachment can be a useful application of certain partial approaches to life so long as it is borne in mind that this intellectual view is not the whole picture:

> It is not a psychopathological state if it is an attitude of mind voluntarily adopted for the specific purpose of investigation. But schizoid intellectuals are bound to be attracted to science as an escape from the pressure of personal emotional relationships which the schizoid person finds difficult. Any analyst who has treated University staff members cannot fail to realize how important the schizoid factor is in their problems. (Guntrip [37], p. 249).

Schizoid tendencies of this kind also underlie the scientists' frequent hostility to recognition of the 'inner world' and to the arts and creative disciplines. They possibly also underlie the retreat of research into human problems (as in educational research) into mechanistic preoccupations such as those based on psychometrics which cannot take into account the emotional complexities of growth in the adult or child and his living creative experience as a person. Perhaps these tendencies explain the hostility of some universities to the psychology of whole persons – to psychoanalysis and psychiatry, and even to a concern with child development, education in the 'whole' sense, or creativity, on the grounds that these have no 'authentic disciplines'.*

Psychoanalytical theory provides the opportunity for reference to a discipline of study of human meanings in another sphere by which to check the assumptions of other humanities. In its studied comparison of case reports and theoretical deductions there is a measure of objectivity: yet the essence of the discipline, as of ours in education and literature, is touch between persons and touch with the inner world of being through symbolism. These aspects of it as emphasised by Fairbairn, make it seem very different from what it was to Freud.

There are those, of course, who still believe that the object of therapy is in 'scientific education' of the patient, rather than a fostering of growth through intuitive processes of love. Answering such a therapist Fairbairn wrote:

> According to Szasz . . . applied psychoanalysis is not properly a form of 'treatment' (in terms of the medical model) at all, but a form of scientific education. This view obviously takes no account of child analysis. But, apart from this, it is impossible to ignore the fact that it is not for a course of scientific education, but for a therapeutic result, that the adult patient ordinarily enlists the analyst's aid . . . a desire to obtain a relief from symptoms. Indeed, it might be held with good reason that the religious analogy would be more appropriate than the educational one, for it would be in complete conformity with the psychological facts to say that what the patient is really seeking is 'salvation' (e.g. salvation from his internal bad objects, from his hate and from his guilt). (Fairbairn [108], p. 374.)

Even the prospective psychoanalyst's interest in psychoanalysis 'must be regarded as ultimately springing from a desire on his own part, largely unconscious perhaps, to resolve his own conflicts; and this consideration must be taken into due account in assessing the 'scientific' orientation of the psychoanalyst'. Thus we are here, as in education and creativity, concerned with a process which becomes 'scientific' only at the peril of moving away from its most important dimension, while yet needing to be disciplined, in terms of the objective collocation of experience, as a means (essentially) of improving its value in actual life-situations:

> the human factor in the therapeutic situation (as represented by the individuality, the personal value, and the needs of the patient) is only too liable to be sacrificed to the method, which thus comes to assume greater importance than the aims which it is intended to serve . . . I find it impossible to agree

---

* As Winnicott says: 'The universities are suspicious of the practical application of psychology in human affairs, especially where individual human beings are being helped; also the universities are suspicious of psychology unless it keeps on the academic rails and eschews working with the dynamic unconscious' (Training for Child Psychiatry in Winnicott [54], p. 195 n.).

with Freud's assumption, cited with approval by Szasz, that the average patient is, in part at least, interested from the very beginning in undertaking a scientific exploration of his own personality. Such an assumption is patently false in the case of a patient who is a child: but, even where the adult patient is concerned, it seems to me simply a manifestation of wishful thinking; and, in my experience, patients in whom this interest is prominent are characteristically obsessional or/and schizoid personalities, in the case of whom such interest is essentially a defence against emotional involvement. (Fairbairn [108], p. 376.)

Although in therapy psychoanalysis may not be 'scientific', yet Fairbairn admits a conscious interest of his own in promoting a more adequate formulation of theory in order to contribute to the therapeutic situation between human beings: 'It is thus predominantly a scientific interest; but this interest is accompanied by the hope that such a reformulation will have the effect of rendering the application of psychoanalytical theory a more effective therapeutic instrument' (Fairbairn [108], p. 376).

In an earlier paper Fairbairn had attempted to define his view of science:

It would be truer to say that I regard ... psychoanalysis as a *scientific discipline* than that I regard it as a 'natural science'. In other words, I regard it as a legitimate field for the harnessing of scientific method to the task of exact conceptionalisation. At the same time I do not regard it as either necessary or desirable for the analyst who aspires to be scientific to adopt the particular method appropriate to *physical* science. Thus I consider that, as in the case of all forms of psychological research, the investigations of psychoanalysis should be conducted at the level of personality and personal relations. (Fairbairn [107], p. 155.)

Fairbairn sees science as an 'intellectual tool'. It does not provide an '(even approximately) accurate picture of reality as it actually exists, still less a revelation of ultimate truth'. Scientific truth he defines as 'explanatory truth':

The picture of reality provided by science is an intellectual construct representing the fruits of an attempt to describe the various phenomena of the universe, in as coherent and systematic a manner as the limitations of the human intelligence permit, by means of the formulation of general laws established by inductive reference under the conditions of maximum emotional detachment and objectivity on the part of the scientific observer. (Fairbairn [107], p. 154.)

One prevalent manifestation of our age (as D. H. Lawrence insisted) has been that of ignoring other modes of knowing and perceiving 'reality', and confusing the 'intellectual constructs' of science which only *describe* certain aspects of reality, with the whole of reality. 'It is possible, of course, to make this intellectual tool the basis of a philosophy of life – and even of a form of religion; and there is a prevalent tendency in the age in which we live, especially among the intelligentsia, to exploit science in this way'. (Fairbairn [107], p. 154).

Certainly, in the realm of psychology, Freud contributed to this invalid erection of scientific method and its divinisation as a philosophy of life.

In the therapeutic situation, as Fairbairn points out, the scientific position is inevitably abandoned – the psychoanalyst is not merely satisfying scientific curiosity, but 'serving human and personal values transcending any scientific value': he seeks to promote integration and health.

Fairbairn chose object-relations psychology as his kind of psychology because of this essential humanity in it: 'Personally I consider that a psychology conceived in terms of object-relations and dynamic structure is more compatible with the recognition of such human and personal values as psychotherapy serves than is any other psychology hitherto available' (Fairbairn [107], p. 155).

But Fairbairn also asserts that he chose this psychology for scientific reasons – if it is scientific to pursue 'human fact': 'its correspondence with the facts and its explanatory value seem to me greater than any other psychology, e.g. a psychology conceived in terms of "impulse" and "instinct".'

Yet while Fairbairn chose object-relations psychology because of its scientific explanatory truth he also recognises that there are in psychotherapy processes of symbolising and relationship which are not scientific, but which belong to those areas of intuitive dynamic which link psychotherapy with religion and culture. As we know from history, he says:

> Effective psychotherapy can take place in the absence of all scientific knowledge. . . . I consider further that what is sought by the patient who enlists psychotherapeutic aid, is not so much health as salvation from his past, from bondage to his (internal) bad objects, from the burden of guilt, and from spiritual death. His search thus corresponds in detail to the religious quest. (Fairbairn [107], pp. 155–6.)

As Guntrip says, while Freud could adopt only a negative and hostile attitude to religion, Fairbairn

> recognises in the religious terminology of 'salvation' an expression of the natural, naive and reflective way in which human beings spontaneously felt about their personality problems.
> Thus for Fairbairn religion is an impressive activity and experience of human beings throughout the centuries, and is to be approached not with hostility as a mere nuisance, irrelevance and brake on progress, but with sympathetic insight in order to understand what human beings have actually been seeking and doing in their religious life. (Guntrip [37], p. 253.)

Fairbairn saw that psychoanalysis should not seek to explain religion and culture away, but to learn from them by phenomenological study.

Here, perhaps, psychoanalytical theory is gradually escaping from a fallacy. Suzanne Langer characterises it as a fallacy to suppose that by explaining the origins of a thing we have explained it and have said all there is to be said about it. Freud began to cast a little light on the infantile origins of some cultural symbolism. But there is a growing recognition, as Guntrip indicates, that while

> it is important that manifestations of guilt and anxiety in moral and religious experience should be studied psychoanalytically . . . when one considers that human behaviour in art, marriage, sport, hobbies, money-making and even science – in short, any and every form of human behaviour – can be similarly affected by the same motivation, it is clear that there is more to be said than psychoanalysis can say. (Guntrip [37], p. 255.)

With Freud, many analysts 'have used psychoanalytical considerations to explain away'. To Guntrip psychoanalysis provides a source of understanding by which 'science stands for the discovery of the necessary knowledge without which love [in the therapeutic situation, D. H.] may be ineffective'. This knowledge and this intuitive dynamic of love are increasingly recognised as *adult* needs – of which adult cultural pursuits are the expression. Of course, the origins of the cultural impulses may be in primal needs: but this is only because the origins of self-aware consciousness and human identity are primary processes themselves. As Fairbairn says:

> The characteristic standpoint of the psychoanalytical school is to look for the sources of religious need in the dynamic unconscious of the individual. It is, of course, in the same direction that this school of psychoanalytical thought looks for the source of artistic inspiration and of all the achievements of human culture in general – the guiding principle being that cultural phenomena represent the symbolic and sublimated expression of repressed wishes of a primal character. (Fairbairn [107], p. 156.)

There are two factors here in the dynamic unconscious to which special importance was attached by psychoanalysis. First, the persistence of the original attitude to the parents displaced towards supernatural beings as the child became disillusioned about the powers of his actual parents. Secondly, the persistent influence of a 'repressed Oedipus situation accompanied by conflict, and an inner need to obtain relief from the attendant guilt'. As Guntrip says, these indicate that the symbolic activity in culture and religion has to do with the human being's 'innate need to find good object-relationship', although they do prejudge the question of whether religion is infantile *per se*, and rule out the possibility of religious experience in the mature personality.

Two psychoanalytical theorists have altered the whole perspective of this problem – in taking the exploration of the inner life to earlier and more primal areas. The work of Melanie Klein and Fairbairn has taken the investigation of intrapsychic processes into more primary, because earlier, human needs. In doing so they have been concerned with processes of integration of the identity which, although they begin in very early infancy, can never be 'solved' or brought to an end, but belong to the continual dynamics by which human consciousness and personality are sustained throughout life. Processes of introjection and identification to do with the parents are still relevant and involved, of course, but the problem of achieving mature "independence" is recognised to include a continuing primal need for dependence. That is, the need for relationship is a primary libidinal need, and 'good object-relations have an intrinsic and not merely a defensive value.' The individual's relationship with the universe is in complex with his object-relations capacities, in which the first object was his mother: and these capacities are in complex with his relationship with his inner world (towards the degree of integration the ego is able to achieve there). Thus, whether or not we can become independent while yet accepting our need for others, our need for dependence depends upon what kind of experience of absolute dependence we had at first.

A more positive attitude to culture also inevitably arises from object-relations psychology. Rather than 'sublimation' these are seen as primary human ways of finding a meaning in life and discovering and sustaining our humanness. Those symbolic activities which are integral to religion and culture are a necessary and primary dynamic.

Before we can explore Fairbairn's thought, however, we must first acquaint ourselves with the work of Melanie Klein, by whom later thinkers in object-relations psychology have been so much influenced. And before we tackle the work of Melanie Klein it will be necessary to make ourselves familiar with certain unusual and complex concepts which have arisen from this field of study. What, for instance, do we mean by 'object-relations'?

This term arose in the historical development of psychoanalytical thought as it came to explore the psychodynamic complex between subjective and objective as the very basis of the growth of human personality. In its more general sense, psychologically, the word 'object' means 'that which is before the mind at any time, perceived, imaged, or thought, as distinct from the act of perceiving, imagining or thinking . . .' (Brewer [7]).

But there is another meaning – of a *love object* (cf. as in *object cathexis* – 'where love is diverted from its normal sexual aims'). In object-relations psychology the object is first of all the mother from whom love is learnt, later other persons, and then the whole world (the earth itself being 'mother earth'). But since we are dealing with potentialities, and with what is going on within the mind the 'object' means the focus or goal of the intra-psychic dynamics, or the *potentiality* towards the mother, the loved person or persons, and the world. 'Object-relations' psychology therefore concerns itself with the subjective *capacities* of the self, the dynamics of which are modified by the ego, to relate to objects or an object.

To be able to relate to a real person or a real world one needs to be a whole subject, an identity: only a *me* can recognise the *not-me*. There is a stage before this is possible: at the other extreme maturity is that independence which fully recognises the distinction between the self and the not-self, while yet accepting the human need for dependence upon an object. Relationship with an object is a primary need in us as confirmation of our identity: the child pieces himself together as he pieces his mother together. In solitary confinement, on in the white blankness of the Arctic wastes (as Fairbairn says), the identity can begin to disintegrate because of a deficiency of dynamic relationship with 'the object', which is also a deficiency of symbolism by which to work on object-relations capacities. Also one's perceptions of the world one lives in depend upon the degree to which one has made the world one's own: that is, the reality of the world depends upon our bringing to it what Keats called 'a greeting of the spirit', the capacity for interpreting sense data, by which one makes one's world in making one's self. The capacity to find the objective object begins with the subjective object. Human beings cannot exist objectless.

Freud's thinking was dominated by the key biological formula *adaptation of the organism to the environment*. Hence, his picture of a struggle for survival between repression and libidinal instincts – his model of human nature involves a structure which implies impulses *which have to be adapted to*, and an organism which must adapt to its environment.

The key formula of the newer object-relations psychology is the relationship of the person to the human environment and the nature of the identity that relates to the object as the basis of future relationship to the whole world. Thus to this psychoanalysis 'The significance of human living lies in object-relationships, and only in such terms can life have a meaning' (Guntrip [110], p. 87).

Fairbairn went so far as to say that the individual's libidinal goal is not pleasure, not merely subjective gratification, but the ability of the 'individual in his libidinal capacity' to relate to an object. Our primary aim is then not to release impulses, nor to adapt, but to become integrated enough to fulfil our identity in relating, and in expressing these aims by libidinal channels. This would seem to accord with Suttie's earlier criticism of Freud in *The Origins of Love and Hate*, in which he sought to point out how the reality of man's altruism and primary satisfaction in social living some-how escaped Freud's attention, or needed to be denied by him.

Balint, it should be pointed out, however, criticises Fairbairn for underestimating our needs for libidinal expression – albeit within relationship – because his (Fairbairn's) theories inevitably arose from the psychoanalytical situation in which, obviously, the patient's primary need is his relationship *with his analyst* as object – from relationship with whom libidinal expression is barred. Balint also suggests that Fairbairn under-estimates being.*

But even if we concern ourselves with being, this leads on to doing, in any real indivi-dual in dynamic relationship with the world, and so the development of the capacity to relate to the world as 'object', since doing naturally follows from being. Whatever view we take, the primary problem is not a conflict between 'reason' and 'instinct', but the struggle to become whole enough to relate to a real world, and a problem of the relationship between inner and outer reality.

---

* Winnicott also suggests that psychoanalysis has overemphasised object-relations because it over-emphasises 'doing' as a solution to problems of identity which is male: there is, he postulates, a female element in everyone concerned with *being*. Being comes first with the mother, and doing later from the father. For Balint's criticisms see Balint [199].

E

Object-relations psychology, moreover, postulates that such complex problems as those of human behaviour cannot be understood except in terms of the effects of 'internalised objects', a concept which will be explored further below. Attempts to explain behaviour in terms of environmental influences, conditioning, or even interpersonal influences cannot explain the basis of our capacity to relate satisfactorily to others or to the world. Here, as we shall see later, one of the mainsprings of a healthy moral sense, from the object-relations point of view, is the urge to make 'the object' good and whole symbolically, within one – reparation, which is a process of seeking integration. This concept of 'internal objects' is so lacking from many approaches to human nature that they cannot begin to explain obvious phenomena. For instance, the present writer once discussed the problem of children and hate with a research worker who believed that the brain was an 'information processing system'. He also believed that the mind was in the brain, as he showed by the way he used the words 'brain' and 'mind' without distinction. In discussion with him I emphasised my belief that children needed creative opportunities to engage with the problem of hate. The systems expert expressed a fear that a preoccupation with hate could become, as it were, enclosed in the circuit of the mental system, so that, by 'feedback', hate could grow until it overwhelmed the individual. Something of this kind, he believed, lay beneath such a manifestation as Nazism.

In his mental scheme there was no place for reparation, the symbolic work done by all human beings on internalised objects, nor could be conceive of bodily feelings and memories inextricably bound up with the problem of feeling real and good in relation to an object felt as real and good towards which there were psychosomatic love urges. Yet, according to object-relations theory, such reparative-impulses to love and be loved lie beneath all human thinking and dealings with hate.

We can perhaps put this human fact in commonsense terms by speaking of our relationship with ourselves. The 'internal' problem inevitably arises because we begin by internalising the mother. Human nature is human nature because each individual can only grow his capacities to be human in the complex context of his mother's care. The moral sense inevitably springs from this, with inevitable problems of guilt and hate which at times threaten the identity in ways such as we have seen. As Melanie Klein says:

> his mother . . . is the original and paramount source of the goodness that [the baby] receives from the outer world . . . the more successfully it [retaining this goodness] is carried through, the less ground is left in the baby's mind for greed and hatred. But . . . the unconscious feelings of guilt which arise in connection with the phantasied destruction of a loved person play a fundamental part in these processes . . . for feelings of guilt give rise to the fear of being dependent upon this loved person whom the child is afraid of losing, since as soon as aggression wells up he feels he is injuring her. (Klein and Riviere [51], p. 117.)

The discovery of the mother as a real person, and the discovery of the self as a whole (who has within the whole the problem of hate) is the way in which these fears are overcome.

How the individual pieces his identity together from 'primary home experiences' was explored in an important study made of evacuation in the 1939–45 war, by Winnicott and Clare Britton:

> By a primary home experience is meant experience of an environment adapted to the special needs of the infant and the little child, without which the foundations of mental health cannot be laid down. Without someone specifically orientated to his needs the infant cannot find a working relationship to external reality. Without someone to give satisfactory instinctual gratifications the infant cannot find his body, nor can he develop an integrated personality. Without one person to love and hate, he

cannot come to know that it is the same person that he loves and hates, and so cannot find his sense of guilt, and his desire to repair and restore. (Winnicott and Britton [127], quoted in Bowlby [6], p. 173.)

Thus finding that 'it is the same person that he loves and hates' is integral with finding that it is the same person who loves and hates. This he finds by developing his own identity by internalising the mother. This concept of the process of internalising is still a subject of much debate. Guntrip follows Fairbairn:

> But things are mentally internalised and retained in two different ways which we call *memory* and *internal objects*. Good objects are, in the first place, mentally internalised and retained only as memories. They are enjoyed at the time, the experience is satisfying and leaves no problems, and can later be looked back to and reflected on with pleasure. . . . Outer experience is enough to meet our needs. (Guntrip [110], p. 88.)

Fairbairn differs from Melanie Klein on this point: she believed in internalised good objects, Fairbairn believed there was no need to internalise unless the object showed 'bad' aspects:

> Objects are only internalised in a more radical way when the relationship turns into a bad-object situation through, say, the object changing or dying. When someone we need and love ceases to love us, or behaves in such a way that we interpret it as a cessation of love, that person becomes, in an emotional, libidinal sense, a bad object. This happens to a child when his mother refuses the breast, weans the baby, or is cross, impatient and punitive or is absent temporarily or for a longer period . . . it also happens when the person we need is emotionally detached and aloof and unresponsive. (Guntrip [110], p. 88.)

Since he cannot yet accept a world or a self which is ambivalent, and because his solutions tend to be magic ones of projection, a baby attributes hurtful things to predators: for this reason Melanie Klein spoke of the 'paranoid-schizoid' position. When any of the above problems are experienced

> as frustration of the most important of needs, as rejection and desertion or else as persecution or attack. . . . Then the lost (or hostile) object, now became a bad object, is mentally internalised in a much more vital and fundamental sense than memory. An inner psychic world has been set up, duplicating the original situation.
> But it is an unhappy world in which one is tied to bad objects and feeling therefore always frustrated, hungry, angry, and guilty and profoundly anxious.
> It is bad objects which are internalised because we cannot accept their badness and yet cannot give them up, cannot leave them alone, cannot master and control them in outer reality and so keep on struggling to possess them, alter them and compel them to change into good objects, in our inner psychic world. They never do change. In our inner unconscious world where we repress and lock away very early in life our original bad objects, they remain always rejecting, indifferent or hostile to us according to our actual outer experience. (Guntrip [110], p. 89.)

These internalised objects are not phantasies or memories; products of identification, they are integral aspects of the structure of our personality. 'The child is emotionally identified with his objects, and when he mentally incorporates them, he remains identified with them and they become part and parcel of the very psychic structure of his personality' (Guntrip [110], p. 89).

Phantasies are manifestations of the workings of these inner dynamics (and our attempts to deal with them): 'The phantasies in which internal objects reveal their existence to consciousness are activities of the structures which constitute the internal objects. . . .'

So the fundamental psychopathological problem is: 'How do people deal with their internalised bad objects, to what extent do they feel identified with them, and how do they complicate relations with external objects? *It is the object all the time that matters, whether external or internal, not pleasure.* (Guntrip [110], p. 89; my italics.)

From this point of view Fairbairn constructed a theory of the psychoses and psycho-neuroses which implies much revision of Freud, though it is still the subject of much debate.

But we may find its principal concepts most illuminating for problems of culture. Having explained the nature of the processes of internalisation of bad objects we may now go on to describe how (according to Fairbairn's theories) psychic problems can arise, such as lead to mental illness in exaggerated forms, but which are present in all of us to some degree. There are two dangerous situations in early infancy, and responses to them are either *schizoid* or *depressive*.

The infant needs love: the mother's function is to convince the child that he is loved for his own sake. If this process goes awry, then a schizoid tendency may develop in the personality. Guntrip explains the schizoid problem thus:

> When you cannot get what you want from the person you need, instead of getting angry you may simply go on getting more and more hungry, and full of a sense of painful craving, and a longing to get total and complete possession of your love-object so that you cannot be left to starve. *Love made hungry* is the schizoid problem and it rouses the terrible fear that one's love has become so devouring and incorporative that love itself has become destructive. (Guntrip [110], p. 90.)

The schizoid person therefore fears love (though he wants to be loved) and avoids or alienates contact. The schizoid problem tends to be associated with a weak sense of identity, for it begins from the stage at which the child has hardly begun to form his own identity under the influence of the mother's love: since love is so feared, the sense of separate identity can hardly be developed. Even the love that can build bridges and continuity can thus seem also to threaten incorporation and annihilation.

The next normal development leads on to further problems of love and hate. Once the 'separation' stage develops, since there is a 'two-body' relationship, the *me* can feel concern for the possible effect of his anger on the *not-me*. But as yet the baby has no full sense of distinction between reality and phantasy: nor does he feel a whole continuous self. Moreover, he has no sense of the reality of the consequences of its phantasies and wishes. So, we have the depressive problem:

> When you want love from a person who will not give it and so becomes a bad object to you . . . may become angry and enraged at the frustration and want to make an aggressive attack on the bad object, to force it to become good and stop frustrating you . . . this is the problem of hate or love made angry. It is an attack on a hostile, rejecting, actively refusing bad object. It leads to *depression* for it rouses the fear that one's hate will destroy the very person one needs and loves. (Guntrip [110], p. 90.)

So depression is the fear of loving lest one's hate should destroy. Schizoid aloofness is the fear of loving lest one's love should destroy, which is the deeper problem, since it belongs to the whole problem of forming an identity at all. Both fears underlie all our relational agonies and problems of identity.

Here it will help if we acquaint ourselves with two main stages or 'positions' in object-relations theory. Melanie Klein and Fairbairn recognize, roughly speaking, two stages of early psychic development – the depressive and the schizoid (or, as Melanie Klein called it, the 'paranoid-schizoid position'). Melanie Klein wrote not of a 'stage' but a 'position': this rather baffling word means not an historical moment in an individual's life which is past and done with, but a pattern of inner consequences of processes belonging to a certain early stage whose legacy forever remains in the personality, in its subjective patterns, because the only way the personality could grow was around these patterns. Thus, depressive illnesses, which may be found to have their origins at the depressive stage, are embodied in the 'depressive position' – which may have to be lived through again, in an adult patient, in later life. (Winnicott prefers to call the depressive position the 'stage of concern' because its essential characteristic in normal life is the positive discovery of the capacity for ruth.)

The schizoid position is taken to be the origin of schizoid illnesses and the depressive position the origin of depressive illnesses (though it is not left out of account of course that all such illnesses may have other origins than purely endopsychic ones).

Both 'positions' or 'stages' occur in early infancy – the schizoid stage during the first four months. During this period, as Winnicott suggests, the mother is in a state of 'primary maternal preoccupation' – that is, she endures a state of extension of personality in identifying with her baby which in normal circumstances would be a schizoid illness. The significance of this very important insight will appear later.

It will also help at this stage if we look a little more closely at the problem of hate. Hate is not the opposite of love, which would be indifference, not wanting relationship, or feeling nothing, as Guntrip points out: 'Hate is love grown angry because of rejection. We can really only hate a person if we want their love.'

In such object-relations theory hate is no innate manifestation of a death instinct, but an excessive urge to incorporate, in the need of love: 'Hate is an expression of frustrated love need, an attempt to destroy the bad rejecting side of a person in the hope of leaving their good responsive side available, a *struggle to alter them*' (Guntrip [110] p. 91).

In the light of this we may regard murder, war, bombing, genocide, cannibalism as inverted forms of love – as attempts to alter 'bad' objects by force. The consequent predicament here is suggested by this: 'The anxiety is over the danger of hate destroying both sides, and the easiest way out is to find two objects and love one and hate the other' (Guntrip [110], p. 91).

This is one process of 'splitting'.

In the schizoid person there is so much fear of devouring everyone and so losing everything in the process that there can be a general withdrawal from all external relationships – a retreat into that indifference which is the true opposite of a love which is felt to be too dangerous. The schizoid substitutes exhibitionism or role-playing for actual relationships: but even in these he will feel hopeless. Thus a sense of 'futility' is the specific schizoid affect (this way of self-defence is evident in much that is schizoid in contemporary culture): 'Just as the depressive is identified with the object he attacks and so hurts himself . . . (and so fears loss of the object) the schizoid, in addition, fears loss of his ego, of himself . . .' (Guntrip [110], p. 91).

Ways out of these predicaments are found by most normal people, though we all experience them at times. We find our way out of them by coming to 'identify less with the object', becoming capable of and accepting bad and good in others and in ourselves, and discovering our own True Self and our inner resources. We become able to distinguish between the ego and the object (i.e. in an adult relationship, between ourselves and our partner whom we can then treat as a person not as part of ourself or a 'part object') and by the growth of the capacity for the mutual acceptance of dependence upon one another in relationship, as by two whole persons relating to one another as whole persons, in mutual reognition. We become better able to bear our fear of our own hate, to avoid splitting, and to find integration.

In all these developments creative symbolism, in life and culture, has a positive role, not least because these processes lead towards a sense of meaningful existence. Fortunately, as it appears from the new object-relation psychology, the fact of general sanity is an earnest of sufficient intuitive primal energy in human beings to seek maturity, wholeness, integration, the capacity for object-relationships, and a sense of meaning in life. The essential basis of this sanity is in the 'ordinary good home', and its intuitive contribution which serves the family and individual development, not least by providing 'primary home experience'.

In this natural energy of self-realisation culture and what it contributes to symbolism may be seen as an instrument to build bridges between the subjective and objective worlds. In this sense (as Ferenczi indicated) object-relations psychology restates the Christian injunction 'Love thy neighbour as thyself' – for we can only love our neighbour in so far as we have come to terms with our own inward bad-object problem, our quest for integration, our inward guilt and hate, and our depressive and schizoid tendencies. Here we will benefit insofar as we can relinquish our impulses to solve our problems of identity in false ways by forms of hate at the expense of others, often (as in our culture) against considerable encouragement to do so.

In the processes of gaining insight the ego exerts an integrative function, and the work done between the ego and the diverse intra-psychic dynamics of the self is done by phantasy, dramatisation of endopsychic processes, by the 'as-if' activity of symbolism, from dreams to high art.

One major preoccupation of object-relations theory is of tremendous importance, and that is its increasing emphasis on the need for experiences, in terms of *being* – creative experiences and interpersonal experiences of the kind the mother fosters in earliest infancy. The kind of psychotherapy we are concerned with here is moving on from the concept of what is done between therapist and patient as 'education' based on 'interpretation' – mind-work – to a deeper concern with personal relationship on which identity is based, which fosters the natural processes of growth, and from which a sense of meaning can emerge. As Winnicott says:

> We could now explain why my interpretations, made on good grounds, in respect of use of object, oral erotic satisfactions in the tranference, oral sadistic ideas . . . why such interpretations were never mutative. They were accepted, but: So what? Now the new position had been reached the patient felt a sense of relationship with me, and this was extremely vivid. It had to do with *identity*. (Winnicott, quoted by Guntrip [38], my italics.)

Guntrip says that this observation points to the 'centre of the concentric circles of psychoanalytic theory and therapy'.

In order to estimate what is happening it is, I believe, most valuable to take account of Guntrip's schematic picture of the way in which psychoanalytical theory is developing. He sees it as finding its 'way in' from the investigation of man in society, towards the investigation of the core of identity, the 'absolute beginnings of ego-identity in infancy'.

> The outermost circle is the life of the individual as a member of his social world. From there investigation proceeds into his capacities for human relationships, as shaped by his experiences of childhood, raising the problems of personality illness on first neurotic and then psychotic levels. This brings us to the heart of the acute difficulties the human infant has in struggling to establish personality in the earliest years, and thence to the centre of all these circles, the absolute beginnings of ego-identity in infancy. (Guntrip [38], p. 246.)

Guntrip diagrammatises the history of psychoanalytical thought thus:

1. *The Individual in Society*, object-relations in real life, with variable degrees of adjustment and maladjustment, and not too serious character neurosis and psychoneurotic symptoms. Human life in general as we see it and take it at face value, coping practically with it, rather than looking too deeply into its anxieties and tensions.

2. *Oedipal Problems*, looking below the surface of the day to day dealings of human beings with each other, to the emotional capacities of the individual for object-relationships, as fashioned within and limited by the family set-up and ties to parents and siblings; healthy normal Oedipal developments; pathological Oedipal patterns grown-in to the structure of the emotional personality, and operative in the outer world.

FREUD

3. *Personality Illness, the Failing Struggle to Function Socially*, to maintain good-enough object-relations, and to stand up to real life pressures when they play upon pathological patterns of grown-in tensions in the unconscious
   (a) *Psychoneurotic anxiety states* over sexual and aggressive antisocial impulses, with their somatic resonances.
   (b) *Ambivalence, love–hate conflicts, guilt and depression*, primitive ruthlessness, fear of destructiveness and the need to make reparation, manic-depressive mood swings, not yet of psychotic intensity. The transference neuroses, hysteria, obsessions, phobias, paranoid attitudes in neurosis.

1, 2, and 3 are pre-eminently the sphere of Freud, taking into account the fact that, increasingly from 1920 his thinking revolved around *Ego-Analysis*.

In 3, however, the work of *Melanie Klein* begins to go beyond Freud.

MELANIE KLEIN

4. *Deeper Level Illness, the Struggle to Keep Possession of an Ego*.
   (a) *Exploration of the earliest stages of ego-development*, the early infantile anxiety-positions, and infantile origins of psychosis. The Depressive and Paranoid positions in development, internal objects and *object-splittings*, and the phantasy 'inner world'.

   4 (a) embraces the main original Kleinian contribution.

   (b) *Schizoid problems*, detachment from real object-relations, and withdrawal to living in the secret inner phantasy world. *Ego-splittings matching Object-splittings*. Regressed illnesses.

FAIRBAIRN

   4 (b) is particularly the sphere of Fairbairn.

   The isolation of the schizoid ego in the unconscious. Winnicott's 'true self in cold storage'. My development of Fairbairn's theory to include a split in the infantile Libidinal Ego, leading to Regressed Ego.

   At this point we must note that the work of Melanie Klein grew out of the analysis of young children in general, and the work of Fairbairn grew out of the analysis of schizoid adults in the light of Melanie Klein's finds. In all this, research was delving further and further back into earliest infancy. There were many workers in this field, but for the further stages I have designated 5 and 6, *the work of Winnicott on the earliest mother-child relationship* seems to me to yield the ideas that become the key concepts for understanding these deepest levels of psychic life.

5. *The Beginnings of the Ego*. The differentiation of subject and object out of the state of primary identification, stimulating the beginnings of specific ego-development. The growth of the experience of *basic ego-relatedness*, and therewith of the capacity both to enter into object-relations and also to be alone, without anxiety and insecurity. Difficulties at this stage, before the Ego is strongly consolidated, will then lead to object-splitting and ego-splitting, as studied by Klein and Fairbairn.

6. *Before the Differentiated Ego, THE ABSOLUTE START OF THE EGO*, factually in an object-relation which the infant cannot yet experience as an object-relation but can experience (in sophisticated adult language) as *symbiosis, identity*, with (in favourable cases) a stable object, the good enough mother; making possible the beginnings of the experience of 'being', or 'security' and of 'self-identity'. With the good mother all this takes place in a condition of maximum protection against anxiety. It is sometimes said that bad-object experience provides the first powerful stimulus to the differentiation of a separate ego. If that were so, the ego could never have any other than an anxious base. *To be capable of development to full maturity, the ego must begin to differentiate out of a basic experience of full security in the mutual identification of mother and infant.* Primary identification is a relationship with a subjective objective object, an experience in which, for the baby, subject and object are as yet all one (in his experience). This, (stage 6, the centre of the five concentric circles discriminated in theory) allows of the emergence (stage 5, the first clearly definable phase of development) of the 'objective object' and the 'objective subject', i.e. the specific Ego.

WINNICOTT

This diagrammatic statement will make it obvious that not all object-relations theory can be covered here in a book which also attempts to relate its findings to problems of education and culture. But the diagrams serves to indicate that much of our prevalent cultural and social theory, and many of our underlying assumptions, are based on the the *first two sections only*, and a little of section 3, all of which is now superseded in psychoanalytical thought. Sections 3 and 4 have been the subject of this book so far, and below I shall try to relate some of the aspects of personality growth explored in sections 5 and 6 to culture and education.

If we despair in the face of the complexity of psychoanalytical theory, however, we can now at least reassure ourselves with the reflections that these insights more and more serve to vindicate intuitive sympathetic processes – those of love and being. We can turn back from them with relief to individual creativity and to our normal daily human gropings with an informed sense that these are the most important things in the world.

CHAPTER 10

Melanie Klein: Phantasy and Aggression

FAIRBAIRN's work enabled psychoanalytical theory to turn towards problems of identity and existence. His work, however, owes a great deal to the earlier developments in the work of Melanie Klein, whose emphasis on phantasy began to lead to an 'object-relations' psychology. From her work with children Melanie Klein developed a number of important theoretical concepts which we need to grasp.

Here we plunge into 'the bewildering complexity of processes which operate, to a large extent simultaneously, in the early stages of development', already referred to. Yet, as Guntrip emphasises, 'all who are practially concerned with the fact that living is a matter of human relationships need to grasp the significance of at any rate the essential discoveries contained in the new developments of psychoanalysis' (Guntrip [37], p. 195).

Melanie Klein's contribution derives its originality (and its relevance to education and creativity) from the fact that she was especially concerned with the analysis of children. Since psychoanalysis traces the origins of personality problems to infancy, it is appropriate that the study of infants should generate further developments: Winnicott's life-long study of babies and their mothers has advanced psychoanalytical thought even further since. But Melanie Klein, by taking into account children's symbolic acts of play rather than the verbal associations of adult patients, explored the unconscious worlds of children even as young as $2\frac{3}{4}$ years. (It was Sandor Ferenczi, who wrote so many fascinating essays on symbolism and the function of love in psychotherapy, who first suggested to Melanie Klein that she might have an aptitude for work with children.) One feature of such work is obviously that it cannot be 'scientific education'! If it is successful, there must be another primary factor.

The effect of working with children was to discover the ease with which they move between the unconscious and conscious worlds: 'Phantasies that work through only very slowly and partially, and often very keenly intellectualised and disguised, in the dreams and free associations of adults, come out with startling directness and detail when played out openly by the small child' (Guntrip [37], p. 196).

Melanie Klein's approach at the beginning was orthodox Freudian, and she never did essentially escape from Freudian dogma. She accepted with Freud that libidinal and sexual should be equated. She takes for granted Freud's 'instinct theory' which had just assumed its final form as 'life and death instincts' in 1920. Guntrip summarises her early approach thus:

Repression is regarded as aimed essentially against pleasure-toned sexual libidinal impulses. Anxiety is converted, frustrated sexual libido, and sublimation is the sexual cathexis* of ego-instincts, activities and interests. On the basis of this theoretical position she shows how play, phantasy and intellectual development in the very small child are inhibited by the repression of sexual curiosity and set free by its release. (Guntrip [37], p. 196.)

The sexual curiosity Melanie Klein found developing over four questions:

(1) Where do babies come from?
(2) What are babies made of?
(3) What is the difference between male and female?
(4) What part does the father play in making of a baby?† (Guntrip [37], p. 196.)

From Melanie Klein's investigation of these preoccupations emerged her significant exploration of the roles òf phantasy and aggression. Question (4) raised the greatest difficulty: and Melanie Klein discovered 'a specially intense anxiety' maintaining a 'heavy repression' on the disturbing matter of the father's role in the genital relationship between himself and the mother. Here she was later to discover considerable underlying aggression, and consequent fear of aggression, associated with phantasies of the primal scene – that is the vision of the father and mother in coition, phantasied in oral terms (i.e. in terms of that oral incorporation which is the child's essential libidinal way of dealing with the world, expressing relationship, and seeking survival).

Melanie Klein's first theories were developed from her analysis of a five-year-old boy called Fritz. He was outwardly an unaggressive little boy, but in his analysis he brought out a flood of aggressive phantasies. These revealed oral, anal and genital sadism, and general aggressiveness directed at his father and symbolic father-figures. He also brought out clear primal scene phantasies in which he both identified with, and displaced, both parents. In retribution for his indulgence in these phantasies he came to fear his father's retribution – and came to fear his father's penis as a symbol of this retribution. He feared that his father might castrate him. As Guntrip says: 'It is evident that the child must be victim, not aggressor, in the face of his own anxiety and guilt.'

So Fritz took up many rituals to hold off his paranoic fears. Moreover, in his phantasies of the primal scene, he could only conceive of this as a kind of aggressive incorporation (or 'eating'). For a child, Melanie Klein believed, parental intercourse is phantasied as being as sadistic as is its own incorporating urges – as hungry as its own eating, and as likely to lead, as he feels hungry love or hate may lead, to damage to the love-object with consequent annihilation of them – and (since he is dependent upon them) of himself. So, in taking the father's place not only did Fritz fear revenge (as in the Oedipus situation *vis-à-vis* his father): he also fears there may be damage to the mother either from his own sadistic phantasy or from his part in the phantasied primal scene. In turn, he fears her talion revenge on him: that she will eat him as she eats the father's penis.

Thus in anxiety over these incorporative fears he 'takes flight into the homosexual position'. That is, he becomes so afraid of 'the castrating mother' who lurks behind the fear of the punishing father, that he cannot tolerate, relate to, or identify with, Woman.

---

* *Cathexis:* the accumulation of an amount of mental energy on some particular idea, memory, or line of thought, usually directed at its suppression – or 'holding it off'. I do not find the phrase 'sexual cathexis' very clear here: presumably what Guntrip means is the cathexis of ego-instincts which are taken to be expressed in sexual terms – D.H.

† Here it is perhaps adding a lay comment at the risk of interrupting the progress of this chapter. From the insights of Winnicott and Fairbairn one can, I think, here add the observation that it is impossible to conceive such questions without also thinking (5) What am I made of? (6) Where did I come from? (and where might I go to?) That is, recognition of such infant preoccupations inevitably leads on to recognition of problems of identity and its continuity, and of existentialist or tragic issues.

The hate and aggression he has felt towards his mother becomes turned back on himself. (Here the awkward word 'position' is used because, while it can only be a matter of terminology to call a child of five 'homosexual', his psychic pattern at this stage is one which, if it were to persist into adult life, might well be the basis of homosexual character-istics.)

The theoretical conclusions which emerged from this were as follows: 'Anxiety and guilt are manifestly due to aggression rather than to sexuality *per se*, arising from the development of sadistic parental images which persecute and punish the child for his own aggression with monstrous ruthlessness. The origin of complexes lies far back in the pre-verbal period' (Guntrip [37], p. 197).

Melanie Klein later linked the phenomena she observed in Fritz and her other child patients with Freud's emerging concept of the super-ego. As we shall see, there are many disagreements centring round this concept, but here we may note the importance of this trend of thought in psychoanalysis. For, although the basis of Freud's theory is a psychology of instinct and impulse, his postulated structure of personality was also the starting point of the dynamic theories of object-relations psychology. Thus earlier com-mentators waver between concepts of such postulated entities as 'organs' and 'centres of functioning', 'substructures', and 'systems': with Freud a new dynamics of divided elements in the self originates:

> These three psychic substructures or systems [the id, ego, and super-ego] are not conceived of as independent parts of a personality that invariably oppose each other, but as three centres of psychic functioning that can be characterised according to their developmental level, to the amount of en-ergy invested in them, and to their demarcation and interdependence at a given time. . . .The functions of the id centre around the basic needs of men and their striving for gratification. These needs are rooted in instinctual drives and their vicissitudes. . . . The functions of the ego centre around the relation to reality. In this sense we speak of the ego as of a specific organ of adjustment. . . . The functions of the super-ego centre around moral demands. Self-criticism . . . self-punishment, and the formation of ideals, are essential manifestations of the super-ego. (Hartman [117], p.14.)

As we have seen, Freud's thinking about what went on inside the mind was organic. To him the ego acts as a mediator, imposing the reality principle on an unwilling id whose natural impulse was to satisfy the pleasure principle but which was inhibited by the sadistic and cruel, or moral, super-ego. Yet Freud also saw the super-ego as a conse-quence of the Oedipal problem, whose solution it masks: 'It is a castrator *par excellence*, the internalisation of the hated, feared yet loved father-rival who will allow the boy no sexual access to his mother' (Guntrip [37], p. 114).

In this concept originates the wider concept of *introjection* – and that of an inner world which is formed by the internalisation of aspects of outer experience. The concept of the super-ego had already become complex in Freud: Melanie Klein developed from it a whole intricate pattern of inner dynamics which eventually became an entirely new basis of personality theory:

> Freud introduced the concept at first as a development from that of an ego-ideal, and spoke of the super-ego as a differentiating grade within the ego. Gradually the super-ego, standing as it were over the ego with often terrifying authority, came to take on the aspect of an *internal object*, the representative of the parents within the psyche. Freud recognised both paternal and maternal components in the super-ego. Its complexity was further apparent in the difference between its early sadistic forms and its later ego-ideal character, a complexity that could not be properly conceptualised in terms of Freud's id–ego–super-ego scheme. (Guntrip [37], p. 230; my italics.)

What was emerging was a complex theory of internal objects from experience derived from patients in a different dimension from that of Freud's psychobiology.

From the concept of the super-ego naturally evolved the concept of a whole world of *internalised objects*, and from this a world of *inner reality*, in the 'psychic tissue':

> An *internal object* is an *imago*, a mental image of a particularly fundamental kind, which defined psychoanalytically is an unconscious psychic image of a person or part of a person as if the object had been taken into the mind, developed within the inner mental world, repressed and elaborated from infancy onwards, and heavily loaded with emotions. (Guntrip [37], p. 229.)

Guntrip quotes Susan Isaacs:

> Such images draw their power to affect the mind by being 'in it', i.e. their influence upon feelings, behaviour, character and personality, upon the mind as a whole, *from their repressed unconscious somatic associates* in the unconscious world of desire and emotions . . . and which do mean, in unconscious phantasy, that the objects to which they refer are believed to be inside the body, to be incorporated. (Isaacs, quoted in Guntrip [37], p. 229.)

From such concepts, as Fairbairn points out, there arises a picture which is no longer an organic picture of intrapsychic structure, but one of an internalised world which is the basis of personality: as we take in milk to form the substance of our bodies, so do we take in aspects of the world, to form our psychic substance – inevitably bringing into that 'tissue' dynamics from our formative experiences:

> On the basis of the resulting (i.e. resulting from Melanie Klein's work) concept of internal object there has been developed the concept of a *world of inner reality* involving situations and relationships in which the ego participates together with its internal objects. These situations and relationships are comparable with these in which the personality as a whole participates in a world of outer reality, but the form which they assume remains that conferred upon them by the child's experience of situations and relationships in the earliest years of life. It should be added that the world of inner reality is conceived as essentially unconscious; but this does not preclude its manifesting itself in consciousness in the form of dreams and phantasies. Morbid anxiety, irrational fears and psychopathological symptoms of every kind are also conceived as having their source in the unconscious world of inner reality. Indeed, it follows that human behaviour in general must be profoundly influenced by situations prevailing in the inner world. The fact is that, once the conception of inner reality has been accepted, every individual must be regarded as living in two worlds at the same time – the world of outer reality and the world of inner reality; and, whilst life in outer reality is characteristically conscious, and life in inner reality is characteristically unconscious, it will be realized *that Freud's original distinction between the conscious and the unconscious now becomes less important than the distinction between the two worlds of outer reality and inner reality.* (Fairbairn [12], p. 124.)

In Fairbairn, awareness of this interplay between the inner world and the outer world develops into a preoccupation with the roots of identity – with psychic problems seen as arising from fears of weakness. Fairbairn's picture of the inner world is more complex than Melanie Klein's, though hers is complex enough. Her insight into the child's preoccupation with the 'stuff inside one', how it got there, whether it is bad or good, leads on to Fairbairn's investigation of schizoid problems of 'inner contents' and the relation of these to identity.

Under the influence of Melanie Klein, says Guntrip:

> The super-ego had . . . become . . . a blanket-term covering the complexity of the whole endopsychic world of internalized objects, for the world of inner reality as Mrs. Klein presents it in a scene in which the ego seeks the aid of good objects in its struggle with persecuting bad figures. . . . An 'internal environment' is created in which the ego feels to be living under the shadow of powerful parental figures who are cruel persecutors at the deepest mental levels but steadily take on the aspect of ruthless punishers and guilt-inducers in later stages of development. But at the same time this complex structural differentiation includes a function of self-persecution and self-punishment in which the ego identifies with its internal enemies. One may say that the bad objects who arose our rage in outer reality then become necessary to us to enforce control on our impulses. (Guntrip [37], p. 231.)

That is we 'introject' them:

We can then forestall their punishment-cum-persecution by taking over their repressive functions ourselves. This entire process is duplicated in inner reality. If, for the moment, we exclude this function of self-judgment which is properly called 'conscience', whether primitive or matured, we may then say that the super-ego covers the whole world of internal objects, good and bad. (Guntrip [37] p. 231.)

The super-ego concept was then extended by Melanie Klein to cover a whole inner dynamic which becomes the whole basis of object-relations theory.

It is thus clear that for Mrs. Klein the super-ego covers a confusing multiplicity of good and bad internal objects, persecutors and pseudo-, semi- and fully-moral figures, some inducing terror and some inducing guilt (i.e. fear of death or of castration on the one hand, and fear of punishment and disapproval on the other). Her work is thus a challenge to still closer analysis. (Guntrip [37], p. 231.)

Any closer analysis would surely explore the need to the relationship between these multifarious inner complexities and the problems of identity they symbolise. Melanie Klein herself indicates the complexity in her writings:

I believe that . . . early phobias contain anxiety arising in the early stages of the formation of the super-ego. The earliest anxiety-situations of the child appear round the middle of the first year of its life and are brought on by an increase of sadism. They consist of fears of violent (i.e. devouring, cutting, castrating) objects, both external and introjected; and such fears cannot be modified in an adequate degree at such an early age.*

The difficulties small children often have in eating are also closely connected, according to my experience, with their earliest anxiety situations and invariably have paranoid origins. In the cannibalistic phase children equate every kind of food with their objects, as represented by their organs, so that it takes on the significance of their father's penis and their mother's breast and is loved, hated and feared like these. Liquid foods are likened to milk, faeces, urine and semen, and solid foods to faeces and other substances of the body. Thus food is able to give rise to all these fears of being poisoned and destroyed inside which children feel in relation to their internalized objects and excrements if their early anxiety-situations are strongly objective.

Infantile animal phobias are an expression of early anxiety of this kind. They are based on that ejection† of the terrifying super-ego which is characteristic of the earliest anal stage . . . the displacement on to an animal of the fear felt of the real father. . . . The fact that the anxiety-animal not only attracts to itself the child's fear of its father but also its admiration of him is a sign that the process of ideal-formation is taking place. Animal phobias are already a far-reaching modification of the fear of the super-ego, object relationship, and animal phobias. (Klein [45], pp. 219–21.)

Guntrip comments: 'in this passage the theory of the super-ego has taken up into itself the whole range of phenomena now called "fear of internal objects", and also needs felt towards them . . . i.e. all the child's experience of reaction to the object-world as duplicated internally in its mental organisation.' He adds a note to distinguish such 'possession' from traditional notions of 'being possessed': in object-relations psychology the internal energies are the individual's own, turned on himself: 'It is our own disturbed emotion that both consitutes and perpetuates this persecutory inner world.'

In the way Melanie Klein develops her exploration of endopsychic structure we see how in her work phantasy and aggression became specially emphasised.

Her work was done within orthodox 'classical' Freudian theory: but she was also much influenced by the impact of the 'structural theory' which Freud worked out between 1920 and 1926. As we have seen, this structural theory points to an object-relations *psychodynamic* approach to the structure and development of personality. Yet Freud seems not to have been able to recognise the degree to which his ego-analysis and

---

* The present writer is surprised at the extent to which psychoanalytical writers never mention teething pains, which to the baby whose ego is a mouth ego, being intensely painful, must seem like a visitation whose violence can only be attributed to persecution from outside forces.

† Guntrip points out here that Melanie Klein's terminology here met severe criticism from Edward Glover. The term here would surely be 'projection', but Melanie Klein presumably wished to imply that his psychic process has its roots in symbolism derived from anal ejection.

structural theory made necessary a revision of his instinct theory because of traits in his own personality, which raises the interesting question of Freud's influence on his followers. For whereas, as Guntrip says, Melanie Klein's 'original genius lay in her capacity for direct understanding of the unconscious in the very small child', her thinking about her clinical work was hampered by her adherence to classical theory. There are lacunae, and areas where her conceptionalisation of her own discoveries is not clear. Significantly perhaps (as we can see from the perspectives of later work) the areas where she is open to criticism are those which concern the *mother* and her role – one of Freud's extraordinary blind spots. That is, she overemphasises the endogenous origins of psychic disorder and neglects attention to the 'facilitating environment': and she attributes the origins of hate not to frustration or failure in these processes – but to the death instinct.

Melanie Klein's great importance is in the direction she takes, in exploring the way in which intense aggression is aroused in the infant at an astonishingly early age: 'fused with his sense of personal need particularly in the form of infantile sexuality, to create a sadistic emotional life which makes the infant terrified both of himself and of the fate of his love-objects, and fills him with persecutory anxiety over their phantasied retaliation against him' (Guntrip [37], p. 198).

Being an orthodox Freudian, Melanie Klein at first set out to see the origins of guilt and anxiety in the consequences of primary libidinal-sexual pleasure drawing 'repression upon itself, for repression is directed against the tone of sexual pleasure associated with the activity and leads to the inhibition of the activity or tendency' (Klein [46], p. 88). This in its turn is based on the orthodox concept of the Oedipus conflict – as Guntrip says, in her view 'the child's sexual activity calls forth castration anxiety because of its fear of the jealousy and punitive interference of the parent of the same sex'. It became obvious, however, that this view was far too simple. The repression of aggression was obviously far more important in the infant than repression of sexuality, and simple attraction and rivalry did not explain the Oedipus situation, which, from her observation, became extremely complex. By 1926 she had concluded that 'impulses of hatred and aggression are the deepest cause and foundation of guilt'.

In fact, as we shall see, in Melanie Klein's reconsiderations of her theory, psycho-analytical theory was already moving away from Freud's emphasis on the libidinal drives of sexuality as the basis of psychic structure and away from his concept of a pleasure principle being only modified *unwillingly* in favour of the reality principle. We are moving towards the later emphases on the primary need for relationship and on integration of identity in their positive energies. For now what is being explored is how, in the infant mind, there arises that combination of sexuality and aggression we call sadism – and in exploring this we are also exploring the experience summarised by Fairbairn later when he says that the child's ego is a 'mouth-ego'.

The infant's first anxieties arise because his very modes of (oral) relationship inevitably seem to threaten his existence of himself and his love objects. Here Guntrip's comment is most illuminating: the child, he says, cannot abstract his mind from his body. 'The child is an intensely "embodied person". . . emotionally preoccupied with embodied persons. His phantasies are all of bodies, attacks on bodies, getting something out of one body and into another body with fears of retaliatory reversals of this procedure, of robbing and injuring bodies and healing and repairing the damage done to them' (Guntrip [37], p. 202).

The child, I would add (from Winnicott's insights) does not wholly distinguish between reality and phantasy. And his first all-important relationship is the intense, instinct-impelled one of suckling at his mother's breast. As Winnicott has indicated, nursing has a very special atmosphere – one in which an extension of the mother's personality becomes a psychic envelope in which both mother and child live for a time. Such later observations make it even more relevant to speak as Guntrip does of the sucking relationship between infant and mother as a kind of 'coitus'. Thus 'A pattern of relationships is created in the child's feeding and phantasy which is then applied in turn to urethral, anal and genital functions and relationships, to feeding, cleanliness training and genital coitus between parents (not seldom witnessed or heard, but sooner or later always phantasied), *and to all kinds of personal relationships*' (Guntrip [37], p. 202).

The child phantasies the primal scene in terms belonging to his own experience of 'coitus' with the mother, by analogy. Since his own 'coitus' was mouth coitus, concerned with incorporation, he conceives of such things, in similar terms, and in ways conditioned by his experience of nursing. Consequently

> the child experiences rage and jealousy (in proportion as he has already become insecure) due to the fact that he feels the parents are getting something from each other (by exchange and incorporation of bodily substances and organs – the only terms in which the infant can experience anything) while he himself feels exited, stimulated with needs and longings, but left out, ignored and left unsatisfied. He usually reacts with bodily expressions of rage such as wetting and dirtying, while in phantasy he attacks the parents who seem to be combined against him. (Guntrip [37], p. 203.)

In these phantasies (and those of the combined parents are most horrible) the child's mind becomes far more Cimmerian than even Freud was able to reveal:

> There were dark fears of possibilities that the most gruesome fairy tale had not dared to explore, cruel impulses where hate and murder rage freely, irrational phantasies that mock at reality in their extravagance. Mrs. Klein's unsparing presentation of the cutting, tearing, gouging, devouring phantasies of infants is apt to make most people recoil. (Jones [46], introduction.)

These phantasies are the basis of much symbolism in myth and art: and they are also the phantasies acted out in life by the adult psychopath who is still in the devouring or cannibalistic state of mind of the infant – which accounts for the universal fascination and horror which his crimes arouse.

Anxiety and guilt arise in every child, evoked by his destructive impulses – 'an anxiety made up of his fear of being himself destroyed by their violence, and the fear of destroying his objects together with the projection of his sadism on to them and the fear that they will retaliate destructively on him' (Guntrip [37], p. 201). The problems of such anxiety and guilt remain throughout life inevitably bound up with love-objects and relationships, and remain an aspect of adult relationship and sex with which we needs must deal. And while in the infant they become linked with sexual curiosity, so too in the adult does sexual curiosity become linked with guilt and anxiety.

Though Melanie Klein does refer in some instances to 'unfavourable conditions of nutrition' here and the severe obsessional neurosis of a mother there, she was, says Guntrip, 'so busy analysing the endopsychic situation' that the environment was taken too cursorily into account. She takes account of the effect of witnessing the primal scene, and of the birth of siblings. But what is missing is what Winnicott was later to supply: 'subtle characterisations of traumatic environmental factors such as Winnicott's mention of "erratic mothering", or the existence of unconscious hate and rejection of the child in the mother, or the effect of maternal types on the quality of mothering given to the child' (Guntrip [28], p. 203).

Melanie Klein gives too much the impression that the child's troubles are internally generated, that neurosis develops by almost wholly endopsychic process, and that inner conflicts are automatic and self-generated. As Guntrip suggests, the view that external reality is secondary in its influence to inner experience is highly controversial. As Lomas says: 'Persons do not, in her thinking, ever really emerge from their internal phantasy world.'

Melanie Klein's adherence to the death-instinct, Guntrip suggests, actually 'vitiates' her discussions of anxiety. She discusses sadism in terms of the 'polarity between the life-instincts and the death-instincts' and quotes approvingly a passage of Terese Benedek: 'Anxiety, therefore is not a fear of death but the perception of the death-instinct that has been liberated in the organism – the perception of primary masochism.'

To Melanie Klein at times, says Guntrip, 'the super-ego as inwardly directed aggression seems to become a purely subjective development of the death instinct' – and this 'in spite of the fact that her work provides a fully satisfactory developmental analysis of sadism and masochism without any need to call in this so-called instinct' (Guntrip [37], p. 205).

As we have seen, others, notably Winnicott, have come to find the concept of the death instinct unnecessary. Yet orthodox Kleinian theory is based on it: and it thus shows a surprising tenacity. Yet, as Guntrip concludes, 'Mrs. Klein's "deviation" from Freud consists, in fact, of the radical development of Freud's own greatest deviation from himself' – that is, the development of the theory of the super-ego into a 'fully psychological view of mental development'. Yet she retains Freud's own blindness to the difference *in principle* between this and the earlier instinct theory.

As Guntrip shows, this concept is clung to with the tenacity of 'biological mysticism', when after a searching analysis of the origins of aggression, the cause is suddenly assigned to the death instinct, which turns up in parentheses: 'under the pressure of intense anxiety (ultimately deriving from the death instinct)'.

Kleinian writers contradict themselves – Joan Rivière, for instance, in one place saying 'Freud . . . was careful not to make it (the death instinct) a first principle of psychoanalysis . . . ' only to say two pages later, 'Freud put forward the duality of the life and death instincts as the fundamental antithesis in the unconscious . . . after which he constantly and repeatedly referred to it as the foundation of intrapsychic conflict. . . . '

As Guntrip urges, the death instinct 'does not represent anything that is clinically presented but something that, from the clinical point of view, is an *a priori* assumption.'

Joan Rivière says that the problem arises because the destructiveness and cruelty in babies seems an enormity to our minds. This, however, 'ceases to be such an insoluable mystery when, as Mrs Klein shows, Freud's hypothesis of a destroying force in our minds, always in interaction with a life-preserving force, is allowed due significance'.

This concept, she says, of a 'destructive force within every individual, tending towards the annihilation of life, is naturally one which arouses extreme emotional resistance'. Emotional resistance is felt, says Guntrip, surely to the fact of 'deep repressed aggression' and not to any particular theory of it. It would rather seem that having swallowed the truth of the aggression, the death-instinct concept seems to add nothing illuminating. The enormous aggression and cruelty in babies can be adequately explained as a developmental phenomenon.

> It is sufficient explained by the fact of the infant's defective or immature sense of reality, and its lack of developed ego-control to moderate the rapid increase of emotional tensions. . . . The infant's

inexperience of objective reality and his incapacity to recognise either his own exaggerated interpretation of his frustrations or the effects of aggression, leaves him unprotected against the blind interaction of the projection of his own rage on to objects, and the introjection of his objects as he now sees them coloured by his aggression in addition to their own. He is then at the mercy of phantastically violent internal persecutors and this means that his emotions cannot be kept at realistic and appropriate levels. (Guntrip [37], p. 210.)

If we follow Melanie Klein, however, we begin to leave behind the concepts derived from psychobiology and instinct theory and begin to employ terms borrowed from psychotherapy, which belong to dimensions the teacher and poet can understand in relation to his own experience – identification, introjection, projection, phantasy, anxiety, and so on. The growth of personality comes to be explored in ways we can understand: no one who knows children finds it ridiculous to have it pointed out to him how strange and terrifying their phantasies can be; how full of aggression they can be; and how they develop their identities by taking aspects of their parents and other people 'into' themselves.

There are, of course, many problems left unsolved by Melanie Klein's investigations, and here we may find difficulties with her work. One difficulty arises over the postulation by Melanie Klein of a premature excitation of sexual tensions, as a consequence of oral sadism.

Defences such as projection, introjection, the spreading of dammed-up tensions to urethral, anal, muscular, genital and other bodily functions lead to the creation of an imaginary or hallucinated world of inner mental experience, according to Freud's hypothesis that the infant hallucinates fulfilment when frustration is prolonged . . . oral tensions . . . cause a precipitate unfolding and development of genital tensions in a way that leads to unconscious knowledge of genital functions. The receptivity of the mouth to the breast leads on to that of the vagina needing to receive a penis, and the teeth biting and penetrating the breast lead on to the penis penetrating a hole in the body, via intermediate linking experiences including anal ones. (Guntrip [37], p. 211.)

The result of Melanie Klein's supposition that such phantasy awareness of genitality comes early to the frustrated child means that the Oedipus problems of conflict between the child's own needs for physical satisfaction come into conflict with his unconscious knowledge of the genital functions of his parents at a very young age – to a time which would seem far in advance of the biological maturation that one would suppose the only possible grounds for such awareness. This early 'oral-genital' stage seems to some psychologists difficult to accept when the concept of 'sexual exitation' seems to suggest an organic sexuality existing before biological maturation of sexual organs. However, the important aspect is the phantasy, symbolic development in the dynamics of the inner world, in which 'oral frustration arouses in the child an unconscious knowledge that its parents enjoy mutual sexual pleasures' (Klein [45], p. 188).

From this arises problems of anxiety about aggression and its consequences, and the exploration of these is the whole basis of Kleinian object-relations theory.

Melanie Klein's most significant theoretical chapter in *The Psycho-analysis of Children* was 'The Significance of Early Anxiety-Situations in the Development of the Ego' – and, as Guntrip says, this title is almost a summary of her theory. The infant from the beginning becomes anxious about the consequence of the powerful feelings he has in complex with his incorporative needs. He cannot fully distinguish between the *me* and the *not-me*: he cannot fully distinguish between phantasy and reality. He suffers pain and frustration but has no sense of cause or connection, and has only a rudimentary capacity to symbolise. From this world of the earliest chaos of emerging consciousness – consciousness not yet differentiated from bodily existence – emerge in Melanie Klein's theory two kinds of anxiety – *persecutory* and *depressive*.

These two forms of anxiety, as we shall see later, became interpreted by Fairbairn as belonging to two significant stages in development: the first the stage of the formation of an identity which is capable of holding together and continuing; the second the stage of discovery of the self in relation to the object, the dawn of recognition of the difference between the *me* and the *not-me* with all that is involved. But the essential aspect of Kleinian theory which needs to be grasped here is that it carries object-relations theory back (through Freud's narcissistic and autistic phases) to the beginnings of separate bodily life, and finds, in the consequences of the initial anxieties, developments which are the basis of the structure of the personality itself. In Winnicott and Fairbairn the way in which primal anxieties are dealt with (by 'splitting' and internalisation and such processes) are to be seen as *positive* developments – not manifestations of the need to 'adapt', so much as *psychic processes without which there would be no human identity at all*: that is, as integrative processes. And since these processes are a primitive symbolism in themselves, they are the basis of all cultural manifestations.*

We have seen above (p. 57 ff.) how the child's earliest consciousness is 'embodied': in order to follow these earliest stages in theory we have to grasp concepts in ways which belong to these 'embodied' stages. How, for instance, does an 'internal object' relate to 'splitting'? These are related, since splitting arises from the attempts by the ego to deal with either good internalised objects which have been 'lost' or bad internalised objects which seem to threaten the self from within.

To object-relations psychology the capacity to be whole and to relate to an object as a whole is a problem of overcoming and avoiding ego-splitting. Yet splitting is inevitable, and is also the basis of the mysterious and rich complexity of human make-up itself, including the capacity to symbolise. This concept of splitting was foreshadowed in Freud's structural pattern of the id, ego, and super-ego; but whereas his pattern suggests rigid entities concerned with the control of (impersonal) impulses and with adaptations, the newer object-relations theory concerns itself with dynamics – with developmental processes of personality such as we are familiar with in poetry in the struggle to become whole, in relation to the world as a whole.

Some contemporary psychology, especially of the sociological kind, recognises that psychic disorders are caused by environmental breakdown. Thus Karen Horney says 'Neuroses are generated by disturbances in human relationships' (Horney [41]). But Guntrip says she is thinking in terms of relations to external objects at the conscious level, and seems to imply that the breakdown in relationships comes first and is the determinant. Since the work of Melanie Klein, object-relations psychology has been concerned with what Guntrip calls, 'a far less obvious danger – a repressed world of internalised objects'.

Here the picture of the structure of personality becomes very complex and, as we shall see, is still the subject of dispute as between various theorists. But there is common ground in that psychodynamic theories assume that the identity is formed by psychic incorporation, of the mother in the first instance, by identification. From that mysterious condition (indicated by Melanie Klein and conceptualised by Winnicott) of 'primary

* It is relevant to note that to R. D. Laing these processes seem to appear as purely negative ones: 'in short he tries to protect himself by every means that he has, by projection, introjection, splitting, denial and so on.' In *The Politics of Experience* he never sees these as the *basis* of identity.

maternal preoccupation', the infant takes in aspects of the mother as object which become aspects of his inner self. Unless this process can be accomplished he can not begin to exist, and so any breakdown of this process of internalising objects threatens psychic annihilation and can mean inanition and death. Inevitably, since mother and infant are 'imperfect' – that is, since they live in the real world and mothers are inevitably at times not there when wanted, tired, ill, hungry, delayed, more of less loving, and not magic or controllable, while all babies are sometimes rejected, there will be times when a 'badness' in the object presents itself. Since an infant is absolutely dependent (and will die if he is abandoned) he cannot tolerate badness in the object 'out there', and so takes this into himself as if *to deal with it within*. Thus internalised, it becomes an *internalised bad object*.

To grasp these concepts we need to ponder further the nature of internalised objects. Guntrip writes:

> In some sense we retain all our experience in life and 'carry things in our minds'. If we did not, we would lose all continuity with our past . . . and no relationships or experiences could have any permanent values for us. Thus in some sense everything is mentally internalised, retained and inwardly possessed: that is our only defence against complete discontinuity in living. (Guntrip [110], p. 88.)

Winnicott points out that the infant needs to build a concept of the real mother as a person out of his memories of her loving attention: this alone can help him develop sufficient by way of a sense of continuity to carry him through his vicissitudes. These include a sense of 'flop' when he is fed, a time when, since his life-seeking hunger is abated he may feel he no longer exists. Here it is as if he felt that his vitality was 'in' the energy of his hunger, so that being satisfied, which brings the decline of this energy feels like a loss of life. Anyone who has experienced the inconsolable sadness of a baby crying after his feed can understand the observation that he may be feeling that he may now cease to exist (and this despite his actual feed: what has 'gone' is the life-hold of phantasy).* The primacy of feelings, in which annihilation may seem to threaten unless urgent psychic effort is made, is a significant perception of object-relations psychology.

The process of internalising still needs more exploration, however, before we can continue to grasp Melanie Klein's theories:

> But things are mentally internalised and retained in two different ways which we call *memory* and *internal objects*. Good objects are, in the first place, mentally internalised and retained only as memories. They are enjoyed at the time, the experience is satisfying and leaves no problems, and can later be looked back to and reflected on with pleasure. . . . Outer experience is enough to meet our needs. (Guntrip [110], 88.)

Guntrip is here following Fairbairn, who differs from Melanie Klein on this point: she believed in internalised good objects. Fairbairn believed there was no need to internalise unless the object showed 'bad' aspects. To Fairbairn the process works thus:

> When someone we need and love ceases to love us, or behaves in such a way that we interpret it as a cessation of love . . . when his mother refuses the breast, weans the baby, or is cross, impatient or punitive or is absent temporarily or for a longer period (these may be experienced as) rejection or desertion, or else as persecution or attack. Then the lost (or hostile) object, now became a bad object, is mentally internalised in a much more vital and fundamental sense than memory. An inner psychic world has been set up, duplicating the original situation.
> But it is an unhappy world in which one is tied to bad objects and feeling therefore always frustrated, hungry, angry, and guilty and profoundly anxious. It is bad objects which are internalized because we cannot accept their badness and yet cannot give them up, cannot leave them alone, cannot master and control them in outer reality and so keep on struggling to possess them, alter them and compel them

---

* One of Winnicott's patient's chief terrors was that of satisfaction – because it threatened annihilation.

to change into good objects, in our inner psychic world. They never do change. In our inner unconscious world where we repress and lock away very early in life our original bad objects, they remain
always rejecting, indifferent, or hostile to us according to our actual outer experience. (Fairbairn
[19], p. 89.)

These internalised bad objects are not mere phantasies or memories: products of
identification and introjection, they are integral 'embodied' aspects of experience which
have become the very structure of our personality: 'The child is essentially identified
with his objects, and when he mentally incorporates them, he remains identified with
them and they become part and parcel of the very psychic structure of his personality'
(Fairbairn [19], p. 89).

Phantasies, with all their cultural concomitants, are manifestations of the workings
of these inner dynamics (and our attempts to deal with them):

The phantasies in which internal objects reveal their existence to consciousness are activities of the
structure which constitute the internal objects . . . so the fundamental psychopathological problem is:
how do people deal with their internalized bad objects, to what extent do they feel identified with them,
and how do they complicate relations with external objects? . . . it is the object all the time that matters,
whether external or internal, not pleasure. (Fairbairn [19], p. 89.)

The above quotations from Fairbairn show how the theory of the processes of 'internalising objects' and the nature of the dynamics by which we 'deal' with them led him to
his conclusion that the 'ultimate goal of the libido is the object'. They also indicate how
cultural issues relate to intrapsychic problems: for if it is true (as Fairbairn also says)
that dreams are a 'dramatisation of endopsychic conflicts', then symbolic creativity, too,
may be seen as largely the dramatisation of 'dealing with internalised bad objects', and
of how these 'complicate relations with external objects'.

As Wisdom wrote, Melanie Klein gave this process of introjection a dominant place:

Freud and Ferenczi had introduced introjection into analysis, where it played an important minor
role. Mrs. Klein gives it a dominating position: she holds that all sorts of objects are introjected, i.e. that
there are 'internal objects' resulting from the introjection or phantasied incorporation of either of the
two parents or parts of them. A part of a person (such as a breast) is called a 'part object'. These
introjected (or internal) objects, whether whole or part, are felt to be good or bad because the child
projects his own feelings into them. (Wisdom, quoted by Guntrip [37], p. 215.)

Aggression, in Melanie Klein, takes over the role of sexuality in Freud, for the anxieties
about loss or destruction by the self of internal good objects, or with the persecution of
the self by internal bad objects, result from *attacks by or on the self* – whose origin is in the
hate aroused in 'embodied phantasy' terms by frustration of primal needs for satisfaction
and love.

Melanie Klein and Fairbairn here develop a theory of two stages or 'positions'. The
word 'position' is used because there is never a 'stage' which is completed. If the psychotherapist is trying to trace a disorder, he looks for a pattern of symptoms, and these tend
to indicate a stage or stages in infancy from which the manifestations spring. But the
consequences of the 'stage' are still in the person: so, the term 'position' is used.*

For Melanie Klein there were two 'positions' – the *paranoid-schizoid* and the *depressive*.
In the development of her concept of the first of these Melanie Klein again makes a
significant departure from Freud – in the direction of a psychology which makes

* 'The term position was chosen because – though the phenomena involved occur in the first place during
early stages of development – they are not confined to these stages but represent specific groupings of
anxieties and defences which appear and reappear during the first years of childhood' (Klein [45], preface).

important links here with problems of identity as they are explored in creativity (as, for instance, in the poetry of Blake or the novels of Dostoevsky).

> *Persecutory anxiety* arises if one is under direct attack oneself, if aggression goes against the ego. It is fear for one's own safety. Kleinians, parting company here with Freud, believe that the internal danger to which the ego can feel exposed in the unconscious may be so great as to develop into a fear of death a terror of extinction and annihilation. (Guntrip [37], p. 217).

This persecutory anxiety is apt to dominate the first three months of life. What comes later is *depressive anxiety*, a fear not for oneself but for one's love-objects (on whom, however, one depends):

> When the mother begins presently to be experienced as a whole person and the good and bad parts, aspects or phases of her dealing with the infant are brought together, an ambivalent relationship to the mother arises to replace the earlier 'splitting' of the object into unrelated good and bad objects. In the earlier position the infant could feel desire towards the good object and terror towards the persecuting bad one, without these two reactions influencing each other. Now that love and hate can be felt towards one and the same changeable object, the anxiety arises that in hating one's object, as bad one may destroy it as good. (Guntrip [37], p. 216.)

Depressive anxiety is therefore a pathological version of grief and mourning, and is, indeed, aroused in late life by the loss of persons who are emotionally important to one by parting or death. 'It is essentially a separation-anxiety accompanied by severe guilt.' It also involves danger to the self: 'depressive anxiety also involves direct danger to oneself, since, through identification with the love-object who is the victim of one's hate and aggression, one becomes involved in the fate of that object. This serves as a punishment for aggression by turning it against oneself internally' (Guntrip [37], p. 217).

Melanie Klein's picture of psychopathological behaviour, then, is of the blind imposition on external persons and situations of the second and wholly internal world built up in infancy. The therapeutic process consists of drawing the individual out of his interior life into realistic contact with the outer world.

Some writers, such as Edward Glover, have accused Melanie Klein of inventing a 'matriarchal variant of the doctrine of Original Sin' in that she offers the concept of a 'three-months-old love-trauma due to the infant's imagined greedy destruction of a real loving mother whom it really loves'. This concept may be difficult to accept, but surely only so if we fail to take into account the momentousness of the primary processes of the formation of consciousness. As soon as we have taken these into account and observed the terrible consequences if things go wrong, we can see that complex phantasy processes must be at work, and that there must needs be a price to pay for the fact that the development of identity is based essentially on these processes of delusion. So, inevitably, we all suffer dreams and visions of destructive monsters, which are symbols of our own inward incorporative or cannibalistic urges which are no more than a bodily hunger to live. Without resorting to patients' dreams, we need only look at nursery rhyme and fairy tale to see the symbolism of hunger in its most terrifying forms.

Fairbairn will be seen to take the problems raised by Melanie Klein further, while Winnicott turns many of her original insights round and offers them in positive terms, as in his popular writing for mothers and those in child care:

> It is a healthy thing for a baby to get to know the full extent of his rage. . . . For a few minutes he really intends to destroy or at least to spoil everyone and everything, and he does not even mind if he destroys himself in the process. Don't you see that every time a baby goes through this process he gains something? If a baby cries in a state of rage, and yet the people round him remain calm and unhurt,

this experience greatly strengthens his ability to see that which he feels to be true is not necessarily real, that fantasy and fact, both important, are nevertheless different from each other. (Winnicott [92], p. 47.)

At the level of conscious discovery of reality we may accept from such insight into familiar experience that a child's exploration of rage is necessary for his 'disillusion' and his proper discovery of the difference between phantasy and reality. It follows that it is likely that unconscious phantasies are even more terrible and more important. And here it is most significant to the problem of life if we accept Melanie Klein's insight that 'sadism and neurotic aggression are post-natal phenomena in reaction to inadequate and unsatisfying mothering, felt by the infant as real frustration of the need for either or both good and tenderness' (Guntrip). Where we may, however, see elements of belief in Original Sin in Melanie Klein's theory is in her belief that infant sadism is innate in that it is a manifestation of Freud's death instinct.

The most profitable developments in psychoanalytical theory, however, have been where significant departures from Freud have been taken. With Melanie Klein the most significant was that she and her collaborators realised that the infant relates to an object from the beginning, and was not objectless and autoerotic. Thus the depressive phenomena which Freud had traced to the Oedipal situation came to be considered as related to earlier problems – the earliest problems of the 'developing perception of the mother as "whole-object"'. This in turn leads on to Fairbairn's exploration of the schizoid problem as underlying all depressive ones.

In 1946 Melanie Klein was using the term 'paranoid position' for the persecutory phase of the first few months, when all impingements (including its own pain and anger) seem to the child like persecution by external forces. Fairbairn at the time was using the term 'schizoid' position. Melanie Klein decided to combine the terms, to speak of a 'paranoid-schizoid' position. This position she held to precede the 'depressive position', in which the infant becomes 'anxious on behalf of its love-objects, and not merely for itself, and guilt arises'.

From Melanie Klein's concepts of these two stages and the relationship between them arise fresh views of development. For one thing depressive manifestations (the psycho-neuroses) now appear *as attempts to master earlier and deeper disturbances*. That is, the infant has, when he reaches the depressive position, a 'backlog' of earlier (schizoid) problems. In normal development the 'work' that is begun at the depressive position marks an advance in emotional and intellectual life – and thus (as Winnicott eminently argues) the 'capacity to be depressed', while it can be psychopathological, is also a feature of everyone's make-up, and is a vital aspect of consciousness. There is 'useful' depression, and this is very much a concomitant of most creative activity – which itself may be seen as symbolic work on depressive *and earlier* problems of being.

Also, Melanie Klein's concepts indicate that object-relations exist from the beginning of life, and so there is a problem from the beginning of maintaining an integrated self, against splits (rather than a self driven impulses merely seeking to 'adjust' by forfeiting potentialities).

These fresh developments are already implicit in her summaries of 1952:

If persecutory fears are very strong, and for this reason (among others) the infant cannot work through the paranoid-schizoid position, the working through the depressive position is in turn impeded. This failure may lead to a regressive reinforcing of persecutory fears and strengthen the fixation points for severe psychoses (that is to say, the group of schizophrenics). . . . While I assumed that the outcome of the depressive position depends upon the working through of the preceding phase, I nevertheless attributed to the depressive position a central role in the child's early development. For with the introjection of the object as a whole the infant's object-relation alters fundamentally. The synthesis between the loved and hated aspects of the complete object give rise to feelings of mourning and guilt which imply vital advances in the infant's emotional and intellectual life. This is also a crucial juncture for the choice of neurosis or psychosis. (Klein [47], p. 294.)

> ... object-relations exist from the beginning of life, the first object being the mother's breast which to the child becomes split into a good (gratifying) and bad (frustrating) breast; this splitting results in a severance of love and hate. . . . (Klein [47], p. 293.)

Resulting from these theories has grown the view that the ego itself was a whole entity from the beginning, and not growing together piecemeal as seen by other theorists (cf. Glover's 'ego-nuclei'). If the ego is a unity, this obviously implies, as we shall see, conclusions very much at variance with Freud's theory of the ego and the id. This ego has the function of integrating, especially when, in the depressive position, the infant

> introjects the object as a whole, and simultaneously becomes in some measure able to synthesise the various aspects of the object as well as his emotions towards it. Love and hatred come closer together in his mind, and this leads to anxiety lest the object, internal and external, be harmed or destroyed. Depressive feeling and guilt give rise to the urge to preserve or revive the loved object and thus to make reparation for destructive impulses and phantasies. (Klein [45], preface.)

Thus the primary unity of the ego and its integrative function is bound up with the concept of the 'depressive position' and its relation to the perception of wholeness in the self and the object, and with the concept of reparation. As we shall see, in re-naming the depressive position the 'stage of concern' Winnicott seeks to emphasise its positive and creative importance as the discovery of ruth, the discovery of others and possible effects of one's own impulses on them, all this as the basis of many symbolic creative activities. We shall also see that this stage is the basis of social impulses, so that here, as Winnicott says, 'civilisation begins anew in every child'.

This concept of a self from the beginning, moving (in optimum conditions) towards integration requires, as Guntrip indicates, radical revision of Freud's theories and structures. From the first even instinctual actions are involved in object-relations: even at first 'guided by his oral instincts, the infant turns to the outer world and makes contact with another human being. He sucks at his mother's breast. . . . 'Is this an id activity (since the id is the seat of the instincts)? Or, since 'by definition it is the surface part of the id, i.e. the ego which performs the contacts with the outer world', *an activity of the ego*?

This debate is reported by Guntrip from Paula Heimann, who concludes:

> When we consider the earliest processes we cannot make a sharp distinction between the id and the ego, because in our view the ego is formed from experiences. The earliest contacts (introjections and projections) start this process. The infant's first sucking is then neither an id-activity nor an ego-activity – it is both, it is an activity of the incipient ego. (Heimann in Guntrip [37], p. 240.)

'Energy and structure' are all one, concludes Guntrip: the so-called id is the primary libidinally needy self and the Freudian ego is a self that seeks adjustment to outer reality. 'The libidinally needy self, as it strives for satisfaction, comes to be opposed and repressed. Freud discovered it in the unconscious and mistook it for an impersonal id because it was not a conscious ego.' (Guntrip [37], p. 241.)

'The primary libidinal id-ego is as much an ego, a self, as any later developed ego-aspects of the psyche. It has an object, the breast and it can introject its object', says Guntrip, who points out the confusion in Paula Heimann in the passage quoted above, who speaks of the id as if it were already functioning as an ego, and on its way to start up ego-development. Guntrip goes on: 'But surely introjection and projection made sense only when they are seen as activities of an ego in dynamic relations with objects. The literal implication of her words would be that the id functions as an ego in order to give rise to the ego' (Guntrip [37], p. 241).

This points to a confusion between object-relations theory as it was developing and orthodox Freudian structure which the Kleinians could not yet throw off. Meanwhile, of course, in our intellectual atmosphere and in popular thought at large Freudian concepts and structure, as of the instinctive id which functions as if apart from the ego (and for which the self is hardly responsible), are firmly entrenched.

Fresh attitudes arose in many post-Freudian writers without their being fully aware of the implications. Susan Isaacs wrote: 'Some measure of "synthetic function" is exercised upon instinctual urges from the beginning. The child could not learn, could not adapt to the external world (human or not) without some sort and degree of control and inhibition, as well as satisfaction, if instinctual urges progressively developed from birth onwards.' (Klein [47], p. 110.)

If this is true it is a recognition that, implicitly, 'free' education (for example) is based on a misconception: indeed, as manifest in creativity in education at large 'control and inhibition' are positively necessary as sources of developing discovery of the reality of others and of social and moral codes. (But perhaps more positive terms such as 'modification and regulation' could have been used here?)

The Kleinians here part company with Anna Freud, who cannot relinquish the concept of the id and primal instincts. She cannot accept that the so-called id is a 'primitive libidinal ego sustaining a definite object-relation to the breast from birth'. Kleinian theory carries object-relations and the ego back to the very beginning: but yet Kleinian theorists seemed unable to deduce that instinct theory was thereby rendered superfluous. To the world at large these issues are important, for psychodynamic theories tend to substitute for Freud's deterministic causality based on a 'biological' determinism a complex picture of energies *about which something can be done* in terms of making it more possible for destructiveness to be reduced. That is, whereas if all our psychic woes were attributable to a death instinct, an impersonal id, and to instinctual drives, it might be that we could do no more than put up with them and accept that man is unchangeably ruthless and predatory (with Anthony Storr). If, however, they are consequences of breakdown in complex processes of identity and relationship in the self from the beginning, to which a 'facilitating environment' in integral, it ought to be possible by social measures (such as the promotion of better child care and the fostering of good personal relationships between parents and potential parents) to reduce the incidence of psychic failure and mental disease to some degree – without falling into the heresy of human perfectibility.

Many Kleinians, as Guntrip shows, have retained Freud's theories of the life and death instinct, his endopsychic structure of super-ego with distinction between ego and id, and his hedonistic or pleasure-principle theory of motivation. They haver over certain fundamental problems, as over whether there is a primary stage which is narcissistic, autoerotic, and autistic, or whether these (clinically observable) phenomena are not 'disguised relationships with objects internal to, and identified with the self'. But the importance of their work is that from it have come important concepts which imply a complete revolution of theory as it stems from the pioneering work of Freud himself.

From our examination of the development of her theory we can now look at the major concepts in Melanie Klein's work, bearing in mind their implications for our concern with symbolism and creativity.

The first is that of *psychic reality* – Guntrip's definition of which is most valuable:

> The mind or psyche has a reality of its own, separate and distinct from the reality of the outer material world. It has its own permanencies, its own energies, and its own enduring and not easily alterable organization. The psyche has, one might almost say, a kind of solid substantiality of its own which we cannot alter at will, and which we have to begin by accepting and respecting. Thus, we cannot ourselves, by wishful thinking, become anything we would like to be, we cannot by an effort of will make ourselves *feel* differently from the ways in which we discover that we do feel. We do not choose what we shall feel, we simply discover that we are feeling that way, even if we have some choice in what we do about its expression. Our feelings are instantaneous, spontaneous and at first unconscious reactions which reveal the psychic reality of our make-up. At any given moment we are what we are, and we can become different only by slow processes of growth. All this is equally true of other people who cannot, just because we wish it, suddenly become different from what they are. Psychic reality,the inner constitution and organization of each individual mind, is highly resistant to change, and goes its own way much less influenced by the outer world than we like to think.
>
> Our conscious mental operations do not convey the full force of this stubborn durability of psychic reality, since it is relatively easy to change our ideas, to alter our decisions, to vary our pursuits and interests, and so on; but we can do all that without becoming very different basically as persons. Our mental life appears to be a freely adaptable instrument of our practical purposes in the outer material world, as no doubt it should be. The closer, however, we get to matters involving the hidden pressures of emotions, the more do we recognize the apparent intractability of psychic reality. The infatuated man cannot subdue his infatuation, the person who worries cannot stop worrying, the hyper-conscientious person who works to death cannot relax, the man with an irrational hate cannot conquer his dislike, the sufferer from bad dreams cannot decide not to have them. This is conspicuously the case with neurotic persons, who manifest a marked helplessness towards their own psychic reality and emotional life. (Guntrip [37], pp. 218–19.)

Although psychic reality is a Freudian concept, it becomes more important and significant through Melanie Klein's work, because it becomes the basis of identity rather than a sublimation of other primary impulses, or a mere defence mechanism for them, and because it introduces the concept of man living in 'two worlds at once' discussed above by Fairbairn.

This concept is, of course, bound up with Melanie Klein's second important concept – of *internal objects and their part in psychic structure* which we have already examined. Phantasied ego-object relations become internalised in such a way as to become 'embodied': although we see them as 'imaginary' in terms of real outward things, they are no longer 'imaginary' when they are taken into the psyche as permanent features of the organisation of an identity. They possess 'psychic reality', as we find when we try to change them, as if they were actually in the bodily being.

A mother 'introjected' thus may be far more terrible than any real mother could ever be. in one of Melanie Klein's child patients the 'introjected mother, whose role she enacted for me in many ways . . . exercised a harsher and more cruel influence upon her than any real mother had ever done . . . ' (Klein [46], p. 144).

We have seen how, according to Melanie Klein, the parents are internalised at the time when sadistic aggressive phantasies accompany the child's awareness of their mutual satisfaction. Because he is so 'bodily minded' the attacks the child makes in phantasy are in bodily terms. Because he is dependent upon his objects and cannot distinguish between phantasy and fact, he fears in consequence damaging his objects, with consequent retaliation upon himself. The result is profound anxiety. Clinically this means 'a neurosis is conceived as a repressed inner world of internal object-relationships constituting anxiety – or danger-situations of both a persecutory and depressive order, in which the ego launches phantasied attacks by oral, anal and ultimately genital means on its parent images, and fears retaliatory attacks in turn from them' (Guntrip [37], p. 221).

But in terms of our consideration of the role of phantasy in actual living, as in education or the arts, we need to take into account the effects of this world of internal objects on the reality sense. The impulse to make restitution (the reparative urge) normally helps the child to seek inward integration, with consequent development of the capacity to discover the reality of the outer world. If, however, anxiety is severe there may be a disturbance of this process:

> The child attaches to its imaginary objects not only feelings of hatred and anxiety but positive feelings as well. In doing this it withdraws them from its real objects, and if its relations to its imaginary objects are too powerful, both in a negative and a positive sense, it cannot adequately attach either its sadistic phantasies or its restitutive ones to its real objects, with the result that it undergoes disturbance of its adaptation to reality and of its object-relations. (Klein [45], p. 192).

As Winnicott indicates, a baby needs to discover the limits of its rage: a child who is unusually good may be suspected of having something gravely wrong with it. A child needs to exert both love and hate on its 'real objects' in order to find inner and outer reality. Out of its inward work towards integration the capacity to deal with the real world develops: as Guntrip says, the Kleinian picture is of the infantile mind in the first few years

> as the creation of a phantastic and intensely emotional internal world of bad, aggressive, destructive ego-object relations, counteracted by an equally phantastic inner world of ideally good-object relations, both more and more removed from realistic relationship with outer reality, yet increasingly influencing the child's and finally the adult's perception of outer reality, and hence behaviour towards it. (Guntrip [37], p. 222.)

Since 'work' in this inner world is done symbolically, we have here one clue to the link between creative imagination and behaviour, of great significance for education, culture, and ethics.

In therapy, the consequence of Kleinian theory is that neurosis is no longer to be seen as a phenomenon of disturbed emotions which can be relieved by abreaction, as was once believed. Neurosis is a phenomenon of pathological personality structure: the whole consciousness has grown organisationally disturbed. Thus neurosis is so hard to cure because it requires regrowth. 'Absolute cure would involve radical regraving of the total personality structure, if such a thing be possible' (Guntrip [37], p. 222).

In culture and education, if we accept Melanie Klein, we can no longer believe that imaginative experience contributes to living by enabling people to 'get things out of their system', or to gain insight by merely living through vicarious experiences, or that the imaginative experience of cruel, violent, obscene, or horrifying experiences can provide an 'outlet' or 'safety valve'. The truth is rather that a subtle dynamic process of constructive ordering and maintenance is continuously going on in the inner world, where reparative effort seeks to overcome threats of disruption. If phantasy material arouses great inward anxiety, it may be necessary for so much energy to be diverted to dealing with the inner world that there is a 'disturbance of adaptation to reality and of . . . object-relationships'.

As we know, this does happen with children when actual circumstances are distressing.

> In those cases in which the significance of reality and real objects as reflections of the dreaded internal world and images has retained its preponderance, the stimuli from the external world may be felt to be nearly as alarming as the phantasied domination of the internalized objects, which have taken possession of all initiative and to whom the ego feels compulsively bound to surrender the execution of all activities and intellectual operations. (Klein [46], p. 263.)

Here the implications for culture may well reverse the whole trend of our thinking, e.g. about 'necessary' or 'useful' violence in entertainment. Cannot something of the same happen to children who are exposed to symbolic phantasies which are calculated to *seem* real? Films and television often both seem to offer what is real: they can be used to make phantasies of horror, of sexual activity, and of violence seem 'real'. A child observes a news item on television followed by a play which contains brutal violence or sexual sadism. He cannot in any case so easily distinguish between reality and phantasy. Cannot such experiences be 'stimuli from the external world' which are felt to be 'nearly as alarming as the phantasied domination of the internalised objects'? And could they not contribute to a kind of 'surrender of initiative and the execution of . . . activities and intellectual operations'?

Could not a similar process in adults, by the arousing of inward anxieties in a sensational culture, lead to a disturbance of the reality sense? And, by contrast, does not genuine creative symbolism contribute to the development of powers of effectiveness in dealing with the outer world? Melanie Klein's theories, which suggest a delicate balance in the way we build bridges between inner and outer reality, should, I believe, make us think seriously, and with some alarm, about the increasing tendency in our culture, because of its commercial basis and consequent need to draw the attention of large numbers of people, to function often by provoking deep anxieties.* Do these not provoke in consequence the diversion of reparative effort away from 'real objects', and foster withdrawal from life? Is not this the effect of the increased proportion of schizoid art in our culture, with its exploitation of hate and its inversion of all values?

Melanie Klein's emphasis on the primary role of *phantasy* also makes for a complete reappraisal of the role of imaginative creativity in human life. This concept is of tremendous importance in a world which has come, because of its concentration on 'outer goodness', to develop contempt for 'inner solutions'. Melanie Klein's work has demonstrated that in a world which regards fantasy as 'unpractical', it is actually supremely impractical to fail to take into account the primary need of human beings for symbolism, and to see phantasy as primary to effective consciousness. As Guntrip says:

> Psychic Reality, and its structuring in terms of internal objects and internal object-relations, is made manifest in phantasy, of which day and night dreams and the play of children are the most clinically relevant examples. With these, however, we must link other forms of phantasy, the myths and legends of primitive peoples, folk-lore, and the imaginative creations of literature and art in all ages which together constitute a continuous revelation of the phantasy-life of the human race, and throw tremendous light on the workings of the Unconscious. All these taken together display an inventive, creative, imaginative activity of the human mind which is not, like science, concerned with the accurate portrayal of the outer material world by intellectual activity, but rather with an expression, every bit as accurate, of the inner mental world, the world of emotional events which forms the inner hard core of personality-functioning. The prosaic mind may dismiss all that as 'mere imagination' or as 'fantasy' or even as 'fantastic nonsense' and – to come back to our starting-point – dreams. The practical mind is apt to contrast 'hard facts' like money and guns with the 'useless' products of the imagination, 'such stuff as dreams are made of'. But the so-called hard-headed, practical man is usually just as helpless in face of emotional realities. His evaluation of the products of emotion involves a two-fold error. He believes that he is free from phantasies and dreams, whereas he is only unconscious of what goes on in his inner world and is phantasy-ridden without knowing it. This is usually discernible at least in such forms as confident prejudice and narcissistic self-evaluation. Further, he believes dreams and phantasies can be contrasted with hard facts as unreal, and dismissed as of no importance. But these same products

---

* At the time of writing a film has just been launched in which a woman becomes pregnant by the Devil. Such play on 'bad internalised object' phantasies inevitably has the effect of driving sensibility back to primitive fears and to the barbarism of irrationality, akin to that of the witch-hunting and other psychopathological horrors of Dark Ages of the past.

of imagination are themselves 'hard facts' in a psychological sense, of a peculiarly inescapable kind, having 'psychic reality'.

. . . [the] world of the imagination, which we cannot either eliminate or suppress, is the eruption of precisely that 'psychic reality' which Freud and Melanie Klein have so stressed, a psychological 'hard fact' which we are obliged to take into account. When it develops, as sometimes happens, to the full force of the disintegrating and even homicidal delusions of the insane we can no longer underestimate its power. (Guntrip [37], pp. 222–3.)

There are two relevant problems here: one is that political ideologies and scientific theories, as well as religious, artistic and literary manifestations may no less be the expression of an essentially subjective phantasy. The other is that there are problems still unsolved about the concept of *unconscious* phantasy. Guntrip seeks to approach it by defining phantasy as 'the form in which we express unconscious emotion when it becomes conscious'. But there would seem to be a state in which we were deeply disturbed, as by a child's accident in which he bleeds profusely, which has a distressing effect on us, as if it confirmed destructive phantasies which *we were already having*, but of which we were not conscious. What we have, perhaps is an 'active psychic structure' or dynamic, which *as soon as it takes conscious symbolic form* becomes a phantasy: until that moment it is a complex of embodied tensions, structures and proclivities. Guntrip seeks to explain it thus:

. . . The complex emotional state which would find expression, if it is expressed, in consciousness in a specific phantasy can be unconscious, but it would seem that phantasy is the form in which we express unconscious emotion when it becomes conscious. Phantasy is a psychic structure in action in consciousness, a conscious expression of the fact that our deep-down complex emotional and impulsive activity at the moment is the same as it would be if in outer reality we were having a relationship of a certain kind with persons of a certain kind, as imagined in the phantasy. This can be expressed only by a 'story' either 'seen' in the mind's eye, i.e. hallucinated, as in a dream, or consciously thought through as in day-dreaming. It is always a story of some form of ego-object relations in which the 'object' is imagined, and is in fact an 'internal object' in the sense already made clear. It seems preferable to say, then, that the primary content of the unconscious mental processes is an emotionally active psychic structure, and that phantasy is its emergence into consciousness. (Guntrip [37], p. 224.)

The fourth relevant concept from Melanie Klein is that of the existence in us of an *inner world* and this is of great relevance to culture and education. Imaginative works can be seen as symbolic dramatisations of this inner world. As Guntrip says:

If we consider a novel, say *Wuthering Heights*, an elaborate phantasy which has been given literary form and an existence independent of its creator, we see at once that a phantasy is a world inhabited by persons and its action consists in their relationships to one another. Such places as Wuthering Heights and such persons as Heathcliffe and Cathy and the other characters of the story have a tremendous vitality of their own, and make a powerful and living impact on us. If, now, we consider a phantasy in an unsophisticated form, in its immediate mental form as we see it in a disturbing dream that wakes us up while its action is still in progress in our minds, we recognize these same characteristics. The dream as we perceive and experience it *is*, so to speak, a place, and it *is* a number of people or animals or other figures in active relationships. So real is all this that the half-awake dreamer starts up and and looks about the room expecting to see the sinister figure who frightened him in his dream. The dream, at the moment of dreaming, has hallucinatory vividness and reality, though its reality lies in the fact that we are experiencing it as our own personality make-up in action, and not in its having outer material reality. (Guntrip [37], p. 224.)

The characters in a dream are schizoid divisions of our inward selves enacting a drama of intrapsychic energies: so, too, the characters and other symbolic entities, themes or preoccupations in a work of art relate to dynamics in the *inner world*:

Past aspects of our 'self' and our past objects of impulse and feeling live on inside us as a repressed unconscious present. To express it differently, the object-relationship situations of past years back to infancy, in which we were bound together with the important persons who were the chief objects of our needs and desires, loves and angers, have entered into our mental make-up, albeit elaborated and distorted by our own emotions as to the mental images we formed of them. They are preserved within us as dynamic parts of the hidden structure of our personality. They are endowed with psychic reality and that sense continue to exist long after the original real figures have materially ceased to be, as in vivid dreams of long dead parents. (Guntrip [37], p. 226.)

This *inner world* bears continually on our attitudes to and behaviour in the real outer world:

> We live in these two worlds at the same time, one mental and the other material, the one a perpetuation of the past and the other an exploration of the present, and we are involved in both of them in situations and relationships which rouse in us excitements, emotions and impulses of all kinds. It is impossible to keep the two worlds of outer and inner reality, of conscious and unconscious mental life, entirely separate. They interact and overlap in everything we do. If, however, the overlapping of outer by inner reality is too crude and uncontrolled, our perceptions of the outer world become badly distorted; and therefore our reactions to it become falsified in disturbing and even dangerous ways. (Guntrip [37], p. 226.)

From this it will seem obvious that cultural symbolism can contribute positively or negatively to the dynamics of the relationship between inner and outer life. We know this from a child's behaviour. If, for instance, we tease a child, by pretending there is a spider on his glove – if he is afraid of spiders – we may laugh, and show that the 'spider' was only, say, a tomato calyx. But we have aroused his anxiety – and he dare not now touch his glove because he feels it contains some danger which reflects a threat from something 'bad' within him. This is part magic, part symbolism: but not only symbolism, for the poison *is* now 'real' enough. Thus, obviously, culture can arouse in children and adults anxieties which require such inward attention that the relationship between inner and outer worlds becomes distorted or broken down.

As Guntrip says:

> Events in the outer world play upon, stir up and draw upon themselves projections of the phantasied events and situations that form parts and aspects of our inner world – often to our own and other people's exceeding discomfiture. Melanie Klein writes:
> The young child's perception of external reality and external objects is perpetually influenced and coloured by his phantasies, and this in some measure continues throughout life. External experiences which arouse anxiety at once activate even in normal persons anxiety derived from intrapsychic sources. The interaction between objective anxiety and neurotic anxiety – or, to express it in other words, the interaction between anxiety arising from external and from internal sources – corresponds to the interaction between external and psychic reality. (Guntrip [37], p. 226, quoting Klein [47], p. 289.)

Through cultural symbolism we continually build bridges between external and psychic reality. The implications of Melanie Klein's work is that it is possible for those bridges to be damaged or closed and for the capacity to deal with the outer world to be wrecked by a storm in the inner. These implications are further explored in the present writer's *The Masks of Hate*. There it is demonstrated how, by working at the unconscious level, it is possible for those working in commercial culture to 'activate even in normal persons anxiety derived from intrapsychic sources', and for this to be made the basis of mass appeal. Freudian 'hate' theory could be taken to be a vindication for this, wher as by Melanie Klein's kind of theory, based on a therapeutic 'loving' concern with children and their creative development, this misuse of symbolism is shown to be full of potential dangers. So, if we believe in the death instinct the dehumanising elements in our culture are excusable on the grounds that 'human nature is by nature like that'. If we reject it, such dehumanisation is exposed as an irresponsible and evil process undermining our potentialities and hope.

From the point of view of our investigation of the nature of symbolism in creative

expression we need here to note the light Melanie Klein casts on the diversity of phantasy·
It has been a marked limitation of Freudian theory that it has not been able to get far
beyond a reductive approach to art, as by 'explaining' *Hamlet* in terms of its Oedipal
symbolism. But in the light of psychodynamics, in which we see symbols as dramatising
endopsychic structures and situations, cultural theory must become less crude.

Melanie Klein indicates that the origin of the symbols in phantasy is earlier and their
nature is in consequence more complex. They are more complex because at the time
when earliest phantasies develop the child is only able to relate to *part objects*, and these
part objects are conceived in embodied terms, because the child experienced largely
bodily terms and cannot yet separate intellectual concepts and bodily life. Only gradually
do we come to be able to relate to whole persons: and the progress towards recognising
the object as a whole person *is* the creative problem, since it involves discovering oneself
as a whole person, too. This 'split libido' problem will also be explored further below.

Melanie Klein's theory emphasises the primary energy of the quest for integration in
us. This progress in adult life reflects the progress the infant made earlier in coming to
discover his mother as a whole person: 'We must presume that at first all the baby knows
or experiences is a breast (a "part-object") and that it takes time and development
for the baby to become aware of the mother in her completeness (a "whole-object")'
(Guntrip [37], p. 226).

Yet the 'part-object' symbolism persists in our adult consciousness, as we know from
our dreams:

> . . . we find the dream and hallucinatory experiences of adult patients 'peopled' not only with com-
> pletely personal figures, but also with 'part-objects' in the form of detached breasts, penises or bodily
> parts, or their symbolic representations in the form of animals or inanimate objects. Thus one patient,
> as she was dropping off to sleep would start wide awake as a result of the frightening experience of
> seeing a unattached penis coming at her. During her analysis she learned to drive a motor-car and
> then for a time she would see instead of a penis a motor-car rushing at her as she dozed off. That it
> represented the penis, however, was clear from the fact that in the act of starting awake she would find
> that she was clutching her vagina to protect herself. Several times in dreams the penis was represented
> by a snake or a rat on the bed, while one male patient saw himself in a dream attacked by a penis on
> which the glans had a rat's mouth and eyes. Here we see a series of graduated representations from the
> penis, through the penis-rat, the rat and snake, to the inanimate motor-car. A further series is indicated
> by the dream of yet another patient, who saw a breast with a penis instead of a nipple and on another
> occasion dreamed of a breast with a snake for a nipple. The resolution of a penis into a breast pure and
> simple as the part-object corresponding to the infant's earliest experience always occurs ultimately in
> any analysis that goes at all deep. It should be added that the so-called 'part-object' is not a part-
> object to the infant but a whole-object. It is only from the adult observer's point of view that we
> recognize that the infant's first object is only a part of the whole mother. (Guntrip [37], p. 227.)

Part-object symbolism also underlies the much more complex symbolism of serious
art, often combined with the symbolism of 'whole objects' and 'significant persons':

> As the infant's experience expands to the taking in of the whole of his mother, he does not necessarily
> lose his earlier partial mental representations of her. They lie under increasing repression, and in the
> unconscious at a later stage part-objects and whole-objects both exist in a psychically active way.
> Moreover, the whole-objects become more and more complex. Phantasied persons in the inner world,
> representing at bottom aspects of parents, become complicated by the addition of aspects of other
> early and later experienced significant persons. (Guntrip [37], p. 227.)

We should not then merely see the symbolism of a work of phantasy as relating to
autobiographical experiences: what is symbolised are the dynamics of 'internal objects'
combined with significant figures who have been identified with and introjected.

> The figures with whom we have relationships in our phantasies are called appropriately, by Melanie

Klein, 'internal objects' because we behave with respect to them, emotionally and impulsively, in the same ways as we do towards externally real persons, though in more violent degrees of intensity than would be socially permissible.

> . . . These internal 'parental' figures are not, of course, exact and truthful copies of the real parents. They represent dissociated aspects of parents and others seen through the medium of the baby's emotional experience of them. They are doubly falsified in that they are both partial, and also distorted by the baby's own feelings. An internal image of an angry parent has no redeeming features as the real parent had, and also it is built up in the baby's mind by his own emotional tensions into a monster or devil. One patient, in a nightmare, saw his mother's face, at first in its ordinary aspect, and then gradually growing redder, angrier, larger, more and more threatening, till it seemed to fill his world and overwhelm him in a volcanic eruption of accusing rage out of which shot the words: 'What have you done?' He woke with violent palpitation and profuse perspiration. In fact his mother was a much-enduring woman who worked hard to help him get an education while her husband was in a mental hospital. Yet the dream represented an intensification of one aspect of his actual experience of her. (Guntrip [37], p. 228.)

Moreover, the aspects of objects in phantasy may not be 'in' the original objects at all, but feelings from within projected over the object and then internalised:

> This inner world is for the most part a world of terrors. Its objects are built up, according to Melanie Klein, by projection and introjection. The baby, faced with an angry or unloving mother and a frustrating breast, projects his own anger on to the mother, and then introjects her, takes her in mentally, endowed with his own aggression as well as hers. Another way of putting this is to say that our expectations of other people's behaviour to us is greatly influenced by our fear that they will retaliate for the aggression we feel against them: and it is in this light that the infant internalizes parents. The unconscious inner world is people, at deep mental levels, by frightful persecutors who are exaggerated out of all realistic proportions into monsters, devils, sinister figures and wild beasts of the most violent kind, such as terrify us in nightmares and have been enshrined in myth and folk-lore from earliest times. All personal and sexual relationships in this deep unconscious inner world are of a sado-masochistic character. Even when our emotional reactions are evoked by events in our outer present-day world, the tone and intensity of the emotion is, to a far greater extent than is generally known, determined by our reactions to these 'bad' figures in the unconscious. This is why very emotional people so often behave unrealistically. (Guntrip [37], p. 228.)

As we have seen dealings with these internal objects hovers between persecutory anxiety, and then depressive anxiety when it begins to appear that the objects destroyed or attacked in phantasy are much-needed parents and love-objects. In detail, the attacks and counter attacks go on in phantasy which is embodied, as the infant's whole life is embodied (while his ego is a 'mouth-ego'):

> . . . all the biological possibilities open to the infant are made use of. Phantasies of tearing in pieces, sucking out, biting, eating, swallowing and devouring belong to the earliest oral level. A little later phantasies of destroying by urination and defecation occur, and later still sadistic versions of genital sexual destructiveness develop. These phantasies express what Melanie Klein calls the 'early anxiety-situations' of the infant. Thus one patient, a young married woman who had been exceptionally severely neglected by her mother as a child because afraid of a sudden impulse to strangle me, remembered she had always felt hungry as a child, and reported a dream in which a slimy black lizard came at her to eat her. She then went back to an incident of very early life which she had previously reported, namely an occasion when she had defecated in her cot and jumped out of it and run downstairs. She now added further details that she had looked at the black bits of excreta in the bed and suddenly felt they were alive and would eat her, and she climbed out of the cot in fear. Clearly the excreta represented to her bad internal objects that would retaliate on her, the terrifying internalized breast that would eat her because she wanted hungrily to eat it. This patient, who had never heard of Melanie Klein or of oral sadism, herself remarked: 'I wanted to eat everything as a child, I expect I wanted to eat my mother.' (Guntrip [37], p. 228.)

As Winnicott points out, the infant does in fact need to 'eat his mother' both physically and psychically and yet cannot do so without the inevitable penalties, in phantasy, of a fear of annihilating her, and himself in the process.

To overcome these fears, of wrecking the inner world and the outer world with it, we build our inward strength by *reparation*, and here again is a major concept of tremendous importance for culture – because if we accept this concept, then we accept that constructive altruistic effort, much of it symbolic, is, in culture, and indeed in social life, the foundation of viable human identity: 'An important aspect of Melanie Klein's views is that not only is anxiety always at bottom due to unconscious phantasied aggressive and destructive relationships, but also that anxiety and guilt over internal and external aggression is counteracted by reparative phantasies and activities. Injured love-objects must be restored and made whole again if the personality is to be at peace.'

For those of us concerned with culture and education the conclusions we must draw from Kleinian theory are of the greatest significance. One is that our sense of being human, and our effective dealings with the world depend upon what degree of order and 'goodness' we can achieve in the inner world. Man's inner life is primary and in this life symbolic reparation is the basis of his living power. As Fairbairn says:

> Indeed, it follows that human behaviour in general must be profoundly influenced by situations prevailing in the inner world. The fact is that, once the conception of inner reality has been accepted, every individual must be regarded as living in two worlds at the same time – the world of outer reality and the world of inner reality; and, whilst life in outer reality is characteristically conscious, and life in inner reality is characteristically unconscious, it will be realized that *Freud's original distinction between the conscious and the unconscious now becomes less important than the distinction between the two worlds of outer reality and inner reality.* (Fairbairn [19], p. 124.)

Melanie Klein's work leaves a number of concepts to be clarified, as we have seen. One is her complex view of the super-ego (which has become a confusing multiplicity of good and bad internal objects). This has been explored further by Fairbairn in his structural theory. Melanie Klein also makes the complexities of the inner world owe more to the projection and interjection processes of innate sadism (associated with the death instinct) than problems of *handling and management*, a bias corrected by Winnicott.

There is the major problem indicated by Lomas, 'love [for her] is not a spontaneous emotion but is based on a need to make reparation for aggressive wishes and phantasies'.

But the social and cultural implications of Melanie Klein's work are still much more hopeful than those of Freud. Yet her optimism has not yet prevailed at large over the pessimistic implications of Freudian theory, and its persistence in Kleinian thought round the concept of the death instinct.

Perhaps the best summary of her cultural and social implications is her own lecture, a paper given to the Departments of Social Anthropology and Social Studies in the University of Manchester in 1959, 'Our Adult World and its Roots in Infancy'. In this paper she summarises her work in popular terms, and in it she seeks to relate problems of the inner world to culture and society.

It is, she says, necessary in order to understand society which 'consists of individuals in relation to one another' to understand personality, for this understanding is the foundation for the understanding of social life. Since infancy is the time when development begins, she emphasises 'insights into the infantile mind and its connection with the mental processes of the adult'. She insists that 'mental life is influenced by earliest emotions and unconscious phantasies', and then outlines her theory in non-technical terms.

Melanie Klein begins with the hypothesis that the newborn baby experiences 'both in the process of birth and in the adjustment to the post-natal situation, *anxiety of a persecutory nature*'. 'This can be explained by the fact that the young infant, without being able to grasp it intellectually, feels unconsciously every discomfort as though it were inflicted on him by hostile forces'.

If comfort is given to him, this gives rise to 'happier emotions'. 'Such comfort is felt to come from good forces and, I believe, makes possible the infant's first loving relation to a person; or, as the psychoanalyst would put it, to an object.'

Melanie Klein sees that 'the unconscious of the mother and of the child [are] in close relation to each other' – a foresight of Winnicott's 'primary maternal preoccupation'. The child develops in this his first relationship in his life. But:

> At the same time frustration, discomfort and pain, which I suggested are experienced as persecution, enter as well into his feelings about his mother, because in the first few months she represents to the child the whole of the external world: *therefore both good and bad come in his mind from her, and this leads to a twofold attitude toward the mother even under the best possible conditions.* (Klein [50], p. 4.)

This ambivalence persists in later life. Because the capacity to love and the sense of persecution have roots in these primary processes. Hate arises from frustration,* and envy from the child's awareness of his dependence on the all-powerful object. Moreover, 'destructive impulses towards anybody are always bound to give rise to the feeling that that person will become hostile and retaliatory' (Klein [50], p. 4).

We have to take account, certainly, of destructive impulses which are *an integral part of mental life*, even in favourable circumstances. In everyone there is a perpetual struggle between love and hate.

The ego exists and operates from birth onwards, and has the important task of 'defending itself against anxiety stirred up by the struggle within and by influences without'. As we have seen, this is on the way to attributing an integrative function to the ego, by contrast with Freud's attribution to the ego of an adaptive function – which Melanie Klein clings to here, by her word 'defending'. But she also speaks of the ego being 'the *organised* part of the self', of it *maintaining the relation to the external world*, and of it including 'the whole of the personality', including the instinctual life – all significant departures from Freudian theory.

Introjection and projection function from the beginning of post-natal life:

> Introjection means that the outer world, its impact, the situations the infant lives through, and the objects he encounters, are not only experienced as external but are taken into the self and become part of the inner life. Inner life cannot be evaluated even in the adult without these additions to the personality that derive from continuous introjection. Projection, which goes on simultaneously, implies that there is a capacity in the child to attribute to other people round him feelings of various kinds, predominantly love and hate. (Klein [50], p. 5.)

Thus an inner world is built up which is partly a reflection of the external one, and this means continual interaction between external and internal factors.

> This interaction continues throughout every stage of life. In the same way introjection and projection go on through life and become modified in the course of maturation; but they never lose their importance in the individual's relation to the world around him. *Even in the adult, therefore, the judgement of reality is never quite free from the influence of his internal world.* (Klein [50], p. 6.)

At this point Melanie Klein quotes Susan Isaacs, who said: 'A phantasy represents the particular content of the urges or feelings (for example, wishes, fears, anxieties, triumphs, love or sorrow) dominating the mind at the moment.'

---

* At this point it is perhaps indicative that Melanie Klein attributes the origin of hate to problems arising in the environment and not to the death instinct, in this late paper, though she does in the next paragraph resort to the phrase 'innate aggressiveness . . .'.

F

> Unconscious phantasies are not the same as day-dreams (though they are linked with them) but
> an activity of the mind that occurs on deep unconscious levels and accompanies every impulse experi-
> enced by the infant. . . . Phantasies – becoming more elaborate and referring to a wider variety of
> objects and situations – continue throughout development and accompany all activities; they never
> stop playing a great part in mental life. The influence of unconscious phantasy on art, on scientific
> work, and on the activities of everyday life cannot be overrated. (Klein [50], p. 6.)

Object-relations start from the beginning, too. The mother is taken into the child's
inner world as a good and dependable object, and an element of strength is added to the
ego. Melanie Klein assumed that the ego develops largely round this good object,

> and the identification with the good characteristics of the mother become the basis for further helpful
> identifications. . . . A strong identification with the good mother makes it easier for the child to identify
> also with the good father and later on with other friendly figures. As a result his inner world comes
> to contain predominantly good objects and feelings, and these good objects are felt to respond to the
> infant's love. (Klein [50], p. 6.)

If such processes continue into adult life, we may here perhaps reflect on present-day
cultural trends.

Melanie Klein observes of the identifying process: 'All this contributes to a stable
personality and makes it possible to extend sympathy and friendly feelings towards
other people . . .' (Klein [50], p. 7) – linking good identifications, sympathy and that
gratitude which can overcome envy.

However good the child's feelings towards his parents, aggressiveness and hate remain,
as in the Oedipus situation, which Melanie Klein takes back, as we have seen, to very
early life. It is also complicated by identification of the boy with his father and the girl
with her mother, giving rise to elements of homosexuality in normal development
(explored by Winnicott later in examining male and female aspects in the identity.)

Projection, Melanie Klein urges, is different from identification. The latter involves
taking aspects of others into oneself: projection is putting yourself in the other person's
shoes. This can lead to insights into their feelings, needs and satisfactions. But 'if projection is predominantly hostile, real empathy and understanding of others is impaired'.
So to 'lose oneself in another' is to become incapable of objective judgement, and so on.
'If the interplay between introjection and projection is not dominated by hostility or
overdependence, and is well balanced, the inner world is enriched and the relations with
the external world are improved' (Klein [50], p. 7).

Melanie Klein then turns to splitting – the need, under duress of persecutory anxiety –
to keep the loved object separate from the dangerous 'bad' one, and so to split love from
hate. The infant can only keep alive in the face of ambivalence (which he cannot tolerate)
by clinging to the good object and his capacity to love it. 'This is an essential condition
for keeping alive, for without at least some of this feeling, he would be exposed to an
entirely hostile world which he fears would destroy him. This hostile world would also
be built up inside him.'

Fairbairn was to develop this area and to postulate the infant's need from the beginning
to be 'convinced that he is loved for his own sake'. Failure here may mean the failure to
become a person at all, or may even mean actual death by inanition. But survival
does not depend upon mere external factors. As Melanie Klein says:

> There are, as we know, babies in whom vitality is lacking and who cannot be kept alive, probably
> because they have not been able to develop their trusting relation to a good mother. By contrast, there
> are other babies who go through great difficulties but retain sufficient vitality to make use of the help
> and food offered by the other. I know of an infant who underwent a prolonged and difficult birth and

was injured in the process, but when put to the breast, took it avidly . . . other infants in such circum-stances are not able to survive because they have difficulties in accepting nourishment and love, which implies that they have not been able to establish trust and love towards the mother. (Klein [50], p. 8.)

Here there are important bearings on cultural and moral problems. Where things go wrong at birth and in early nurture in individuals we may have the development of attitudes to life in them *which are their only means to survive*. Mere survival itself may demand splitting or (as Fairbairn was later to suggest in his analysis of the schizoid mentality) *the substitution of hate for love*. These are really false strategies of survival. Because such manifestations are a matter of life and death, of the very survival of the identity, those whose minds function in this way must seek to preserve their splits and reversed relationships with the world *at all costs*: hence the energy, tenacity, and ruthless cunning of schizoid individuals whose inverted values and destructive or self-destructive impulses have all the false vitality of a hold on life which is yet a drive to death. Here, indeed, we have what can be called a 'death impulse'.

The destructive impulses at the paranoid-schizoid stage are associated by Melanie Klein with greed and envy: 'There is no doubt that greed is increased by anxiety – the anxiety of being deprived, of being robbed, and of not being good enough to be loved' (Klein [50], p. 8).

This kind of greed indicates a failure of the early complex between mother and child. The breast is never enough:

As soon as the gratification is gone, he becomes dissatisfied and is driven to exploit first of all the mother and soon everybody in the family who can give him attention, food or any other gratifica-tion. . . . The infant who is so greedy for love and attention is also unsure about his own capacity to love; and all these anxieties reinforce greed. This situation remains in fundamentals unchanged in the greed of the older child and of the adult (Klein [50], p. 8.)

Here we can make many social and cultural deductions. In the cultural sphere Freudian hedonistic theory vindicates these impulses: to Melanie Klein they manifest failures of processes of growth, and impulses of envy and hate.

Envy, related to greed, arises from the feeling, at inevitable frustrations, that the mother is keeping the milk for herself. This can be exacerbated by the sadistic feelings a child has over his parents' mutual satisfaction. In life it becomes

a strong urge to spoil other people's enjoyment of the coveted object – an urge which tends to spoil the object itself . . . nothing can be fully enjoyed because the desired thing has already been spoiled by envy.
. . . if envy is strong, goodness cannot be assimilated, becomes part of one's inner life and so gives rise to gratitude. (Klein [50], p. 9.)

This spoiling impulse can, of course, be found in culture.

To feel gratitude towards the mother, for sustaining one's life, is a means towards being able to feel gratitude towards others and to free oneself from the undermining forces of resentment and envy. Such developments go with integration of the inner world:

In normal development, with growing integration of the ego, splitting processes diminish, and the increased capacity to understand external reality, and to some extent to bring together (these) contra-dictory impulses, leads also to a greater synthesis of the good and bad aspects of the object. This means that people can be loved in spite of their faults, and that the world is not seen only in terms of black and white. (Klein [50], p. 9.)

Melanie Klein then speaks of how she came to see the 'depressive position' as a normal part of development. The infant cannot distinguish between his desires and impulses and their actual effect, so when he is possessed by destructive and greedy impulses he becomes afraid of the harm these might do, or might have done, to his loved objects. So he is urged to 'make reparation for harm done'. This kind of guilt is the valuable basis of dynamic conscience, and is the foundation of a 'healthy moral sense'.

The implications of this on child rearing are that parents must strive to keep a balance between too much and too little discipline. If there is excessive indulgence,

> while the child may take advantage of his parents' attitude, he also experiences a sense of guilt about exploiting them and feels a need for some restraint which would give him security. This would also make him able to feel respect for his parents, which is essential for a good relation towards them and for developing respect for other people. Moreover, we must also consider that parents who are suffering too much under the unrestrained self-expression of the child – however much they submit to it – are bound to feel some resentment which will enter into their attitude towards the child. (Klein [50], p. 11.)

The application of this to education will be obvious: the child benefits if adults behave as adults in lessening his guilt about exploiting adults, while more 'free expression' in education or the home may only make children insecure and adults resentful. There are implications for creativity at large. Mere 'self-expression' in the absence of 'good relationship' based on a meeting of the disciplines of symbolism and of response to symbolism, makes only for dissociation of the creative function – insecurity in the artist and resentment in the spectator, because the situation disallows reparative collaboration. The breakdown of responsibility between artist and audience in our time reduces reparative, and so creative, possibilities.*

Indeed, Melanie Klein's theory vindicates many traditional concepts of relationship between individuals in a creative situation, while implicitly condemning 'free self-expression' based on a romantic belief in 'letting off steam', or the freeing of a 'natural' man, or 'sensuality' in 'release', or 'acts of insurrection' merely. Positive identifications are important – and so every individual has a great responsibility for his own conduct and expression because others need to identify with him in a positive way:

> At every stage the ability to identify makes possible the happiness of being able to admire the character or achievements of others. If we cannot allow ourselves to appreciate the achievements and qualities of other people – and that means we are not able to bear the thought that we can never emulate them – we are deprived of sources of great happiness and enrichment. . . . Such admiration also stirs up something in us and increases indirectly our belief in ourselves. (Klein [50], p. 12.)

Here we may reflect on our present-day culture which offers us so few positive identifications, and is inclined to reject the concept of reparation altogether, in favour of a ruthless ambitiousness which finds its vindication in pseudo-scientific theories of man's natural animal aggression. The ethos of our culture is based on manic acquisitiveness so that identity becomes attached to a symbolism of magic and envy, while our whole environment is deficient in opportunities for truly creative reparation, including opportunities for experiencing the painful problems of loss and guilt necessary for satisfaction. Melanie Klein here indicates how right Buber was in suggesting that our culture inhibits us in 'confronting the problem of existence'.

One major element in the symbolism to which we attach identity is, of course, ambition. Ambition Melanie Klein associates with anxious greed. 'There is no doubt that ambition gives impetus to achievement but, if it becomes the main driving force, cooperation with others is endangered. The highly ambitious person, in spite of all his successes, always remains dissatisfied, in the same way as a greedy baby is never satisfied.' (Klein [50], p. 13.)

* See *The Masks of Hate*, pp. 161–176 especially.

As we shall see, this can be put in a different way in terms derived from thinkers who have followed: ours is a world in which the bustling external activities of 'false male doing' are preferred to the quest for 'being'.

Melanie Klein's final emphasis is on the need for the pursuit of richness to be an inner concern to establish 'inner goodness' by sincerity and integrity. If her terms sound unfamiliar or old-fashioned, then this is a comment on a world which disastrously neglects, in its social life and culture, the deep realities with which her theory and therapeutic work were concerned – in a far more penetrating way than Freud, whose essential hedonism is widely taken to vindicate the abrogation of genuine provision for inner creative needs:

> One consequence of a balanced development is integrity and strength of character. Such qualities have a far-reaching effect both on the individual's self-reliance and on his relations to the outside world. The influence of a really sincere and genuine character on other people is easily observed. Even people who do not possess the same qualities are impressed and cannot help feeling some respect for integrity and sincerity. For these qualities accuse in them a picture of what they might themselves have become or perhaps even still might become. Such personalities give them some hopefulness about the world in general and greater trust in goodness. (Klein [50], p. 14.)

As Melanie Klein concludes: 'The effect of a good character on others lies at the root of healthy social development.'

The social implications of Melanie Klein's positive approach to the human need for opportunities to make reparation, and to feel inner strength from this, are well expressed in this passage from the book in which she collaborated with Joan Rivière on *Love, Hate and Reparation*:

> It seems . . . that we may be nearing the point at which external goodness – prosperity and material gains – will have taken the place of internal goodness as an ideal . . . the inner life of man may come into contempt. . . . Our need to love, as the strongest security against the anxiety of hate and destructiveness within, together with the problems of guilt which are inseparable from love, and the standards of conscience and morality that spring from our guilt, all suffer from neglect, are denied, and may starve in their turn though material prosperity increase. Klein and Rivière [51].)

Already, in 1968, this sounds almost quaintly old-fashioned, so severely have moral standards and attitudes to human needs been subjected to demoralisation and dehumanisation based on assumptions that our 'animality' is more real than those 'inner needs' which Melanie Klein helped to make pre-eminent in psychoanalytical thinking. Melanie Klein's 'realism' about hate and aggression, as we have seen, is of a very different order from that of popular views based on animal behaviour.

It will by now be obvious to the reader that if we accept the work of Melanie Klein we must revise our whole model of human nature. Indeed, revision becomes necessary as soon as we accept object-relations theory, since the theory of development evolved by Melanie Klein, which is one of ego-development by environmental object-relations, and is not directly reconcilable with what she took over from Freud, whose psychopathology rests on a theory of *ego-development by hereditary predestination*. As Guntrip says (in a review of *Introduction to the Work of Melanie Klein* by Hannah Segal): 'Melanie Klein, dealing directly with the fantasy life at its source in early childhood, showed that it reveals the structure and working of personality and neurosis . . . her internal object-relations discoveries demanded a consistently psychodynamic ego theory, a theory of man as a personal self' (Guntrip [113]).

In this theory (a) there is a real ego at birth and (b) 'instincts are by definition object-seeking'.

But the chief stumbling block to revision is the concept of the death instinct:

> (Hannah Segal) overlooks the fact that this cannot be true of the death instinct, which by definition does not seek a proper relationship but the destruction of the object. Clinical experience is pushing the Kleinians towards a type of theory from which the 'death instinct' holds them back. If there be a death instinct there cannot be a properly whole ego at birth, nor can object-seeking be the basic nature of our instinctive endowment. Segal raises questions about the death instinct which she does not face. This remains the crucial issue. (Guntrip [113], p. 259.)

Hannah Segal, in summarising Melanie Klein's theory, does not see the death instinct as created out of unsatisfactory experiences in object relations in real life, 'a view which would make clinically verifiable sense.' Instead, it is taken over from dogma: 'Kleinian "metapsychology" is an inverted pyramid resting on an insubstantial apex, the concept of a "death instinct", the most speculative and subjectively determined of all Freud's ideas' (Guntrip [113], p. 259).

The origins of mechanisms of the splitting off of 'bad' aspects of experience, according to this Kleinian theory, begin with the fear of one's own death instinct: '[The ego] has from the beginning a tendency towards integration. At times, under the impact of the death instinct and intolerable anxiety, this tendency is swept away. . . . Faced with the anxiety produced by the death instinct . . . the ego splits itself and projects that part of itself which contains the death instinct outwards' (Guntrip [113], p. 259).

This theory, in which everything begins with the ego's fear of its own death instinct, Guntrip pronounces merely another version of the dogma of 'original evil', strictly parallel to the theologian's dogma of 'original sin' – for it is a wish to believe that 'Human nature contains an enormously powerful innate destructive force which is anti-social and anti-libidinal'.

If this is so, then the experience of objects, and the capacity for relating to others and the world as objects, becomes split because of man's nature and not because of environmental accident or intrapsychic stress. The influence of the environment is only secondary. Yet clinical experience seems to Guntrip to verify that 'bad and good object phantasy life arises out of the infant's difficulties in dealing with his real outer world'.

If Kleinian dogma were correct, then in therapy 'we are up against fixed and final limits to what can be achieved' because 'one cannot analyse the death instinct'. 'If it existed, it would be an ultimate and ineradicable datum. . . . '

Melanie Klein's work does not yet release us from this attitude altogether and, as Lomas says, she does not 'bridge the gap between the Freudian and the existential point of view'. But from Freud's postulation of the dynamics within the psychic structure came her object-relations psychology – and the investigation of ego-splitting: so that after 1920 and in recent theory more complex dynamic processes take the place of impulse control as the centre of interest. This also means an increasing concern with the schizoid processes themselves – that is, with earlier problems relating to the forming of an identity and the capacity to relate, beneath the depressive problems: 'The "depressive" diagnosis fixes our attention on our badness, the "schizoid" diagnoses on our weakness: a frightening change of emphasis' (Guntrip [116], p. 99).

That this development is 'frightening' explains why, although psychoanalytical theory has developed so rapidly towards object-relations dynamics, it is still dogged (as in Kleinian theory) by anachronisms such as the concept of the death instinct. It explains, too, why the world of popular thought at the journalistic and best-seller level prefers to stick to Freudian theory, and to the belief in man's essential beastliness.

As we shall see, one major human problem is that of the attractiveness of the false solutions of hate as in our cultural preoccupation with the heroics of 'exaggerated abnormality'. Exaggerated abnormality at least solves the terrifying problem of weakness for a time, in a false way. By contrast, in the light of theories which developed beyond Melanie Klein, true solutions can only be found in that 'creative reparation' that seeks our true nature and which accepts that mature independence which accepts the need for dependence. As we shall see, the paradox is that to a mentally ill person the hate-solution of his or her own 'badness' can seem to be life and identity itself. But there is something of this same false solution tendency manifest in Kleinian theory by which the psychodynamic forces making for identity and life are felt not to be adequately explained unless there is included in the scheme an innate impulse towards destruction and death. In theory this kind of self-deception is one which manifests a need to deny dependence.

Fairbairn's achievement was to penetrate these human self-deceptions still further.

CHAPTER 11

Love and the Structure of Personality
The Theories of W. R. D. Fairbairn

WE HAVE already seen that Fairbairn's approach to human psychology, following Melanie Klein, finds primary those processes which belong to the inner world and to the sphere of symbolism and meaning. Thus Fairbairn is prepared, as Guntrip says, in a way Freud was not, 'to allow for the existence of a normal cultural, and . . . religious experience . . . '.

Of a particular case ('Notes on the Religious Phantasies of a Female Patient', 1927) Fairbairn says: 'It is plain that we are not here dealing with the normal religious experience of the devout person orientated in reality, but with experiences of an unusual and grandiose character in which the imagination has been exalted at the expense of the facts of real life . . . an actual dramatisation within the individual of the themes underlying the religious experience' (Fairbairn [19], p. 188).

This patient's religiosity was psychopathological: yet it was a manifestation of the 'terrific power resident in the primary need and search of the human child for a good father' (Guntrip [59], p. 255). On this case history of Fairbairn's, Guntrip comments: 'So overpowering was this need for good-object relationship that it seized possession of the patient's entire life, world and available energy, ultimately destroying her physical existence in its utterly uncompromising struggle to gain satisfaction' (Guntrip [37], p. 255).

This paper of Fairbairn's was written before Melanie Klein's work. The patient in question never knew her father because her parents separated soon after her birth: her whole life was a quest for a father, and she eventually died after uttering two significant phrases: 'Perhaps I shall marry father' (after a dream) and 'I want a man'.

Since the woman became a fanatical devotee of masturbation, tormented by mingled erotic and religious hallucinations, it seemed to Fairbairn then (while his thinking was still based on Freud) that she may have died from sexual frustration: 'Can she have been said to have died of unsatisfied sexual desire? Or did she die of masturbation? Or did she kill herself by means of repression?' (Fairbairn [19], p. 196).

These answers seemed equally unsatisfactory, and what eventually emerged in Fairbairn's thought according to Guntrip's summary was the conclusion that: 'So basic is the object-relations need that a human being can even die in consequence of the complete frustration of the primary libidinal need for a basic (parental) good-object relationship during the development period' (Guntrip [37], p. 254).

As we have seen, Melanie Klein postulates something of the same, in suggesting that a failure in object-relations between mother and baby can bring about a loss of urge to live. In this patient's symptoms it was possible to see 'phases of her tortured personal, emotional and sexual need for this vital object-relation' (Guntrip). There was also a schizoid failure to distinguish between phantasy and reality: yet the implication of the passages from Fairbairn above are that the kind of religious experience which was psychopathologically disturbed by such elements is by no means itself a mere sublimation. There could have been a natural religious experience ('an expression of human nature as rooted in the primary need for good personal relationship') which could have found natural channels had it not been for the earliest deprivation.

So, Guntrip concludes, Fairbairn's point of view becomes one from which 'human behaviour in art, marriage, sport, hobbies, money-making and even science – in short, any and every form of human behaviour – can be similarly affected by . . . motivation (that can be studied psychoanalytically)'. But, at the same time, '*it is clear that there is more to be said than psychoanalysis can say*, especially with reference to religion. Freud and most psychoanalysts have used psychoanalytical considerations simply to explain away. Fairbairn uses psychoanalytical considerations as one factor among others in helping to determine the nature and function of religion in human life' (Guntrip. [37], p. 256).

This is an important and significant direction in psychology for those concerned with education and the arts.

Some of Fairbairn's earliest papers were on art and aesthetics, revealing a desire to work out a psychology of art, and from this concern with human meaning comes his contribution to the existentialist direction in psychoanalytical thought.

In his book *Psychoanalytical Studies of the Personality* Fairbairn typically both gives us his major papers over the years and gives an account of how his thought developed. Guntrip points out now, even as early as 1929, Fairbairn was beginning to question the orthodoxy of Freudian insistence that the primary libidinal urge was sexual. One can see from this how, when he came upon the work of Melanie Klein, he would find her sympathetic:

> One cannot help feeling that Freud would have been better advised to describe the satisfaction which the child derives from sucking as 'sensuous' (i.e. 'of the senses') rather than as 'sexual'. All pleasure afforded by the satisfaction of appetites is essentially sensuous pleasure, whatever the nature of the appetite concerned. Since the fundamental activities of the infant are all appetitive, the satisfaction derived from their indulgence may be described as sensuous. To call it sexual, as Freud does, involves a mistaken narrowing of the conception concerned. The truth seems to be that in infancy sensuous satisfaction is undifferentiated. . . . For similar reasons the 'libido' should be regarded as the biological life-impulse, from which, in individual development, the sex-instinct is differentiated, rather than as something strictly sexual from the start. Freud, however, regards the libido as sexual from the outset, because the adult sex-instinct develops from it. (*Edinburgh Medical Journal*, June 1929, p. 540.)

Here already we see the origins of a challenge to the confusions arising out of Freud's broadening of the term 'sexual' until it became the mystical entity 'Eros'. Fairbairn was henceforth to develop the theme that '*sex is but one form of libidinal experience, and the way in which an individual uses his sexuality as depending upon his character and personality as formed by his experience in object-relations*' (Guntrip [37], p. 259).

Also we see here the beginnings of Fairbairn's attention to the child, and his insight into the immensity of the infant's psychic achievements – an area of perception in which his work complements that of Melanie Klein and Winnicott, and commends itself to the attention of those concerned with education and creativity.

Indeed, in Fairbairn's work one is deeply impressed by the way in which, even from the dense and closely organised argument about theory, a significant picture emerges

of the child and his deepest emotional needs at the centre of the whole preoccupation.
One glimpses from time to time the perplexed, courageous, life-seeking human animula –
as one does so marvellously from the writing of Winnicott. It is this essential act of imaginative insight which has led these writers to the deepest problems of being and identity,
so they can offer so much to those concerned with creativity. This focus also brings their
work to be centred more in the normal and positive than in the psychopathological.
It thus escapes the morbidity of so much psychoanalytical theory derived from the
experience of psychoneurotic adult patients and from compulsive self-inquiry, such as
that of Freud himself. Fairbairn's work never loses its warm contact with 'the person',
with the child within the adult, nor with the origins of the personal life, in the crucial
mother–child relationship: 'The greatest need of a child is to obtain conclusive assurance
(*a*) that he is genuinely loved as a person by his parents (*b*) that his parents genuinely
accept his love. . . . Frustration of his desire to be loved as a person and to have his love
accepted is the greatest trauma that a child can experience' (Fairbairn [19], p. 39).

One is therefore sympathetically drawn to Fairbairn because, even in the harshest
rigours of his disciplined argument, with all its independent Scottish severity, he never
loses sight of the essential human truth that within each of us lurks the weak and frightened child, representing those aspects of the personality whose growth processes have
never completed themselves. In various degrees, though this aspect of our inward creature
urgently seeks to become mature, it cannot escape proclivities for infantile dependence,
and cannot find its way to the 'mature dependence' of the adult on 'the object', the love
partner, which assures support to the fulfilment-seeking identity. His persistent humane
concern with how this unfulfilled child-self disturbs the inner world of the adult brings
Fairbairn to draw attention to the deepest problems of all, which is to say the earliest
problems of all – that is, schizoid problems originating in the first few months of life,
which seem to him to underlie all personality disorders. In that all these disorders are
found in all of us to one degree or another, he thus illuminates a universal aspect of
human nature and, if we can absorb it into our thinking, it helps illuminate many
aspects of our cultural, imaginative life, and the relation of these to living.

To absorb his theories once more requires considerable effort of re-examining assumptions and of making ourselves familiar with new concepts: the reward, however, is to
escape from the kind of preoccupations with causality and culpability, moralising versus
demoralising, such as are aroused by Freud's preoccupation with the libidinal sexual
basis of human motivation. That is, we shall have much less difficulty over sex and in
relating these psychoanalytical concepts to cultural matters than we have when we are
discussing, say, Freudian concepts which, in so far as they concern libidinal impulses
and erotogenic zones, tend to focus our attention on 'sexual reality', and thus tend to
provoke a conflict over responsibility and causality. The value of Fairbairn's work is that
he implies that preoccupations with 'functions' themselves (as with 'sexual urges') can
be something of a disguise of deeper and more primary problems of identity and relationship. As we shall see, for him the erotogenic zones and the genitals are less primary as
foci for the pleasurable satisfaction, goals for the libidinal impulses, than (natural)
pathways for the primary quest of the 'individual in his libidinal capacity' *for an object*,
to whom to relate. '*The ultimate goal of the libido is the object*': this sentence of Fairbairn's,
if we accept it, must prove one of the most significant ever written in psychoanalytical
theory.*

* Fairbairn later altered it to read '. . . of the individual in his libidinal capacity . . .'.

The crucial paper in Fairbairn's *œuvre* is his attempt to establish the aetiology (a theory of the origins) of schizoid factors in the personality. Fairbairn's paper derives from his own observations of patients with severe schizoid problems, the origins of which seemed to be earlier than those of patients with depressive problems. As Fairbairn says, these schizoid processes seemed to him (in 1940) to provide the most interesting and fruitful material in the whole field of psychopathology.

Before giving an account of this crucial paper on schizoid problems, however, I would first like to examine a more general statement from a later chapter, 'A Synopsis of the Development of the Author's Views Regarding the Structure of the Personality' (Fairbairn [19], p. 162). This will help us to begin to think about the origins of the personality in his modes rather than in those of largely Freudian psychology to which we are habitually accustomed.

As we have seen, perhaps the most important question in object relations psychology is that of the origins of aggression. Melanie Klein established the importance of aggression in the make-up of the infant and the part aggression plays in the baby's phantasy – and consequently in his psychic growth. Where does this hate come from? As we have seen, the Kleinians still cling to the death instinct as the ultimate origin of 'innate' hate. But there is a clash between classical Freudian theory, clinical experience, and theory which arises from the observation of those like Winnicott who can see enough evidence to postualte hate as frustrated love, about which something can be done by 'good management', rather than as a savage innate propensity, which must then be pessimistically accepted as a natural aspect of animal man about which we can do little except seek to 'control' it or put up with it.

Fairbairn finds hate to be a consequence of the inevitable realities of the formative relationship between mother and baby. Aggression and hate arise gradually through inevitable 'flaws' in this relationship:

> I do not consider that the infant directs aggression spontaneously towards his libidinal object in the absence of some kind of frustration; and my observation of the behaviour of animals confirms this view. It should be added that in a state of nature the infant would never normally experience that separation from his mother which appears to be imposed upon him increasingly by the conditions of civilisation. (Fairbairn [19], p. 110.)

That is, if it were never frustrated (an impossible state of affairs in reality) a baby has no natural innate impulse to aggression directed towards his mother which must, somehow, be released, or else sublimated.

> Indeed, it may be inferred that in a state of nature it would be rare for the infant to be deprived of the shelter of his mother's arms and of ready access to her breast until, in the ordinary course of development, he himself became increasingly disposed to dispense with them. Such perfect conditions are, however, only theoretically possible for the human infant born into a civilised cultural group; and in actual fact the libidinal relationship of the infant to his mother is disturbed from the first by a considerable measure of frustration. (Fairbairn [19], p. 110.)

Aggression arises from this frustration.

Since the word 'libidinal' was commonly used earlier in psychoanalysis to mean 'sexual desire', we need here to emphasise that it is used by Fairbairn rather to mean 'vital impulse' or 'life energy'. We must also take care to see that Fairbairn regards the goal of this impulse to be 'the object' – that is, relationship with another – at this stage the mother. Aggression, Fairbairn considers, 'does not appear capable of being resolved into libido', and so aggression must be in itself a 'primary dynamic factor'. But he regards it as 'subordinate' to libido and 'essentially representing a reaction on the part of the infant to deprivation and frustration in his libidinal relationships – *and more particularly to the trauma of separation from his mother*' (Fairbairn [19], p. 172; my italics).

Inevitably, of course, all babies suffer the sense of frustration and separation as they come to discover their separate identity and find they cannot 'control' the mother, and so become what Winnicott calls 'disillusioned'. But, as inevitably, the distress this causes engenders in all, to greater or lesser degree, aggression, and raises the problem of ambivalence – and of splitting. Fairbairn's account of the processes by which this arises seem more developed and more convincing than those of Melanie Klein:

> It is . . . the experience of libidinal deprivation and frustration that originally calls forth the infant's aggression towards his libidinal object and so gives rise to ambivalence. At this point the subjective aspect of ambivalence becomes important; for to the ambivalent infant the situation presents itself as one in which his mother functions as an ambivalent object. (Fairbairn [19], p. 172.)

Here we have a theoretical shorthand summarising a great deal of torment and confusion in the unformed consciousness of the baby, experienced as it is rediscovered in the regression of adult patients during therapy sessions. Here we need to remind ourselves that at the stages here being described the infant develops his phantasy life out of his deep bodily feelings, while the conceptual capacities he is developing out of his phantasy powers are very rudimentary (he cannot separate thought things from bodily things). His sensitive and acute bodily life focuses on his mouth, and his mouth is his contact from time to time with his mother's breast, and in this a source of the beginnings of social and personal relationships. From this contact he begins to develop rudimentary awarenesses of his dependence on the mother, not yet associated with any adequate of his difference from her, but experiencing deprivation and frustration which must press upon him gradually the predicament of being 'other'.

Certainly what would be intolerable in this situation is a mother on whom life and well-being depends who is capable of confusing and confounding love and hate – that is who is in a state of ambivalence. Since he is uncertain as to what is *me* and what is *not-me*, how is a baby able to cope with these complex circumstances of frustration as they break into his consciousness? His mother *must* frustrate him in order to live her separate life – as in answering the door, or when she is tired and has had enough, or puts him down too hastily. We have all, at some time or other, faced this intolerable prospect of having presented to us the situation in which the mother 'functions as an ambivalent object'. Out of his confusion, and in the dim perception of the unreliability and insecurity of his situation the baby fears loss of identity.

So, when the mother fails to satisfy the libidinal needs, this situation

> imposes a severe strain upon his capacity for endurance . . . being a situation in outer reality, it is one which he finds himself impotent to control, and which, accordingly, he seeks to mitigate by such means as are at his disposal. . . . He . . . follows the only path open to him and, since outer reality seems unyielding, he does his best to transfer the traumatic factor in the situation to the field of inner reality, within which he feels situations to be more under his own control. This means that he internalizes his mother as a 'bad' object. (Fairbairn [19], p. 110.)

Fairbairn puts this process elsewhere in a slightly different form:

> To ameliorate this intolerable situation, he splits the figure of his mother with two objects – a *satisfying* ('good') object and an *unsatisfying* ('bad') object; and with a view to controlling the unsatisfying object; he employs the defensive process of internalization to remove it from outer reality, where it offers prospects of being more amenable to control in the form of internal object. (Fairbairn [19], p. 172.)

There are differences here, we may note, between various theories on this early introjection – differences which suggest that there is a great deal more yet to be discovered about this area of experience. Melanie Klein, who first emphasised the importance of processes of introjection in the infant psyche, considered that the child took into its inner world both the 'good' and the 'bad' object.

Fairbairn differs from Melanie Klein in believing that there is no need for the infant to internalise the 'good object':

> In my opinion, it is always the 'bad' object (i.e. at this stage the unsatisfying object) that is internalized in the first instance; for I find it difficult to attach any meaning to the primary internalization of a 'good' object which is both satisfying and amenable from the infant's point of view. There are those, of course, who would argue that it would be natural for the infant, when in a state of deprivation, to internalize the good object on the wish-fulfilment principle; but, as it seems to be, internalization of objects is essentially a measure of coercion and it is not the satisfying object, but the unsatisfying object, that the infant seeks to coerce. (Fairbairn [19], pp. 110–11.)

Later, however, Fairbairn modified this view to include the concept of a pre-ambivalent stage, when the 'good and bad objects have not yet been separated in the infant mind'. As Guntrip puts this:

> Rather it must be the pre-ambivalent object that is at first internalized, for the reason that, while it is in some measure satisfying, it is also in some measure unsatisfying, which creates the need to internalize it in an attempt to make it more satisfactory, i.e. to deal with the problem 'in the mind' because it cannot be dealt with in outer reality. Only after internalization is it split into a good object and a bad object in the inner phantasy world and therewith ambivalence arises. The good object is then desired, while the bad object is hated and rejected. (Guntrip [37] p 296.)

Fairbairn himself, however, takes the process even further: for, as he says, it is not only that the bad object is 'hated and rejected'. From his exploration of schizoid problems he knew that manifestations of hate are, as it were, reversed attempts to discover love. So, since the 'bad' object is internalised in an attempt to coerce it, *it also becomes desired*. (Here there are many cultural and social implications.)

> I speak here of 'the satisfying object' and 'the unsatisfying object', rather than of 'the good object' and 'the bad object', because I consider that, in this connection the terms 'good object' and 'bad object' tend to be misleading. They tend to be misleading because they are liable to be understood in the sense of 'desired object' and 'undesired object' respectively. There can be no doubt, however, that a bad (viz. unsatisfying) object may be desired. Indeed it is just because the infant's bad object is desired as well as felt to be bad that it is internalized. The trouble is that it remains bad after it has been internal ized, i.e. it remains unsatisfying (Fairbairn [19], p. 111.)

This situation produces a really terrifying situation of complex ambivalence.

> The unsatisfying object has . . . two facets. On the one hand, it frustrates; and, on the other, it tempts and allures. Indeed its essential 'badness' consists precisely in the fact that it combines allurement with frustration. Further, it retains both these qualities after internalization. After internalization the unsatisfying object, the infant finds himself in the quandary of 'out of the frying pan into the fire'. In his attempts to control the unsatisfying object, he has introduced into the inner economy of his mind an object which not only continues to frustrate his need, but also continues to whet it. (Fairbairn [19], p. 111.)

Just as, in dealing with an intolerable situation in the external world the infant split the material object into the 'good' and the 'bad', so now he splits the internal object into (a) the needed or exciting object and (b) the frustrating or rejecting object. 'He then represses both these objects (employing aggression, of course, as the dynamic of repression)' (Fairbairn [12], p. 112).

From this internal conflict even the ego splits into 'a multiplicity of egos', because the libidinal ego and a dynamic Fairbairn calls 'the internal saboteur' develop: 'In the

process of repressing the resultant objects, the ego, so to speak, develops pseudopodia*
by means of which it still maintains libidinal attachment to the objects undergoing
repression' (Fairbairn [19], p. 112).

As we shall see, Fairbairn's endopsychic model in consequence becomes so complicated
that it is grasped only with great difficulty. Yet each of the dynamics he postulates can
be seen (if we bear in mind the 'bodily' concomitants of these phantasy-dynamics as
explained by Melanie Klein) as of very great relevance to any discussion of symbolism –
since symbols in religion and art are manifestly related to these dynamics of the inner
world.

The complexity, however, makes one despair at times of either grasping Fairbairn's
concepts, or (certainly) of conveying them to the general reader. The exploration of these
concepts is much helped, however, by the clarity of Fairbairn's thought itself, and his
capacity to see the problems in his own theory, as here:

> Amends must now be made for an apparent inconsistency in my exposition of the principle of
> dynamic structure. Although I have spoken of internalized objects as structures, I have treated them
> simply as objects of dynamic ego-structures, and not in themselves dynamic. I have done so partly in
> order to avoid too complicated an exposition, but mainly in order to focus attention on the activity of
> the ego-structures – which is, after all, the most important thing, especially since the internalization
> of the object is itself a product of this activity. In the interests of consistency, however, I must draw
> the logical conclusion of my theory and acknowledge that, since internal objects are endopsychic
> structures, they must be themselves in some measure dynamic, and it should be added that they must
> derive their dynamic quality from their cathexis by ego-structures. (Fairbairn [19], p. 177.)

We are dealing with an internal dramatisation. The model is, interestingly enough,
closer to the intellectual model of the nature of matter in modern physics than to the
'billiard ball' model of Helmholtz as Fairbairn himself points out ([19], p. 176). That is,
it is a model conceived in terms of mutually reacting dynamics, within a structure, not of
entities in static or mechanical relationship.

We are also helped by the continual reminders that Fairbairn, despite the complexity
of his intrapsychic models, is not attempting to 'explain anything away'. He merely
wishes to contribute to insights, while recognising that the primary intuitive and 'higher'
processes of the psyche go on unaided and inexplicable: 'Personally, I am very far from
being one of those who considers that higher values can be accounted for wholly in terms
of their psychological origins; and, indeed, if it were so, it would be a poor outlook for
human culture. Nevertheless, psychological origins provided a legitimate field for investigation on the part of psychological science' (Fairbairn [19], p. 189).

* *pseudopodia*: literally, 'false feet'.

CHAPTER 12

Schizoid Factors in the Personality
Fairbairn's analysis of the Logic of Hate

FAIRBAIRN says that 'mental processes of a schizoid nature' increasingly came to occupy his attention. Schizoid conditions 'constitute the most deep-seated of all psychopathological states', and so they provide an unrivalled opportunity 'not only for the study of the foundations of the personality, but also of the most basic mental processes'. The exploration of schizoid cases,* he says, offers the therapist the opportunity of examining the widest range of psychopathological processes in an individual, as essentially schizoid problems are only reached when all methods available to the patient of defending his personality have been exploited by him. Schizoid persons, he says, contrary to general belief, have great psychological insight because they are so introverted – preoccupied with inner reality – and so familiar with their own deeper psychological processes. (Neurotics by contrast tend to have some of the deeper processes excluded from their consciousness by the 'most obstinate defences and stubborn resistances'). Fairbairn also found schizoid persons eminently capable of transference, and thus presenting unexpected possibilities for therapy.

Fairbairn then goes on to discuss types and characteristics which need not concern us here, except to note that it would seem that increasing acquaintance with schizoid factors in the personality will reveal an increasing number of patients in psychoanalysis whose psychoneuroses will ultimately turn out to have a deeper schizoid factor. Fairbairn says, for example, 'The personality of the hysteric invariably contains a schizoid factor in greater or lesser degree, however deeply this may be buried'.

When we take into account in this way all those whose character traits are considerably influenced by underlying schizoid factors, says Fairbairn, the resulting 'schizoid group' becomes a very large one. It includes 'a high percentage of fanatics, agitators, criminals, revolutionaries, and other disruptive groups'. Schizoid characteristics, usually in a less pronounced form, are also common among members of the intelligentsia. 'Thus the disdain of the highbrow for the bourgeoisie and the scorn of the esoteric artist for the philistine may be regarded as minor manifestations of a schizoid nature.'

It may therefore be that while schizoid personal problems are often the driving force of so many intellectuals, that 'minority culture' inevitably manifests dominant schizoid

---

* Schizophrenia proper, psychopathic personalities of a schizoid type (not excluding epileptic personalities), the schizoid character (not psychopathic), and those in a transient schizoid episode (as in adolescent nervous breakdowns).

characteristics in the attitudes to life it expresses, and also the relationships of its adherents with the rest of the world. As we have already noted, Fairbairn points out that . . . intellectual pursuits as such, whether literary, artistic, scientific or otherwise, appear to exercise, a special attraction for individuals possessing schizoid characteristics to one degree or another' (Fairbairn [19], p. 6).

Fairbairn proceeds with his examination of the peculiar characteristics of individuals who 'fall under the schizoid category' and the aetiology of the condition. Among the various characteristics of those who come into the schizoid category are these: '(1) an attitude of omnipotence, (2) an attitude of isolation and detachment, (3) a preoccupation with inner reality.' These may be conscious and overt, but not always; for often they are unconscious, and also complicated by compensations and such manifestations. Thus the attitude of omnipotence may be over-compensated and concealed under a superficial attitude of inferiority or humility; and it may be consciously cherished as a secret. Similarly the attitude of isolation and detachment may be masked by a 'façade of sociability' and other disguises. The most important characteristic is the preoccupation with inner reality, and this 'is none the less present whether inner reality be substituted for outer reality, identified with outer reality or superimposed upon outer reality'. In this, as Fairbairn points out, his concept of 'schizoid' corresponds remarkably closely with the concept of the 'introvert' type as formulated by Jung (*Collected Papers on Analytical Psychology*, 1917, p. 347).

Fairbairn now deals with the criticism that, if his categories are to be accepted, then everyone is schizoid – a criticism which he accepts. The problem is the depth of the splitting of the ego. But, as he points out, schizoid tendencies reveal themselves in the most integrated persons, under extreme hardship or deprivation ('under conditions of grave illness, or of Arctic exploration, or of exposure in an open boat in mid-Pacific, or of relentless persecution, or of prolonged subjection to the horrors of modern warfare'). But generally it is true to say that, just as Winnicott refers to 'those manic-depressive people whom we call normal', so, by Fairbairn's account, we are *all* to some degree schizoid. He himself would put this in another way by saying '*the basic position in the psyche is invariably a schizoid position.*'

The *schizoid position* according to Fairbairn is a basic first stage in the growth of consciousness, and would be only 'not there' in a theoretically perfect person (of which there can be no such thing) whose ego suffered no basic splitting (which, since ego-splitting is to be seen as the basis of the structure and dynamics of personality, would mean that he would have no personality). Thus anyone who is a human being experiences schizoid problems:

> There are probably few 'normal' people who have never at any time during their lives experienced an unnatural state of calm and detachment in face of some serious crisis, or a transient sense of 'looking on at oneself' in some embarrassing or paralysing situation; and probably most people have had some experience of that strange confusion of past and present or phantasy and reality, known as *déja vu*. And such phenomena, I venture to suggest, are essentially schizoid phenomena. (Fairbairn [19] pp. 7–8.)

The commonest of common schizoid experience is the dream, which Fairbairn takes to imply that 'everyone without exception is schizoid at the deeper levels'.

> As Freud's researches have shown, the dreamer is commonly represented in the dream by two or more separate figures . . . the figures appearing in dreams represent either (1) some part of the dreamer's personality, or (2) an object with whom some part of his personality has a relationship, commonly on

a basis of identification, in inner reality . . . at the level of the **dreaming** consciousness the ego of the dreamer is split. (Fairbairn [19], pp. 8–9.)

The word 'schizoid', of course, comes from the Greek *skhizo*, split (and schizophrenia from *skhizo*, split and *phren*, mind), and the earlier conception of schizoid states saw them as marked by a dissociation between the intellectual processes and the affective, with the latter disorganised, with a shut-in personality often resulting. But, as Fairbairn points out, psychoanalysts since Abraham (who was for a time analyst to Melanie Klein) have become increasingly preoccupied with the 'libidinal attitude of oral incorporation' peculiar to schizoid cases. Schizoid individuals, that is, seem to have difficulties in their capacity to deal between inner and outer reality marked by characteristics which seem to belong to what Abraham defined as the 'early oral stage'.

These difficulties have a close connection with the splitting of the ego. But, Fairbairn insists, we must not only see the function of the ego as being that which Freud mostly stressed (being so much influenced by nineteenth century biology) as its *adaptive* function – 'the function which it performs in relating primal instructive activity to conditions prevailing in outer reality, and more particularly social conditions'. We must look at the ego in a more dynamic way, and see its association with schizoid conditions in a more dynamic way (and here Fairbairn is, of course, beginning to approach psychic development in a new dimension of his own, leading to a significant revision of Freud). The ego also performs *integrative* functions, 'among the most important of which are '(1) the integration of perceptions of reality, (2) the integration of behaviour'. Another important function of the ego is discrimination between inner and outer reality. Splitting of the ego has the effect of compromising the progressive development of all these functions.

The 'ego' we may define as the dynamic aspect of an individual which is conscious of the experience of the self, is in touch with external reality, is conscious, and includes 'the representation of reality as given by the senses' and 'existing . . . as memories, together with . . . influence and impulses from within . . . which have been accepted'.* It is this ego and its complex functions which are deranged by the splitting brought about by schizoid conditions, in an equally complex way.

By Fairbairn's approach we have a scale by which to measure normality, through complete integration is a theoretical possibility only, impossible in life:

> Accordingly, we must recognize the possibility of development resulting in all degrees of integration of the ego; and we may conceive a theoretic scale of integration such that one end of the scale represents complete integration and the other end represents complete failure of integration, with all intermediate degrees. On such a scale schizophrenics would find a place towards the lower end, schizoid personalities a higher place, schizoid characters a still higher place, and so on: but a place at the very top of the scale, which would represent perfect integration and absence of splitting, must be regarded as only a theoretical possibility. (Fairbairn [19], p. 9)

Fairbairn's intention in postulating such a scale is merely to help us 'appreciate the general position as regards splitting of the ego'.† As he points out, there are complications – as, for instance, that 'quite a number of schizoid manifestations, as . . . Freud pointed out, are really defences against splitting of the ego'.

Fairbairn here points out that although ('with the implications of Bleuler's classic conception of Schizophrenia') splitting of the ego is the most characteristic schizoid

---

* The definition given here is by Brewer [7]. I have omitted the significant last phrase 'and are in control' because I believe this not to be the right word.

† Presumably R. D. Laing, who queries the concept of normal, would challenge the existence of any such scale.

phenomenon, psychoanalysts have always largely confined their attention to the libidinal orientation involved in the schizoid attitude.

> Under the influence of Abraham's psychogenetic theory of libidinal development, clinical mani-festations of a schizoid order have come to be regarded as originating in a fixation in the early oral phase. It is presumably during this first phase of life, and under the influence of its vicissitudes upon the undeveloped and inexperienced infant, the splitting of the ego commences to occur; and there must thus be a very close association between splitting of the ego and a libidinal attitude of oral incorporation. (Fairbairn [19], p. 10.)

Fairbairn believes that 'the problems involved in splitting of the ego deserve much more attention than they have so far received'. Here we may remind ourself of comments by Melanie Klein on 'Some Schizoid Mechanisms': the libidinal urges here referred to as bodily feelings:

> The phantasied onslaughts on the mother follow two main lines: one is the predominantly oral impulse to suck dry, bite up, scoop out and rob the mother's body of its good contents. . . . The other line of attack derives from the anal and urethral impulses, and implies expelling dangerous substances (excrements) out of the self and into the mother. Together with these harmful excrements, expelled in hatred, split-off parts of the ego are also projected on to the mother or, as I would rather call it, *into* the mother. . . . In psychotic disorders the identification of an object with the hated parts of the self contributes to the intensity of the hatred directed against other people. (Klein [45], p. 300.)

I quote this (which, Guntrip says, casts much light on schizophrenic reactions in the clinical situation) to remind us here that in considering, with Fairbairn, libidinal and splitting aspects of schizoid characteristics, we need to do so with a sense of these not being only philosophical concepts, but proclivities rooted in deep bodily feelings with consider-able symbolic qualities in phantasy. Moreover, as Guntrip says:

> The schizoid phase has its own characteristic form of aggression. The frustrated hungry infant does not *aim* to destroy the breast but to possess it. He may however . . . in phantasy see himself destroying it in the act of seeking to possess it. . . . . One of my schizoid patients woke up in terror one night feeling herself nothing but one big hungry devouring mouth swallowing up everyone and everything. (Guntrip [37], p. 342.)

These 'mouth impulses' represent the 'libidinal orientation' of the schizoid attitude: Fairbairn insists on the need to examine not only the 'incorporative' characteristics deriving from the 'schizoid position' – which have their origins in the 'early oral phase' of Abraham – but the associated problems of splits in the ego and its capacity for object-relations. 'The ego of the infant may be described as above all a "mouth ego". . . . So far as the infant is concerned, the mouth is the chief organ of desire, the chief instrument of activity, the chief medium of satisfaction and frustration, the chief channel of love and hate, and, most important of all, the first means of intimate social contact' (Fairbairn [19], p. 10).

The mother's breast and the infant's mouth are the focal points of his libidinal object and his libidinal attitude. If there is a libidinal fixation in this early oral phase, then the features which characterise this phase persists in an exaggerated form in the individual's attitudes and modes of behaviour throughout his life.

The nature of the far-reaching effects of 'libidinal fixation in the early oral situation in question' are as follows:

(1) Although the mother as a whole person is really his 'libidinal object', in proportion
    as disturbances occur in his relationship with his mother, there is a tendency for
    the breast itself to assume the role of *libidinal object*. 'The libidinal object tends to

assume the form of a bodily organ or *partial object* (in contrast to that of a person or whole object).'

(2) 'The libidinal *attitude* is essentially one in which *"taking"* predominates over "giving".'

(3) 'The libidinal attitude is characterised not only by taking, but also by *incorporating and internalising*.'

(4) 'The libidinal situation is one which confers tremendous significance upon the states of *fullness and emptiness*.'

As we shall see, these manifestations have considerable bearing on creativity (which is all 'inner contents'). (Compare for example, Sartre's obsession with bodily fluxes.)

> In circumstances of *deprivation* emptiness comes to assume quite special significance for the child. Not only does he feel empty himself, but he also interprets the situation in the sense that he has *emptied his mother* – particularly since deprivation has the effect not only of intensifying his oral need, but also of imparting an *aggressive* quality to it. Deprivation has the additional effect of enlarging the field of his incorporative need, so that it comes to include not simply the contents of the breast, but also the breast itself, and even his mother as a whole. The anxiety which he experiences over emptying the breast thus gives rise to *anxiety over destroying his libidinal object* . . . the fact that his mother customarily leaves him after suckling must have the effect of contributing to this impression. (Fairbairn [19], p. 11–12; my italics except for the last phrase which is italicized in the original.)

Winnicott's attention to phantasy as an accompanying element does contribute some additional depths and complications to the symbolism of this state – not least the infant's sense of a 'hole' or 'an emptiness where once was a body of richness', but also in the baby's deeply disturbing uncertainty as to the degree of stability of objects in a world in which he feels he is contributing by wanting or by phantasy of incorporation, to its mutability.

What it is important to note here is that to the schizoid individual at this stage, because he 'empties the breast' (and because his mother leaves him after feeding him), 'the libidinal attitude acquires the implication that it involves the disappearance and destruction of the libidinal object'.* This implication 'tends to become confirmed at a later stage, when he learns that food which is eaten disappears from the external world, and that he cannot both eat his cake and have it'. The conclusion is the fundamental schizoid fear that *love is destructive*.

Fairbairn next tackles the above headings one by one, and in following his analysis of these features of the early oral attitude we can see their cultural relevance. Since these features are embodied in phantasy and approaches to life, and since they are in all of us (because we all have schizoid problems as our deepest and earliest problems) they have a universal *symbolic* relevance. That is, when we come to examine symbolism in creative work, or even the symbolism of actual human actions in life, we shall find that they are often manifestations of problems belonging to this phase. For example, in order to explain the underlying anxieties behind a poem it may be necessary to discover that these arise from the fact that there is a conflict between the object in the poem (who is a 'partial object') and the actuality of a whole person, either imagined, or real. That is, the writer is aware to some degree that there is a conflict between how he wants the 'partial object' to behave, and how any actual whole object (a real woman) would behave. (There is much about this problem in Yeats' poetry.) In life, also, we find a person trying to treat someone in a relationship as if they were a 'partial object', with consequent

---

* We may perhaps suggest that the problem of 'flop' after satisfaction indicated by Winnicott (see above, p. 115) is presumably exacerbated by deprivation and would contribute to schizoid anxiety.

failure to establish relationship with a whole person: indeed, this is one essential relational problem, and so is most relevant to ethics.

The first problem Fairbairn pursues is this question of 'The Tendency to Orientation Towards a Partial Object (Bodily Organ)' ([40], p. 12 ff.): 'Its effect is to promote the schizoid tendency to treat other people as less than persons with an inherent value of their own . . . ' (Fairbairn [19], p. 12).

Fairbairn here discusses some cases: one patient 'treated other people more or less as though they were animals', which meant, as animals are often symbols in dreams of bodily organs, as we have seen, as 'bodily organs' or 'partial objects'. Fairbairn concludes that they 'illustrate the tendency with schizoid characteristics to treat libidinal objects as means of satisfying their own requirements rather than as persons possessing inherent value' (Fairbairn [19], p. 13).

There are other implications which we shall examine later: one is of *contempt* for the object because it does not have 'inherent value' as a whole person. The other is the 'sense of superiority' to others which is a schizoid characteristic: contempt and scorn can be schizoid characteristics.

This orientation towards partial objects Fairbairn characterises as regressive and determined by unsatisfactory relationships with parents in ways which will be obvious from what has been said earlier from Melanie Klein and Fairbairn himself about the consequences of a situation in which 'the mother . . . fails to convince her child by spontaneous and genuine expressions of affection that she herself loves him as a person'. This 'renders it difficult for him to sustain an emotional relationship with her on a personal basis; and the result is that, in order to simplify the situation, he tends regressively to restore the relationship to its earlier and simpler form and *revive his relationship to his mother's breast as a partial object*' (Fairbairn [19], p. 13).

This situation may arise worst of all from a mother 'who conveys the impression of both possessiveness and indifference'.*

Here there is a particular need to explore the nature and origins of behaviour and symbolism generated by the urge to regress to relationship with a 'partial object'. In truth such behaviour displays contempt for the object, and a regressive need to return to the breast which satisfies, out of a failure of maturity. Yet in cultural symbolism and adult behaviour the regressiveness is hidden by the compensatory assertion of such behaviour as 'larger than life'. What is revealed by such behaviour is weakness of identity: the consequent fear impels the false assertion that such behaviour is a strength. These considerations are relevant to such phenomena as the behaviour in life and the reputations of some modern writers, and may be related to the symbolism by which they compensate for the failure to discover mature independence in relationship 'with persons with an inherent value of their own'.

Fairbairn's clinical reference here is to a schizophrenic youth who had the bitterest antagonism towards his actual mother while dreaming at the time of lying in bed in a room from a ceiling of which poured a stream of milk – the room in question being one just beneath his mother's room. This symbolises not only regression to the need for a partial object, but also so a depersonalised object.

This type of regressive process may perhaps be described as *Depersonalization of the Object*; and it is characteristically accompanied by a regression in the quality of the relationship desired. Here again

---

* See Levy [56]. Over-mothering was found by him to be a form of compensation in some cases for unconscious hostility.

the regressive movement is in the interests of a simplification of relationships; and it takes the form of a substitution of bodily for emotional contacts. It may perhaps be described as De-emotionalization of the Object-relationship. (Fairbairn [19], p. 14.)*

Fairbairn next explores the consequence of the schizoid tendency in giving rise to a *predominance of taking over giving in the libidinal attitude.* Schizoid individuals find 'giving', in the emotional sense, very difficult because they are fixed in the oral (incorporative) phase. Here, again, in order to understand we must find our way back to the bodily feelings of the very young child whose ego is a mouth-ego and whose concepts centre round its alimentary functions.

The oral incorporative tendency, as Fairbairn points out, is the most fundamental of all tendencies, and the next in importance are the excretory functions. As does Melanie Klein, Fairbairn sees these as underlying modes of dealing with the world symbolised in phantasy and action. Though biologically speaking the aim of the excretory activities is the elimination of useless and noxious substances from the body, the child 'soon learns to regard them as the classic means of dealing with bad libidinal objects' and, moreover,

> their earliest psychological significance for him would appear to be that of creative activities. They represent the first creative activities of the individual; and their products are his first creations – the first internal contents that he externalises, the first thing belonging to himself that he gives. In this respect the excretory activities stand in contrast to oral activity, which essentially involves an attitude of taking (Fairbairn [19], p. 14.)

This is also the (opposite) difference between an oral incorporative attitude which implies valuation of the object, and the excretory attitude towards an object which implies its devaluation and rejection. But 'what is relevant for the immediate purpose, however, is the fact that at a deep mental level, taking is emotionally equivalent to amassing bodily contents, and giving is emotionally equivalent to parting with bodily contents' (Fairbairn [19], p. 14).

When one sees this in the light of the 'emotional equivalence between mental and bodily contents', then one can see how one preoccupation colours the other. The individual with a schizoid tendency finds difficulty in expressing emotion in a social context, because giving has the significance of 'losing contents'. For this reason he finds social contacts exhausting: 'if he is long in company, he is liable to feel that "virtue has gone out of him", and that he requires a period of quiet and solitude afterwards in order that the inner storehouse of emotion may have an opportunity to be replenished.' So 'In the case of those with whom the schizoid tendency is masked, defence against emotional loss gives rise to *repression of affect* and an attitude of detachment which leads others to regard them as remote – and, in more extreme cases, even as inhuman' (Fairbairn [19], p. 15).

Fairbairn discusses two techniques by which 'individuals with a schizoid propensity' overcome difficulties involved for them in emotional giving. These are (a) the technique of playing roles, (b) the technique of exhibitionism. These, again, have considerable cultural implications (as, for instance, in examining such writers who also suffer from alcoholism such as Scott Fitzgerald and Dylan Thomas).

By the 'technique of playing roles' says Fairbairn:

---

* As will appear, this paragraph has profound cultural implications. Here I will content myself by remarking that it challenges our complacency about the effects of pornography. As Farber says: 'To serve pornography, sexuality must be torn from the larger human context and exalted into a life of its own.' The implicit de-emotionalisation in the effect of a play on part-object sex, involves a reduction of human values to the level of that desired by such a schizophrenic patient. See *The Masks of Hate, passim.*

> The schizoid individual is often able to express quite a lot of feeling and to make what appear to be quite impressive social contacts; but, in doing so, he is really giving nothing and losing nothing, because, since he is only playing a part, his own personality is not involved. Secretly, he disarms the part which he is playing; and he thus seeks to preserve his own personality intact and immune from compromise. (Fairbairn, [19], p. 16.)

As Fairbairn indicates, a role can, however, be quite unconscious: as illustration of which he gives an account of a patient who appeared to be a devotee of psychoanalysis – but whose devotion was in fact an adopted role which was really a defence against genuine emotional contact and 'genuine emotional giving'.

Closely related to the question of role-playing is that of exhibitionism. Here again there is a direct application to the cultural sphere: 'The attraction of literary and artistic activities for individuals with a schizoid propensity is partly due to the fact that these activities provide an exhibitionistic means of expression without involving direct social contact' (Fairbairn [19], p. 16).

Exhibitionism is a way of 'giving without giving', by means of a substitution of "showing" for "giving". The danger here is that 'the anxiety originally attached to the act of giving is liable to become transferred to the act of showing with the result that "showing off" assumes the quality of "showing up" . . . "being seen" at all may then give rise to acute self-consciousness' (Fairbairn [19], p. 17). There are obvious cultural implications here.

Fairbairn's next heading is 'The Incorporative Factor in the Libidinal Attitude'. Culturally the implications of this phrase may be summed up in another phrase used both as the title of a book and as a present-day advertising slogan: 'Take a girl like you.'

Fairbairn here retraces the origins of the 'taking' impulse in schizoid individuals as 'regressive reinstatement of the early oral attitude', which is brought about by a 'situation of emotional frustration' in which the child comes to feel '(a) that he is not really loved for himself as a person by his mother, (b) that his own love for his mother is not really valued and accepted by her (Fairbairn [19], p. 17).

This is a 'highly traumatic situation' giving rise to further complexities:

(a) The child comes to regard his mother as a bad object in so far as she does not seem to love him.
(b) The child comes to regard outward expressions of his own love as bad, with the result that, in an attempt to keep his love as good as possible, he tends to retain his love inside himself.
(c) The child comes to feel that love relationships with external objects are bad, or at least precarious. (Fairbairn [19], p. 18.)

The effect of this infantile logic is that the child tends to *transfer his relationships with his objects to the realm of inner reality*, an observation which would confirm Melanie Klein's observation above of the problem of devotion by the child of too great a degree of psychic energy to the inner world if the outer world seems to confirm his worst inward fears (see p. 122 above). As Fairbairn says, the mother and her breast as object have already been internalised and this internalisation is further exploited. Since this internalisation coincides with the oral stage (and has all bodily feelings which we have discussed above) and 'the inherent aim of the oral impulse is incorporation', an excessive need to incorporate can become 'woven into the structure of the ego'.

> In the case of individuals with a schizoid component in their personality, accordingly, there is a great tendency for the outer world to derive its meaning too exclusively from the inner world. In actual schizophrenics this tendency may become so strong that the distinction between inner and outer reality is largely obscured. . . . Such extreme cases apart . . . there is a general tendency . . . to heap up their values in the inner world. (Fairbairn [19], p. 18.)

We have already seen this problem as it is manifest in the attitude to life and philosophy of Sartre. But obviously, from this account, this tendency accounts for much in creative and intellectual activity. Yet here there is an important distinction – for though it is the artist who, with schizoid individuals, identifies himself very strongly with his internal objects, he is essentially concerned with building bridges between this internal world and the external world by symbolism. If he is overcome by psychopathologically excessive concern with internal objects, deterioration, depreciating values and sterility may set in.

> In the case of individuals whose object-relationships are predominantly in the outer world, giving has the effect of creating and enhancing values, and of promoting self-respect; but, in the case of individuals whose object-relationships are predominantly in the inner world, giving has the effect of depreciating values, and of lowering self-respect. When such individuals give, they tend to feel impoverished, because when they give, they give at the expense of their inner world. (Fairbairn [19], p. 18.)

This causes some women difficulty in childbirth: but there are analogies in the mental sphere: 'an artist . . . after completing a picture, used to feel, not that he had created or gained something as a result, but that virtue had gone out of him. Such a phenomenon goes a long way to explain the periods of sterility and discontent which follow periods of creative activity in the case of certain artists' (Fairbairn [19], p. 15.)

This sense of impoverishment following creativity is often dealt with, according to Fairbairn, by an 'interesting defence'. 'He adopts the attitude that what he has given or created is worthless. . . . '

Fairbairn quotes an artist who lost all interest in his pictures once they had been painted, treating them merely as 'commodities for sale'. Similarly, some women lose all interest in their babies once they are born.

But there is a variant of this, which is totally opposite: individuals with schizoid attributes may regard what they have produced as if it were still part of themselves. This applies to certain over-permissive mothers ('with grievous consequences for the unfortunate children whose mothers cannot accord them the status of separate persons'), and to artists who regard their works as still 'theirs' even though they are possessed by others. But yet artists and authors can solve schizoid problems by producing works which even though they have passed from the inner to the outer world, may still be regarded as 'part of themselves'.

Associated with these problems is the characteristic schizoid feature of *intellectualisation* – a feature we have glimpsed over Sartre. But here we obtain insight into a whole dominant and dangerous split between thought and feeling in the modern world. It is possible even that this 'dissociation of sensibility' has come about because, since intellectual pursuits do (for reasons which will by now be obvious to the reader) have a special attraction for the schizoid person, the intellectual sphere becomes predominantly schizoid, not least in a world which bases solutions to problems of identity on activity rather than being. Here extensive quotation is necessary: 'Intellectualisation', says Fairbairn, 'implies over-valuation of the thought processes'. This has become a dominant aspect of our higher education: 'this over-valuation of thought is related to the difficulty which the individual with a schizoid tendency experiences in making emotional contacts with other people . . . he has difficulty in expressing his feelings naturally towards others, and in acting naturally and spontaneously in his relations with them. This leads him to work out his problems intellectually in the inner world. . . . '

This is an attempt (so far as conscious intentions go) to 'pave the way for adaptive behaviour in relation to external objects'. But, as will seem to follow, if we accept Guntrip's account of psychic reality above (p. 123), since emotional conflicts springing from deep sources in the unconscious defy solution in this way, 'he tends increasingly to substitute intellectual solutions of his emotional problems for attempts to achieve a practical solution of them within the emotional sphere in his relationships with others in the external world' (Fairbairn [19], p. 20).

This will be later associated with the elements of 'false male doing' in our intellectual and cultural life. As Fairbairn says the consequences of this overvaluation of the thought processes are '(1) the thought processes become highly libidised; and the world of thought tends to become the predominant sphere of creative activity and self expression, (2) ideas tend to become substituted for feelings and *intellectual values for emotional values*' (Fairbairn [19], p. 20; my italics.)

The latter phrase is most relevant to many problems of cultural criticism. On the one hand, it enables us to see the value in such an emphasis as that of D. H. Lawrence on 'whole being' and the need to defend him against those (easily found in universities) who judge him by 'intellectual' rather than 'emotional' values – that is, by values which are based on a preference for intellectual rather than affective experience. Similarly, it enables us to see how it can be that our intellectual minority can acclaim writers such as Iris Murdoch whose grasp of emotional reality is so thin and whose feeling for experience is so anti-human and so full of hate. Where 'being' was valued highly, such writers, if they were examined in the light of emotional reality, would surely be quickly exposed as inadequate in their sense of humanness.

With schizophrenics there is a manifest split between thought and feeling: the name itself means a split in the mind. But Fairbairn insists that 'the split in question is fundamentally a split in the *ego*', a split between '(1) a more superficial part of the ego representing its higher levels and including the conscious and (2) a deeper part of the ego representing its lower levels and including those elements which are most highly endowed with libido and are hence the source of affect' (Fairbairn [19], p. 21).

Such a split can only be explained by regression: towards 'simplification'. In so far as this schizoid split is prevalent in a cultural ethos, it means a loss to the community of deeper sources of emotionally creative material. It is this kind of split which underlies the abdication of the symbolic role of the artist in favour of consciously intellectual tricks with media, devoid of metaphorical engagement with those elements in the inner life 'which are most highly endowed with libido'.

Schizoid individuals are often more inclined to construct intellectual systems of an elaborate kind than to develop emotional relationships with others on a human basis. There is a further tendency ' . . . to make libidinal objects of the systems they have created'. Fairbairn draws an analogy with the phenomenon which we all know in adolescence of 'being in love with love'. But, he goes on to say, 'Infatuations of this kind may lead to unpleasant enough consequences for the ostensible love-object; but, when we find a really schizoid personality in love with some extreme political philosophy, the consequences become more serious, because the toll of victims may then run into millions'.

'When such a fanatic has the inclination and the capacity to impose his system ruthlessly upon others the situation may become catastrophic – although at times it may admittedly be potent for good as well as evil.' Written in 1940 this obviously referred to both fascism and communism: the peril is still underrated, and is still with us in many dangerous forms – in Marxism in its varying forms, and in *avant-garde* and revolutionary dogmas, whose essence is a preparedness to sacrifice the human to an idea.

A sense of 'inner superiority' is always present in individuals with a schizoid tendency, even when this is unconscious. This is based upon '(1) a general *secret* overvaluation of personal contents, mental as well as physical; and (2) a narcissistic inflation of the ego arising out of *secret* possession of, and considerable identification with, internalised libidinal objects (e.g. the maternal breast and the paternal penis).'

These discoveries were made by Fairbairn in the course of therapeutic work in penetrating the defences of patients. But they have great cultural relevance.

The internalised libidinal objects which the schizoid individual has taken into himself have, he feels, been 'stolen'. For him to lose contents by giving feels like being emptied: so, if he has taken libidinal objects into himself then he feels guilt at having emptied others. This accounts for the need for 'secrecy' and the secretive and mysterious air Fairbairn associates with 'markedly schizoid individuals'.

The internalised objects feel infinitely precious – as precious as life itself, and their internalisation is a measure of their importance. This obviously links the secrecy to anxiety about the identity: and because of his secret possession of these internalised objects the schizoid individual feels 'different' from other people: the 'odd man out', the 'outsider', the person who is 'left out'. This associates with the schizoid individual's difficulties in emotional relationships in the group. And such an individual will often try to circumvent such difficulties by attainment within the intellectual sphere.

Fairbairn finally turns his attention to 'Emptying of the Object as an Implication of the Libidinal Attitude'. We have seen how the incorporative quality of the early oral attitude implies emptying of the object. Here, too, as we have seen, Fairbairn is very close to Melanie Klein in the analysis of the 'bodily' phantasy of early childhood and its philsosophical-poetical feelings. As does Melanie Klein, Fairbairn recognises that a major problem here is the fear of emptying the mother's breast: the infant thus comes to 'entertain anxiety over being responsible for the disappearance and destruction, not simply of his mother's breast, but of his mother herself – anxiety considerably increased by the effect of deprivation in imparting an aggressive quality to his libidinal need' (Fairbairn [19], p. 24).

This anxiety, Fairbairn points out, finds classic expression in the myth of Little Red Riding Hood: 'the little girl finds to her horror that the grandmother she loves has disappeared, and that she is left alone with her own incorporative need in the form of a devouring wolf.'

As the fairy tale (as least in England) has a happy ending, so the infant should discover that the mother, whom he fears he has eaten up, does eventually appear again. Nevertheless, there is a problem here (which Winnicott has explored yet further): 'in their infancy children, although they do not lack intelligence, yet lack the organised experience from which they might otherwise derive reassurance against their anxiety. In due course they acquire sufficient conscious knowledge to realise that in actual fact their mothers do not disappear in consequence of the apparent destructiveness of their incorporative needs.'

In the discovery of the real mother, through experience of her living management, the child builds up a reassurance of his continuing existence. (Something of the same process goes on in adult love relationships – in which the apprehension of the real relationship, and the 'otherness' of the object, build a sense of continuity that strengthens identity.)

154 Human Hope and the Death Instinct

The experience of the traumatic situation arising out of deprivation during the early oral phase becomes subject to repression once the conscious knowledge is gained. 'But the anxiety attached to this situation persists in the unconscious, ready to be reactivated by any subsequent experience of an analogous kind' (Fairbairn came to see war neuroses as manifestations of this anxiety reactivated by a situation that re-enacted deprivation.) In the schizoid person it is this anxiety which is particularly liable to be reactivated.

Fairbairn ends his essay on 'Schizoid Factors in the Personality' by examining the essential forms of logic of this condition – logic which will be found of considerable cultural relevance.

The child's oral relationship with his mother is his first experience of a love relationship and the foundation on which all his future love relationships will be based. It also represents his first social relationship and thus forms the basis of his subsequent attitude to society. If, then, he comes to feel that he is not really loved and valued as a person by his mother, and if he feels she does not really appreciate and accept his love as good, then he comes to feel that the reason for his mother's apparent lack of love is that he has destroyed her affection and made it disappear.* 'At the same time he feels that the reason for her apparent refusal to accept his love is that *his own love is destructive and bad*' (Fairbairn [19], p. 25; my italics).

'This is an infinitely more intolerable situation than that of a child fixated in the late oral phase', Fairbairn goes on. Here he is using the 'early oral phase' and 'late oral phase' from Abraham, more or less to coincide with Melanie Klein's 'paranoid–schizoid position' and 'depressive position' (the latter to be renamed by Winnicott the 'stage of concern'). The child fixated in the late oral phase ('biting' phase) 'being essentially ambivalent, interprets the situation that it is his hate, and not his love, that has destroyed the mother's affection. It is then in his hate that his badness seems to him to reside; and his love is thus able to remain good in his eyes. This is the position which would appear to underlie the manic-depressive psychosis, and to constitute the depressive position.' (Fairbairn [19], p. 25.)

That hate is destructive, threatens the object, and, with the object the self, is the depressive problem. Far worse is the fear that love is destructive: 'The position underlying schizoid developments . . . [is one] in which the individual feels that his love is bad because it appears destructive towards his libidinal objects; and this may be appropriately described as *the schizoid position*' (Fairbairn [19], p. 25).

This, Fairbairn says, represents an 'essentially tragic situation' and provides the theme of many of the great tragedies of literature. (Fairbairn instances the 'Lucy' poems of Wordsworth, and quotes the sentence from Oscar Wilde's *Ballad of Reading Gaol*, 'Each man kills the thing he loves'.)

Schizoid patients experience great difficulty in emotional giving because they fear their gifts are deadly. So the individual with a schizoid tendency has another motive for 'keeping his love inside himself' besides that of feeling it is too precious to part with. 'He also keeps his love shut in because he feels that it is too dangerous to release upon his objects. Thus he not only keeps his love in a safe, but also keeps it in a cage.' (Fairbairn [19], p. 25–26.)

So, too, he feels that the love of others is bad: as with Red Riding Hood, the libidinal object (grandmother) turns into a devouring wolf. So a schizoid individual erects

* I have slightly compressed this argument. Fairbairn is in fact giving an account of what happens in the mind of a child *fixated in the early oral phase* so that this stage is reactivated in later stages.

defences not only against his love of others but also against their love for him. (A patient of Fairbairn's used to say, 'Whatever you do, you must never like me'.) So, when a schizoid individual makes a renunciation of social contacts, it is because he feels he must neither love nor be loved. Indeed, he will take active measures to drive his libidinal objects away from him. He draws on the resources of his hate, and by quarrelling with people, draws their hate, instead of their love, on him. 'All this he does in order to keep his libidinal objects at a distance.' He can only permit himself to be loved from afar off. 'This is the second great tragedy to which individuals with a schizoid tendency are liable. The first is, as we have seen, that he feels his love to be destructive of those he loves. The second arises when he becomes subject to a compulsion to hate and be hated, while all the time *he longs deep down to love and be loved*.' (Fairbairn [19], p. 26; my italics.)

Fairbairn finally unravels some of the most complex motives of the schizoid by which he substitutes hate for love: here we have insights of tremendous value in the moral, educational and cultural sphere:

> There are two further motives, however, by which an individual with a schizoid tendency may be actuated in substituting hating for loving – curiously enough one an immoral, and the other a moral motive . . . the immoral motive is determined by the consideration that, since the joy of loving seems hoplessly debarred to him, he may as well deliver himself over to the joy of hating and obtain what satisfaction he can out of that. He thus makes a pact with the Devil and says 'Evil be thou my good.' The moral motive is determined by the consideration that, if loving involves destroying, it is better to destroy by hate, which is overtly destructive and bad, than to destroy by love, which is by rights creative and good. (Fairbairn [19], p. 27.)

'When these two motives come into play, therefore, we are confronted with an amazing reversal of moral values', as Fairbairn says (significantly the essay we are exploring was written at the time of most terrifying moment of the manifestations of Nazism). 'It becomes a case, not only of "evil be thou my good" but also of "Good be thou my evil".'

This 'third great tragedy' to which individuals with a schizoid tendency are liable is of particular relevance again today at a time of so much fanatical moral inversion.

The 'schizoid diagnosis' reveals that such inversions are a false solution to problems of weakness of identity. Ours is a world which gives too little support for the sense of being by a cultural atmosphere which fosters creativity and the 'feminine element'. On the contrary false solutions, based on hate and the reversal of human values, are everywhere at a premium – and commercially most successful. In 'protest' and 'revolution' schizoid elements are leading to nihilism. Fairbairn's analysis of schizoid characteristics is thus also an analysis of our whole ethos, coloured as it is prevalently by the preponderance of schizoid individuals in our cultural and intellectual life. This preponderance itself is a mark of the 'ontological insecurity' of our time. At root, in consequence, as Fairbairn indicates, there is a tragic impulse to invert all human values and to promote an anti-morality – with destructive effects which are today everywhere visible, while we seem incapable of detecting their origins. Fairbairn makes the sources of this hate in our world only too plain.

CHAPTER 13

The Psychology of Dynamic Energies
Fairbairn's Conclusions

FAIRBAIRN's whole theory of personality structure is far too complex to give here, but it is important to give the gist of it. Instead of Freud's simple division between id, ego, and superego, we have in Fairbairn a system with six or more components in conflict, and yet again these are not to be understood as 'entities' at all, but rather as conflicting energies. As Fairbairn himself says: 'the ego-structures I envisage . . . are all conceived as inherently dynamic structures resulting from the splitting of an original and single dynamic ego-structure present at the beginning.' The essential difference here is that Fairbairn is exploring the problem of the self turned against itself in some of its capacities: by contrast, in Freud's scheme, the id, 'being impersonal', as Guntrip says, 'cannot be dealt with as either ego or object but merely as unstructured raw psychic material'. In Fairbairn everything arises from the 'pristine unitary ego' and its objects, some aspects of which have become internalised and which feel they are integral with the structure of the body. There is no primary impersonal 'id' reality: the realities in this sphere are realities of human identity.

The main dynamics of Fairbairn's system are given by Guntrip thus: 'all human infants encounter varying degrees of bad object relationship, and developments on the basis of disturbed emotional reactions take place. The maternal object, on account of her unsatisfying aspects, is internalised mentally, and split into an accepted and rejected object, thus giving rise to ambivalence.' (Guntrip [37], p. 328.)

Ambivalence, as we have seen, is an attribute of the mother that threatens the child's sense of being able to survive: so, to defend the self against the pain of threatened insecurity, further divisions of the internalised object take place: 'The rejected object is further split into two separate imagos in virtue of her having both an exciting and a rejecting aspect. The mother's capacity to excite the child's needs is, however, here associated with her rejective failure to satisfy them, so that both the exciting object and the rejecting object are bad objects' (Guntrip [37], p. 328)

These, surely, can be associated with Melanie Klein's concept of envy.

> The child's realistic anger and aggression against the mother who excites need which she does not meet, then becomes the dynamic of the child's internal struggle to reject the bad object whom he feels rejects him; i.e. his aggression becomes the dynamic of his *repression* of both the Exciting Object and the Rejecting Object. The remainder of the original object, shorn of its disturbing, exciting, and rejecting aspects, is then retained as a good object to an idealized form at the level of consciousness, and is called by Fairbairn the Ideal Object. While the Exciting Object and the Rejecting Object are

156

repressed into the unconscious as bad figures, the Ideal Object is projected back into the real external objects, and every effort is made to see the actual mother . . . as a good, undisturbing figure in the outer world. The real parent is 'idealized' in equal proportion to the badness of the bad parent figures who have been repressed. (Guntrip [37], p. 328.)

Where there has been severe failure in early object-relations, then we may find the Ideal Object so strong that devotion to it takes the form of the 'Holy Mary complex' to which Freud referred – a complex which makes it impossible for a subject to relate to any real partner in all her ambivalence.

The most important of all Fairbairn's concepts is the Regressed Libidinal Ego – which is the focus of many psychic woes:

> Corresponding to this tripartite splitting of the internalized object, there inevitably follows a similar tripartite splitting of the originally whole and unitary ego. The ego at first cathects [i.e. devotes a portion of its psychic energy to] the whole object, and continues to cathect the parts into which it is split; but this involves the ego in disunity, conflict, division. When the Exciting Object is repressed, part of the ego which remains attached to it by reason of the libidinal need which it excites becomes repressed with it. It is appropriate to call this the Libidinal Ego, since it is part of the ego in which is chiefly concentrated the ego's primary urge towards the good object. This Libidinal Ego, however, is in a constant state of unsatisfied desire, so that its need becomes ever more aggressively orally incorporative and it is drawn back ever more deeply into the revival of the original primary identification with the mother in proportion as no satisfying object relationship is obtained in reality. It is in the regressed Libidinal Ego that Infantile Dependence persists most obviously as an undermining undercurrent in the adult personality. (Guntrip [37], p. 328.)

This complex division of the self against itself arises, Fairbairn believes, out of the impulse to *withdraw* into an inner world, when the outer world has become too terrible because of 'impingement' and a failure of object-relations – as by encountering an indifferent mother or a mother who cannot 'be' for her child, reciprocate his love, or 'reflect' him. However, as he tries to withdraw, he fears loss of all objects, and if this happened, as Guntrip says, 'presumably the infant would die'. From the beginning, according to Fairbairn, there is a 'pristine unitary ego', but as it discovers this predicament it 'splits' in two. Part of the human self in embryo is directed at dealing with the outer world, and part withdraws into the inner mental world.

This seems easily acceptable as a picture of divided energy. But here again things become complicated by the fact that a human being cannot exist without objects. The split-off 'part' of the self left to deal with the outer world does not involve the real self. It is merely a 'screen of front-line troops', to use an analogy from Guntrip, and it is 'conformist'. It simply responds in a reactive way to the meaningless bustling activity of 'impingement'. It is Freud's 'reality-ego', Fairbairn's 'central ego', and Winnicott's 'False Self' – a kind of 'caretaker', often concerned simply to keep things going until the self can be more fundamentally realised. It can never realise the True Self or the whole individual.

But this leaves the True Self, which is in touch with the area of 'being' within, however unfostered, without an 'object' – and this is intolerable. As Guntrip says:

> 'Psychic reality', instead of registering the active function of dealing with the outer world, becomes a 'place' to live in. As Melanie Klein has shown, the infant internalises his objects and builds up an inner world of object-relations.' Fairbairn regards the infant as internalising his unsatisfying objects in an effort to master them in inner reality because he cannot master them in the outer world. In the result however, they are felt to be as powerful and terrifying in inner reality as in outer. (Guntrip [38], p. 71.)

These internalisations feel as if they are part of the very structure of the self. The infant can only become himself by taking others into himself and building up a structure based on remembering and experiencing. Now he finds that he must take aspects of others into himself in order to construct a self capable of living. His split-off inward self must have an 'object': yet this object consists of all he can take into himself from the outer world – bad experiences. As Guntrip says, 'a serious predicament has arisen'.

No further retreat seems possible. So a fresh series of manœuvres are made with the purpose of staying alive in the face of impossible odds. The object has proved unsatisfying, so, according to Fairbairn it becomes divided into three aspects within: libidinally exciting, libidinally rejecting, and emotionally neutral – good and undisturbing. This last internalised aspect is, of course, magic in the sense that it represents all that the object is desired to be. It is thus 'projected' back over the actual mother. This concept of projection is very important for culture, as we have seen. Of course, this raises questions of how we 'see' the nature of another person at all. Inevitably, when we 'see' people, we are not simply responding to sense-data coming from their appearance. Our interpretations here are immensely conditioned by our inward 'psychic tissue' and subjective needs to *see what we want to see there*, or are capable of seeing there and then projected back over the world. In consequence, we may not be able to 'see' the actual individual at all.

Winnicott virtually extends this insight to suggest that we are able to see the world creatively and to perceive out of our capacity for apperception only in so far as we have been creatively reflected ourselves.

Out of its predicament faced with inadequate outer objects and internalised bad objects, the subject – the ego of the infant faced with not-good-enough mothering – divides into a number of split-off elements, one of which is Fairbairn's 'central ego' or 'conformist false self'. This false self establishes relationship with the external object – yet not the object recognised as real, but a 'screen' over whom the infant has projected the image of *an object he desires to be there in the outer world*. But, of course, such a relationship with a projection may not really be a relationship at all. As Guntrip says:

> The . . . Ideal Object is projected back into the real object and what has all the appearance of an external object-relationship is maintained with it by the central ego, the ordinary ego of everyday living. Nevertheless, it is not properly objective relation, for the object is not fully realistically perceived but only experienced in the light of a partial image projected from inner reality. Thus, once some measure of schizoid withdrawal has been set up, such contact with the outer world as is maintained is defective. (Guntrip [38], p. 71.)

Meanwhile the internalised elements of the ego are seeking to relate to those aspects of the object which have themselves been internalised.

The *exciting object* arouses libidinal needs, and to this element of the object becomes attached the *libidinal ego*. This is the split-off part of the self which seeks to live vitally and to fulfil itself. It is, as Guntrip says, 'characterised by ever-active and unsatisfied desires which come to be felt in *angry and sadistic ways*.' This libidinal ego is felt to be like a *great hungry mouth* capable of swallowing everyone and everything. It feels like a sadistic mouth directed at an exciting *breast* – that is, part of the object split-off from the whole object or person.

The other element of the internalised object, however, in Fairbairn's model, was a *rejecting object*. The infant, we must realise, has at this stage learnt nothing, and has still to learn *to be* from the object entirely – despite its own primary needs to fulfil itself. When its love is rejected it concludes that love is harmful and that it is itself bad. It then seems that in order to live it must become involved in rejection. The infant therefore identifies with the rejecting elements of the bad mother, and turns these cruel and hostile elements – the hate he feels he has taken from her – on himself. There is thus a link between the paranoia of this 'paranoid–schizoid position', as Melanie Klein called it, and the cruel self-denying forces within individuals which Freud called the super-ego, sadistically turned upon the self. Where the infant cannot find a benign world, the malignancy he experiences in this world is taken into the self, and he feels that his life is bound up with directing this very malignancy against his own hunger to be. As Guntrip says:

> Attachment to the rejecting object results in an *anti-libidinal ego* based on identification which reproduces the hostility of the rejecting object to libidinal needs. Inevitably the libidinal ego is hated and persecuted by the antilibidinal ego as well as by the rejecting object, so that the infant has now become divided against himself. This is easy to recognise in the contempt and scorn shewn by many patients of their own needs to depend for help on other people. (Guntrip [70], p. 72.)

From such anti-libidinal impulses arises the 'taboo on weakness' to which Guntrip draws attention – our unwillingness to admit that we are only human, with human needs. And associated with this, in Fairbairn's 'model', is the tendency in us to deny the regressed libidinal ego because of its vulnerability and its needs. This is the 'unborn self' of the schizoid individual, but is found in all of us. It can be associated with Winnicott's True Self, and represents that aspect of being which is undeveloped, and unrealised, to the extent to which we suffer from ego-weakness. The struggle for ego-maintenance centres round the problem of the regressed libidinal ego as the focus of ego-weakness. Fairbairn's theories have made a considerable contribution to clinical theory. Here we are concerned with their cultural and social implications. In the plane of behaviour this energy of splitting in the libidinal capacities of an individual can be illustrated as Guntrip illustrates what he calls 'the phenomenon long known as "split libido" ':

> The commonest example of this is the case of the man who feels no sexual attraction towards a wife whom he loves in an affectionate manner, and is only capable of feeling sexually excited by a woman he does not truly love and whom he may in fact hate, despise and treat with varying degrees of aggressive behaviour. His relationship with this woman may vary from pleasurable sexual excitement, through various degrees of sadistic fusion of sexual and aggressive feeling, to frank disgust, bad treatment, hate and rejection, but none of these reactions disturb his relationship with his wife whom he does respect and love, albeit in a calm and much more neutral way. A variation of this 'split libido' theme is provided by a case I have quoted elsewhere.
> A male patient reports that his relationship with his wife is one of constant rows and antagonism, while he finds another woman at work sexually exciting; but neither of them are his ideal woman for a wife. His ideal wife is described in terms of the internal ideal object who is perfectly supporting but in no way emotionally disturbing. His actual wife is the rejecting object and the other woman is the exciting object. Hereby he reveals the tripartite split in his own ego setting up needs for three quite different types of women.
> In fact the relationship was more complicated than that, for he could change round his objects, so that at times his wife was sexually exciting woman and the woman at work aroused his anger. . . . Always both of them had to be quite separate from the phantasied ideal wife. . . . All variations on this theme disclose, when carefully studied, the same three fold division . . . it is a commonly recognised fact that many men will turn with disgust from the woman as soon as they have had a sexual relationship with her, while in other cases a couple may have to quarrel violently before they can feel sexual towards each other. Always, however, there is the third type of relationship, of respect, consideration and duty without any strong emotion. (Guntrip [37], p. 324-5.)

This kind of analysis obviously differs markedly from Freud, as does Fairbairn's approach to dreams, which he regards as dramatisations of endopsychic structures and situations. Fairbairn himself states his differences thus:

> (1) Although Freud's whole system of thought was concerned with object-relationships, he adhered theoretically to the principle that libido is primarily concerned with pleasure-seeking, i.e. with the relief of its own tension. This means that for him libido is theoretically directionless, although some of

his statements undoubtedly imply the contrary. By contrast, I adhere to the principle that libido is primarily object-seeking, and that the tension which demands relief is the tension of object-seeking tendencies. This means for me that the libido has direction.

(2) Freud approached psychological problems from the *a priori* standpoint that psychical energy is essentially different from psychical structure. On the other hand I have come to adopt the principle of dynamic structure, in terms of which both structure divorced from energy and energy divorced from structure are meaningless concepts. (Fairbairn [108]).

Fairbairn characterises Freudian theory as both static and mechanical: Fairbairn shows himself here concerned to bring psychoanalytical theory back to the study of living persons whose dynamic needs to sustain an identity are more real than any supposed impersonal or 'animal' drives beneath the 'cracks' in their civilised appearance.

Freud's divorce of energy from structure represents a limitation imposed upon his thought, says Fairbairn,

by the general scientific atmosphere of his day. It is a curious feature of modern times that the scientific atmosphere of a period appears to be always dominated by the current conceptions of physics. Be that as it may, the scientific atmosphere of Freud's day was largely dominated by the Helmsholtzian conception that the universe consisted of a conglomeration of inert, immutable and indivisible particles to which motion was imparted by a fixed quantity of energy separate from those particles. However, modern atomic physics has changed all that; and if psychology has not yet succeeded in setting the pace for physics, it is perhaps not too much to expect that psychology should at least try to keep in step. So far as psychoanalysis is concerned, one of the unfortunate results of the divorce of energy from structure is that, in its dynamic aspects, psychoanalytical theory has been unduly permeated by conceptions of hypothetical 'impulses' and 'instincts' which bombard passive structures, much as if an air-raid were in progress. Thus, to choose a random example, we find Marjorie Brierley speaking of 'instincts as the stimulus to psychic activity'. From the point of view of dynamic structure, however, 'instinct' is *not the stimulus* to psychic activity, but itself conststs in characteristic activity on the part of a psychical structure. Similarly, 'impulse' is not, so to speak, a kick in the pants administered out of the blue to a surprised, and perhaps somewhat pained, ego, but a psychical structure in action – a psychical structure doing something to something or somebody. . . . The terms 'instinct' and 'impulse' are misleading hypostatisations which only serve to confuse the issue. Still more misleading are the plural forms 'instincts' and 'impulses'. (Fairbairn [108]).

As we shall see, the notion that the most 'real' and 'natural' impulse bearing upon us is 'instinct', which is inevitably frustrated by the restraints of 'society', remains the basis of thinking about man even in such a 'revolutionary' writer as R. D. Laing, who claims to be an existentialist psychoanalyst. If we accept Fairbairn's theory that there is a pristine unitary human ego from the start, and that all our problems arise from within this psychical structure, some far more radical thinking is necessary about human civilisation and its 'discontents'.

CHAPTER 14

The Heart of Being
The Insights of D. W. Winnicott

IT SEEMS appropriate and significant that, while Winnicott is obviously a major influence behind the present work, the present writer has not sought to summarise Winnicott's theories. Yet at the same time Winnicott's papers on psychoanalysis are so radical that every time one reads one it seems as if all one's thinking about human problems needs thorough reconsideration as a result.

The reason for this dilemma is, I believe, in the fact that Winnicott embodies the approach discussed by Rycroft thus:

> If neurosis is the result of parental deprivation, then perhaps analysis is a form of replacement-therapy and the effective agent in treatment is the analyst's concern, devotion and love. But this view of the matter leaves unexplained why the analyst should consider himself to be the possessor of a store of *agape* or *caritas* so much greater than that of his patients' parents. Analysts who hold that their capacity to help patients derives from their ability to understand them, and that this ability depends on their knowledge of the language of the unconscious are really being more modest. (Rycroft [72], p. 18.)

Winnicott's attitude to analysis is that of 'creative reflection':

> The glimpse of the infant's and child's seeing the self in the mother's face, and afterwards in a mirror, gives a way of looking at analysis and at the psychotherapeutic task. Psychotherapy is not making clever and apt interpretations; by and large it is a long-term giving the patient back what the patient brings. It is a complex derivative of the face that reflects what there is to be seen. I like to think of my work in this way, and to think that if I do this well enough the patient will find his or her own self, and will be able to exist and to feel real. Feeling real is more than existing, it is finding a way to exist as oneself, and to relate to objects as oneself, and to have a self into which to retreat for relaxation. (Winnicott, in Lomas [57], p. 32.)

Winnicott's emphasis is thus on understanding the patient's meanings, and on the living personal contact: 'I would not like to give the impression that I think this task of reflecting what the patient brings is easy. It is not easy, and it is emotionally exhausting. But we get our rewards. Even when our patients do not get cured, they are grateful to us for seeing them as they are, and this gives us a satisfaction of a deep kind.' (Winnicott, in Lomas [57], p. 133).

We are as far away as we could be from reification! And in Winnicott we recognise an approach to experience which confirms our own in education:

> For a long while the small child needs someone who is not only loved but who will accept potency. . . in terms of reparative and restitutive giving. In other words the small child must go on having a chance to give in relation to guilt belonging to instinctual experience, because this is the way of growth. There is dependence here of a high order, but not the absolute dependence of the earliest phases.

G   161

This giving is expressed in play, but constructive play at first must have the loved person near, apparently involved if not actually appreciative of the true constructive attainment in the play. It is a sure sign of a lack of understanding of small children (or of deprived children who need regressive healing experiences) when an adult thinks to help by giving, failing to see the primary importance of being there to receive. (Winnicott [90], p. 271.)

Winnicott also shows a remarkable capacity for understanding the meaning of a baby's activities before it can speak:

I place a spatula for him, and as he takes it his mother says: 'He'll make more noise this time than last', and she is right. Mothers often tell me correctly what the baby will do, showing, if any should doubt it, that our picture gained in the out-patient department is not unrelated to life. Of course the spatula goes to the mouth and soon he uses it for banging the table or the bowl. So to the bowl with many bangs. All the time he is looking at me, and I cannot fail to see that I am involved. In some way he is expressing his attitude to me. Other mothers and babies are sitting in the room behind the mother some yards away, and the mood of the whole room is determined by the baby's mood. A mother over the way says: 'He's the village blacksmith.' He is pleased with such success and adds to the play an element of showing off. He puts the spatula towards my mouth in a very sweet way, and is pleased that I play the game and pretend to eat it, not really in contact with it; he understands perfectly if only I show him I am playing his game. He offers it also to his mother, and then with a magnanimous gesture turns round and gives it magically to the audience over the way. So he returns to the bowl and the bangs go on.

After a while he communicates in his own way with one of the babies the other side of the room, choosing him from about eight grown-ups and children there. Everyone is now in a hilarious mood and the clinic is going very well.

His mother now lets him down and he takes the spatula on the floor, playing with it and gradually edging over towards the other small person with whom he has just communicated by noises.

You noticed how he is interested not only in his own mouth, but also in mine and in his mother's, and I think he feels he has fed all the people in the room. This he has done with the spatula, but he could not have done so if he had not just felt he had incorporated it, in the way I have described. (Winnicott [90].)

This capacity to understand the most primitive problems of existence and the human meanings involved has taken Winnicott to the 'very start' of the development of identity. Winnicott has been able to expose so much that we take for granted, 'that had a beginning and a condition out of which it developed'. The problems of illusion and reality, and the symbolism by which we build bridges between subjective and objective are immense. As Winnicott says:

In the most primitive state . . . the object behaves according to magical laws, i.e. it exists when desired, it approaches when approached, it hurts when hurt. Lastly, it vanishes when not wanted. This last is most terrifying and the only true annihilation . . . [To] the vast problem of the initial steps in the development of a relation of external reality, and the relation of phantasy to reality. . . . we must add ideas of incorporation. But at the start a simple *contact* with external or shared reality has to be made, by the infant's hallucinating and the world's presenting, with moments of illusion for the infant in which the two are taken by him to be identical, which they never in fact are.

. . . The subject of illusion is a very wide one that needs study; it will be found to provide the clue to a child's interest in bubbles and clouds and rainbows and all mysterious phenomena, and also his interest in fluff, which is most difficult to explain. . . . Somewhere here, too, is the interest in breath, which never decides whether it comes primarily from within or without, and which provides a basis for the conception of spirit, soul, anima. (Winnicott [90], p. 154.)

The reader will have become aware that when he is employing such insights Winnicott is writing something eminently like poetry, and writing in such a way as to cast valuable light on poetic symbolism, and all the 'language of the unconscious'. (Compare, for instance, the light cast by the above on nursery rhymes, on certain images in folksong, on the poetry of Blake and Sylvia Plath, and even on the nature of music and song itself.)

Guntrip notes at this point that the work of Melanie Klein grew out of the analysis of young children in general, and Fairbairn's came from work with schizoid patients the origins of whose psychic difficulties were in earliest infancy. Guntrip believes that in the exploration of these the work of Winnicott on the earliest mother–child relationships yield ideas that 'become the key concepts for understanding these deepest levels of psychic life'.

Psychoanalytical investigation is pressing towards the earliest (schizoid) problems, says Guntrip, 'pushing us back inexorably to the absolute beginnings, the very start of the human personality'. As it does so it opens up new perspectives of the origins of culture as it emerges from the very foundations of human identity. In recent years psycho-analysts have shown an active concern with the infant 'from the moment of birth': this involves the study 'of the emotional dynamics of the infant's growth in experiencing himself as "becoming a person" in meaningful relationship, first with the mother, then the family, and finally with the ever-enlarging world outside' (Guntrip [38], p. 243).

Here the problem is one of the terms to be used, and even the ways in which we should think about these states. For the neonate is

alive, physically separated from the mother, but not yet capable of distinguishing himself and the mother as separate objects; nor even as yet able to experience himself as an object, and only vaguely as a subject; perhaps at the very beginning only able to experience transitions between states of comfort and discomfort in what he will later discover to be the infant-mother relationship. . . . *How, out of this obscure beginning, does a human being come to be a person?* (Guntrip [38], p. 243.)

As Guntrip points out, in the later work of Fairbairn we explore '*the isolation of the schizoid ego in the unconscious*', and thus find ourselves in the desolate and terrible wilderness of the problems of perplexities of True and False Self.

Winnicott speaks of a 'true self in cold storage' which can be observed through analysis: Guntrip himself sought to develop from Fairbairn's complex model of the structure of human make-up a theory of 'a split in the infantile Libidinal Ego, leading to a Regressed Ego'.

As Guntrip points out, in *Schizoid Phenomena, Object-relations, and the Self*, in order for psychotherapy to discover its own aims, psychoanalysis needs to penetrate to the 'beginnings of ego-identity in infancy', where such problems of existence are encountered. As it explores these areas of identity it finds itself pursuing paths which are also being followed by philosophers and by those concerned with meaning and symbol, as we have seen. Cultural criticism urgently needs to take account of these explorations and to see the relevance of a writer like Winnicott.

Winnicott is not, of course, the only writer in psychoanalysis who is working on the earliest problems of identity and existence. His work is parallel to the whole stream of existential psychoanalysis, and here it is interesting to note that there seems to be more that is sympathetic to Winnicott in Transatlantic Existential sources, where Martin Buber is more of an influence than Jean-Paul Sartre. There is a very relevant paper by an American writer of the psychodynamic school on 'Alice and the Red King' (Solomon [123]). Professor Solomon concludes with a statement that seems very close to Winnicott: The development of the knowledge of one's existence. . . is derived from the introjection of the primary object which had previously incorporated the subject. Stated differently, the child's sense of existence is contingent upon internalising the mother who has inter-nalised him. . . . '

Because the origins of identity are in such strange identifications, from this can arise the threat of 'loss of one's existence . . . from the disappearance of one's image from another person's mind'. Solomon quotes a patient's dream:

> There is a giant lying on the grass. There is a big round circle above him indicating that he is dreaming (like in the comic strips). I'm in the dream just doing ordinary things. I get the idea that I exist only in his dream. It is important for him to stay asleep, because if he wakes up, I will disappear. This is a tremendous fear. (Solomon [123], p. 65.)

This obviously recalls the episode in *Alice Through the Looking Glass*:

> 'I'm afraid he'll catch cold with lying on the damp grass,' said Alice, who was a very thoughtful little girl. 'He's dreaming now,' said Tweedledee: 'and what do you think he's dreaming about?' Alice said, 'Nobody can guess that.' Why, about *you*!' Tweedledee exclaimed, clapping his hands triumphantly. 'And if he left off dreaming about you, where do you suppose you'd be?' 'Where I am now, of course,' said Alice, 'Not you!' Tweedledee retorted contemptuously. 'You'd be nowhere. Why, you're only a sort of thing in his dream.' . . . 'I *am* real!' said Alice, and began to cry.

Though Professor Solomon does not use the term, this is obviously a schizoid phantasy – to do with non-existence and identity. As Hannah Segal has pointed out, we find many such schizoid phantasies in children's nursery rhymes and fairy-stories.

Professor Solomon sees that the origin of the image of the Red Knight, with Alice existing only in his mind, must be in the earliest relationship between infant and mother, and he links this with the human need for 'confirmation'. An American writer called Hora says: 'Existential anxiety stems from the need to have our existence confirmed by our fellow man. We are driven to reach out with our voices, and experience a connection through being heard by another power.'

The child is not completely clear as to the distinctions between phantasy and reality, and is continually receiving shocks from his recognition of mutability. As Fairbairn points out, for instance, he finds that when food is eaten it disappears. So there comes to him the perplexing thought that 'the object may disappear when not wanted'. If he feels he only exists in so far as he exists in, or is confirmed by, his image in the object's mind – if the object disappears, what then? His own memory of the mother fades when she goes away: what happens if he fades in hers? Such childhood perplexities are often evident: Solomon quotes an experience at home:

> When our younger son, Dan, was 2½ years old, his mother entered the room and found him engaged with two imaginary companions. He turned to his mother and said: 'Sh – be quiet – Tuesday and Dirty are sleeping – they're sick!' She entered the game with Dan and played it very seriously. Dan could not stand it very long. He was slightly alarmed. 'Mommy, this is only make-belief – Mommies are real!' It seems that he was afraid that his mother would disappear like his phantasy companions. This in turn would threaten his existence. (Solomon [123], p. 68.)

Obviously, where the sense of the mother having been satisfactorily taken into the self, and of her being there permanently to support the ego, is weak, this kind of fear may be intense, as in Professor Solomon's patient. Such a person may suffer from severe 'ontological insecurity'.

But while their own individual existence problem is acute, such individuals also express our universal need to have our identities confirmed. They cannot be satisfied by confirmation in terms of external possessions, or even by family contact and home surroundings. Their anguish is in seeking a deeper sense of at-oneness with the whole universe in which they feel terrible isolated and alone because of primary ego-weakness. To overcome this problem of existence they have to ask what it is to *be human*.

Such individuals are thus able to help us with our existence problems, and this is particularly valuable at a time when so many traditional sources of confirmation, and poetic modes of exploring the inner life have broken down or come into disrepute. As Professor Solomon points out, the concept that man's existence is confirmed by God's looking is found in many religions. In the Hindu religion 'the dream of the supreme creative power (Isvara) controls the entire cosmos'. In Christianity, man is confirmed by God's awareness. St. Thomas Acquinas quoted the New Testament, 'Upholding all things by the word of His power': 'As the air becomes light by the presence of the sun, so is man illuminated by the presence of God, and in his absence returns at once to darkness' (*The Summa Theologica*).

Solomon also refers to Bishop Berkeley, who reasoned that objects exist only because we perceive them. 'He next went on to say that individual human existents exist in the mind of human persons as well as in the mind of a Supreme Being. From this he believed that he adduced a proof of the existence of God.'

'Thou God seest me' is thus an expression of *esse est percipi*, to exist is to be perceived by someone's mind. This human feeling about existence has its origins in the need for the infant to find himself confirmed, indeed, to begin to find himself, in the regard of the mother who reflects him.

Here, says Professor Solomon, the existentialists seem to differ from the psychoanalytical point of view. The atheistic existentialists cannot come to the theological conclusion that man's existence is confirmed by God's regard. They turn to the 'natural' factors of the organism – the anatomical and physiological realities – but they are unable to explain existence along 'natural' lines, and so take refuge in older metaphysical ideas. They concern themselves with ontology – 'the science of being or reality' – but in fact they 'resort to mystic mental gymnastics and on the other take basic phenomena for granted'.

> Ontology . . . is considered to be that branch of knowledge which investigates the nature, essential properties, and relations of being as such. In this connection May (*Existence, a New Dimension in Psychiatry*, 1958) and others offer the statement that man must be understood in terms of those characteristics which make him human and without which he could not exist.

But even so, because they seem unwilling to explore the nature of primary inward and unconscious experience,

> The 'atheistic' existentialists, namely Heidegger, Sartre and others, have a more difficult time explaining existence. In fact, they do not explain it at all. They say, 'We exist because we exist'.

Of this conclusion Solomon says,

> The 'I am because I am', says nothing. This is resorting to *a priori* reasoning, which has no place in our scientific world. It violates the basic principles of mathematical logic, which states that we cannot use one system of calculations to prove something within the same system. Stated differently, certain seemingly inconsistent statements made in a logical system cannot be discovered by the logic of that system.

Though Professor Solomon does not say so, the combination of two of his paragraphs do seem to suggest that the Sartrean existentialists become incomprehensible in their attempt to explain existence because they themselves are merely expressing their own inability to feel primitive ego-integration. Guntrip considers this branch of existentialism to be a rationalisation of schizoid attitudes ([38], p. 48). Solomon says:

> Heidegger refers to the union of man with his environment as the phenomenon of 'being-in-the-world', Sartre refers to two aspects of existence, 'being-in-itself' and 'being-for-itself.' Being-in-itself possesses reality and is what it appears to be. Being-for-itself or 'nothingness' is presumably synonymous with human consciousness. To me this is a totally incomprehensible concept. It may be Sartre's particular way of dividing the natural from the ontological. The difference lies in the concept that Sartre

says that man conquers his feelings of nothingness or non-existence by the use of the will, whereas the theologians turn to faith in a Supreme being.

As Solomon says of such existentialists, they express the problem of being in negative terms, and really say nothing about the positive fact or awareness of existence.

> Non-existence is the basic threat to survival, the threat of the disintegration of the self. In infancy and in neurotic persons it is the threatened loss of the primitive ego integrity. The disturbances of the state of being or existence, whether they emanate from the outer world or from within the individual still do not explain the positive fact or awareness of existence itself.

As I shall try to argue, what the Sartrean kind of existentialist does is to rationalise into a philosophy his own sense of disturbance of identity or state of being. Without security at the core of being the identity has to be held together by will. Their 'existential anxiety' is what Solomon's patient was expressing by her dream. Their solution, like hers, represents what I believe Winnicott would call 'false male doing' – a way of coping with the world which is a necessary substitute for a (female) sense of being:

> Xenia . . . projected a good image of herself into the mind of the father, as demonstrated by her dream. It also became evident that she reintrojected the male image of her father into herself. This led to her acquiring his masculinity as a spurious identity. She also displaced and projected her hostility to her mother on to her father, fortifying her own fears of his actual power over her. Defensively, her helplessness was also projected outwardly, allowing her to feel powerful and bossy over other people. This form of tyranny over the assumed helplessness of others gave her a reason for her existence and created a form of temporary ego mastery.

Psychoanalysis itself is approaching a 'natural' explanation of the phenomenon of existence, from which it is possible to judge the existentialist position, as expressed in Sartre's assertion that man is '*abandoné*'. He is only *abandoné* in so far as he feels that someone should be reflecting him: where an individual has a strong sense of identity this feeling does not predominate. Because none of us have perfect ego-strength we all experience despair and awareness of our tragic predicament: but only those who suffer from desperate existence anxiety are likely to put this in the peculiarly negative way conveyed by Sartre's terms.

Buber has said of Sartre, that he 'speaks willingly of the whole and nothingness', but 'I do not know either what the whole is, or what nothingness is. The one seems to me as inhuman and fictitious as the other, and what I aim at is the simple *quantum satis* of what this man can accomplish and take unto himself in this hour of his life.' This 'final severe judgement' on Sartre by Buber reveals the essential difference the fashionable existentialism of Europe, and that influenced by Buber in America, where a great deal of work has been done on problems of existence. (This seems not yet to be known at all in Britain – see, for example, the most interesting contributions from a wide field to the *Journal of Existential Psychiatry and Psychology*.) The essential difference between Sartrean existentialism and Buber's philosophy is perhaps indicated by the following passage from Jean Wahl's account of Buber and the Philosophies of existence: 'In his study of man Sartre, says Buber, always begins with the subject-object relation. It is well known that many existentialists believe the fundamental fact about men to be that one is an object for another. But this is to eliminate to a very large extent the reality of the interhuman, the mystery of contact.' (Buber [10], p. 502.)

Buber's concepts of *meeting* and *relation* obviously imply something different from one 'making an object of the other'. His concept of the I–Thou belongs to the realm of shared being and creative reflection: Sartre seems able only to conceive of a kind of relationship in which one individual *makes use* of another:

The important thing, if one considers the relationship between two human beings [Buber argues] is not to see that the one makes an object of the other, but to see why this never completely succeeds. Such is the privilege of man. Sartre fails to see the relation between the I and the Thou, which is the most fundamental relation of which the other is but a subsequent elaboration. Hence the sort of solipsism which Buber attributes to Sartre. For him there would be insurmountable barriers between men. Each has to do only with himself; there is no immediate relation one with another. (Wahl in Buber [10], p. 502.)

Buber also criticises Sartre's account of the invention of values. Buber says: 'One cannot believe in, espouse, a meaning or a value unless one has discovered it rather than invented it. The value must have come to me in my meeting with being.' Although here 'being' for Buber would be empty without God, I believe we can see that, in the light of Winnicott's insights, it can have a meaning, in that the moral sense can only arise from the healthy experience of 'being' in the primary stages of existence. The values and meanings we discover can only arise from this initial creative reflection of a growing human identity in the togetherness with the mother at first. They are thus at one with our ontological security.

Professor Solomon indicates the source of our capacities for ontological security when he says: 'There is a distinct connexion between the feeling of existence on the part of the child and the appreciation of the existence of the mother. The emotional or perceptual experience of the infant-mother union must occur before the awareness of one's own existence is established. . . . '

Solomon refers to a writer named Silverberg who speaks of 'The subsequent derivatives of the [basic instinctive motivations of the infant] are the wishes to *be* seen, to *be* touched, and to *be* swallowed by the mother. . . . The knowledge of the satisfactory mutual coexistence of mother and self forms an early beginning of the ego. . . . '

Winnicott's recent work has done much to illuminate this primary area of the experience of being, not least by his denotation of the state of Primary Maternal Preoccupation as the matrix of identity.

As Guntrip emphasises: 'The deepest thing in human nature is "togetherness". From that starting point the psyche passes through the separation of birth into "aloneness" which would be intolerable unless beneath it, as its foundation, there still persisted that oneness of the child with the mother, and through her with "mother-nature." '

Guntrip explores this at-oneness as symbolised in the Brughes Madonna: and we may say that the image of Virgin and Child symbolises throughout European history the basis of our kind of identity in this primary 'togetherness'.

In the deepest unconscious [says Guntrip] [this connexion] is never lost, and human beings struggle to return to it when their 'ego' is most desperately menaced. Only when this foundation of security is retained is it safe for the reality outside to impinge on the ego of consciousness: and two human beings can be together in silence and yet know that they are 'in touch' and 'relating' and 'communicating' in deep feeling without words or actions, at that deep level.

We are now approaching those insights into the first formative relationship between mother and child which Winnicott has so usefully explored. These theories belong to the later stages of Guntrip's schematic representation of the growth of psychoanalytical thoughts. Guntrip collects together some of the most important quotations from Winnicott's theoretical work (see especially the first three chapters in *The Family and Individual Development*, particularly 'The Relation of a Mother to her Baby at the Beginning' and Chapters 2, 3, 4, and 17 of *The Maturational Processes and the Facilitating Environment*).

'Ego immaturity is naturally balanced by ego-support from the mother': 'The maternal ego implementing the infant ego and so making it powerful and stable.' 'Is the (infant) ego strong or weak? The answer depends on the actual mother and her ability to meet the absolute dependence of the actual infant at the beginning, at the stage before the infant has separated out the mother from the self.'

Winnicott's most important observation is of the strange state of extension of personality which he believes to be the essential matrix of the human identity – the state already mentioned as the context of psychic parturition:

> We notice in the expectant mother an increasing identification with the infant . . . a willingness as well as an ability on the part of the mother to drain interest from her own self on to the baby. I have referred to this as 'primary maternal preoccupation'. In my view, this is what gives the mother her special ability to do the right thing. She knows what her baby could be feeling like. No-one else knows. (Winnicott [93], 15).

As the baby grows the mother emerges from this state: 'It is part of the normal process that the mother recovers her self-interest, and does so at the rate at which the infant can allow her to do so. . . . The normal mother's recovery from her preoccupation with her infant provides a kind of weaning. (Winnicott, quoted by Guntrip [38], p. 223.)

Where all goes successfully,

> I would say the ego is both weak and strong. All depends upon the capacity of the mother to give ego-support. . . . Where the mother's ego-support is absent or weak or patchy, the infant cannot develop along personal lines . . . It is the well-cared for babies who quickly establish themselves as persons. . . . Only if there is a good-enough mother does the infant start on a process of development that is personal and real. (Winnicott, quoted by Guntrip [38], p. 224).

Where things go wrong, the consequence is a false start: 'If the mothering is not good enough, then the infant becomes a collection of reactions to impingement, and the true self of the infant fails to form or becomes hidden behind a false self which complies with and generally wards off the world's knocks' (Winnicott, quoted by Guntrip [38], p. 224).

'Reactions to impingement' take the form of 'doing' instead of being, of various forms of 'false self' activity, including certain forms of intellectual activity that is a substitute for whole dealings with life. Also involved is the capacity to believe in a benign environment, and to be alone, relying on one's inner resources: 'Maturity and the capacity to be alone implies that the individual has had the chance through good-enough mothering to build up a belief in a benign environment' (Winnicott, quoted by Guntrip [38], p. 226).

The capacity to feel this depends upon there being, deep down, an 'ego-supportative environment' which has become 'built in to the individual's personality': 'there is always someone present, someone who is equated ultimately and unconsciously with the mother, the person who in the early days and weeks, was temporarily identified with the infant, and for the time being was interested in nothing else but the care of her own infant' (Winnicott, quoted by Guntrip [38], p. 226).

The result of this taking into oneself of the mother who allows the infant to involve her in this way is, says Guntrip, a conviction, in terms of feeling, not idea, of the 'reality and reliability for him of good objects in the outer world': 'This is not the same as a capacity to phantasy good objects. We must distinguish between enjoyable remembering on the basis of actual good experience, and compulsive anxious phantasying and thinking as an effort to deny actual bad experience' (Guntrip [38], p. 227).

The cultural and social implications are surely beginning to be obvious. Hate, including 'intellectual hate', is a manifestation of insecurity, and an inverted protest of life, rather than the manifestation of a primary destructive urge.

Psychic problems arise in us primarily as defence mechanisms by which we seek to protect ourselves against impingement, against 'bad experience'. They are 'strategies of survival' to take Laing's useful term, against a false bustling activity in the mother who cannot 'be' for her infant. From this arise the problems we have already looked at, of the 'regressed ego': 'When the infant finds himself in a relationship to outer reality which imposes on his greater strains than he is capable of bearing, he mentally withdraws from the outer world into his inner psychic life' (Guntrip [37], p. 430).

We may look at the processes involved in two ways. To Fairbairn the problem is to be seen in terms of the ego's need for the object. The infant's needs in consequence become so intensified that they seem to be dangerous to love-objects: 'the schizoid withdrawal from object-relations is motivated by the fear *that one's love is destructive.*'

But the object is also needed to confirm the subject's identity, and we can also see the problem in terms of the ego's need to preserve itself. Winnicott looks at the matter in this way. 'He regards good mothering', says Guntrip, 'as consisting of *adjustment* to the infant without *impingement.*' 'The mother must supply the baby's needs at a time when he feels them, but not force attentions on him when he does not want them. If she does the latter, she *impinges* on the baby's sensitive psyche . . . Fairbairn has also recently stressed . . . the pressure of the parents' needs and problems on the child . . .' (Guntrip [37], p. 430).

If the child withdraws from the outer world into himself, then 'the first move towards the creation of the schizoid position has been made'. If the breaking off of object-relations were complete, it would be followed by a collapse of the ego, 'so that the child could hardly be kept alive'.

> He must therefore detach a part of himself to remain in touch with a reality from which he retreats. . . .
> What Fairbairn calls the Central Ego, Winnicott the False Self, and Freud the 'reality-ego' is left with depleted energies, like a forward screen of front-line troops 'in touch with the enemy' and struggling to hold its position by whatever manœuvres seem useful. *The emotional heart of the personality has drawn back inside out of reach of being hurt.* (Guntrip [37], p. 430.)

What Guntrip believes is that a split in the psyche occurs, so that a libidinal self draws back leaving a de-emotionalised self to maintain a 'somewhat mechanical touch with the outer world':

> If however, the withdrawn ego remained without objects it would become depersonalised and no doubt undermine the Outer Reality Ego as well. To ward off this danger a world of internal objects has to be set up and an inner world created. . . . Here, as Fairbairn says, the ego tries to master its bad objects (in their duplicate psychic version) since it could not master them in outer reality, but only to find itself tied to a fifth column of persecutors secretly attacking it inside the inner world where safety had been sought in retreat. The world of internal bad objects is set up. (Guntrip [37], p. 431.)

Guntrip here quotes a patient:

> I don't know that I want to come to terms with this blasted world of daily life. It's better to keep my own fairy story going. Better not to see people or things as they really are. Retired into your fairy-story of wicked witches and bad dragons. Why the hell should I go into the outer world? Why should I have any further dealings with my impossible father? Why go out and meet strange people I probably won't like? Better to go to a theatre and read a book. But my troubled dream world is my real fairy-story world. (Guntrip [37], p. 431.)

As Guntrip says, the psychotherapist finds his patients *imprisoned* in this world of internal bad objects:

> Having had to grow up, not on the basis of feeling safely in touch and secure in a reliable good rela-

tionship with mother, but on the basis of feeling that his inner self is not understood by anyone and he must work hard to organize himself to keep himself mentally alive and functioning, it seems impossible to the patient to reverse this situation. To give up operating one's own ego-maintenance system seems like inviting collapse and extinction. (Guntrip [38], p. 235.)

Guntrip is speaking here of the problem of offering therapy to the schizoid individual: fear of relationship and the experience of trust let down makes the individual feel 'what if the therapist should prove in the end to be of no more use than mother was?' But from this observation we can see how irrelevant it is to accuse such an individual of being unwilling to relinquish this withdrawal, and this inner world, and to come into the world of ordinary life, and normal values. As Guntrip says:

> *The entire world of internal bad objects is a colossal defence against loss of the ego by depersonalization.* The one issue that is much worse than the choice between good and bad objects is the choice between any sort of objects and no objects at all. Persecution is preferred to depersonalization. The phenomenon of internalization of bad objects has hitherto been regarded as arising out of the need to master the object. We have now to see it as arising even more fundamentally out of the need to preserve an ego. (Guntrip, [37], p. 432.)

As Guntrip points out: 'The ultimate unconscious infantile weak ego is very clearly experienced consciously as a fear of dying, when its threat to the stability of the personality is felt.' This can be associated with 'fear of breaking down into a regressed illness, or more mildly still feeling unable to cope and worrying over everything. On the other hand, when exhaustion begins to develop as it periodically does, out of the struggle to master this internal breakdown threat, then it may be experienced as *a wish to die*' (Guntrip [38], p. 238).

This is felt 'in less uncompromising terms', says Guntrip, as 'a longing to regress, to escape from life, to go to sleep for an indefinite period, or more mildly still as a loss of interest and active impulse, a wish to get out of things and evade responsibility'.

The most poignant aspect of the Regressed Ego as manifest 'most undisguisedly' in schizoid suicide is that the 'life-tiredness' expressed in the withdrawal, and even in suicide attempts, is an attempt at rebirth. Guntrip quotes several instances of patients who made suicide attempts but in such a way as to ensure that they were found before they died, and quotes others who said:

> 'I've often felt it would be lovely to put my head in the gas oven and go unconscious. But I couldn't do it, because I couldn't be sure of being able to turn the gas off at the right time, before it killed me.'
> Another patient . . . on several occasions went downstairs . . . and lay down beside the gas oven and turned on the gas. . . . (Guntrip [38], p. 238.)

Guntrip comments:

> Schizoid suicide is not really a wish for death as such, except in cases where the patient has utterly lost all hope of being understood and helped. Even then there is a deep unconscious secret wish that death should prove to be a pathway to rebirth. One patient in the middle of a paranoid-schizophrenic episode had a vivid compelling phantasy of slipping into the local river and drifting downstream to re-emerge at some point out of the waters as a new creature. . . . What is the mental condition which drives a human being into such a dilemma as needing to stop living while not wanting to die? (Guntrip [38], p. 239.)

New perspectives are also rapidly being developed here, as with the appearance of the new paper by Winnicott (not yet published) referred to above called 'The Split-off Male and Female Elements to be found clinically in Men and Women: Theoretical Inferences'. This very startling paper, which affects our thinking about sexuality, identity, and modes of experience in an extraordinary way, deals with a middle-aged man, 'a married man with a family and successful in one of the professions'. This patient had had a great deal of psychoanalysis, but he knew that 'what he came for he has not reached': 'If he cuts his losses the sacrifice is too great.'

Winnicott records, in his marvellous way of conveying extra-normal experiences, that what he lived through with this patient was new for him. It struck him one day that his patient was talking about *'penis envy'*. The term was 'appropriate in view of the material and of its presentation'. But this is a term 'not usually applied to men'. Winnicott records how he handled this: 'On this particular occasion I said to him: "I am listening to a girl. I know perfectly well that you are a man but I am listening to a girl, and I am talking to a girl. I am telling this girl: You are talking about penis envy." ' (Winnicott [128]).

The whole of his paper is based on this experience. The patient responded: 'If I were to tell someone about this girl I would be called mad.'

Winnicott, being a psychoanalyst with the experience of many severely ill individuals behind him was able to respond thus:

> The matter could have been left there, but I am glad, in view of subsequent events, that I went further. It was my next remark that surprised me, and it clinched the matter. I said: 'In fact it was not that you told this to anyone; it is I who see the girl and hear a girl talking, when actually there is a man on my couch; the mad person is myself.'
> . . . The patient said that he now felt sane in a mad environment. In other words he was now released from a dilemma. And he said, subsequently, 'I myself could never say (knowing myself to be a man) "I am a girl". I am not mad that way. But you said it, and you have spoken to both parts of me.'
> This madness which was mine enabled him to see himself as a girl from *my position*. He knows himself to be a man, and never doubts that he is a man. (Winnicott [128]).

Winnicott says he had to live through a 'real personal experience' to see this. The insights could only have been achieved by one who was able to really believe that analysts learn everything from our patients' and for his courage in being willing to meet their madnesses half-way. His theoretical conclusion was this:

> His mother . . . saw a girl baby when he was an infant before she came round to thinking of him as a boy. In other words this man had to fit into her idea of a girl. (He was the second child, the first being a boy.) We have very good evidence from inside the analysis that in her early management of him the mother held him and dealt with him in all sorts of physical ways as if she failed to see him as a male. On the basis of this pattern he later arranged his defences, but it was the mother's 'madness' that saw a girl where was a boy, and this was brought right into the present by my having said, 'It is I who am mad.'

Winnicott later discovered that the girl he was talking to did not want the man released. The girl always hoped that analysis would find out that 'this man, yourself, is and always has been a girl'. 'The only end to the analysis that this girl can look for is the discovery that in fact you are a girl.'

Winnicott decided to surrender himself to the implications of this case. 'The first thing I noticed was that I had never before fully accepted the complete dissociation between the man (or woman!) and the aspect of the personality that has the opposite sex. In the case of this man patient the dissociation was nearly complete. I saw that what I was dealing with could be called a *pure female element*.'

As Winnicott says, the ways in which these male and female elements are split-off (and sometimes organised into multiple splits) is 'vast and complex', but the implications for considerations of identity and object-relations psychology are profound.

Here we have to try, lacking any terminology for this, to enter into primal states of consciousness. Before there is a sense of self, of the difference between the *me* and the *not-me*, there is a state of 'being at one with' for which Winnicott uses the phrase 'subjective object'.

> The term subjective object has been used in describing the first object, the object *not yet repudiated as a not-me phenomenon*. Here in this relatedness of pure female element to 'breast' is a practical application of the idea of the subjective object, and the experience of this paves the way for the objective subject – that is, the idea of a self, and the feeling of real that springs from the sense of having an identity. However complex the sense of self and the establishment of an identity eventually becomes as a baby grows, no sense of self emerges except on the basis of this relating in the sense of BEING. This sense of being is something that antedates the idea of being-at-one-with because there has not yet been anything else except identity. Two separate persons can *feel* at one, but here the baby and the object *are* one. The term primary identification has perhaps been used for just this that I am describing and I am trying to show how vitally important this first experience is for the initiation of all subsequent experiences of identification.
>
> Projective and introjective identification both stem from this place where each is the same as the other. (Winnicott [128]).

Guntrip, discussing this paper, puts the situation in different terms:

> A good enough relationship with a stable mother is the basis of the possibility, through primary identification, of the first nascent experiences of security, self-hood, identity, the definitive start of the ego, making possible in turn a growth in object relationships, as the differentiation of a subject and an object proceeds and the baby acquires a 'not-me' world and feels to be a 'me' over against it. Before that, the ego is there as a potentiality latent in the psyche since the infant starts off as a 'whole human being' (Winnicott). That is really what Fairbairn meant in speaking of a 'pristine unitary ego'.* (Guntrip [38], p. 249.)

Here we have attention to the first origins of 'ontological security' and of security of identity – and these seem to Winnicott to be bound up with the first 'experience of *being*' that comes 'via the female element of men and women and of male and female infants'.

By contrast, 'the object-relating of the male element to the object presupposes separateness'. 'The male element *does* while the female element *is*.'

> As soon as there is an ego organization available the baby allows the object the quality of being not-me or separate, and so experiences id-satisfactions that include anger relative to frustration. Drive satisfaction enhances the separation of the object from the baby, and leads to objectification of the object. Henceforth, on the male element side, identification needs to be based on complex mental mechanisms (involving splitting of the idea of the object) mental mechanisms that must be given time to appear, to develop and become established as part of the new baby's equipment. On the female element side, however, identity requires so little mental structure that this primary identity can be a feature from very early, and the foundation for simple being can be laid (let us say) from the birth date, or before, or soon after, or from whenever the mind has become free from the handicaps of its functioning due to brain damage associated with the birth process.

Here Winnicott refers to very subtle details of handling which determine the capacity to be in the neonate. Behind his considerations here are the concept of a good-enough, and not-good-enough mother, and of primary maternal preoccupation.

In his first paper on the subject Winnicott defines this 'very special state of the mother' ('which deserves a name') thus:

> It gradually develops and becomes a state of heightened sensitivity during, and especially towards the end of the pregnancy, it lasts for a few weeks after the birth of the child.
> ... the memory mothers have of this state tends to be repressed. ...
> This organized state (that would be an illness were it not for the fact of the pregnancy) could be

---

* For this reason Winnicott believes that our origins must be discussed in human terms: 'I can see no instinct drive in this ... I doubt very much whether imprinting is a matter that affects the new born infant at all. I will say here and now that I believe the whole subject of imprinting is irrelevant in the study of early object-relating of human infants.'

compared with a withdrawn state, or a dissociated state, or a fugue, or even with a disturbance at a deeper level such as a schizoid episode in which some aspect of the personality takes over temporarily. (Winnicott [90], p. 302.)

This special relationship between mother and child involves something like an extension of the mother's identity so that it is shared by the child. This is telepathic, or extra-sensory (an aspect noted by Guntrip) – as no one who has experienced a close relationship with a very young baby will deny. In terms of living experience, primary maternal preoccupation means (as Guntrip points out) *being something for the baby* rather than *doing something for*: everything that enables the infant to feel securely 'in being'.

> At first the infant knows no difference between himself and the breast, but feels he 'is' because the breast 'is. Here is the origin of all 'knowing by identification'. Thus there are two ways of 'knowing'. *The male way of knowing* is its highest development in objective analytical scientific investigation. *The female way of knowing* is the sense in the mother's intuitive knowledge of her baby. (Guntrip [38], p. 261.)

Here Guntrip quotes Winnicott:

> Primary maternal preoccupation . . . is the thing that gives the mother her special ability to do the right thing. She knows what the baby could be feeling like. No-one else knows. Doctors and nurses may know a lot about psychology, and of course they all know about bodily health and disease. But they do not know what a baby feels like from minute to minute because they are outside this area of experience. (Winnicott [107], quoted by Guntrip [38], p. 15.)

Thus we may say that 'feeling' is the 'female element, a state of being', says Guntrip, 'of being in touch by identification, while "thinking" is a male element, intellectual activity.' (Here we may reflect on how this both confirms Lawrence's attention to the subjects of *being* and (intellectual) *will*, and also illuminates Lawrence's own problems over his own female and male elements).

A woman who cannot accept her female element, her capacity to be, may well fail in primary maternal preoccupation. In such a case:

> Maternal failures produce phases of reaction to impingement and these reactions interrupt the 'going on being' of the infant. An excess of this reacting produces not frustration but a *threat of annihilation*. This in my view is a very real primitive anxiety, antedating any anxiety that includes the word death in its description.
> In other words, the basis for ego establishment is the sufficiency of 'going on being', uncut by reactions to impingement. (Winnicott [90], p. 303.)

'The mother's failure to adapt in the earliest phase does not produce anything but an annihilation of the infant's self. . . . Her failures are not felt as maternal failures, but they act as threats to personal self-existence.' From the dangers inherent in such absolute dependence arise fears of dependence and fear and hatred of woman – both often found in our culture.

Winnicott's conclusion is 'After being – doing and being done to. But first, being.'

As Guntrip says, 'If "being" exists "doing" will follow naturally from it. If it is not there but dissociated, then a forced kind of "doing" will have to do duty for both.' He quotes a speaker in a television programme ('The Sense of Belonging') who said: 'I plunged into marriage and motherhood and tried to substitute doing for being.'

> It was the sense of 'being', the female element, that had either never been evoked in her, left out from the start of her development, or else had been lost through the withdrawal, and regression into the unconscious depths of the heart of her libidinal nature. It remained a dissociated potentiality in the absence of which any amount of busy 'doing' was like the superstructure of a house with no foundation. . . .

When 'doing' is substituted for 'being' the experience of 'doing' 'degenerates into a meaningless succession of mere activities . . . performed . . . as a futile effort to keep oneself in being: to manufacture a sense of "being" one does not possess.'

> This may become a manic of obsessional compulsive activity, for the 'mind' cannot stop, relax or rest, because of a secret fear of collapsing into non-existence. It is the individual's capacity for experiencing a sense of 'being' that is primarily dissociated, left unrealized at the start of development. He cannot get at his capacity to feel real. . . .

It is this failure to find in oneself a sense of 'being' that leads to such a feeling of ego-weakness that the individual feels life-tiredness, the desire to withdraw – or the schizoid impulse towards that suicide that seeks rebirth (or perhaps that adequate experience as a neonate of primary maternal preoccupation which can give birth to the identity).

The failure of being, and consequent weakness of the female element, for which 'doing' is an attempt to compensate, by male 'doing', may be related to Winnicott's conception of True and False Self. As a strategy, activity of the False Self serves to deal with the world: 'only if there is a good-enough mother does the infant start on a process of development that is personal and real. If the mothering is not good enough, then the infant becomes a collection of reactions to impingement, and *the true self of the infant fails to form*, or becomes hidden behind a false self which complies with and generally wards off the world's knocks.' (Winnicott [93], p. 17.)

The origins of this False Self may be traced to the *pathological preoccupation* of the ill mother (to the mother who cannot use her female element?): 'It is part of the normal process that the mother recovers her self-interest, and does so at the rate at which the infant can allow her to do so. . . . The normal mother's recovery from her preoccupation with her infant provides a kind of weaning.' (Winnicott [86], p. 223.)

As Guntrip says, Winnicott points out that 'the ill mother cannot *wean* her baby', i.e. cannot let him grow to an increasing strength and security so that he can become independent of her because either she has not been able to give him the primary necessity for his security, the state of identification, and intuitive understanding. 'Her infant has never had her so weaning has no meaning' – or else she weans him too suddenly to free herself from him 'without regard for the gradually developing need of the infant to be weaned' [86], pp. 15–16).

Weaning is a process of necessary disillusioning, towards maturity, and the 'capacity to be alone', having built up a 'belief in a benign environment, through various stages from absolute dependence, towards independence'.

We find it difficult to grasp or gain insight into the state of the human mind in these very early stages, because even to contemplate it makes us feel dissociated. The strange atmosphere of Coleridges' poem *Frost at Midnight* evokes the atmosphere of 'primary preoccupation' with a baby as a form of intense identifying. Even to understand such states we have to re-enter (as in *Alice in Wonderland*) modes of experience in which our accepted distinctions between the *me* and the *not-me* dissolve by creative regression – a terrifying experience if it were possible. Those with experience of their own children will know that at times a mother obviously feels as if she *is* her baby or the baby will eat her. The baby, when hungry, will sometimes seem to see the object of his desire in the air obliquely behind one – an uncanny experience.*

* My daughter of 13 thought our baby at three months was seeing a ghost – which of course he really was: except that what he was seeing was in his mind, and so vividly yearned for that it was (for all he knew) in the room. A baby sees this vision obliquely because he turns his head obliquely to put it up to the breast, which he has to 'create' to find and take from. Winnicott gives insights into many infant feeding problems which are poetic-philosophical – e.g. that the baby has to 'make' the breast before he can take it and that he does not know at first that all things which happen to him are happening to the same baby.

By its exploration of such problems of the origin and nature of existence, object-relations psychology has thus become a form of philosophical anthropology with genuine subjective disciplines. Yet it can never become an intellectual scheme which stands in the place of experience. As an American writer says, in terms which suit well with Winnicott's approach:

> It so happens that psychiatry cannot be formalised either as a clinical system, or as a method of treatment. When a formalistic clinical attitude is assumed in psychiatry, the psychiatrist loses his usefulness as a healer; but, strange as it may seem, he may gain in stature as a psychiatric expert. For if he feels he can classify mental diseases with precision, and if he feels he can look upon the individual as the sum total of so many logical categories, and formal principles he can fit himself and his opinions perfectly into the mold of the verbal metaphysics of certain aspects of the law. On the other hand, psychiatry will never be able to abandon its search for the individual in the individual person, and therefore psychiatry will always be confronted with the fact that every human being is unique, that no matter how many general laws of human psychology we may discover we must take our general knowledge and distil out of it that very individuality and uniqueness which make up the person whom we study. (Zilboorg [98], p. 126.)

From such theories we can see that what happens in the first four months between mother and child weaves into the 'psychic tissue' a complexity of capacities, of internal dynamics, of attitudes to life which can obviously be affected by 'society' and which are engaged with by the cultural dynamics of each individual, by his 'ego-maintenance' activity. But society does not directly *cause* our problems of identity. Culture and social conditions can, however, foster growth or inhibit it. But in all these complex processes there is always hope because negative forces are but distortions which arise when positive forces are thwarted. There is no need for a death instinct to explain ego-weakness or even the most terrible suicidal or destructive human manifestations. *Where these appear there has been a failure of love and growth*: and it is within human power to make it possible to make these failures good.

The problem of life is thus not that we have to *accept* that man is instinctively violent, destructive, and death-seeking. The problem is how we can help to foster sufficient strength of identity in ourselves to bear to be able *to be*.

PART IV

Identity and Society

*Implications for Social Theory, Social Psychology, Education,
Ethics, Politics, and the Humanities and Culture*

CHAPTER 15

Identity and Social Theory

HAVING traced the development of object-relations psychology, we can now turn to consider its implications for us who work in the humanities. What effect should these theories have on our thinking, about man in society, about ethics, politics, education, and culture? If psychoanalytical theory has penetrated to the very core and origins of the human identity, does this give us more hope for the future? If, as Fairbairn believed, 'psychology should at least try to keep in step [with physics]', is there anything as revolutionary as modern physics in this philosophical anthropology?

I believe that these theories are so full of fresh insights into man's nature that they require a painstaking reconsideration of almost every sphere of thought about human affairs. Moreover, I believe that they are seminal in a revolutionary way. That is, they present us with no dogma, no intellectual system, and no impossible or daunting ideals. They present us merely with a way of gaining insight into our experience: with a discipline of inquiry only. But they also indicate how, in the circumstances of the living individual and in social policy at large, it might be possible to achieve a kind of 'mastery', painfully, and by drawing on all our human resources. Thus they offer us hope – maybe, in the present circumstances a slender hope, but a hope nonetheless – that we can survive, and continue to be 'at home in the universe'.

We must be prepared, however, if we apply these theories in other spheres, to find that many of our present assumptions and the actions and decisions based on these are chimerical. This is true, I believe, particularly of the sphere of political and social organisation. There are many hopes and ambitions which many of us retain in our minds in the belief that the fulfilment of these would bring about an improvement in the human condition. The realism of object-relations psychology makes the whole task of the betterment of human life seem dauntingly complex and difficult. On the other hand, it does present possibilities for genuine developments, based upon a sound recognition of human 'facts' of a subjective kind. For what emerges as of major significance is how people *feel* about their experience. For one thing it is possible to feel 'real' even when poor, and deficient in all that the 'better living' of the politicians offers us. It is even possible to find affluence a threat to one's sense of being human. But it is not possible to feel real in a creative way if one is not free – free to discover and realise one's potentialities.

Here, especially, we may find more adequate foundations for ethics and politics: certainly we shall find that many assumptions about morality or social goals abroad in our society are no more than vindications of false solutions which impel us further and further away from the realisation of our True Selves and our essential human nature.

The heart of the revolutionary theme in object-relations psychology lies in Fairbairn's remarks quoted above, that ' "instinct" is not the stimulus to psychic activity' – nor is 'impulse' a 'kick in the pants administered out of the blue to a surprised, and perhaps somewhat pained, ego, but a *psychical structure in action*'. Even the terms 'impulse' and 'instinct' are 'misleading hypostatisations'. What we have to think of is 'a psychical structure doing something to something or somebody' while we must not think of 'structure divorced from energy' nor 'energy divorced from structure'. We must cease to think of processes at all divorced from persons. Moreover, when we think of libido we must think of it as being 'object-seeking' – so that the 'tension which demands relief is the tension of object-seeking tendencies' in which 'the libido has direction'. We need one another to feel real. Our primary reality is not the *id* but the need *to be*; not the animal inside us but the human yearning. (Now Rollo May invokes Husserl's concept, 'intentionality'.)

As we have seen, Freud's approach to man as an object of natural science led to a way of thinking about him as if he were an organism behaving in certain ways in response to organic stimulus affecting him from the environment. Attention was focused on *reactions* and adaptation. There is a sense in which to think thus is appropriate, for man lives in a body, and, for example, if the air becomes thin, he will gasp for breath. But such a response belongs to the body, and man's body is both 'a natural object and not a natural object'* – the man who lives in the body must also be looked at as an entity belonging to another sphere, which is that of personal experience. Freud's errors arose from his metapsychological ambition to explain the realm of subjective experience in terms of organic functioning. This mode of thinking, however, remains doggedly with us, as when a student writes 'Society has repressed our sexual instincts so much . . . ', or when Laing accounts for the origins of schizophrenia in terms of 'society' repressing 'normal instincts'.

If we forgo explanations of the psychic life in terms of 'instinct' and 'impulse' then we are forced to talk about 'a psychical structure doing something to something or somebody' – and this psychical structure is not to be divided from its energy, which is seeking an object, and which is prompted by libido in the direction of an object. That is, we must talk about what goes on in a human person who is driven by energies within himself, energies which take certain forms, and which have certain directions, the major direction being to seek confirmation of identity through relationship. Since this confirmation includes not only that which comes from a person, the mother at first, and later other persons, but also the ultimate object which is the whole world or 'Mother Earth', we can say that the direction of the energies and structures impelled by the libido is a confirming relationship with the whole of external reality. As we have seen, this discovery of the 'not-me' is integral with discovery of the whole 'me' – so, I believe we can say, there is in the primary energies of man a direction towards integration and the discovery of reality, which reality includes other human beings who will confirm the identity. The primary need is to feel real in a real world.

One conclusion from this recognition of the object-seeking energy in man must be that living in society satisfies a primary impulse in each individual. From what we have said it will now be obvious to the reader that we must forfeit some of our most commonplace

---

* A useful example here is that of a child who needs an inoculation but who fears the needle as a rape of the tegument. So terrible can this fear be that, because of traumatic effects, the injection simply must not be given, and the consequent risks accepted as being less dangerous than the psychic damage likely. This is not my own point of view but comes from Winnicott by way of private communication.

sources of false comfort over the psychic life. For one thing, we can no longer justify our dissatisfactions, shortcomings, or wickedness by attributing these to overbearing 'pressures' from the primary 'realities' of 'instinct'. For another we can no longer attribute our evils to the way in which we have been 'unnaturally' forced to 'conform' to 'society' in any simplistic way.

We would be nothing as human beings if it were not for 'society'. That this is so is surely confirmed by the example of the 'wild man' who grew up as an animal from childhood in France in recent years: he died in 1968 without becoming able to speak or relate to other human beings. He never *was* in any human sense. Left to our 'instincts' and outside 'society' we would not survive as *human*. On the other hand, there is a biologically generated force within us which created human culture as a tool and which re-creates civilisation within each of us.

From these revolutionary human 'facts' we can go a little further, taking in elements from the work of Winnicott, and his uncanny penetration, through imagination, into the formative moments of personality.

We cannot even begin to look 'at' the mental processes as a detached flux of mechanical processes at all, in any reductive way. In the background of any psychological investigation we must recognise that each human subject belongs to a life-pattern in a unique existence. He has a mother and father, and a particular experience of the 'maturational processes and the facilitating environment'. He has his 'given' nature and inherited make-up. He also has a 'condition', to use Sartre's term – he is a Negro, or an Eskimo, or a London Irish, poor or rich. He lives in a society whose economy has failed, or in a Communist society, or an affluent society, or among a working-class community brought to misery and poverty, or in a secure peasant economy, or in suburbia, or in a war, or in a society where starvation, disease, and death are everyday torments. Moreover, he has within himself a 'psychic tissue' and an 'ego-maintenance system' conditioned by these life-patterns.

We can see that it is always dangerous to extract from the whole living man abstract entities such as 'super-ego' unless we qualify what we say in some such was as to remind ourselves that we mean 'the individual in his capacity to turn his moral energy on himself'. It is disastrous to try to account for human behaviour in terms of non-personal basic forces such as the id or instincts. As psychology restores essential humanness to its models, as with Fairbairn's complex dynamic theory, it is obliged to become aware of significant elements in the 'psychic tissue' created by the formative life-pattern – and here the primary element is how *the subject was handled as a baby*. The primary energies of the 'pristine unitary ego', are the self, and a self which is not merely 'kicked around' by impinging forces such as 'society' or 'instinct', but which seeks from its own inner energy, towards *integration* and the *capacity to feel real in a real world*. But whether or not the ego can achieve these human goals depends totally on how it *became* in complex with the first experience of the mother.

This is the most revolutionary human truth of all, and it is the most uncomfortable. All human history looks different in the light of the discovery of the problem of 'primary maternal preoccupation' and the conditions in which mothering could, or could not, be 'good enough'. Yet this is a state which is so uncanny and intangible that even those who have experienced it suppress the memory of it, while those who are presented with it day by day often deny it or fail to see its significance.

Yet this is the truth we have to live with, now Winnicott has dared to give it a name.

Where this complex state of interaction between mother and infant has gone wrong, there has been disaster. It maybe that at times in history this process has been interfered with on a mass scale. For instance it may be that there was such social disintegration among working-class communities in the Industrial Revolution (as E. P. Thompson shows in *The Making of the English Working Class*), that psychic consequences of maternal failure have perhaps persisted since for generations, as manifestations of weak identity, in some social groups. Or it may be that in certain individuals the consequences of maternal failure have left them with such an urgent – even cosmic – need to feel real by false solutions, that nothing less than 'eating' the whole world would do. When historical conditions have enabled them to enlist others, because of their collective weaknesses at certain periods, we have the psychotic phantasies such as those in which Napoleon, Hitler, and Stalin have involved millions. It may be that the vast wars in our time are huge attempts to feel real in a collective way, at a time when social trends had uprooted and destroyed the complex of 'being' by the disruption of family life, so that identity had to be attached to 'doing' while 'doing' inevitably culminated in conflict between expanding 'activities' – leading to immense manifestations of hate.

What the connections are here between problems of nurture and manifestations of collection psychopathology will require painstaking investigation. But a whole new field is opened up for urgent exploration the basis of which is in psychotherapy as a research method. One strange fact which is relevant here is that among primitive peoples, although the forms of mental illness differ, proportions of psychosis and neurosis are roughly similar to ours, though psychosis seems to be increasing in some areas in Africa.*

The problem remains of how these areas of human reality are to be explored. Of course, something can be discovered from the observation of external behaviour, as by the investigation of the way mothers handle their children. But because of the very nature of the more significant aspects of human existence with which we are here concerned it is evident that we shall need to rely increasingly on subjective disciplines. The I–Thou can only be found and explored in this way. Fairbairn draws our attention to the primary energies of integration, and the object-seeking nature of the libido. Buber speaks of our need for 'confirmation'. Winnicott postulates a True Self in every human being. The primary problem in human psychology appears as the problem of the 'secret core', where the experience of the mother's handling is to be found, either as an adequate core of being, or a lack of a sense of being. However much there is dissociation, chaos, and disintegration, there is a human psyche or 'unitary ego' there to experience these, and a True Self lurking in the darkness, yearning to be born, to be made whole in its existence by some kind of 'confirmation'. How else can this fundamental human problem be approached except through that 'projective identification' which demands imagination? As Guntrip indicates, if science is to take account of 'human fact' it will have to include those facts which are only accessible to imagination. But the thought of the amount of 'person-to-person' effort needed to plumb these problems is daunting.

Here we may look beyond theory and imagine all the many hundreds of thousands of human beings, essentially like ourselves, incarcerated in prisons, mental hospital wards, lying under the arches of bridges doped with methylated spirits, waiting to be executed, still in hospital after thirty years, addicted to heroin, on the verge of suicide, living 'underground', autistic adolescents, or psychopathic children cut off from the world.

---

* See *Psychosis and Social Change Among the Tallensi*, Meyer Fortes and Doris Meyer, *Cahiers d'Études Africaines*, Vol. VI, 1966, p. 5. Also *Psychiatric Disorder Among the Yoruba*, Leighton Lambo *et al.*, 1963.

All these individuals, however dehumanised, degraded, insane, evil, or wasted to society, have a True Self that waits, sometimes hopeless, sometimes defended by a seemingly callous False Self, sometimes virtually dead, never to be revived. But the human being is, all the same, there. There should have been in these individuals that human entity with unlimited potentialities, created by a woman's capacity to reflect a human identity by her intuitive capacities. But there is not. There is only a dim energy or structure that yearns to integrate and to become human. But this is hidden under a complex and desperate pattern of 'strategies of survival' conducted by the False Self, so that what survives physically can hardly be called human psychically. All social theories need to remain aware of this identity problem in each human individual. Yet, as Buber has indicated, more often than not the ideation of I–It imposes a deadening falsification on this unique realm of the I–Thou in which human truth alone can be found. Once we revive it in our minds, urgent social problems become evident at once (e.g. What is the point of criminal law and punishment?)*

Such insights from 'philosophical anthropology' should revolutionise ethical and social thought. For one thing – to what shall we be responsible? As we shall see, Sartre believes that man creates himself by his actions, and takes on responsibility for acting on behalf of every other member of the human race, whom he commits by his actions. But there is another responsibility revealed to us by Winnicott's work. That is the responsibility in each of us to our own True Self – and, to take Sartre's point, to the True Self of every other human being. Far from there being 'nothing within us on which to rely' as Sartre believes, Winnicott's insight into the origins of the sense of 'being' and the association of this with the True Self, gives us an inward basis for moral discrimination which is of enormous significance. And while this insight is quite independent of religious belief it can be accepted equally by atheist or Christian, as a primary reality of human nature, for whatever its origins may be taken to be, the True Self in each is there as a human fact.

This is not to say that to follow Polonius's maxim 'To thine own self be true' is as easy as his kind of commonplace moralising suggests. But this insight certainly exposes the falsity of many prevalent assumptions about problems of ethics and human behaviour. For what we take to be 'free' or 'enlightened' behaviour so much at large in the world of culture and popular opinion is by this light often revealed as vindication of 'False Self' behaviour rather than fulfilment of the True Self. It is a justification of false ways of feeling real, rather than an indication of how we might, by pursuing integration and the experience of 'being', become a little more real in a world felt to be real. The effect of the 'realism' of pseudo-science, which proclaims that man's essential nature is bestial, moreover tends to reduce responsibility to our true humanness. If aggression is innate, then we are at the mercy of impersonal 'organic forces' within us, and if we give way to the false solutions of hate, this is only 'natural'. This prevalent popular attitude, vindicated by Freud, tends implicitly to dehumanise us and to promote solutions which are anti-human. This kind of pessimistic realism also tends to reduce the confidence and energy of those who are seeking genuine human solutions.

Of course, great problems are raised as of how it is possible for a person whose very survival depends upon False Self behaviour to achieve touch with his True Self. But it does not help for us to try to escape such problems by endorsing his false solutions,

---

* There is an even more uncomfortable thought behind this paragraph, which takes account of those with whom there is no chance of ever becoming human, because of organic and incurable faults.

however heroic, as valid, nor by endorsing schizoid attitudes to life and inversions of value. If we accept object-relations psychology, we can no longer escape our human responsibilities by claiming that we are driven by 'instincts' which overpower us, or by saying that 'society' created by 'them' is so repressive that we had to protest by 'insurrectionary' behaviour. Such behaviour may be no more than a false solution, a mere anti-social attempt to feel real while being essentially destructive or degrading to the True Self. We cannot escape our responsibility by taking refuge in simple determinism, saying 'My parents let me down', or 'I was a foundling', or 'Society oppressed me', since even beneath the toughest of False Selves we must allow for a True Self which is lost for ever unless we recognise its existence and its right to *become*, be born, if any chance should come.

Thus in the field of legislation and social organisation, culture, and politics, we have to ask whether, if we believe in universal human rights – Will this measure *help to foster the capacity in individuals to discover their True Selves*? Does this promote integration and 'being'? Will this help individuals to discover their humanness? Here is the basis for a new liberalism which does not suffer from the hypomanic qualities of the present state into which liberalism has now fallen, with its blindness to the schizoid problem and its tendency towards demoralisation in the name of 'amoral' freedom. Even the most tolerant social measures need real teeth by which to foster and help defend the True Self in each individual against the more destructive manifestations of the False Selves in the schizoid minority and the False Self in each 'normal' individual. Thus, to pass a law against racial discrimination enables those who are weak in their ego-structures to resist the temptation to find strength by attacking others over whom they have projected their internal bad objects. But permissiveness alone does not solve everything. Tolerance of homosexuals may enable many to satisfy their libidinal need for relationship and thus, perhaps, even to become more mature and overcome some of the splitting which prevents their integration. On the other hand, restrictions on pornography may help restrain those whose False Solutions require that they should exploit and make use of others by involving them in the depersonalising of sex, the lowering of human value, hatred of woman, and the impulse to thrust harm into others. If they are restrained, they may become able to avoid false solutions of living at the expense of others. When an individual such as Polanski, who made a film about a woman having a baby by the Devil, says, 'It is a terrible assault on people's liberty to tell them what they can experience' we may suspect he means 'It is intolerable for the community to seek to limit my needs to feel real by thrusting fear into others'. Many cultural problems of an ethical kind are indicated by the implications of object-relations psychology. Freudian psychology, because of its basis in instinct theory, tended to obscure them, or to seem to vindicate such impulses, even though these offended the deepest ethical principles and were a form of antisocial behaviour.

All such problems need thinking out afresh, in the light of the recognition of our primary human needs to feel whole and real, and to realise the True Self in the realm of 'being'.

Object relations psychology dispels the prevalent delusion, which seeks blindly to free human potentialities for forms of 'insurrection' by which to alleviate the 'burden of sacrifice' unwillingly forced on us by 'society' which has obliged us to have to make 'instinctual sacrifices'. From the point of view of 'philosophical anthropology' there is nothing to 'release': it is rather that a dynamic of ego-maintenance and unfolding of a personality needs to be fostered and nourished. Opportunities need to be provided so that human beings may discover, by symbolic creative effort, 'what it is they really want'. Unless we provide for these needs, our contributions to human affairs will be valueless. Object-relations psychology in this sphere confirms Buber's approach to the ethical problems of the individual in society: conduct and actions should not be judged 'according to their use or harmfulness for individuals and society, but according to their intrinsic value and disvalue'. Winnicott's postulation of a True Self gives this word 'intrinsic' meaning. Buber says, 'We find the ethical in its purity only there where the human person confronts himself with his own potentiality and distinguishes and decides in this confrontation without asking anything other than what is right and what is wrong in his own situation' (Buber [10], p. 172).

Such an approach goes with a new kind of faith in human nature.

This kind of approach to human nature is also a move in psychology closer to the humanities: philosophical anthropology is, as we have seen above, concerned with the kind of experience which can only be explored by the subjective disciplines. In Winnicott's use the terms 'true' and 'false' we have semantic and evaluative aspects which require consideration in terms of sign and meaning in relation to the Kantian question 'What is man?' As Charles Rycroft says in his introduction to *Psycho-analysis Observed*: 'Winnicott . . . has found it necessary to introduce the distinction between a "true" and "false" self. But "true" or "false", like the "authentic" and "inauthentic" of the existentialists, are semantic and evaluative concepts, not scientific causal ones. Perhaps the principle of psychic determinism applies to the "false self", while the "true self" has free will.' (Rycroft [72], p. 16.)

Rycroft indicates that much of Freud's work was in fact semantic, which is another way of indicating as Farber does Freud's capacities for the poetic, and confirming what Home says about Freud's concern with the meaning of symptoms.

> It can indeed be argued that much of Freud's work was really semantic and that he made a revolutionary discovery in semantics, viz. that neurotic symptoms are meaningful disguised communications, but that, owing to his scientific training and allegiance, he formulated his findings in the conceptual framework of the physical sciences. In some aspects of his work Freud saw this himself clearly. His most famous work he entitled *The Interpretation of Dreams* not *The Cause of Dreams* and his chapter on symptoms in his *Introductory Lectures* was called *The Sense of Symptoms*. He was also well aware that many of his ideas had been anticipated by writers and poets rather than by scientists. (Rycroft [72], p. 14.)

The trouble has been that 'both psychology and medicine are faculties which suffer from an inferiority complex in relation to science' so that the necessary fully active disciplines have not been pursued. Meanwhile, from our point of view, psychoanalysis has tended to alienate itself by pretending to be a science concerned with causality.*

The semantic approach is also helping to bring psychoanalysis out of many futile controversies related to problems of cause and the degree to which adult capacities are

---

* One of the problems here is that so long as psychoanalysis regards itself as a science it lends itself to being exploded by experimental psychologists. As Rycroft says: 'They (analysts who reject the semantic approach) thereby lay themselves open to attack from critics like Professor Eysenck who see quite clearly that psychoanalysis cannot satisfy the canons of those sciences which are based on the experimental method but who believe that if they can demonstrate its inadequacy as a causal theory, they have proved that it is nonsense. To my mind, one of the merits of the semantic view . . . is that it completely undercuts the Eysenck-Psychoanalysis controversy by showing that both parties are not only, as Eysenck himself has said, arguing from different premises but from wrong premises. On their side analysts are claiming that analysis is what it is not, and, on his, Eysenck is attacking it for failing to be what it has no need to claim to be. And both parties are assuming that it is only the physical sciences which are intellectually respectable.'

determined by early experiences and to bring therapists increasingly to concern them-selves with getting into touch with the patient, and understanding what it is he is trying to communicate in the here and now. For as the term 'position' was meant to indicate, primal 'causes' are manifest in the here and now life. That is, the semantic (or poetic) approach is bringing psychoanalysis closer towards a study of practice, of 'strategies of survival' and meaning of symptoms in adult life and dynamics of ego-maintenance. The therapist, for instance, is less concerned with interpretation, as if his major role were to uncover some hidden origin of a problem, but more concerned with creative reflection of dynamic re-growth in the here and now, and fostering the creative symbolism by which the patient works on his problem of life.

Here, as we have seen, Winnicott's influence here has been most valuable. His concept of therapy as creative reflection is one which involves the doctor in a role which is at times arduous, painful, and even dangerous – like that of any parent. Winnicott gives the impression of a meeting between persons which is neither 're-education' nor the implication of an intellectual system. It is a form of love.

As Lomas says: 'He believes, as did Freud, that it is necessary to revive an early infan-tile memory. This does not mean that particular well-defined incidents need emerge from repression, but that there must be a return to the infantile experience of simple, passionate openness preceding the disappointment that led to withdrawal and splitting'. (Lomas, in Rycroft [72], p. 134.)

Winnicott's terminology of 'true' and 'false' says Lomas, needs to be submitted to circumspection. Is it a distinction that will enrich our theory of personality? Lomas relates it to Freud's term 'defensive':

> A defence is a manœuvre to prevent the expression of an 'instinctual' impulse considered likely, for one reason or another, to have undesirable effects in life. The impulse in question will then be repressed (or suffer some other vicissitude such as projection), with the consequence that actual behaviour will no longer be a relatively accurate expression of personality, but will give a false, disguised and distorted picture of it. (Lomas, in Rycroft [72], p. 134.)

This way of putting it, in this context, surely reveals that not least in Freud's theory are there many evaluative and semantic assumptions, despite the attempt to give the theory a basic quantitative aspect: 'false, disguised and distorted' imply a norm which by contrast is 'true, undisguised and accurate'. Freud attempted to imply that, say, 'distorted' meant something like the disguise of hatred by piety. But this is to imply, as we have seen, that it is the hatred which is more 'real', because it is more obviously animal, and like what seems real in the external world. Thus, to Freud, 'true' implies 'instinctual' and so 'real' while 'false' means 'civilised' and so unreal – a dichotomy which reappears in Laing, who speaks of the 'false self adapted to an alienated society'.

Lomas explores the problem further thus:

> A person who, for instance, has repressed viciousness may present a mild and equable demeanour In terms of the dichotomy under consideration his 'instinctive' self is the true one, his defences and their consequences false. But suppose that his viciousness is not primary but itself merely a disguise or a relatively meaningless escape valve? Does one not again have to put the question: 'Is his behaviour true or false?' (Lomas, in Rycroft [72], p. 134.)

Freud did not formulate his ideas in terms of trueness or authenticity because of the biological framework. But also perhaps there was another reason, in Freud's negative or defensive approach to experience:

He regarded growth less as a continuing evolution than as a gradual victory of each stage over the past; the pleasure principle must succumb to the reality principle; each new self discards the old, even if traces of it remain to harass and embarrass. Freud is caught between the authenticity of the past and of the present, and *his thinking does not allow for the unfolding of a true self which remains intact as the core of personality*, a unique entity gathering meaning as it grows, discarding only those aims and illusions that are peripheral to its being, whose quality is measurable not by stage of development, degree of libidinization, or physical mode of expression, but by its experienced meaningfulness and manifest spontaneity. (Lomas, in Rycroft [72]; my italics.)

That is, not only does Freud not have a language for the expression of interpersonal relationships, as Laing complains, but neither does he have a language in which one can speak of a continuous unitary self. He could not find the True Human Self. 'In a theory of continuity the main dichotomy is not between past and present or id and ego but between what is true and what is false.'

This 'truth' or 'falsity' exists within the self: truth or falsity is not to be attributed to social influences nor to conflict between 'real' nature and the impositions of repression through the super-ego which falsify this 'natural' self. Here we may note that Laing's 'existentialist' social theory coincides with Freud's rather than Winnicott's, as when he speaks of the need for 'dissolution of the false ego, *that which is adapted to society*'. Here Fairbairn's insistence on the unitary nature of the pristine ego is of great importance, because this establishes that there is a 'true' self in everyone, even where it is thwarted or suppressed by circumstances. What is disastrous is not to 'conform to society' or to 'lose one's instinctual spontaneity' – but to lose the sense of meaning and validity of one's human identity.

A first move would seem to be the acceptance of Fairbairn's view that the infant starts life in an integrated, pristine state which dissociates only in the face of adverse circumstances, and to equate this state with that of the true self, which is spontaneous, concerned with meaning and the agent of its own action. The integration is primary but not absolute, in that certain determinants of behaviour – such as reflex actions – have their own relative independence. These elements constitute behaviour which in animal life is called 'instinctual', but it does not follow that the spontaneous urge of the true self lacks biological foundations. (Lomas, in Rycroft, [72], p. 136.)

The problem now becomes that of telling 'At what point does the distortion of the original urge become so marked as to justify the view that a "false self" is operating?' Lomas believes that the answer to this 'would appear to be somewhat arbitrary, depending upon whether one is an idealist or a cynic' (though, as we have seen above from Suttie, it is the cynic who is essentially denying the nature of experience for his own purposes).

But it would perhaps be least confusing to restrict the term 'false' to behaviour designed, for whatever reason, to conceal the existence of the true self and therefore to deny meaning. The reasons for this kind of aim would include the avoidance of a real experience of life that was too awful to contemplate, the preservation (as Winnicott has shown) of a hidden but intact true self, and the attainment of some kind of meaning and satisfaction from the spurious personality which is erected. Although some satisfaction may be gained in this way, true meaning cannot. In such a state the person is 'depersonalised': his identity is based on delusion and parasitism, dependent on the use of mechanisms known to psychoanalysts by such terms as introjection, identification, narcissism, masochism, etc.; he has become a quisling, and has, in Anna Freud's phrase 'identified with the aggressor', the latter being, in this context, the world which has prevented him from becoming himself. . . . Actual behaviour will necessarily be a function of both the true and the false. (Lomas, in Rycroft [72], p. 137.)

This way of looking at human problems of identity and behaviour and their social context is obviously radically different from that of Freud and traditional psychoanalysis. Its essential concern is with 'meaning' – the sense of being real, of one's action and being as significant, of being 'confirmed' by one's relationships and in one's actions –

and in one's relationship with oneself. Once we have grasped this way of approaching the emotional life and behaviour we ought to be able to see at once that, if we accept it, a radical revision of our ethical belief and social theory is necessary, with concomitant changes to our approaches to culture and education. We can become at once more compassionate, and yet more discriminating. The essential question is, What is it to be human? and answers are to be judged in terms of our common awareness of human 'fact'.

What is most real about human beings is by no means 'instinct' or 'animality' – but that in us which is capable of complete truth to itself, such as the unflinching devotion of Cordelia and her kind of love which transcends death – or the preoccupation with an integration of identity, as in Mahler, which renders death insignificant. In such symbolism is the highest expression of the meaning in human life.

With object-relations psychology as a form of philosophical antropology we are indeed moving in a different orbit from that of the early reductive theories derived in a mechanical way from natural science, with all their abysmal implications for society. Today we find the scientist quoting Shelley's 'There is a spirit within man at enmity with nothingness and desolation' (Towers and Lewis, [83]). In so far as psychoanalytical theory can be regarded as belonging to the sciences, it brings science into the realm of the poet, in the direction of asking, with the psychotic, 'What is it to be human?' and with King Lear, 'Who is it that can tell me who I am?'

CHAPTER 16

'Society' and our 'Instincts'

THE popularity of the 'realism' of those who believe man to be no more than an animal raises in a new way the problem of what we believe about society and our 'instincts'. As we have seen, Freud found the origins of neuroses in the undue 'suppression of the sexual instinct' necessary for man to live in society:

> Our civilisation is, generally speaking founded on the suppression of instincts. . . . The sexual instinct is probably more strongly developed in man. . . . It places an extraordinary amount of energy at the disposal of 'cultural' activities. . . . The task of mastering such a mighty impulse as the sexual instinct is one which may well absorb all the energies of a human being. (Freud [27], p. 82.)

Those who failed to 'master' their instincts were offered the choice of becoming neurotics or heroes. Typically Freud sees the problem of man in terms of the defence mechanisms of an organism in an environment which he cannot believe to be benign. Thus in Freud's view, social life 'can never be more than unending warfare between instinct and morality'.

Of course, Freud's picture of 'instincts' breaking out and disrupting the individual life seems to be an accurate account of *how things are* with *some* people (and with all of us at times). The error, says Guntrip, lies in his implicit assumptions of *why* they are so. 'Man's recalcitrant and aggressive compulsions may not after all be due to instinct in the sense of innate and essentially unmodifiable drives, but may be due to a psychological factor not at the time appreciated' (Guntrip [37], p. 71).

So while it is true that 'large numbers of human beings experience a strong and persistent pressure or sexual need . . . in a way that finds no gratification within the limits of . . . civilised sexual morality . . . many *rebel* against restriction . . . more repress their needs and fall ill of neurosis', the problem remains of the interpretation we put on this. What we believe here has important social, political, and philosophic implications. If our destructive drives are 'innate instincts', then there is little we can do except tolerate rebels, promote demoralisation, avoid 'inhibition', or endure the spread of neurosis. A stricter morality would only make the rebel or the neurotic unhappy. So is there no alternative but the 'relaxation of morals'? If we merely allow more relaxation of sexual morality, then what? Guntrip suggests that the result of such relaxation, because of the falsity of its underlying assumptions, has already been: 'a weakening respect for marriage, the "acting out" of neurosis in sexually indiscriminate behaviour, which is rationalised as emancipation, an every-increasing supply of unwanted children who are denied their rightful parental background and are likely to have to endure in themselves the neuroses their parents are supposed to escape by means of sexual freedom'.

That is, to some extent, as Guntrip says, to come degree, a description of the actual situation brought about by two world wars and the effect of 'enlightened' popular opinion. But the truth, 'as the psychotherapist knows it', is that 'the relaxation of sexual morality since 1908 has not led to a diminution of neurosis'. Moreover, as Guntrip asks 'Is the relaxation of morality . . . to apply to the "instinct" of *aggression* as well as sex?'

What happens here, if we continute to believe in a death instinct whose aim is the organic detensioning of that life which 'disturbed' the universe? Must we not accept the extinction of life, as by nuclear warfare, as the inevitable expression of this? Some cultural critics, such as Susan Sontag, are actually spoken of as being 'attuned to the extinction of the species', while extreme *avant-gardists* speak of the Final-release Beauty of the Bomb. To such writers war is thus natural and inevitable – and so the extinction of the human race is imminent.

We cannot, of course, escape the truth that some individuals do have powerful negative drives and 'death-impulses' – but are they individuals with 'more powerful instincts' – or weak individuals trying to hide deeper problems? Guntrip asks: 'May it not be possible that "instinctive" is (being) confused with "neurotic"?'

Freud said that 'Men are not gentle, friendly creatures wishing for love . . .' (Freud [31]).

But is this state of affairs due to 'normal' 'innate' 'instincts' or their neurotic development in *some*? It seems surely odd, suggests Guntrip, that 'our greatest achievements should arise' as 'sublimations'. Should we not rather see social life, culture, morality, and religion as expressions of fundamental and primary human impulses? The fact about man is surely that he is distinguished from the animals by his culture? As Cassirer said: 'The new acquisition transforms the whole of human life. As compared with the other animals man lives not merely in a broader reality: he lives so to speak in a new dimension of reality.'

Guntrip re-examines the historical development of instinct theory. Freud and McDougall, he says, made instinct the basis of their psychological theories, but difficulties arose because, as one comes higher up the scale of animal life, intelligence becomes increasingly a modifying factor. In the conscious human being phantasy, as an integral aspect of personality structure, modifies instinct from birth. Even McDougall came to use another term – 'propensity' – when dealing with human beings. In his *General and Social Psychology*, Guntrip points out, Thouless wrote (in 1935): 'There seems to be no sufficient reason for saying that all motive forces behind human activity come from the inborn propensities, nor even from the more moderate statement that such motive forces as come from innate propensities are necessarily the strongest ones. . . . It seems better to avoid the word "instinct" in connection with human behaviour.' (Thouless [81], p. 41.)

Allport, on personality, in 1949, wrote: 'The doctrine of drive is a rather crude biological conception . . . the personality itself supplies many of the forces to which it must adjust. . . . Whatever the original drives or 'irritabilities' of the infant are, they become completely transformed in the course of growth into contemporaneous systems of motives.'

In recent psychoanalytical work the 'innate' factors in human behaviour are no longer regarded as fit merely to be called instincts. As Guntrip says: 'The sucking reflex in the new-born infant is instinctive, but the "sucking need and the sucking attitude to life" of the adult neurotic is certainly no simple instinctive phenomenon' (Guntrip [37],

p. 74). To which one might add that since more becomes known about the sensitivity of the foetus before birth and its capacity even for anxiety (as one gathers from Winnicott) it seems obvious that we are born with a degree of phantasy and an inward structure of apprehension which predominate over 'instincts' from the moment of birth. Even from the beginning symbolic aspects of behaviour and I–Thou experience 'of togetherness' seem more important than of instincts – as, when Winnicott points out, a baby cannot begin to suck until he has 'made' the breast, and has to make his self and his world by working on his framents of experience to unite them into a whole single self which is felt to be having the experiences of a single world which he is experiencing.

Of course, as Guntrip admits, impulses towards disruptive or destructive behaviour surge up within the psyche – we feel them to arise in our bodily life, and so they are easily mistaken for 'instincts'. But psychologists at large have long ceased, however, to equate impulse and instinct. Thus Professor John Cohen, in *Human Nature, War and Insight* (1946), found occasion to 'cast doubt on the value of instinct theory altogether as an explanatory principle in human conduct', and the sociologically inclined psychoanalyst in America, Karen Horney, regards Freud's 'mighty impulses' not as instincts but as 'neurotic trends'.

This is not to deny neurotic suffering, or the strength of such impulses which seem instinctive as there are, say, in some people's tormented and restless sexual activity. But to object-relations psychology these modes of behaviour tend to be seen not as the expression of primary drives but rather manifestations of ego-weakness and of flight from life. Here we need to re-examine attitudes such as those prevalent at the moment to sexual morality: are these 'realistic'?

Guntrip says in an earlier work, of the hunger that expresses itself (for instance) in compulsive sexual promiscuity:

> We cannot realise our nature as personal except in relationship with other persons. . . . The appetitive compulsion symbolises our reaching out after personal relationship, as is conspicuously the case in sexual compulsions. It is the individual who is inwardly isolated from other people who has no genuine flow of sympathetic friendly feelings towards others, who cannot really love, who is driven towards in desperation to clutch at physical contact to make up for inability to achieve emotional rapport.

Thus depersonalised sexual activity (as in promiscuity) may be seen as a search for love and a sense of identity which is false because it never finds its true aim, which is to fulfil the primary need for relationship. Such behaviour is not a 'release of instincts' but rather a displaced way of contracting into relationship and society: a false 'doing' in place of 'being', and the activity of a False Self.

This point of view hardly endorses the prevalent fashionable 'permissive' view which sees 'free' sensual behaviour in defiance of moral restraints, as a valuable way of 'throwing off inhibitions' and finding our 'natural' freedom.

What seems to be a more adequate approach to sexual reality is suggested by Guntrip thus: 'Relationship is achieved with both the mind and the body, and a sexual relationship is one among other pathways of escape from emotional and personal isolation into the security and fulfilment of sharing one's life intimately with another person.'

The minority of 'rebels' comes from those who cannot accept these goals of personal development often because they are schizoid individuals who fear contact, 'giving', and the recognition of the need for dependence. Yet, if we take the person who has grown up and developed from the 'ordinary good home', we can see the positive norm thus: 'A human being whose basic human relationships in childhood and adult life were, and are, good, satisfying and permanent, does not experience a ceaseless upsurge of painfully imperious and demanding sexual impulses. Sexual desire arises rather as a realistic response to a really appreciated external love-object.'

Freudian theory has been taken to vindicate the value of 'release' in behaviour and expression. From the object-relations point of view, however, ego-maintenance depends upon the activity of exploring one's humanness through symbolism, making reparation, and seeking to maintain touch with one's True Self. By contrast, while such creative activity belongs to 'being', 'bad thinking' is a False Self activity which manifests a schizoid solution to ego-maintenance based on the flight from weakness and human sensitivity. 'Sensuality' and violence in culture could thus actually divert energy from the quest for the True Self and its realisation. These could be a form of arousing primitive anxiety to which psychic energy has to be diverted from more creative and human forms of ego-maintenance, but which yield a momentary sense of being alive. They could be reinforcing the 'taboo on weakness' while blinding individuals to their needs to discover and foster the True Self. In personal behaviour and symbolism 'release' can thus become anti-human and a manifestation of a flight from life.*

Arguments in favour of permissiveness in both culture and behaviour focus on the sexual, in the 'release' of which a new 'freedom' is to be found. The truth of human sexual life would seem to be that the majority find enrichment and peace in relationship, are able to put a great deal of their creative energy into love while finding their primary sense of human satisfaction and meaning in family life and creative relationship. Sex is one expression of the libidinal goal of relationship and of the fulfilment of being. If 'the ultimate goal of the libido is the object', then our primary need is for relationship rather than sex, though sex is a major form of expression of relationship. Most individuals find their human qualities by 'contributing in' to 'the ordinary good home', and in this their sexual satisfaction is a significant aspect. There is no innate 'mighty impulse' which presents such a major problem that it 'may well absorb all the energies of a human being', as Freud believed. Of course, there is a disturbed minority who do feel they cannot cope with inward drives, and there are times (such as adolescence) when perhaps we all feel like that. But to believe that all human beings suffer from a loss of potentialities through sexual frustration is itself an intellectual schizoid chimera in the modern world which disguises deeper problems.

Where there are disruptive impulses in the relational life, says Guntrip, they are primarily 'reactions to situations of frustration perpetuated from childhood in the inner unconscious psychic world which is played upon by the outer world'. And these are, as we have seen, essentially problems of identity and existence – not of 'sex' at all.

Certainly what we cannot allow is the underlying assumption in much cultural comment today that there are unchallenged grounds in psychoanalytical theory for regarding 'rebellious' behaviour as acceptable as a heroic attempt to 'release instinctual drives' against the 'inhibitions' of a civilised society which is 'inimical' to self-fulfilment.

If object-relations theory does imply such a rejection of the assumptions of 'progressive' attitudes to sex, then a revision of the ethics both of culture and behaviour should follow. These need to be based on more realistic insights into how people behave and their motivation.

Guntrip writes: Sexual difficulties can now be seen as due not to the constitutional strength of the sex instinct, but to the developmental immaturity of the whole personality,

* See *The Masks of Hate*, pp. 226 ff.

and more specifically to the internal and unconscious perpetuation in the psyche, of frustrating object-relations of early life.'

That is, an approach to sex which craves for 'freedom' from committed relationship is itself a manifestation of frustrated love in infancy, and may spring from an unconscious fear of relationship, and of one's own needs: 'Neurotic suffering is not due to the repression of strong and healthy constitutional sexuality, but to the struggle to master infantile and immature sexual needs, which are kept alive by the situation in the unconscious inner world.'

If this were so it would therefore not be true that 'a relaxation of cultural and moral standards is the only escape from neurosis . . . ' for 'cultural and moral standards . . . are, at their best, an expression of the way in which reasonable mature individuals behave, the way in which Freud himself behaved in private life.'

We can apply this not only to sex, but also to the problem of violence. We need no longer accept Freud's pessimistic view of human nature, which he shared with Hobbes, Machievelli, Schopenhauer, and Pareto – and also with Hitler and Mussolini, as Guntrip suggests – that individuals only behave well because they are coerced by a minority into civilised moral behaviour. Object-relations psychology obliges us to re-examine the implications of Freud's attitude for social theory at large. As Bantock points out, it is incredible how in our intellectual world Freud's pessimistic and anti-human 'realism' can share the same bed with 'progressive' education or his negative view of human make-up be squared with a belief in the 'freedom' to be obtained by the 'release' of inhuman id instincts.

The social and ethical implication of Freud's view, says Guntrip, is that 'human nature is innately self-seeking, pleasure-seeking (not object-seeking), and is to be socialised only under very heavy pressure; and then only from non-altruistic motives, and under a never-relinquished repressed protest and revolt'.

Recent object-relations theory expresses much more hope in the individual man and much more trust in his natural conscience, and positive drives. 'Recent developments more and more establish the opposite view that good personal relationship is not desired merely for the sake of pleasure but is in itself the basic need and aim of men, whose nature cannot be fulfilled without it, while aggression and pleasure-seeking only result from the frustration of this primary aim.'

Hedonism may be the attempt to vindicate what is seen from the medical viewpoint as 'deteriorated' behaviour. So that we may get to grips with these deeper problems, suggests Guntrip, 'the assumption that civilisation rests on the renunciation of instincts is a misleading ideology that there is now urgent need to discard'.

The importance of discarding instinct theory is even more urgent as psychoanalytical thought discovers that the 'depressive' model of human make-up itself disguises deeper (schizoid) problems.

Guntrip suggests that a complete reorientation of psychoanalytical theory is involved because of this:

> The increasing emphasis of recent years on the schizoid problem represents the emergence of a distinct point of view in psychodynamic studies; a point of view, moreover, which diverges markedly from the traditional centuries-old approach to human problems. Like all other phenomena psychopathological phenomena disclose hitherto unrecognized aspects when looked at from a different viewpoint. (Guntrip, [116], p. 99.)

Psychoanalysis began, says Guntrip, when Freud changed his approach to psycho-

H

neurosis from the neuropathology in which he was trained to the psychopathology in which he 'was to prove the greatest of all pioneer investigators'. In a sense, however, Freud's picture of human nature resembled traditional theory, from Plato's model to St. Paul's doctrine of unceasing war between the flesh and the spirit, to which Freud 'merely gave a scientific dress'.

Freud's picture is therefore of a 'many-headed beast of desires and passions' governed by the 'law of the members': the instincts of sex and aggression functioning according to a 'pleasure-principle' and leading to a Hobbesian world in which life would be nasty, brutish and short': 'The "lion" of Plato's internal scheme becomes aggression taken up by the sadistic super-ego and turned against the id instinct-derivatives. The "law" of the mind and the "charioteer of reason" . . . becomes the ego seeking to operate by a "reality principle".' (Guntrip [116], p. 100.)

As Guntrip says, Freud never gave up this way of thinking, and it is still the basis of much 'rational' debate of the relationship between the individual and society. But supposing this picture of the nature of human psychic problems is essentially false? As Guntrip shows, it leads to pessimism on the one hand, and demoralisation on the other:

> The classical psycho-analytical theory is that anti-social impulses, biologically determined, which certainly might be better tolerated socially than they usually are, must be controlled and in the process such intense guilt and repression are developed that the whole psyche is liable to fall into a state of illness and depressive paralysis. . . . Freud took the side of easing depression and showing more toleration of instincts while strengthening the ego for rational control . . . (as against Christianity which 'took the side of repression, while essentially agreeing on the basic nature of the problem'.) (Guntrip, [116], p. 101.)

This picture of man striving against 'mighty instincts', is still the essential orthodoxy of much 'enlightened' humanist thought everywhere, and it forms the basis of the approach of many writers who seek a 'rational' approach to problems of sex, morality, aggression, and behaviour. When examined, their fundamental belief is that human nature is as Plato described it:

> He describes human nature by a simile. On the outside men look like human beings, but under the skin three creatures are concealed: a monster with many heads, some wild, some tame . . . the desires and passions: a lion – the spirited quality which will fight; and a human being – the rational element. Plato urges us to make the man supreme, and see that, helped by the lion, he controls the many-headed beast. (Sir Richard Livingstone, quoted by Guntrip [116], p. 121.)

The word 'control' is paramount, as in much 'scientific' writing about behaviour, sex, and morality. Our only hope over our unruly monster is in intellectual reason and 'self-control'. But supposing the whole picture itself, far from being 'scientific' is in fact an illusion, a phantasm of Freud's own, which disguises deeper problems, which cannot be dealt with directly by 'law' and 'reason' but only by ego-maintenance?

Guntrip sees the platonic, or Pauline, picture of man struggling against 'mighty instinctual drives' as itself a 'depressive diagnosis' that masks the essential problem. According to Freud's picture we feel, 'thank God we are not weak. We have a mighty sexual instinct and a powerful destructive and aggressive instinct'.

We have seen how this belief is reflected in popular thought, and is used as a vindication by advertisers and commercial culture. The diagnosis of this belief, however is this:

> The incompleteness of the 'depressive' diagnosis is seen the moment we realize that human beings always prefer to feel bad and strong rather than weak. The diagnosis of anti-social 'instincts' has always been man's most convincing rationalization of his plight, a subtle defence against the alarming truth that the real trouble is fear, flight from life at deep levels, and the failure of basic strong ego-formation, resulting in consequent inadequacy, both felt and factual, in coping with life.

The fact that human beings prefer feeling 'bad somebodies' rather than 'weak nonentities' emerges historically and socially. There is the story of the ancient Greek who burned down a temple because he could not gain recognition in any other way, and much crime and delinquency must be motivated by the quest for a sense of power and notoriety for destructive behaviour, to cover the felt inability to achieve true valour by constructive work. (Guntrip [116], p. 101.)

At first, as Guntrip points out, Freud worked within the traditional concepts of human make-up – of natural instincts versus social controls, which had remained the same from Plato to St. Paul, and is still the 'commonsense' view. 'His first concepts evolved in the first stage were those of repression, resistance, the censor, transference, the meaning of dreams and symbolism, infantile sexuality, the 'family' or Oedipus complex and so on' (Guntrip [116], p. 98).

All these concepts belong to a psychology of impulse-control. The essential picture of man in this traditional view which culminated in instinct theory as Guntrip points out, is that of a creature within whom a rational element strives with a 'many-headed beast' within so that the only hope for man is for the 'law of the mind' to prevail.

This is a purely negative view by which the ego exerts an adaptive function, concerned to oblige the 'organism' unwillingly to recognise the 'reality principle' in such a way as to forfeit potentialities. This is surely the least creative of Freud's theories.

What have proved to be most seminal in Freud's theories are the psychodynamic structural concepts by which he sought to explain the way man can divide against himself. While his id, super-ego, ego scheme has come to be found unsatisfactory because it suggests a too simple mechanical division of the self into entities around the impersonal id and death instinct, it was the beginning of insight into ego-splitting – the way the self can become divided and turn on itself. Freud's later concepts such as that of the super-ego, however, marked a significant development from the psychology of impulse-control to the psychology of object relations, since what became apparent was that the failure of a person's reality sense was due to divisions in the self. From this investigation of splitting has grown a sense of dynamic complex between relationship and identity, in the realm of personality and the growth of consciousness which no longer requires instinct-theory as a basis, and no longer requires man to be seen as an organism merely adapting to his environment.

This 'schizoid diagnosis' should prove challenging to the psychology at present used in some forms of 'scientific' investigation of human society – the sociologist and anthropologist. According to Professor Henry – an American Freudian anthropologist – 'America is one of the most psychoanalytically-minded countries on earth.' Yet what America has in mind here is strictly Freudian, and it is possible that this Freudian intellectual theory itself in American has become a defence against deeper insights into human nature and human needs – not least against the recognition of feeling and intuition and the deeper problems of being and identity. Certainly, it would seem futile to try to explain human needs in terms of such a simplified picture of personality structure as this.

Fun is a creature out of the Id, the repository of all untamed instinctual cravings that surge within us. Within every man and woman, says Freud, is an Id, a volcano of seething impulse, held in check only by society, whose controls become our conscience, our Super Ego. In contrast to the Id, which urges us to seek only pleasure, the Super Ego commands that we work hard, save, and control our impulse life. But nowadays, as the Super Ego values of hard work, thrift, and abstemiousness no longer pay off, and technological drivenness presses the Self so hard; nowadays, when the high-rising standard of living has become a moral ideal, the Id values of fun, relaxation, and impulse release are ascendant.

Only a people who have learned to decontrol their impulses can consume as we do. So the consequence of technological drivenness is the creation of a people who, though reared to support it – by being trained to heroic feats of consumption – are quitely undermining it by doing the least they can rather than the most, not only because it is hard to get anything out of the system but also because they have stayed up so late the night before having fun! (Henry [40], p. 44.)

It is worth examining this typical point of view based on Freud to indicate how it obscures rather than illuminates the cultural problems. Professor Henry is nearer the point on his previous page when he speaks of the urge in the self to 'stay alive', by 'adaptive radiation': 'Fun in America is an adaptive radiation, for it is the expression of the American's determination to stay alive.' That is, 'fun' is an expression of what Winnicott might call 'manic denial of deadness' in an environment that threatens depersonalisation while opportunities for real reparation are lacking. I have now put the matter, as we shall see, in 'schizoid' terms – that is, in terms of the basic fear of weakness (and death) of identity.

But while 'fun' is an assertion of manic vitality, so too, surely, is the belief that we have a 'volcano' inside us. Is not the problem rather that we fear there might be nothing inside us? If we see the 'volcano' picture as a myth, we can also perhaps see that the accompanying belief in the need to 'release impulses' in culture is but vindication of a false solution behaviour in society and culture where acquisitiveness is the basis of identity. This prevalent attempt to solve identity problems by incorporation and acquisition, being a false solution, inevitably leads to the dead end of becoming 'quietly undermined'. That is, it is essentially a hate-cycle whose hedonistic fever can never satisfy the urges it seeks to serve, and whose morality is too coarse to refine living.

If we accept Freud as Professor Henry does, then the assumptions of the cultural symbolism of an acquisitive economy are justified by 'realism'. All commerce is doing, when it exploits emotion and attaches identity to acquisitiveness and the 'survival of the fittest', is to champion impersonal id forces against inhibiting super-ego limitations. 'Fun' living is on the side of 'release', against 'police control, legal punishment, denunciatory public opinion, moral disapproval, religious preaching of sin', which 'all conspire to discipline recalcitrant instincts'. Indulging your impulses is good for your libido – against 'society' which imposes restraint. As the advertiser believes this, so does the rebel of the *avant-garde*: hallucinogenic drugs and the depersonalised sex orgy are valuable in the campaign to enlarge experience. But supposing the assumptions about human nature behind all this activity is false? Object-relations psychology suggests that they are, and that the direction of 'release' is anti-human and a complement to war and the dehumanising effect of an economy based on bustling activity and externals.

How many adherents to the enlightenment of liberation through 'fun' ever pause to consider the implications of Freud's attitudes to man in society here – which were that civilisation had to be defended against individuals by coercion?

Guntrip quotes Freud from *The Future of an Illusion*:

Every individual is virtually an enemy of civilisation, though civilisation is supposed to be an object of universal human interest. It is remarkable that, little as men are able to exist in isolation, they should nevertheless feel as a heavy burden the sacrifices which civilisation expects of them in order to make communal life possible. Thus civilisation has to be defended against the individual.

One thus gets an impression that civilisation is something which was imposed on a resisting minority which understood how to obtain possession of the means to power and coercion. (Freud [34], p. 6.)

It seems rather that every civilisation must be built up on coercion and the renunciation of instinct. . . . One has, I think, to reckon with the fact that there are present in all men destructive, and therefore anti-social and anti-cultural trends. (Freud [34], p. 7.)

If we follow Freud, we follow him towards a distrust of man which seems far from confident in democracy, but rather implies that men must be belaboured into being civilised, by a minority of *biens savants*:

> It is just as impossible to do without control of the mass by a minority as it is to dispense with coercion in the work of civilization. For masses are lazy and unintelligent; they have no love for instinctual renunciation, and they are not to be convinced by argument of its inevitability; and the individuals composing them support one another in giving free rein to their indiscipline. (Freud [34], p. 7.)

The only way to better this situation is 'to lessen the burden of the instinctual sacrifices imposed on men, to reconcile men to those which must necessarily remain and to provide a compensation for them' (Freud [34], p. 7).

Failure to question the basis of their 'realism' in this realm has meant that many intellectuals are not able to find radical objections to the hedonism of our commercial society, nor even to its sacrifice of human value to the 'economy'.

Thus Professor Henry speaks of 'personality impoverishment' as though this were a failure to find outlets for the 'volcano' in his view: 'society' causes the problems: 'Along with the emotional problems they create, all cultures provide socially acceptable outlets or anodynes. In America some compensation for personality impoverishment is provided by the higher standard of living'. (Henry [40]).

So, too, he thinks (with Freud) in terms of a minority of 'cultural maximisers': 'All great cultures, and those moving in the direction of greatness, have an élite which might be called the cultural maximisers whose function is to maintain or push further the culture's greatness and integration' (Henry [40]).

Unable to see culture as having its positive origin in the inward reparative and creative drives of each individual, Professor Henry can thus only see education (for instance) as being 'the central conserving force of the culture' and as having 'the function . . . to prevent the truly creative intellect from getting out of hand'. His views on education and culture are essentially pessimistic.

Professor Henry is 'for' creativity, he will not have it 'tamed' or made useful: 'creativity, when it is encouraged . . . occurs only after the creative thrust of an idea has been tamed – and directed towards socially approved ends'.

Social approval is death: the goal is the 'release of impulse' as we have seen: 'The root of life is impulse, and its release in the right amount, at the proper time and place, and in approved ways, is a primary concern of culture' (Henry [40], p. 305).

These approaches to culture are endorsed by the attitude of Laing, in whose 'phenomenological' library Henry's book was published.

The underlying concept here of cultural potential in man is extremely mechanistic and belongs to the crudest theories of nineteenth-century biology. Impulse theory implies that we have a certain quantity of libidinal energy within us which must be employed in one way or another: like a head of steam or gathering of fluid. If it is not released in sexual activity, it must be released by 'sublimation' in another direction – as in culture or religion or some other displacement activity. Art is no more than a sublimation of primitive urges. Religion is a manifestation of infantile dependence out of which the mature man grows. To be fully 'adult' by contrast is to release one's sensual and primary sexual drives – albeit, 'in approved ways'. For decades these attitudes have been felt by the intelligentsia to be 'realistic': now they are exposed both by science and by subjective disciplines as delusions. To science man's culture is the most significant aspect of his development,* while to philosophical anthropology his concern with meaning and being are primary.†

The consequent implications for culture are of tremendous importance. For now phantasy processes and symbolism, instead of being (as they were, typically, for Freud) forms of displacement, defensive modes of self-protection, or sublimation, are seen rather to be positive primary processes in the development and maintenance of the structure of personality. With the work of Melanie Klein the role of phantasy became established as a primary creative and crucial factor in the development of human consciousness and personality. With Winnicott the emergence of the human consciousness in the baby is explored as a creative achievement, in which far, from seeing man as a creature struggling in a hostile environment, one may see the processes of personality development as one of the most marvellous fulfilments of the impulse of life to proliferate and develop – in a way that accords with the attitude of modern biology.‡

As Guntrip says, Freud saw psychotherapy as a way of helping the ego in its struggle against powerful anti-social instincts.

> The only way of avoiding either criminality or illness is to achieve maturity, not in the sense of basic socialisation but in the sense of sublimation, a hypothetical process of detaching enough energy from the original instinctive aims to be redirected to valuable cultural goals. The original instinctive aims can, however, always be found still being energetically pursued under repression in the unconscious. (Guntrip [116], p. 100.)

For Freud – and for St. Paul – there is no possibility of 'cure' while man remains in the flesh. By contrast with Christianity, 'Freud took the side of easing repression and showing more toleration of instincts while strengthening the ego for rational control.'

But to Plato, St. Paul and Freud, as we have seen, 'it seems to be proved beyond all doubt that we are very bad . . . we have *a mighty sexual instinct and a powerful and destructive and aggressive instinct*' (Guntrip [116], p. 100).

This attitude is still with us in those who believe that 'we have . . . an innate behaviour pattern, an open instinct, an inward biological demand placed in our nature by our evolutionary history', so that there is no chance of eradicating this aggressive component – 'we deal with the changeless'.

These beliefs, Guntrip suggests, are an attempt in themselves to overcome the schizoid fear of weakness of identity: 'At least if we are bad we are someone.' From the point of view of object-relations psychology and the study of schizoid conditions, this whole belief that we have to live with mighty bad inner instincts, Guntrip says, may be man's greatest self-deception.

From the point of view of the 'schizoid diagnosis', the truth rather is that we cannot bear our own weakness and the associated fear that we may cease to exist.

---

* 'To assume that studies of animal behaviour imply any decrease in the structure of man would be a view of the utmost naïvety. Man displays emergent qualities for transcending those of the highest animal. The extent of his high powers of abstract reasoning and the fact of his religious awareness and spiritual life, his appreciation of moral and aesthetic values '. . . not only confirm this but suggest that there are also, in his future vast potentialities yet to be realised' (W. H. Thorpe, a leading ethologist, *Learning and Instinct in Animals*, quoted in Towers [83]).

† 'When one speaks of a man one speaks of him *along with* the summation of his cultural experiences' (Winnicott [130], p. 370).

‡ Yet a symposium can be held, and a book compiled, in 1966, on *Biology and Personality* (ed. I. T. Ramsey, Blackwell, Oxford) without reference to Winnicott's insights, or Margaret Ribble, or John Bowlby, or indeed anything in it on inner reality except a reference to hallucinants! As Guntrip says: 'The traditional scientific approach tends always towards an impersonal type of theory, and this is not often honestly admitted to be an expression of a certain philosophical view of man, that the mind is the brain' (Guntrip [37], pp. 16–17).

As we have seen, from object-relations psychology, a new model emerges by which it is not 'pressure' of instinctual drive and its inhibition which lies at the root of our problems, but ego-weakness, splitting and the consequent need to seek integration. In this integration culture has a positive creative role, and a major aim is to 'contribute in' to society.

Guntrip says that:

> Ego-splitting, a concept which Freud presents quite explicitly as fundamental in the last section of his unfinished, posthumous *Outline of Psycho-analysis*, begins to take the place of impulse-control as the centre of interest. It is now possible to see that this actually implies a shift of emphasis from a *psychology of depression* to a *psychology of the schizoid process*. (Guntrip [116], p. 99.)

We may, in the light of this, see our kind of society as one in which, while the constructive means to develop a sense of identity are frustrated, we tend to take recourse to schizoid or 'False Self' solutions. We tend to aggressive and destructive modes of behaviour and expression, which yet essentially manifest a flight from life, or deterioration, in the desperate need to 'feel someone'. Our society is established on 'pseudo male doing' while 'female element being' is comparatively despised as weak. The belief in our innate destructiveness and the hopelessness it promotes is itself a form of 'bad thinking' which enables us to deny our humanness – while at the same time being irresponsibly prepared to relinquish it by default.

Here, perhaps, we can see clues to the connection between paranoia in the modern world and the false solutions to problems of identity in our culture from 'Westerns' to industrial 'go', ambition, acquisitiveness, manic hedonism, and false attitudes to our own reality. We would rather be 'bad somebodies' than 'weak nonentities' – to be human and weak is felt as if it were on the way to loss of identity. 'Enlightenment' based on theories of 'release' of 'impulse' actually make the situation worse by making it more anti-human and schizoid.

As Melanie Klein says, in the infant persecutory anxiety gives rise to 'anger and aggression' which are an attempt to master fear by removing its cause. But in the infant these merely lead to 'the discovery of helplessness and therewith the inturning of aggression against his own weak ego'. The effect of the false posture of being 'bad' and strong can thus lead to a greater degree of turning against one's own humanity – a syndrome I explore further in *The Masks of Hate*.

In our society the effect of taking resort to 'hate processes', as by aggressiveness or 'drivenness' in the social sphere, or as by paranoic 'anger' in the international sphere, or by theories of our ape-like badness, is to seek to remove causes of fear *which cannot be removed in that way*. That is the fear, having arisen from existential insecurity, could really only be slowly worked on in terms of inward integration by creative living and creative symbolism, by finding and living with real people, by love, and by reparative effort in seeking to discover a whole self in relation to a real world. These would mean accepting and living with one's fear of one's own hate and destructiveness and one's weakness. The effect of 'drivenness' and assertion towards a supposed 'external' enemy in modern forms of paranoia and hate culture, merely reinforce splitting, and division within the individual psyche by exporting our hate by projection. Not only does this make the problem of weakness of identity worse, but it diverts energy from actual living to deal with it, while deepening the 'taboo on weakness' – on being human. Thus, the fundamental criticism, from object-relations theory, of the nature of Western society is that because of the false solutions it promotes abroad, it not only causes a failure to discover riches in the world, as Professor Henry indicates, but actually depletes individual energy available for creative living, and so directs it away from real solutions of the problems as by finding richness and peace in our lives by coming to terms with our essential humanness and 'confronting the problem of existence'.

CHAPTER 17

Education, Culture, and Moral Growth

IF WE are to reconsider ethical issues in the light of object-relations psychology and believe that human nature can be trusted to continually recreate civilisation within itself, then we must consider how individual morality develops and functions. Philosophical anthropology does not see hope here in Reason alone. Perhaps it will help us to approach this problem if we begin by referring to a contemporary rationalist philosopher con cerned with the reform of moral education, John Wilson, Director of the Farringdon Institute at Oxford, author of *Logic and Sexual Morality* and part-author of the Pelican Book *The Education of Morality*. Wilson is seeking an approach which is more 'realistic' and more liberal than, say, the traditional Christian approach. He is a logician. He insists that the educator concerned with morals should be that of 'analytic clarifier', while morality is essentially a matter of 'communications'. For him the problem is one of providing children with 'facts' in order to allow them to make their own choices. The adult or teacher should represent no definite moral code, but allow children to decide on their own choices in behaviour, making their decisions by reason and logic.

This approach seems convincing, but when examined in the light of our exploration of the problems of object-relations, it can perhaps be seen to be fundamentally fallacious. It is fallacious in the light of the recognition, in psychoanalysis as in philosophical anthropology, that it is not reason which distinguishes man, but his 'psychic reality' in his existence as a person. It leaves out of account the basis of a moral sense in one's relationship with oneself, and the whole bodily, or 'mouth ego', origins of moral capacity. The 'rationalist' approach tends almost to assume that it is possible for the mind to function as though it were not in the body, nor in a being once nursed through 'psychic parturition' by a mother. Wilson has forgotten Buber's insistence, speaking of Kierkegaard, that 'thought cannot authorise itself but is authorised only out of the existence of the thinking man' (Buber [10], p. 72).

Thus morality to him is too much a self-authorising mental trick separated from existence in the individual human life. In the light of the object-relations model of personality development, it can be seen that such a view fails to take into account most of the significant processes of growth in which creative symbolism plays so large a part. Such an approach based on presenting 'facts' fails to recognise the one significant human fact involved, which is the inner struggle between love and hate. It fails to take into account the close connection between the 'need to feel real' and the need for a personal moral sense. It fails to take into account the child's need to draw on (or reject) the 'moral code and general cultural endowment of our age'. And it fails to put first the need to 'introduce to the child the opportunity for being creative that the practice of the arts and the practice of living offers to all those who do not copy and comply but who genuinely grow to a way of personal self-expression'.

My quotations in the above paragraph come from an essay on *Morals and Education* by D. W. Winnicott, originally a lecture given at the London Institute of Education in 1962 (Winnicott, in Niblett [67]; also in Winnicott [94]).

Winnicott draws our attention to the underlying problems of all morality which are first (as in the psychology of Fairbairn) the question of establishing an identity at all (what Winnicott calls the 'I AM feeling'). Later, morality is in complex with relating to others and becoming capable of 'contributing in'. Without 'belief in', moral issues are meaningless to an individual. The teacher provides for needs whereby

> the child's own and personal solution to the problem of destruction of what is loved turns into the child's urge to work or to acquire skills . . . the need is the essential factor, and the need arises out of the child's establishment within the self of a capacity to stand feeling guilt in regard to destructive impulses and ideas, because having become confident in regard to reparative impulses and opportunities for contributing in. This reappears in a big way at the period of adolescence, and it is well known that the provision of opportunity for service for young people is of more value than moral education in the sense of teaching morals. (Winnicott [94], p. 103.)

Winnicott distinguishes between the development of a personal moral dynamic, and a moral sense which is 'implanted'. A deficiency or absence of a moral sense is a consequence of early failure in processes of maturation probably through environmental deficiency. Such people are ill: they need to be 'given' a moral sense: 'Where there is lack of personal moral sense the implanted moral code is necessary, but the resulting socialisation is unstable' (Winnicott [94], p. 26).

To apply the kind of 'implanting' required by such persons without a moral sense to healthy people (who do have their own personal moral sense) is likely either to induce a false socialization based on mere compliance, or to seem irrelevant to them.

The basis of Winnicott's position is in the observation of Freud's that bad deeds are done because they are forbidden, and manifest the need to '*attach a sense of guilt to something*', in order to mitigate an otherwise oppressive feeling of nameless guilt. Thus wicked acts may bring to a child mental relief in the mitigation of this oppressive sense of guilt. This guilt-sense, as we have seen, is associated with the problem of feeling real. A child who steals may well be symbolically taking something he feels belongs to him by right: that is, the psychic nurture that should have created a secure sense of *being*. There also seems to be an extension of this in Winnicott's observation that takes this further: 'in the more serious and more rare anti-social episodes it is precisely the capacity for guilt-feeling that is lost. Here we find the most ugly crimes. We see the criminal engaged in a desperate attempt to feel guilty.' (Winnicott [94], p. 27.)

This attitude seems to point to Fairbairn's indication of the schizoid problems underlying the absence or presence of guilt. That is, a person who has not discovered the capacity to feel guilty has not discovered his identity in relationship to others. He has not found himself as real; he has not found himself as human. Thus in the symbolism of Dostoevsky's novel *Crime and Punishment*, Raskolnikov by his crime is not only trying to discover the reality of his identity in a real world: in the end he discovers both ruth and love, and, so, his humanness.

We may perhaps see here the relevance of a concern with the symbolism of anti-social acts to the need to preserve a sense of good and bad being 'within the self', and engagement with these elements of the identity. The pointless riots which occasionally flare up in various parts of the world may be expressions of such a 'need to feel real and personal' in a dehumanised environment.

As Winnicott says, one of our problems is that we face the danger of relying on war to give a sense of reality to those who need it in that way: 'a localised war, with all its immense tragedy, used to do something positive for the relief of individual tensions, enabling paranoia to remain potential and giving a sense of REAL to persons who do not always feel real when peace reigns supreme. Especially in boys, violence feels real, while a life of ease bring a threat of depersonalisation.' (Winnicott [94], p. 243.)

In America, during a riot in the Watt's area of Los Angeles, a youth charged with the murder of a lorry driver, said: 'I'm sorry I shot that white dude . . . I wanted to be the big man.' The tentative conclusion of the authorities there was that the Watt's riot was not a race riot but an urban riot whose cause was not racial discrimination or unemployment, 'but the deadly dreariness of the American urban environment'. Such areas as Watts do not ever have the 'warmth and camaraderie which is the other side of slum life' (*The Times*, 17 March, 1965).

In the light of Winnicott's view, the teacher's role may be seen as one of fostering a natural process of the development of a moral sense, which has already accomplished a great deal, and is at one with the development of a sense of identity. The teacher has his own quality of identity and his own moral patterns, of which his pupils may make use, as by identification, if they choose. They can adopt these for their own purposes. But there will be a minority who are not healthy or integrated enough to make use of these for their own purposes. These may require a degree of coercion, into compliance, but in the recognition that the socialisation brought by compliance is 'always weak'. This coercion only does harm if it is extended to healthy individuals because it merely induces a false compliance in them, a false socialisation.

Thus there are certain influences which can be inimical to normal processes of development. This sentence itself suggests a way of looking at the problem of culture at large. What we need to consider is not the effect of a 'bad' work of expression, say, in 'corrupting' others in the sense of encouraging them to be wicked, for if they were wicked this might manifest an expression of the hope to feel guilty or to attach one's guilt to something which would be a manifestation of 'hope'. What we should look at is the effect its symbolism has on the need for us *to discover and work on our responsibility for the good and within us*, to discover our True Self. This we achieve by symbolism as we achieve the capacity to accept these as aspects of an integrated identity that feels real in a real world. Whatever prompts or fosters splitting can be inimical (an obvious example is racialist propaganda). It is not therefore possible to extend mere tolerance to all forms of expression and cultural influences (as we recognise by our race laws). At the end of his essay on guilt, Winnicott discusses this problem over a case history. This concerns a boy patient who had been under compulsion to steal: 'hearing a voice that ordered him about, the voice of a wizard.' The wizard was an hallucinated internalised authority standing in the place of an adequate true conscience (what Winnicott calls 'natural super-ego organisation'). (The full history of the case is given in Winnicott [90], pp. 101–17.) For complex reasons, partly to do with the war, this child 'had missed something at the age of two years' and had to go back to look for it. He suffered depression in consequence of his mother's absence as the 'good object' who could see him through the period of reparation: 'Mother went away. I and my brother had to live by ourselves. We went to stay with my aunt and uncle. The awful thing that happened there was that I would see my mother cooking in her blue dress and I would run up to her but when I got there she would suddenly change and it would be my aunt in a different coloured dress.'

'The child often hallucinated his mother, employing magic, but constantly suffering from the shock of disillusionment.'

The mother had 'gone away' to have a baby: it was then that the boy had stayed with his aunt and uncle: during this time, in fact (as Winnicott discovered), he had 'only just managed to keep the thread of experience unbroken'. 'He was not only hallucinating but also he was needing to be told exactly what to do and his uncle, recognising this, had deliberately adopted a sergeant-major attitude and by dominating the boy's life he had counteracted the emptiness which resulted from the loss of the mother' (Winnicott [90], p. 111).

Here we have the picture of a child who, because of his problems of envy over his mother's creativity, suffers talion* fears so great that they threaten to break his continuity of existence. So in the absence of the real mother he is seeking to make do with hallucin-ated mothers, the uncle in a substitute role, while his inner world is wrecked by the internalised 'bad object': 'the witch, and the cauldron, and the magic spells . . . the woman of early infancy who is terrible to think of in retrospect, because of the infant's absolute dependence' (Winnicott [90], p. 113).

That is, there is a problem here of ambivalence, of the inability to bring together love and hate in the mother and in the self. There is a terror of dependence because the object is too ambivalent to depend upon: in the attempt to deny the 'bad' side of the mother and the internalised 'bad object', there is an attempt to survive. There is a consequent splitting of the ego and relief from the fear of loss of continuity of being. This splitting led to a situation in which survival was 'falsely' given as if by the internalised uncle, who became, as it were, a substitute for a normal 'super-ego organisation':

> The wizard . . . turned out to have the overcoat of his soldier uncle, the one who had dominated his life, thus saving him from the emptiness of depression. He now told me that the wizard had a voice which was exactly that of the uncle. At school this voice continued to dominate him. The voice told him to steal and he was compelled to steal . . . in stealing he was in the direction of finding the mother that he had lost. (Winnicott [90], p. 112.)

My point in referring to this case is not only to draw attention to Winnicott's approach to the problems of anti-social behaviour but also to indicate Winnicott's opinion that '*It would have been easy to have diverted this boy from the path that led to his recovery*' and to examine the cultural implications of this.

This boy patient stole in order to try to find 'true guilt', as by finding the mother, as a real continuing person, and as an object that could be taken into the self as part of an adequate 'super-ego organisation' – that is, as part of a natural moral sense which was felt to belong to a whole self. For various reasons the circumstances of his life had wrecked this possibility, and so the child's moral creativity was split into hallucination and threat-ening bad objects rather than integrated dynamic elements within the self, felt as real. The 'magic' by which he seeks to hold his life together becomes disembodied 'bad' objects, the witch mother and wizard uncle, and the latter commands him (as though from 'outside' the self) to commit 'bad' actions as a means to discovering the mother and discovering the capacity for guilt.

---

* *Talion*: the law of retaliation inflicting punishment of some kind or degree as injury. See Leviticus xxiv. 20 and the Latin phrase *lex talionis*.

Underlying Winnicott's approach here is Kleinian theory that what such a patient needed to do was to complete the stage of 'being depressed', towards development associated with reparation. What the child had 'missed' was the experience of achieving integration by coming to terms with the hate and love within himself and making reparation towards wholeness. As we have seen, Winnicott takes the important positive step of calling the 'depressive position' 'the stage of concern' and regarding it as an achievement: 'being depressed is an achievement, and implies a high degree of personal integration, and an acceptance of responsibility for all the destructiveness that is bound up with living, with the instinctual life, and with anger at frustration' (Winnicott [94], p. 176).

The child under discussion had not achieved this *'acceptance of responsibility'*, and so the 'wizard' commands him as if from outside him, to carry out acts *for which he feels no shame* ('since he obeyed the voice and had not been a coward'). There is an inverted schizoid morality here. To desire not to be a coward is a 'good' thing. The object of the act is bravely to seek love and the attachment of guilt to reality, even by a criminal act which is from the normal point of view 'bad' thing and an act of ('taking') hate. It is humanly more revealing to see such stealing as a 'strategy of survival' than as 'wicked'. The whole problem arises from the lack of opportunities to work through a stage: 'the human individual cannot accept the destructive and aggressive ideas in his or her own nature without experience of reparation, and for this reason the continued presence of the love object is necessary at this stage since only in this way is there opportunity for reparation' (Winnicott [94], p. 176).

It follows that to punish such a child severely is to punish him for a situation which occurred between the ages of 2 and 5, *for which he was in no way responsible.* At the time of the act he is following an inverted schizoid ethic. His fundamental problem arose at the age of 2 or thereabouts when he was not able to make reparative effort to accept the destructiveness and hate within him because of the inaccessibility for some reason of the love object.

Punishment to such a child will seem merely bewildering. It might, indeed, have the effect of reinforcing the split, and making development less possible: 'If he had been thrashed or if the headmaster had told him that he ought to feel wicked, he would have hardened up and organised a fuller identification with the wizard; he would then have become domineering and defiant and eventually an anti-social person' (Winnicott [94], p. 28).

This case and Winnicott's insights have many implications for discipline, dealings with anti-social behaviour and crime. But here I wish to examine the cultural implications. 'It would have been easy to have diverted this boy from the path that led to his recovery. He was of course unaware of the intolerable loneliness and emptiness that lay at the back of his illness, and which made him adopt the wizard in place of a more natural super-ego organisation. . . . '

This child had problems of a kind which are also found universally in all of us in a less exacerbated form. Indeed, his problem is the universal problem, which is that of accepting the hate and destructiveness in ourselves and of making reparation in such a way as to embrace and modify these. The effect of such reparation is to make us feel more integrated and to make others and the world appear more real (and not split as this patient's self and world were split): this is, as we have seen, the basis of personal richness and fulfilment.

There are two points to note here. One is that we can only achieve this at all if we are 'healthy' up to a point (which is the point of being able to be 'usefully depressed'). If we have damage to our 'psychic tissue' then the cure of our dissociation may require lengthy therapy, and is not easily accessible to ordinary culture. The other is that we must not take creative achievements by individuals to stand for their health itself.* That is creativity (true reparation) can do a great deal for us, but even the most satisfying creativity has only a minute and slow effect on the intractable area of the inner world, and if there are immature elements there they will remain so unless some drastic kind of therapy is used. We are here up against the intractability of psychic reality, even while recognising that symbolism is the means by which this reality is sustained in its viability and growth.

But where as with most people, effort is being made by normal creativity to maintain integration, by ego-maintenance, to preserve a sense of identity, and to feel real, is it not here, also, possible to 'divert' energy, culturally, from the 'path which leads to recovery' or, as we may say, to a sense of a 'continuing thread of life'? That is, is it not possible in the cultural sphere for the energy we have for seeking solutions to the problem of identity to be 'diverted'?

If it is possible to divert such a patient by authoritarianism, would it not also be possible to divert him by destructive cultural influences? Supposing this child had been living in Nazi Germany: could he not have been persuaded that the most valuable solution would have been to 'harden himself' and to become 'domineering and defiant'? ('We will have no weakness or tenderness in our youth' [Rauschning].) Supposing no chances of development had come? They did come because his mother, with Winnicott's help, accepted that he needed to go through a period of regression at home. But suppose they had not – could he not have discovered in certain cultural sources (e.g. in the 'pop' world or the drug culture) a vindication for his false solutions of becoming an 'anti-social person'? Could not cultural influences, whether religious or in entertainment phantasy, have persuaded him that it was acceptable to leave the 'wizard's voice' 'outside' himself as 'the voice of the devil', or to accept his thefts as manifesting appropriately an heroic act of establishing that he was not a coward? And cannot this 'diversion' of creative attention to problems of splitting be effected on normal people? I believe, in fact, that many thousands of youth have been so 'diverted' towards false solutions by the ethos of our commercial culture, and that this affects those who are having the hardest struggle to maintain an ego. The objection to commercial culture when it exploits sensibility is that its fortunes are made from the weak.

In the situation in which a sympathetic adult is being 'given' reparative creative effort by the child, the essence of what is happening is a symbolic engagement with 'destructive impulses and ideas' within: the effort to exert love over hate and to build bridges by coming to terms. In this way a creative education can become, as Sir Herbert Read urges us to make it become, a contribution to peace by the engagement with hate towards establishing a balance in individuals which helps resolve aggression.

The need to make reparation and to come to terms with one's hate and destructiveness is the deepest moral issue, and it is far more important than the concern of the moral educator of the predatory kind to 'implant moral values'. As Winnicott says:

---

* 'Excellent artistic productions . . . can indeed denote potential health in the patient . . . but do not stand for health itself' (Winnicott [94], p. 000). Winnicott was speaking to workers in a psychiatric hospital.

No doubt there are and always will be those who by nature and nurture prefer to implant morals, just as there are those who by nature and nurture prefer to wait, and perhaps wait a long time, for natural developments. . . .

In these matters the answer is always that there is *more to be gained from love than from education*. Love here means the totality of infant-and-child-care, that which facilitates maturational processes. It includes hate. . . . (Winnicott [94], p. 100.)

Until he is a 'whole person' to a degree, a child cannot make use of the human knowledge and skills with which education presents him:*

> Education in terms of the teaching of arithmetic has to wait for that degree of personal integration in the infant that makes the concept of *one* meaningful, and also the idea contained in the first pronoun singular. The child who knows the I AM feeling, and who can carry it, knows about one, and then immediately wants to be taught addition, subtraction and multiplication. (Winnicott [94], p. 100.)

Similarly, we need to accept that moral development can only come about once civilisation begins to develop anew within each child: 'In the same way moral education follows naturally on the arrival of morality in the child by the natural developmental processes that good care facilitates' (Winnicott [94], p. 100).

Good care is that love which assures the child (to use Fairbairn's terms) that 'he is loved for his own sake', 'in his own right as a person'. Grave early failure here can mean an incomplete personality, with characteristics which make normal moral 'contributing in' impossible, from a fear of relationship as too dangerous, to the impulse to devalue human things as a consequence of the failure to be convinced of one's own value. Only if a child is given the security of his own identity by good care while he is absolutely dependent as an infant can he become increasingly independent while still accepting the need for dependence. If things go well, he can then begin to discover the real world and establish relationships with real persons from a secure independent relationship: he can make creative use of the civilisation around him and build from it his own moral dynamic. Parent and teacher contribute to this inner dynamic and growth.

There is thus a complex traffic between the child and his environment, and this is one which the teacher cannot take charge of and direct. He only does harm if he attempts to control it wholly. Attempts at control can be authoritarian, or they can take the form of cutting a child off from the civilisation on which he can draw:

> Advocates could be found for not leaving any cultural phenomena lying around for the child to catch hold of and adopt. I even knew a father who refused to allow his daughter to meet any fairy story, or any idea such as that of a witch or a fairy, or of a prince, because he wanted his child to have only personal personality; the poor child was being ordered to start again with the building up of the ideas and artistic achievements of the centuries. The scheme did not work. (Winnicott [94], p. 101.)

John Wilson, despite his claim to be truly liberal, also seeks to control the child's moral development by removing from the context the necessary sources for the child in an adult's adherence to a specific code. For, while we need to allow the child to find his own way, we must not leave him to build the whole of civilisation from scratch. He needs to find the adult representing his own moral code so that he can make use of it (or not as he pleases). There is a special reason, according to Winnicott, why it is important that there should be adult moral codes available to the child. This is because the child's 'innate† moral code' can be crippling.

---

* Bowlby gives evidence from several sources that the capacity for abstract thought and intelligence itself are affected by lack of proper home care in children (see *op cit.*).

† Strictly speaking, surely the word 'innate' is surely wrong here since the fierce moral code develops naturally in early infancy, and he is not born with it?

In the beginning, before the body is separated from thought, phantasy from reality, self from object, the child feels his frustration and anger as if they threatened to destroy the whole world and existence.

Your adult moral code is necessary because it humanizes what for the child is subhuman. The infant suffers talion fears. The child bites in an excited experience of relating to a good object, and the object is felt to be a biting object. The child enjoys an excretory orgy and the world fills with hate that drowns and with filth that buries. These crude fears become humanized chiefly through each child's experience in relation to the parents, who disapprove and are angry but who do not bite and drown or burn the child in retaliation related exactly to the child's impulse or phantasy. (Winnicott [94], p. 101.)

Here there is an implication, surely, that if the parents do actually attack a child, then the situation is likely to be traumatic because reality then seems to confirm the fears of revenge for phantasy attack? Here we may find a clue perhaps to the cultural and moral problem I am approaching: What happens if, in his cultural environment, the child comes upon symbolic manifestations which seem not to humanise but to dehumanise his experience, or to thrust it back into the 'subhuman'?

Here it is important, of course, to distinguish between 'wicked' conduct, which may be a manifestation of the life-problems of a child – and accounts of wickedness in a book, which *is an act of symbolising*.

Moreover, before we can try to relate 'wicked' symbolism to 'bad' behaviour we need to discuss what we mean by 'bad' behaviour. 'Wickedness' is a manifestation of a failure of the environment to make certain maturational processes possible: and actual acts of wickedness, rather than mere manifestations of deterioration, are, in the child signs of hope. 'For the psychiatrist the wicked are ill. Wickedness belongs to the clinical picture produced by the anti-social tendency. It ranges from bed-wetting to stealing, and telling lies and includes aggressive behaviour, destructive acts and compulsive cruelty and perversions. . . . '

In the child this wickedness manifests *hope*:

> The anti-social tendency represents the hopefulness in a deprived child who is otherwise hopeless, hapless and harmless; a manifestation of the anti-social tendency in a child means there has developed in the child some hopefulness, hope that a way may be found across a gap. This gap is a break in the continuity of environmental provision, experienced at a stage of relative dependence. (Winnicott [94], p. 104.)

The break in continuity has resulted in a hold-up of maturational processes. If the gap can be bridged the wickedness disappears. 'The child knows in his bones that it is hope that is locked up in the wicked behaviour, and that despair is linked with compliance and false socialisation' (Winnicott [94], p. 104).

'Compulsive wickedness', says Winnicott, 'is about the last thing to be cured or even stopped by moral education.' 'For the anti-social or wicked person the moral educator is on the wrong side' – he points to despair rather than hope. Later Winnicott says: 'Strong or repressive measures, or indoctrination even, may suit society's need in the management of the anti-social individual, but these measures are the worst possible thing for healthy persons, for those who can grow from within.' (Winnicott [94], p. 104.)

Winnicott's essay requires us to look at the problem of morality, culture, and the child in a much more realistic light – realistic, that is, in being aware of the problems of identity and internalised objects. Repressive morality, or the impulse to 'implant values' by moral education or a controlled moralising culture are the 'worst possible thing for healthy persons'. Positively the best thing is to 'introduce . . . the opportunity for being creative' – and where this engages the dynamics of an individual who is aready 'contributing in' all is well. The best moral educator is not logic but love.

'Wickedness' is the manifestation of environmental failure, and in the child a mani-

festation of hope. It comes from those who have suffered a break in continuity of environment – their environment has not been good enough or continuous enough to foster
their maturation, so they are trying desperately to make contact, so as to find themselves
'confirmed'. In this way, to use Powys's phrase in *Mr. Weston's Good Wine*, 'a sinner is
the true saviour of mankind' – since he expresses his *hope* that it may be possible to
establish once more a 'personal way of life'. Wickedness is but a manifestation of a desperate inner morality, strangely inverted. 'The fiercest morality is that of early infancy, and
this persists as a streak in human nature that can be discerned throughout an individual's
life. Immorality for the infant is *to comply at the expense of a personal way of life*. For instance,
a child of any age may feel that to eat is wrong, even to the extent of dying for the
principle.' (Winnicott [94], p. 102.)

Destruction of this inner morality is the worst sin. It is possible, says Winnicott, to
gain compliance but the result may be disastrous:

> Compliance brings immediate rewards, and adults too easily mistake compliance for growth. The
> maturational processes can be by-passed by a series of identifications, so that what shows clinically is
> a false, acting self, a copy of someone perhaps; and what could be called a true or essential self becomes
> hidden, and becomes deprived of living experience. This leads many people who seem to be doing well
> actually to end their lives which have become false and unreal; *unreal success is morality at its lowest ebb. . . .*
> (Winnicott [94], p. 102.)

Here we begin to see, perhaps, deeper enemies than those who offer amusements which
we fear may encourage a child to be 'wicked'. The worst thing it is possible to do to a
child is to seek to force it to comply so that it fails to discover its True Self. But it is also
surely possible to divert it, or to persuade it to accept the false and unreal, or to detract
from the child's brave creative energy by thrusting it back towards primitive dehuman-
ization by the exploitation of primitive anxieties by cultural symbolism?

There would seem from Winnicott's view to be two extremes of possible harmfulness
to the child. One is to present the child with crude manifestations of the sub-human
which confirm his talion fears rather than humanise them. As when a mother fails to
bring her child through his need to 'rebuild the damaged object' so that he fails to find
or loses the capacity to feel guilt, the result here may be that he feels 'crudely anxious'
and 'this anxiety is merely wasteful'. This I believe to be the effect of much in our culture.

The other extreme is that of inflicting a complaint morality by authoritarian coercion
rather than a fostering of the capacity Winnicott calls 'belief in'. If there is 'belief in'
then the child can make use of whatever household gods there are lying around: without
'belief in' even the best God will seem 'evidence that the parent-figures are lacking in
confidence in the processes of human nature and are frightened of the unknown'.
(Winnicott [94], p. 93.)

Here, I believe, we have an important clue to our need to discriminate in the cultural
sphere. What are we seeking in creative education? What is the best in personal development? The answer to both is the opportunity for each child to discover his True Self to
the greatest degree possible, according to how well he has been equipped to do so by his
earliest environment. This is a complex process in which one major important creative
concern to which education can contribute, has to do with the overcoming of hate by
love, towards

> a satisfactory integration of the idea of destroying the object and the fact of loving the same object.
> The mother is needed over this time and she is needed for her survival value. She is an environment
> mother and at the same time an object-mother, the object of excited loving. In this latter role she is
> repeatedly destroyed or damaged. The child gradually comes to integrate these two aspects of the

mother and to be able to love and to be affectionate with the surviving mother at the same time. This phase [Winnicott is speaking here of early infancy, six months to two years – D.H.] involves the child in a special kind of anxiety which is called a sense of guilt, guilt related to the idea of destruction where love is also operating. It is this anxiety that drives the child towards constructive or actively loving behaviour in his limited world, reviving the object, making the loved object better again, rebuilding the damaged thing. . . .

This reparative activity continues in all creative activity, as a basis for our real dealings wth the world. (Winnicott [94], pp. 102–3.)

The development of integration and realisation of a True Self is thus a complex process requiring both the establishing of the self by taking in elements from the world (as by taking into the self aspects of the parents), and the exploration of the world in terms of inner emotional needs. Such a process as Winnicott emphasises gains most from love and trust than from the impulse to 'implant' by 'acculturation' (which may itself be a manifestation of hate in that it is an attempt to control an independent self-directed creativity which is feared out of an inability to believe in human nature). The foundations of a True Self are laid down in the context of the mother's loving continuity by the inward reparative activity of love exerted over the consequences of hate, so that bridges may be built between the inner and outer worlds, towards mature effectiveness:

It is evident that as the child grows in this way the content of his personal self is not only he. The self becomes increasingly shaped by the environment provisions. The baby who adopts an object as almost part of the self could not have adopted it unless it had been lying around for adoption. In the same way all the introjects are not only exports reimported, they are also truly foreign goods. The infant cannot know this until considerable maturation has taken place, and the mind has become able to deal intellectually and intelligently with phenomena that have no meaning in terms of emotional acceptance. In terms of emotional acceptance the self, at its core, is always personal, isolated and unaffected by experience.

As Winnicott says, such a way of looking at emotional development means that those concerned with child care should leave lying around not only objects and opportunities but also *moral codes* – which are essentially 'given in subtle ways by expressions of acceptance or by threats of the withdrawal of love', and in these lie the basis of ideas of right and wrong. The ideas, however, cannot be separated as mental activity from the capacity to live from the True Self. That is why love has more to offer than 'moral education', and why the rationalist approach fails to take into account the core of the problem. Professor John Wisdom, in his *Philosophy and Psychoanalysis* indicates the kind of poetic-philosophical process that goes on between mother and child here:

The mother says, 'how would you like it?', i.e. 'How much is your complaisance due to the fact that it's you who are pulling the cat's tail and not vice versa?' And in this she is *not* merely putting something into the child but *bringing out* the uneasiness which lurks in *him* just as it did when biting her breast he laid waste his world and with it himself. (Wisdom [94], p. 176.)

Moral education of the moralising kind may obstruct this essential discovery and development of the True Self and its potentialities. This is Winnicott's objection to a good deal in established religion: 'Religion . . . has stolen the good from the developing individual child, and has set up an artificial scheme for injecting this that has been stolen back into the child, and calling it "moral education" ' (Winnicott [94], p. 176).

Moreover, religious moralising may merely convey to the child that its parents or teachers (like Headmaster Keate*) may lack 'confidence in human nature'. The attitude of John Wilson by contrast in asking for the adult to merely be 'an analytic clarifier'

* Who is reputed to have said to a pupil: 'If you do not believe in the Holy Ghost by five o'clock this afternoon, I will beat you until you do.'

seems to me but an inversion of the authoritarian attitude, since it would simply convey to the child a parallel lack of confidence. It is also a form of splitting akin to the splitting of good from evil in religion. Wilson's whole approach, like that of religion, fails too to express a belief in 'original goodness', and he merely counters moral coercion by removing all sources of material for moral growth except split-off intellectual activity.

Winnicott's objection to the splitting off of aspects of the inner 'moral' self in the symbolism of culture and religion are expressed in the following terms:

> Religions have made much of original sin, but have not all come round to the idea of original goodness, that which by being gathered together in the idea of God is at the same time separated off from the individuals who collectively create and re-create this God concept. The saying that man made God in his own image is usually treated as an amusing example of the perverse, but the truth in this saying could be made more evident by a restatement, such as: man continues to create and re-create God as a place to put that which is good in himself, and which he might spoil if he kept it in himself along with all the hate and destructiveness which is also to be found there. (Winnicott [94], p. 94.)

The concept of God, that is, is a pure and idealised split-off aspect of human nature. The great value of Christian myth at best, perhaps we could add here, is that it contains the idea of God becoming man and suffering man's temptations – and from this emerges the concept of the Christian individual's struggle within his own soul for his own salvation – a concept missing from the Old Testament but found in the Gospels. Wilson's rationalist approach is to split-off 'reason' or 'logic' as an ideal into which to project goodness separated off from the living ambivalent individual: his is the corollary to the religious approach as well as its inversion.

According to Winnicott's view: 'Theology, by denying to the developing individual the creating of whatever is bound up in the concept of God and of goodness and of moral values, depletes the individual of an important aspect of creativeness' (Winnicott [94], p. 95).

In so far as religion becomes less an individual search of inner light (as it is perhaps for the Quakers) and rather a matter of loyalty to institutions, dogmas, established moral codes, and forms of exhortation, the less it fosters individual moral potentiality:

> All sorts of feelings and ideas of goodness that belong to the child and his or her inner experiences can be put out there and labelled 'God'. In the same way, nastiness in the child can be called 'the devil and all his works'. The labelling socializes the otherwise personal phenomenon. Practising psychoanalysis for thirty years has made me feel that it is the ideas bound up with the organization of moral education that deplete the individual of individual creativeness. (Winnicott, [94], p. 95.)

What Winnicott suggests is that moralising and 'theology' are defences against insight into the meaning of 'wickedness' (this does not mean, of course, that individuals in society do not need moral standards and codes). But theology and moral exhortation limit insight and moral development:

> There are reasons why the ideas of the moral educationist die hard. An obvious one is that there do exist wicked people. In my language, this means that there are persons in all societies and in all ages who in their emotional development did not reach to a stage of believing in, nor did they reach a stage of innate morality involving the total personality. But moral education that is designed for these ill persons is unsuitable for the vast majority of persons who, in fact, are not ill in this respect. (Winnicott [94], p. 95.)

That is, the moral educator justifies his moralising by 'the existence of wicked persons' without being realistic enough to regard them as ill. He exhorts the good not to be wicked and the wicked not to be wicked too. If he is successful with the wicked he may only induce a false compliance, a 'socialisation' instead of personal phenomena of self-discovery. There is a problem here, however, that a 'wicked' person who is cut off from effective help such as psychotherapy must presumably cling to his false way of 'contracting in' because otherwise he will feel his whole existence is threatened. As Winnicott himself points out elsewhere, it is usually misguided to seek to reform those whose way of 'contracting in' (e.g. prostitutes) is their only way of finding a way to survive as identities at all.

The predatory moraliser is thus virtually wasting energy, defending himself against his own fears of human nature and by no means promoting insight, sympathy, and understanding. On the contrary, he fails to understand both the good and the wicked. His approach is based on the impulse to reform the wicked; thus, as Winnicott implies, he bases his approach on ill persons, and while this is unsuitable for those who are not ill he does not hesitate to apply it to them, taking as his vindication the existence of ill persons. *Those who have an 'innate'* (or should we not rather say 'naturally developed'?) *morality involving the total personality* are only likely to be 'depleted' by a morality which seeks to split off 'goodness' or 'badness' *so that they are less involved in the total personality.* We can see the strange logic of such splitting mechanisms in the boy with the 'wizard' above.

Winnicott criticises theology for taking goodness out of the individual and putting it away in the concept of God, so that its purity may be preserved against the hate and destructiveness which would mingle with the same goodness if it were kept within and perhaps be spoiled. A corollary is to project the hate and destructiveness as a split-off outward agent. The self is to be kept pure by being armoured against destructive attack from without. Much of human cultural, social, and religious history is the record of struggles to do with this paranoic symbolism in which man has sought to preserve his sense of individual or group identity against penetration by evil forces that seem to threaten annihilation from without, from the Devil to 'heathen, Turk or Jew', and this form of splitting is the basis of racialism. While approaches to morality based on logic and reason, such as that of John Wilson, claim to avoid the pitfalls of Christian and authoritarian preoccupations with morality, they often fail to be realistic not only because they do not see the basis of morality in love, but also because they do not see the problem of hate.

Here a remarkable book on the processes of 'coming to terms' from an approach the writer and educationist can easily understand, is Marion Milner's *On Not Being Able to Paint.* She makes clear the distinction between two modes of approach to experience – that of love and that of hate – and the relation of this problem to education, culture and ethics. Without coming to terms there is inevitably a 'laying waste'.

Dr. Milner discovered through some of her own drawings that:

> unlike the external environment, the incorporated one did actually change according to one's feelings, and particularly in response to one's unadmitted feelings. If one had been full of unadmitted hate it could apparently become a desert land with only dead bones in it, since the destructive wishes could be felt as fulfilled merely by thinking them . . . one's inner world could be devasted by unrecognised hate; it is this world culture affects, and this inner world (as I knew from children) colours all our dealings with the outer, 'real' world. (Milner [62], p. 129.)

So the problem of the relationship between love and hate is a problem of preservation of the identity: 'denied hate can . . . work itself out internally, making one feel, in extreme conditions, that one's inner world is wrecked and everything is hopeless; even though the external environment, objectively seen, may be full of promise' (Milner [62], p. 130).

The colouring of the external world by our inner problems, and the colouring of our internal world by taking external things into ourselves (especially experienced at a death), *are* the problem of living. The struggle with them is a process of disillusion, since it brings us to see what we can do and what we cannot, and to distinguish what we are from what we are not. The pain of this disillusion, though it is a process of finding, in creativity and love, is at times intolerable – and so met by hate, in which we revert to the angry phantasies of the frustrated baby: 'behind the bare fact of the discrepancy there could lurk a tremendous potentiality of primitive hate, the feeling accompaniment of the disillusion inherent in the human situation' (Milner [62], p. 131).

The way out of this reaction of hate – which is basically a desire to 'eat up' what we cannot tolerate – is by creativity: this *is* 'building bridges':

> this hate . . . is inherent in the fact that we do have to make the distinction between subject and object. . . . It is surely through the arts that we deliberately restore the split and bring subject and object together in a particular kind of new unity . . . in the satisfying experience of embodying the illusion there has been an interchange. Since the object is thereafter endowed with a bit of the 'me', one can no longer see it quite the same way as before; and since the 'me', the inner experience, has become enriched with a bit more of external reality, there is now a closer relation between wishes and what can really exist and so less cause for hate, less despair of ever finding anything that satisfies. (Milner [62], p. 131.)

The cultural and educational problem, Marion Milner helps us to see, lies in a contest between those elements which foster and those which undermine our bridge building between subjective and objective. The essential moral dynamic in each of us is an inward creative dynamic, and the education and nurture of this presents subtle problems. This creative inward moral dynamic is far more important than the degree to which we are influenced by the explicit logic of moral debate, as we see from Professor John Wisdom on ethics in philosophy and ethics in living. It is interesting to see the degree to which Wisdom echoes Lawrence ('the mind works in possibilities, the intuitions work in actualities, and what you intuitively desire, that is possible to you') and Marion Milner's discovery of the difference between the intuitive and the merely logical.

Wisdom's comments on Mill link his 'naturalistic type of talk' with Lawrence on intuition and Marion Milner on how 'one came to know more clearly what one loved and would want to cherish':

> Mill said that the desirable is the desired and he didn't mean all the nonsense he's been said to mean. He didn't mean that the desirable is what happens to be consciously desired at the moment. He meant that it is what is really desired. What is really desired is what is desired when *all* our inclinations towards it are faced and not some ignored, including desires not to have a desire for such a thing; in other words, our desire for *X* is a real desire when all our desires for all that is for us in *X* have been 'owned' and 'sifted'. What does this mean? (Wisdom [97].)

In Marion Milner we discover the nature of the problems of 'owning' and 'sifting'. And in the essay already referred to by Professor John Wisdom (on Waddington's *Ethics*) we have the problem explored philosophically as the poet or educationist would understand it. In 'ethical living' it is inadequate to listen to any one voice in oneself. An adequate approach to moral problems requires taking account of the whole range of promptings:

> In ethical effort people take note of the voice or prick of conscience – of the immediate response, 'Oh no, mustn't do that.' But they do not always take this as final. They say, 'But there's no harm in it really, it's only my puritanical conscience,' and a small Dionysian voice grows louder, 'It's foolish but it's fun' . . . Oscillation in deciding between philosophical doctrines goes hopelessly on until one gives up suppressing conflicting voices and lets them *all* speak their fill. *Only then can we modify and reconcile them.* (Wisdom [97], pp. 107-8; my italics.)

By such complexity of inward debate is how we make ethical effort; and to this an ethical scheme – and intellectually held code – is only partially relevant. Of course there are 'facts': 'in deciding what to do, one of the things necessary is, of course, to estimate what consequences will follow and primarily what consequences in the way of how people, including onself, will really feel, and that *not* in the way of approval and disapproval'. But discovering 'how people, including oneself, will feel' depends much not only on 'facts' but imagination, and an appreciation of the subjective elements involved, often guided by insights gained from culture, as by imaginative exploration of how others (and oneself) may feel in experiences we have not yet had.

John Wisdom is linking ethical effort with a certain kind of knowledge of experience which is not merely logical or rational. As he says, it springs from the mother's fostering of a child's discriminations among his reactions to objects, and fostering his capacity for sympathetic identification, as when she says, 'How would you like it?'

In the light of the object-relations approach to the problems of moral growth we can, I believe, see the possible basis for discrimination in ethics and culture as being between contrasting processes in our relationship with ourselves. The social implications are important, and Melanie Klein indicates these thus:

> One part of ourselves that we cherish is the wealth we have accumulated through our relations to external people, for these relations and also the emotions that are bound up with them have become an inner possession. We hate in ourselves the harsh and stern figures who are also part of our inner world, and are to a large extent the result of our own aggression towards our parents. At the bottom our strongest hatred is directed against the hatred within ourselves. (Klein and Rivière [51], p. 115.)

The consequence is that we tend to develop a malign cycle, to overcome our fear of this hate: 'We so much dread the hatred in ourselves that we are driven to employ one of our strongest measures of defence by putting it on to other people – to project it.'

The alternative (which is, of course, never totally taken by anyone) is a benign cycle:

> But we also displace love into the outer world; and we can do so genuinely only if we have established good relations with the friendly figures within our minds. Here is a benign circle, for in the first place we gain trust and love in relation to our parents, next we take them, with all this love and trust, as it were, into ourselves; and then we can give from this wealth of loving feelings to the outer world again.

Hatred, by contrast, breeds hatred:

> There is an analogous circle in regard to our hatred; for hatred . . . leads to our establishing frightening figures in our minds, and then we are apt to endow other people with unpleasant and malevolent qualities. Incidentally, such an attitude of mind has an actual effect in making other people unpleasant and suspicious towards us, while a friendly and trusting attitude on our part is apt to call forth trust and benevolence from others. (Klein and Rivière [51], p. 115.)

The cycles of hate breed hate: the recognitions of love spread benevolence: thus the essential moral problem is to become able to bear one's dread of one's own hate. Wholeness is in being able to bear this dread, rather than seeking to export it, in the mounting cycles of malignancy that belong to hate. But accepting one's own hate can 'call forth . . . benevolence' all around one.

CHAPTER 18

'Amorality', Progress, and Democracy

WE MAY accept that, as Joan Rivière said in *Love, Hate and Reparation*:

> Self-deception and unwarranted self-satisfaction easily attend the search for inner goodness. And if the conscience and morality within us are not the representatives of our love, they become vehicles of our hate. . . . They may then, for instance, mislead us into the complacent search for badness, partly indeed as a defence against self-deception. But since we find evil more readily in others than in ourselves, this is no cure for self-deception. (Klein [51], p. 51.)

But the potentialities we have for self-deception in this way should not divert us into supposing that we need have no morality at all. If we do, we may be following yet another self-delusion, in seeking to escape from the problems of guilt and hate altogether:

> All these dangers and difficulties tend to turn us away from the problems of goodness within, for fear of disillusionment, and the helplessness and insecurity that threaten us.
> External satisfactions are being grasped, therefore, while the even more difficult struggle for inner riches and peace of mind has been left to look after itself . . . matters of conscience have gone out of fashion and . . . morality nowadays has a provincial air. . . . In its fear of being deceived this age of 'realism' may have overshot a mark. (Klein [51], p. 51.)

Joan Rivière's insights here throw a good deal of light on some of the influential sources of public opinion in our time. I am thinking of that intellectual milieu associated roughly with intellectual London newspapers such as *The Guardian*. Naturally a newspaper has to serve 'external satisfactions', even while striving to serve liberal thought on the other. Inevitably, however, liberal thought in a commercial medium tends to 'fear disillusionment', because it must sustain a certain kind of optimism for economic purposes. It thus tends to be hypomanic, and so to avoid where it can the complex problems of hate and guilt.

The Guardian even once had a leader announcing satisfaction with the new 'amoral' and 'open' society London was becoming – no doubt, by contrast with the provincial morality of Manchester which it had left behind. Later, in the issue of 26 January 1967, a typical attempt to urge 'amorality' appeared in an article which was a kind of humanist sermon by Werner Pelz. Pelz suggested that 'Nothing has wrought more havoc in Western history . . . than the concepts of good and evil, right and wrong. . . . All the infinite varieties of sado-masochism, of a twisted will to power, find expression and justification in the defence of the good. Moralism denotes ultimate frustration and responsibility, misdirection of our best energies.'

There is surely a need here to make distinctions between the individual moral sense, which is a sign of psychic health; moral codes which are the collocation of values emerging from individual moral senses and necessary to moral growth – and *predatory*

215

moralising. The latter is the impulse to impose on others a moral code, often out of a fear of human nature, expressing an urge to control the minority who have only a weak moral sense, because they are felt unconsciously to be dangerous.

With Pelz, however, 'moralism' is not to be taken to mean 'predatory moralising': he urges us to abandon *all* morality:

> . . . eradicate 'good' and 'evil' and most of the antis would lose much of their gloomy fun and would have to face anew the challenge of their own existence. . . . *Above all:* forget the concepts of right and wrong. . . . And then we could transform prisons into factories and farms with well-run classes and time for creation and re-creation. . . . Parents would not be horrified by the discovery that their children had been stealing. They could laugh, sympathise, and explain clearly why the risk was not worth taking in a society with a fanatical belief in complex and highly organised robbery. Should a child really prefer robbery to other, better pursuits, he will have to practise it within the prescribed framework of industry and commerce. . . .

All morality, he claims, is an irrelevance, while demoralisation would release our creative potentialities. Stealing is only parallel with economic gain. To hug discrimination is our disease:

> Why do we nevertheless hug our disease? . . . Perhaps because moralism is the only pleasure we get out of doing what we dislike . . . and of restricting others to the same kind of fun. Perhaps because, more than sickness and death, we fear the awful freedom of personal decision, or creative unjustifiable choice and action. Perhaps because we have not yet discovered anything which, like good and evil, can focus and spur the energies of a whole community. . . . There will be no significant change, until we desire to learn – above all else – how to release and develop, in ourselves and in our children, all those violent, creative passions by virtue of which we once became and still become men. Nothing can save us from moralism and destruction, except the full deployment of our talents, so that we learn to do well what we love doing, and, like all creators, will want our achievements to overflow and shine on good and evil alike. . . .

Here, in the reference to 'sado-masochism', we have a nod at Freud, the Freud of *Civilisation and Its Discontents*. In the phrase 'challenge of their own existence' and the reference to 'freedom' we have a nod at existentialism (our 'creativity' must be 'violent'). What is necessary is 'the awful freedom of personal decision' – but this requires as an essential that our choice and action must be 'unjustifiable'. This takes the theme of the 'leap in the dark' far out. Kierkegaard believed that when we leapt we would find ourselves in the arms of God. Sartre believes that when we commit ourselves we commit ourselves on behalf of all mankind. Pelz wants us to have a freedom completely devoid of any responsibility to anything human – we leap in rapt and blind egocentricity, – and dehumanisation. There must be no references to any moral code, nor reference to concepts of good and evil, natural and unnatural, normal and abnormal nor inward feelings of that 'true guilt' which enables us to feel real. There must be no recognition of the human facts of our subjective life, and its deeper needs for insight and the discovery of the True Self.

> Eliminate the concepts of right and wrong, natural and unnatural – all premature delusions – from the debate on sexual morality and the debate will cease. There will be no sensational change in behaviour. (Pornography might experience a slump and the circulation of certain papers decline gradually.) We should be left with persons who, in concrete and incomparable situations, have to make reponsible, creative decisions *vis-à-vis* other persons who have to do the same.

If our choice and action is to be 'unjustifiable' how can it be 'responsible'? Responsible to *what*? From any real knowledge of human nature, it is obvious that if we were successfully demoralised things would by no means be as bright as Pelz suggests. Our guilt is inherent in our growth of identity, and our inward moral dynamic is a manifestation of health.

Pelz's impulse is to deny the essential ambivalence from which our humanness is derived, by hypomanic denial of the problem of hate. His approach suffers from all the dangerously unrealistic sentimentality of Rousseauism. Pelz's picture of prisons being happy creative centres of adult education in the absence of 'moralism' is farcical, as is his picture of a society freed from concepts of 'natural and unnatural' in sex. To remove conscious concepts of good and bad would in fact surely make little or no difference to the patterns of behaviour of the criminal or the sexually 'deviant' person. Their patterns of behaviour are their way of contracting into life, of belonging, of trying to find what belongs to them – a human identity. Their behaviour often is symbolic of deficiencies in the early environment – as is the 'sucking' behaviour in an adult whose sexual needs are expressed in 'taking' on incorporative terms, because he has not been freed by his infant experience to develop beyond 'sucking' to be able to share sexual experience with an adult, on an equal basis. His only hope may be to grow slowly towards maturity and wholeness: to complete his moral growth towards health, and to find his True Self.

Pelz would merely endorse such an unfortunate person's false solutions as normative. Thus he would, by demoralisation, merely convey to him that efforts for the progress for which he intuitively yearns, in hope, towards wholeness and greater potentialities, are futile.

In the background is the chimera of human perfectibility. Pelz's golden future in a demoralised society could only be as golden as he suggests *if human nature were not human nature*. There is a problem, of the ideation of good and evil, and the vindication of bad means by the idealism of good ends, from which many horrors have arisen. There is the problem of authoritarian coercion. But it is not true to suggest, as Pelz does, that it is *morality of any kind* that causes the trouble.

'Deviant' modes of behaviour may be seen as individual solutions to problems of how to live. But what happens if the solution chosen if it is chosen by false solutions is that of *living at the expense of others* – and the promotion abroad of the cycles of hate?

The existence of false solutions, such as those of the schizoid individual as delineated by Fairbairn, makes nonsense of Pelz's advocacy of 'amorality'. Pornography, for instance, would not disappear in an 'amoral' world because the schizoid individual would still need to depersonalise sex and to devalue humanity by his symbolism. He would still need to express his hatred of woman and to thrust harm into others. He would also try to make money by involving others in his 'hate' solutions. Here the problem arises – whether we believe in 'amorality' or not – will not False Solutions, because they seem quicker and larger ways of feeling alive, always triumph? Can human beings at large bear to seek to feel real and alive by True Self means, since these always bring the pain of depression, despair, and the recognition of our vulnerability and mortality – despite the satisfactions they bring? Can we bear to be human?

Pelz's position is a hypomanic one: its impulse is to deny that the problems of guilt and hate exist. It will be useful perhaps to dwell here for a moment on the concept of the 'manic' as object-relations psychology sees it. 'Manic denial' is the attempt to insist that one is alive and that one has no human problems. As Hannah Segal says, in her account of the theories of Melanie Klein:

> The resolution of depression by reparation is a slow process and it takes a long time for the ego to acquire sufficient strength to feel confidence in the reparative capacities. Often the pain can only be overcome by manic defences which protect the ego from utter despair; when the pain and threat lessen, manic defences can gradually give way to reparation. (Segal [75], p. 69.)

In cultural terms, a manifestation of manic defence is the buffoonery which tradition-ally accompanies death in folk-drama or in tragedy (cf. Hamlet's grave-diggers). The experience of loss by death leaves us with feelings such as those we experienced when we first came to feel, in the depressive position, that we have ruined the object and our whole world, by our phantasies of hate. Death leaves us an inward problem of ruin, and it takes some time before truly reparative mourning can restore this world. A more immediate relief is found by manic denial of deadness (as in the Wake). As Hannah Segal says: 'manic defence will be used in defence against any experience of having an internal world or of it containing any valued objects, and against any aspect of the relation between the self and the object which threatens to contain dependence, ambivalence, or guilt' (Segal [75], p. 70).

Manic defence in culture is thus a way of denying by assumed liveliness that we have such problems which threaten our identity. Real reparation, however, needs to include a recognition that manic denial of deadness is not enough.

For us to find true solutions to the problem of existence, manic defence needs to give way to true reparation – that is, to a real acceptance and modification of the hate within, that threatened to ruin the inner world under the threat of death. We need to confront 'the problem of existence', including despair and the problem of the meaning of death. While manic elements are important in culture, the manic alone is insufficient to achieve a full assurance of wholeness and strength of identity – since the manic merely denies, and does not engage with, the problem of hate.

Our deepest fear being that we will cease to exist either because there is too little 'stuff' in us or because we are too full of hate, one of our cultural problems is that there is thus a manic appeal in the very assertive energy of hate solutions themselves: these are a desperate assertion that 'at least we are alive'. Here there is much that is relevant to culture in accounts of 'manic defence' in accounts of psychoanalysis.

Winnicott says that the effect of a successful psychoanalysis is to 'lessen omnipotent manipulation and of control', but suggests that this 'devaluation to normality' is akin to the normal process of accepting reality, and may bring a patient to a 'normal' degree of manic defence:

> to a degree of manic defence that is employed by all in everyday life. For instance, one is at a music-hall and on the stage come the dancers, trained to liveliness. One can say that here is the primal scene, here is exhibitionism, here is anal control, here is masochistic submission to discipline, here is defiance of the super-ego. Sooner or later one adds: here is LIFE. Might it not be that the main point of the performance is a denial of deadness, a defence against depressive 'death inside' ideas, the sexualization being secondary?
>
> What about such things as the wireless that is left on interminably? What about living in a town like London with its noise that never ceases, and lights that are never extinguished? Each illustrates the reassurance through reality against death inside, and a use of manic defence that can be normal. (Winnicott [90], p. 131.)

Although such 'primal scene' phantasy can be seen as a 'normal' form of the manic, there would seem to be a problem indicated by Fairbairn's insights into the need of the schizoid individual to devalue and depersonalise. In the dream of Fairbairn's schizo-phrenic patient the 'stream of milk' represented a part object rather than a person, and a tendency to de-emotionalise and dehumanise – to separate the libidinal need from the person. It is a manic symbol of his need to be alive through being loved: but its manic nature is bound up, like that of the Bunny Girl, with it not being *human*. Something of the same kind of symbolism permeates both our culture and our society's attitudes to human individuality. The manic here seems to involve a reduction of human value, which in turn affects our whole social life. Hypomanic attitudes to ethical problems therefore tend to be based on a denial of humanness.

The 'enlightened' approach to sex, or 'amorality', may divert individuals even further from the realm of 'being' and 'confirmation'. Taking to manic sexuality, to alleviate the effects of a dehumanising environment, the individual may find himself further dehumanised by a bogus 'revolution' in pursuit of a chimerical 'freedom'. He finds he has forfeited the progress towards maturity for which his True Self, his 'pristine unitary ego', has striven all his life.

He may also find himself, contrary to all his expectations, contributing to social and political developments which would seem far from 'progressive'. Where we find depersonalisation and dehumanisation we may suspect a flight into 'pseudo male doing' from 'female element being'. We may recall Frankl's view that existential frustration impels sexual activity. To resort to sex detached from emotion and relationship, or to 'bad thinking' about sex is to enter into a schizoid syndrome in which there is expressed a fear of the vulnerable area of the inward creative life itself, and from the whole realm of the I–Thou which is felt to be dangerous.

From this emerges, as I believe, the profound hatred of woman which is expressed so widely in our culture and its symbolism. This hatred of woman can also be seen as manifesting a hatred of the 'female element' in both men and women. At bottom, it expresses a hatred of being human, with human weakness, susceptibility, and sensitivity. We have only to glance around our culture to see many examples of the combination of a hatred of feminity and a hatred of being human.

In so far as men tend to fly from their own feminity, we find them taking resort to false strengths. Here we may also invoke Guntrip's phrase 'the taboo on weakness'. Fear of ego-weakness, vulnerability and ambivalence may drive men to extremes in false solutions – and here I believe we have a clue to the ultimate ethical problem of mass psychopathology. The greatest threat to our freedom is to be found as Polanyi says in the appeal of 'the logically stabler state of complete moral inversion'.

As Winnicott points out, democracy depends essentially on there being a sufficient number of sane and mature individuals to make their own responsible decisions, and a numerous enough community of balanced people to be able to tolerate an anti-social disbalanced minority. A democracy is effective to the degree it can rely on individual attainment of maturity at large. '. . . a democratic society is "mature", that is to say, that it has a quality that is allied to the quality of individual maturity which characterises its healthy members. . . .' Democracy is here defined, therefore as a 'society well-adjusted to its *healthy* individual members'. (Winnicott [93], p. 156.)

This definition implies the origin of the democratic community in the psychic health of the individuals who make it up. A democracy can therefore never be imposed: it can only grow and be fostered (as by creativity) and this psychic health depends upon there being a sufficient number of *ordinary good homes*:

> These *ordinary good homes* provide the only setting in which the innate democratic factor can be created. [*Footnote in the original:* The ordinary good home is something that defies statistical investigation . . . it has no news value, it is not spectacular, and does not produce the men and women whose names are publicly known. My assumption, based on 20,000 case histories taken personally over a period of twenty-five years, is that in the community in which I work the ordinary good home is common, even usual.] (Winnicott [93], p. 160.)

At the 1948 Mental Health Congress, Dr. R. E. Money-Kyrle said: 'Democracy is a

society well-adjusted to its *healthy* individual members.' Winnicott, in discussing some
thoughts on the meaning of the word 'democracy', modifies this thus:

> In psychiatric terms, the normal or healthy individual can be said to be one who is mature according
> to his or her chronological age and social setting there is an appropriate degree of emotional develop-
> ment.
> Psychiatric health is therefore a term without a fixed meaning. In the same way the term 'democratic'
> need not have a fixed meaning. Used by a community it may mean *the more rather than the less mature in
> society structure.* (Winnicott [93], p. 156.)

The problem then becomes 'what proportion of anti-social individuals can a society
contain without submergence of innate democratic tendency?'

This is complex because as well as anti-social people there are those who react to
inner insecurity by the alternative tendency to identify with authority.

> This is unhealthy, immature, because it is not an identification with authority that arises out of self-
> discovery . . . each of these anti-social types needs to find and control the conflicting force in the world
> outside the self. By contrast, the healthy person, *who is capable of becoming depressed,* is able to find the
> whole conflict within the self as well as being able to see the whole conflict outside the self, in external
> (shared) reality. When healthy persons come together they each contribute a whole world, because
> each brings a whole person. ([93]; my italics.)

Democracy is thus taken to depend upon there being enough people of sufficient
maturity not to seek to externalise their conflicts by one anti-social way or another or to
seek to solve them by ruthless egocentricity at the expense of others. Democracy requires
the capacity in a majority to accept and suffer the conflicts within and those without –
even if this brings depression and taxes their ego-weakness. But everything depends upon
there being a majority with a 'healthy moral sense'.

Thus from Winnicott's point of view, the fundamental basis of democracy as a social
system depends upon individual maturity which is created by the mother's role in the
family. For this reason, democracy can only grow and cannot be implanted.

But where we find the flight from democracy it would seem that something has gone
wrong with the relationship between mother and child – a relationship obviously affected
by the prevailing ethos, and the degree to which individuals can allow themselves to
develop and accept the capacity to 'be'. The desire for a dictatorship is associated by
Winnicott with a fear of dependence (because total dependence in infancy was too
terrible). Thus the fear of independence is essentially associated with fear of woman,
because once we were all totally dependent upon a woman. 'One of the roots of the need
to be a dictator can be a compulsion to deal with this fear of woman by encompassing
her and acting for her. The dictator's curious habit of demanding not only absolute
obedience and absolute dependence but also "love" can be derived from this source'.
(Winnicott [93], p. 165.)

Winnicott's ethical and political positives emerge as emotional maturity, independence, and the willingness to accept inner conflict. He celebrates the 'ordinary good home',
and the need for us to cherish the role of creative woman. He sees democracy as a society
which can confidently absorb its anti-social minority.

Winnicott's attitudes will easily be accepted by the teacher in school and the tutor in
adult education. They know that most homes are good homes, and in each individual
there is a powerful impulse towards order, altruism, and love.

The stability and creativity of the democratic community depends upon this being so.
But since human beings are dynamic beings who are continually engaged in a wrestle
with inward and outward experience, especially in the formative years, education plays

a considerable part in helping foster that individual maturity which makes for democracy by extending and training the imaginative energy devoted to subjective life-problems. Winnicott emphasises the value of education in making members of a democracy 'intelligently self-conscious': it is also, of course, necessary to foster a discriminating minority in particular who are aware of human problems and who can defend democracy by vigilance. But besides conscious vigilance, we need to promote inner awakenedness, and the impulse to live creatively: teachers are bound to be the largest body of those who can undertake these tasks.

'But it is not possible for persons to get further in society-building than they can get with their own personal development' Winnicott says ([93], p. 167). Education of the whole being is therefore a major contribution to social growth, since it fosters this personal development in terms of gaining subjective insight.* So education of the whole being cannot be conceived merely in terms of imparting information or skills or a 'new technology'. It is necessarily a matter of subjective disciplines, for to become as capable as possible of 'contributing a whole world' individuals have to exercise their capacity to become aware of inward conflict, and to ponder the nature of the flux between inner and outer reality. Because this valuable activity is associated with 'the capacity of being depressed' it is painful and can be resisted – or we can, and often do, seek to avoid it.†

The essence of education – especially creative education – is give-and-take: is 'touch', contact – processes of love and finding reality. In writing poetry, or painting, dancing, or making music, children are engaged in contest with inward experience, seeking by intuitive processes, to make sense of their inner life. Such activities foster intuitive capacities between teacher and child, and between children, because giving and receiving are so bound up with creating.‡ But besides being valuable as means to an effective education, these creative activities are also primary to adult life. To say this is to reveal that in our society at large we starve of those forms of nourishment for the sense of 'the point of life' which object-relations and existential psychoanalysis emphasise as a primary human need.

Education, of course, must recognise that it only contributes to a process of becoming civilised, a 'going concern' which began with the mother: 'we can if we like think of the child as developing an internal good mother, who feels it is a happy achievement to get, any experience within the orbit of a human relationship . . . *civilisation has started again inside a new human being*. . . . '

The parents' own moral code will be used by the child, 'to humanise the child's own cripplingly fierce morality, his hatred of compliance at the expense of a personal way of life. It is good for this fierce morality to be humanised but it must not be killed.' (Winnicott [95], p. 97.)

We need to ponder further the political implications of the gulf between the attitudes to human nature of the therapist and educator, and those of many prevalent assumptions in the literary and intellectual world. It is a great distance from Sartre and Laing to see

* Here we may consider Bowlby's comment on the need for help when dealing with life-problems such as grief. He says: "In helping the children experience their grief, the grown-ups have a vital role to play . . ." (Bowlby [6], p. 146). The teacher's role is often to "help children to experience . . ." various human realms of feeling.

† This is why some people pronounce art as 'morbid' – they cannot tolerate the 'useful depression' it brings. A colleague reports a member of a grammar school staff as saying, 'Children of decent parents don't write poetry'.

‡ Here one of the major problems in our education is that we seem to have failed to discover what content makes a good education for girls – or indeed for the 'female element' of either sex.

with Winnicott each human being 'civilisation starting again' in each child in this positive sense as the basis of a democracy in which we can find freedom and fulfilment, in the meeting of beings, with no need for a conflict of freedoms. Moreover, there is a definite conflict between the ethics of our commercial acquisitive culture and the truths and aims we pursue in education and child care.

So, in relating education and culture to 'living ethics', we are still faced with the kind of problem discussed by Joan Rivière in 1936:

> External satisfactions are being grasped . . . while the even more difficult struggle for inner riches and peace of mind has been left to look after itself . . . our inner psychological struggles – between our love and our hate – are receiving but little aid from conscious attention and efforts. It is true that the great necessity within us to encourage and nurture love, to give and to receive it, and to suppress, deflect and modify hate, is seeking new outlets externally in our lives; but as an inner problem in each one of us it is obtaining little direct support. In its search for genuine goodness and in its fear of being deceived, this age of 'realism' may well have overshot a mark; there is reality within us as well as without, the facts not only of our ruthlessness and greed, but also of our need to love and to be loving, which we suppress and do not honestly avow. (Klein and Rivière [51], p. 51.)

I have elsewhere accused education of failing to give 'direct support' to inner problems. But in culture at large, and especially in commercial culture, we find not only a lack of direct support, but an active dissemination of false solutions – hate made socially acceptable: a demoralisation that seeks to invert values and make hate itself a 'good'. Here we find a force whose destructive power is as yet unnoticed. Joan Rivière was able to continue in 1936: 'I do not suggest that life itself is in danger of extinction by the destructive forces in man, but that at the moment, love with its power of unification being at a discount and so hard pressed by aggression, the civilised form of life seems to be in danger of disintegration' (Klein and Rivière [51], p. 52).

However much times have changes since, and the dangers are greater, the essential problem remains. There is now a danger of life becoming extinct through the sheer technical power at the service of man's destructiveness. The 'civilised form of life' is once more in danger, but the source of this is now in 'Freudian' America as much as in those dictatorships which seek to deny the inner life of man altogether. The problem still is that 'a good relation to ourselves in a condition for love, tolerance and wisdom towards others . . . [so that we] can be at peace with ourselves and able to love others in the true sense of the word' (Klein and Rivière [51], p. 119).

The trouble is, as Joan Rivière says, 'It is well known that matters of conscience have gone out of fashion and that morality nowadays has a provincial air . . .' (Klein and Rivière [51], p. 51) – and this situation has increasingly opened the way for the exploitation of hate, not least because hate is a better commercial commodity than love or integration. But a deeper problem arises, for the attack on conscience is also an attack on identity and ego-maintenance, while the vogue for 'amorality' involves a threat to democracy – by promoting further denial of our human needs. The growth of a 'healthy moral sense' in society depends upon our recognition of the fundamental ethical problem which is whether our solutions to problems of identity take the path of being mature enough to accept independence and responsibility, or whether we need to live at the expense of others, because we cannot accept weakness and division in ourselves. (Pelz merely denies that this problem of living at the expense of others exists at all.)

Money-Kyrle puts the essence of these problems thus:

> In a form which is relevant to ethics, I would put it thus: deep in the unconscious, the ultimate source of anxiety is our own aggression, especially aggressive greed, which, however, may seem to threaten us, either from within* or from without, like a foreign force.

Then, as a defence against the resulting unconscious intensification of the fear of death, the aggressive component in the ego's will to live may be increased to such an extent that every *external* object tends to be unconsciously viewed as a kind of nourishment to be consumed or as a threat to be destroyed. But, in conflict with this completely predatory egoism, the ego has developed an opposite tendency to embrace and identify itself with other objects, which it then as desperately endeavours to preserve. So an insoluble unconscious conflict threatens to arise, and is averted in the first place largely by mechanisms of splitting which tend to divide the world into enemies to be destroyed and friends to be protected from the external replicas of our own aggression. (Money-Kyrle [97], p. 110.)

By these insights we may approach ethical and cultural problems at a deeper level than that of moralising which can be seen as a form of defence mechanism against the deeper issues on the one hand, or 'amorality' on the other, which is hypomanic and unreal. We can approach problems of cultural expression, and problems of morality and conduct, not in terms of whether people influence each other's behaviour for good or bad, or whether or not they have an 'intent to corrupt' – but in terms of whether they seek to exercise their aggression at the expense of the inner life of others.

It is often necessary for those whose own relationship with reality is disturbed to seek to invert values and to deny their human needs because of the 'intensification of the fear of death' which they feel, accompanied by internal threats. To such people it is a life and death matter, to operate ethically in the 'split' ways Money-Kyrle indicates, not least *because of their fear of their own aggression*. But the aggression is not recognised as a real threat, requiring organised engagement; it is denied by splitting and either made a 'good' or proclaimed non-existent. Their solutions, in the end, tend to be those of the schizoid person who denies his dependence, his feelings, his relational needs, his ego-weakness and his humanity. Essentially the schizoid individual is unable to deal with others as if they had value, because he cannot feel he has any himself: he must therefore seek to degrade human nature, and attack civilised values. He thus threatens democracy and political freedom.

Nowadays the astonishing inversions in our cultural life and our attitudes to morality have gone so far that here and there we are boldly offered such false solutions as a 'new sensibility': cruelty, hate, the depersonalisation of sex, the derangement of the senses, and the undermining of conscience are proclaimed high values.

The *avant-garde* seems committed to the 'solutions' of ruthless egocentricity, violence, and anti-social anarchy, rather than creative effort towards fostering healthy moral development and the 'capacity to be depressed'. Many in the world of modish culture would no doubt reject with some heat that they should concern themselves with the 'ordinary good home' – or anything so ideologically conformist.

Yet, as Winnicott implies, the origins of a healthy moral sense and of the I AM feeling in the 'ordinary good home' *is* a basic truth of human life at large, and so presumably, those concerned with human truth should be able to recognise and celebrate the kind of experiences which in normal life, by the processes of love and symbolism, make us human as, say, Tolstoy, Lawrence, Bonnard, and Gorki concerned themselves symbolically with the reality of our normal daily, domestic, striving life. In our time, however, many concerned with the arts in our ethos are obviously hostile to any suggestion that they should contribute to social life at all by their creativity. It is inevitable that art and the subjective disciplines must be 'insurrectionary' in such a way as to manifest only contempt for the community that starves of creativity, and for democracy?

---

* (*Footnote in the original*): Thus, for example, we speak of hunger 'gnawing' as if it were a devouring enemy inside.

This tendency in the realm of fashionable arts can be associated with the belief in man's 'real' animal nature, with the death instinct in the background in pseudo-science. Although we are often asked to accept this 'realism' in the name of 'progressive enlightenment' it is, in the light of object-relations psychology, essentially anti-human. It is certainly not 'scientific' in any true sense, nor is its rejection of moral values as 'idealistic' or 'unrealistic' vindicated philosophically. As Towers and Lewis say:

> The popular press seems often to imply that it is only in the present age that man has become sufficiently 'daring' to face the 'stark reality' of his kinship with the rest of nature. The views of those who aim to denigrate and vilify man are advertised and praised with expressions such as 'takes the lid off our animal nature' or 'allows us to peer through the veil that hides man from himself'. (Towers and Lewis [83], p. 113.)

Such individuals often purport to be speaking in the name of science. The public is likely either to accept and act on the views, or in rejecting them, reject science itself. As Towers and Lewis say: 'Both possibilities would be disastrous for civilisation.'

There is some justification for some antipathy to science, since there are scientists who also seek to dehumanise man. But these come in for severe criticism from within science itself:

> Many scientists and too many philosophers write . . . and if they believed that man lacks a 'mind' – a conscious, knowing, striving and understanding mind. The absurdity of such a view of any person not blinded by too long immersion in a particular kind of thought process, is manifest. But too often the experts fail to see how disastrous to the ordinary man and perhaps ultimately to civilisation itself, their view may be if put over in semi-popular language incautiously and irresponsibly. Indeed, one feels sometimes that the clever are simply trying to bamboozle the good in order to indulge themselves in the mental tittilation which results from shocking people. (Thorpe, quoted by Towers and Lewis [83], p. 114.)

Professor Thorpe obviously speaks for other scientists who feel, with D. H. Lawrence, that 'One must speak for life and growth, and all this mass of destruction and disintegration'. Towers and Lewis, who quote this, also quote Sir Wilfrid le Gros Clark, in his Presidential Address to the British Association, who said: 'Our task is to give expression to the deep-rooted altruism which is an essential attribute of the humanity of man.'

From the true scientist we may find as humane a concern with man's moral energy and his future as from philosophical anthropology. There are certainly grounds neither in science nor in interpersonal psychology which give support to popular 'enlightened' theories of permissiveness, or the advocacy of 'amorality'. There are no grounds in these disciplines for the prevalent belief that it is only realistic to give way to 'natural' passion in sex or violence, or in cultural expression, or for the tendency to cease to feel responsible for 'ethical living'.

In object-relations psychology, as in Buber's approach to ethics, human life depends upon 'the critical flame' which must 'shoot up ever again out of the depths', the source of which is 'the individual's awareness of what he "really" is, of what in his unique and non-repeatable created existence he is intended to be' – that is, they are related to his quest for the True Self. Ethical solutions can be 'traditional' or 'perceived by the individual himself': either way they are a measure of the sense of what it is to be human. Where we find ethical dynamics undermined – as in the prevalent culture and intellectual atmosphere centred on New York and London – what we can now recognise is a disguised attack on being human, in the pursuit of false solutions.

CHAPTER 19

The Primacy of Culture

ONE of the major changes in philosophical thought in recent decades is the recognition of man as a 'symbolising and mythologising animal'. Psychoanalysis is following this development. Whereas, as we have seen, it tended at the beginning to see culture and religion as sublimations of more primary and real instinctual drives, it has now come to concern itself primarily with *meanings* rather than with the 'release' of functions and drives. Ego-maintenance is a continuing positive process depending upon phantasy and symbol: and when a patient asks 'What is it to be human?' the answer is not given in terms of the fulfilment of a libidinal id, but in terms of personal culture.

Our thinking at large about culture and society does not yet take sufficient account of this change in approach to human 'fact', and has not yet appreciated the degree to which, if culture is a primary human need, our society abysmally neglects it. Here I merely seek to draw attention to various sources, scientific, philosophical and psychological, which insist upon the primacy of culture.

There is no transcendentalism in this view and no 'soul' to be evoked. As Towers and Lewis say, 'We are considering here the intrinsic power of matter to organise itself in increasingly complex hierarchies of forms . . . in us the arrangement has become so complex that it can even reflect upon and analyse itself' ([83], p. 118).

I take it with Suzanne Langer that 'man is an animal' and 'that he has no supernatural essence, "soul", or "entelechy"* or "mind-stuff" enclosed in his skin'. 'He is an organism, his substance is chemical . . . and what he does, suffers, or knows is just what this sort of chemical structure may do, suffer, or know' (Langer [55], p. 40).

This material organisation, whose origin we do not know is, by a great complexity we do not understand, capable of self-awareness. 'What causes this tremendous organisation of substances, is one of the things the tremendous organisations do not know; but with their organisation, suffering and impulse and awareness arise' (Langer [55], p.40).

Suzanne Langer goes on to follow her declaration of faith with a declaration of philosophic heresy, which is:

> That I believe there is a primary need in man, which other creatures probably do not have, and which actuates all his apparently unzoological aims, his wistful fancies, his consciousness of values, his utterly impractical enthusiasms, and his awareness of a 'Beyond' filled with holiness. . . . This basic need, which certainly is obvious only in man, is the *need of symbolisation*. The symbol-making function is one of man's primary activities, like eating, looking, or moving about. (Langer [55], p.41).

Suzanne Langer has earlier quoted Ritchie: 'The essential act of thought is symbolisa-

---

* Aristotle's concept of the soul. 'Informing spirit' (*Oxford Dictionary*).

tion (Langer [55], p. 27). So, symbolisation is the metaphorical basis of conceptual thought, languages, numeracy – and not least of science itself.

Psychoanalytical studies confirm this assumption of the primary nature in man of the need to symbolise. To object-relations theory, symbolism – conscious and unconscious – is more than the basis of thought, and more even than the basis of understanding and insight, but is the basis of the identity itself, and of perception. To some investigators it seems even perhaps the foundation of biological viability, as we shall see. The continuity of human identity seems to depend upon a constant energy of unconscious phantasy which underlies all our dealings with the world, while symbolism is the means by which integration and ego-strength are maintained.

Here we must make plain what we mean by phantasies. For we do not mean mere trivial fancies, day-dreams, and illusions. Phantasy and symbolism in the sense we are to consider them are by no means mere 'pastimes' or visions belonging to reverie, but primary dynamics of human consciousness and modes of apprehension. Melanie Klein, as we have seen, has insisted that 'Phantasies . . . continue throughout development and accompany all activities; they never stop playing a great part in mental life. . . . '

Note that Melanie Klein is talking here about *unconscious phantasies*. Susan Isaacs she quotes as saying: 'There is no impulse, no instinctual urge or response which is not experienced as unconscious phantasy.' This assertion of Melanie Klein's that below the level of our living is a submerged world of continual phantasy seems to be confirmed by experimentation on dreaming.

Some research work has been done in America on dreams and dreaming by the 'sleep and dream laboratory', Boston, Massachusetts.

To the biological observer in Freud's time the function of dreams appeared to be defensive: to the present-day biologist, significantly enough, dreams appear to have a primary function of keeping us alive – and human. The director of the American laboratory writes: 'it appears that D-state or dream-state is necessary for life, as are presumably the states of waking and sleeping, and in this sense its function is to keep the organism living' (*New England Journal of Medicine*).

The research workers discovered the following facts:

> It was first discovered that sleep was cyclical with four or five periods during an average night's sleep, marked by characteristic movements of the eyes and changes in electrical recordings of brain activity. Individuals awakened during these periods almost always reported that they had been dreaming. Subsequent investigation showed that these eye and electrical changes were accompanied by equally characteristic changes in the pulse rate, blood pressure, breathing and muscle potential.

Before the identity is formed nearly all the infant's time is spent in the dreaming state:

> Young children spend as much as 40 per cent of their total sleep time in the D-state, while in the new-born infant the figure rises to 50 per cent and there is some evidence that premature infants spend even more time in this state. Most interesting of all is the possibility that the unborn child 'spends most or all of its time in the D-state, or at least in a state that later develops into dreaming sleep'.

The adult, it would seem, has a continual regular need for the creative work done by dream symbolism in sleep. This could explain the 'need to dream' discovered by the American research workers: 'Among the evidence in support of this suggestion is the finding that an individual who gets to bed much later than usual, or has slept badly the night before, tends to have his first D-period much sooner than usual after falling asleep, '*as though he had built up a "need to dream"*.'

Dreams are necessary to health, and certainly to psychic health. The explanation given here that dreams 'relieve tensions' (which obviously belongs to instinct theory) however, could perhaps be challenged, and in its place could it be suggested that it is the creative psychic work of dreaming, seeking order, and meaning in experience, that maintains the whole being.

> Much more impressive is the evidence suggesting that the D-state is essential to healthy living. Some eighty years ago it was claimed that dreams were a safety valve of the mind, allowing the tensions accumulated during the day to be relieved and that 'a human being deprived of the possibility of dreaming would have to become mentally disturbed after some time'.
> Recent experiments with human volunteers are in agreement with this suggestion. Five such volunteers were deprived of their dreaming on five consecutive nights by awakening them whenever their recordings showed that they were entering the D-state. During the first night they only required four or five awakenings, corresponding with the usual number of periods of the D-state that a normal adult has.
> On successive nights, however, they required more and more awakenings up to 20 or 40, suggesting that the individuals were making increasingly frequent attempts to have D-periods. During the day they became increasingly irritable, behaving as if they had been deprived of sleep although actually they had slept six or seven hours a night.
> They were studied for a further period and during their 'recovery nights' they were found to have much longer D-periods, suggesting that they were trying to make up for lost D-time. That this condition was not due to the frequent wakenings is indicated by the fact that during a subsequent period they were subjected to the same number of awakenings at night but not during D-periods, and these upset them in no way whatever.

This research work certainly seems to confirm that phantasy work is primary to identity as Melanie Klein suggests. Fairbairn says of dreams that they are 'dramatisations of endopsychic situations' as we have seen:

> Under the influence of Melanie Klein's conception of psychic reality and internal objects, I came to regard dreams, and for that matter waking phantasies also, as essentially dramatizations of endo-psychic situations involving both (a) relationships between ego-structures and internalized objects and (b) interrelationships between ego-structures themselves. (Fairbairn [19], p. 170.)

In examining the nature of phantasy we need to consider the implications of the concept of psychic reality in which our phantasies exist, which was originally Melanie Klein's. This concept is indivisible from her emphases on phantasy, aggression, and internalised objects which mark her development beyond 'classical' Freudian psychoanalysis. We may link our exploration of the unconscious symbolism behind all culture with that patient's remark to Mrs. Klein: 'I wanted to eat everything as a child. I expect I wanted to eat my mother.'

In fact, of course, we do become a person, as Winnicott points out, by 'eating' the mother both physically and psychically speaking. That is, good and bad in our personalities are taken in by identifying with the mother and 'taking her in' as we took in her milk. We have seen the importance of the observation that the child's ego is a mouth-ego, so that all his primitive approaches to the 'object' and the world are in terms of symbolic incorporation, and conceived very much in terms of bodily life (since his capacity to intellectualise does not exist at the time when the primary stages in the formation of an identity are taking place).

The essence of Melanie Klein's view is that our psychic problems must be examined in terms of anxiety and its sources in unconscious phantasied aggression, which arises as we become perplexed at the consequences of our own rage and of our cruel phantasies when frustrated. This perplexity occurred at a time when we confused phantasy and reality, and were not entirely sure of the distinction between ourselves and others. Also, when our feelings were aroused by sexual feelings to do with our parents, we feared in this all kinds of consequences, of an 'eating up', damaging kind: 'Moreover, however, according to Melanie Klein . . . anxiety and guilt over internal and external aggression is counteracted by reparative phantasies and activities. Injured love-objects must be restored and made whole again if the personality is to be at peace . . . (Guntrip [37], p. 229).

These 'injured love-objects' are felt to be 'within' the self, by the processes of internalising discussed above. That is, since the origins of them belong to a time when all our concepts were 'embodied' ones, they have come to feel part of our bodies. The restoration of them is in complex with our relationship to the whole external world, since the problem arose when the mother was the whole world. A wrecked inner world damages our relationship with the outer world.

Our effective dealings with the outer world depend upon the degree of organisation we can achieve within by continual phantasy work through symbolism of all kinds. As Guntrip says: 'This helps us to see what endopsychic dramatisation may be: on the basis of the resulting concept of internal objects there has been developed the concept of a world of inner reality involving situations and relationships in which the ego participates together with its internal objects.'

This comment embodies the concept Fairbairn has of the ego as an integrative force. This inner drama underlies the part we play in the world: 'These situations and relationships are comparable with those in which the personality as a whole participates in a world of outer reality, but the form which they assume remains that conferred upon them by the child's experience of situations and relationships in the earliest years of life.'

Symbolism is an activity which continually establishes bridges between these two worlds.

The complex problem now arises, of course, of the relationship between cultural symbolism and such creative processes of symbolism in the inner world of the individual.

Here we may find useful a Kleinian analysis of the function of symbolism in the dynamics of identity by Hannah Segal in a paper on Symbol Formation (Segal [121]), and this we can relate to the 'need to dream'. The ability to form symbols and use them as symbols is gained by the achievement of a certain stage of consciousness: roughly, the depressive position. If certain stages in this development do not complete themselves, then symbols as standing between experience and our awareness of it are not viable. That is, the schizophrenic who has no identity may have no capacity for metaphor:

> example . . . from a schizophrenic patient in an analytical situation: One session, in the first weeks of his analysis, he came in blushing and giggling, and throughout the session would not talk to me. Subsequently we found out that previous to this hour he had been attending an occupational therapy class in which he was doing carpentry, making a stool. The reason for his silence, blushing and giggling was that he could not bring himself to talk to me about the work he was doing. For him the wooden stool on which he was working, the word 'stool' which he would have to use in connexion with it, and the stool he passed in the lavatory were completely felt as one and the same thing that he was unable to talk to me about it. His subsequent analysis revealed that the equation of the three 'stools' . . . was at the time completely unconscious. (Segal [121]).

There is a stage then, when word and thing are not separate, a reminiscence of which is felt in all verbal taboos, on sexual word, blasphemous words, and so forth. This explains the (schizoid) human feeling that to take someone's name in vain may be felt to be likely to damage them, or oneself, by retribution.*

To arrive at the capacity to use language metaphorically requires the accomplishment of a certain awareness of relationship between oneself and the world, and oneself and aspects of one's inner self. These stages of awareness have not been achieved by the psychotic who consequently tends to confuse word, thing, and self. He has an inadequate sense of differentiation between the *me* and the *not-me*. As Hannah Segal says: 'disturbances in differentiation between ego and object lead to disturbances in differentiation between the symbol and the object symbolised and therefore to concrete thinking characteristic psychoses. . . . If symbolism is seen as a three-term relation, problems of symbol formation must always be examined in the context of the ego's relation with its objects'.

This process of the ego's relation with its objects take very complex paths. Melanie Klein's theory of the paranoid–schizoid and manic-depressive positions explains them thus (and these processes are closely related to symbolism):

> The chief characteristics of the infant's first object relations are the following. The object is seen as split into an ideally good and a wholly bad one. The aim of the ego is total union with the ideal object and total annihiliation of the bad one, as well as of the bad parts of the self. Omnipotent thinking is paramount and reality sense intermittent and precarious. The concept of absence hardly exists. Whenever the state of union with the ideal object is not fulfilled, what is experienced is not absence; the ego feels assailed by the counterpart of the good object – the bad object, or objects. It is the time of the hallucinatory wish fulfilment, described by Freud, when the thought creates objects which are then felt to be available. According to Melanie Klein, it is also the time of the bad hallucinosis when, if the ideal conditions are not fulfilled, the bad object is equally hallucinated and felt as real.
>
> A leading defence mechanism in this phase is projective identification. In projective identification, the subject in phantasy projects large parts of himself into the object, and the object becomes identified with the parts of the self that it is felt to contain. Similarly, internal objects are projected outside and identified with parts of the external world which come to represent them. These first projections and identifications are the beginning of the process of symbol formation.

From the cultural point of view we may note that the growth of the capacity to use language and symbols of all kinds is a product of the immense processes of 'inward work' by which we become human persons. The schizophrenic cannot be creative because he cannot symbolise: because he cannot do either he has no whole human identity. At later stages symbolism is a way to 'find' and accept 'within the self' what otherwise may be projected and 'identified with the external world' – a means of dealing effectively with the *not-me* from the *me*. Since cultural symbolism is so bound up with our humanity we should be very concerned about the degree to which culture is abused or neglected, since to lose the capacity to use symbols is to become less human.

At first the symbol is not recognised as a symbol or metaphor, but is 'felt to be the original object itself' (Hannah Segal calls these feelings 'equations'). Thus a child patient of Melanie Klein's showed acute anxiety when a pencil was sharpened: to him the pencil 'was' Melanie Klein and she was now cut up. This phenomenon is common with children who will eagerly accept in play that a piece of wood or a spider 'is' a witch, who can be got rid of by burning. And, of course, this capacity to 'equate' belongs to the

---

* As Hannah Segal points out in the paper under discussion, a Paraguayan tribe, the Abipones, cannot tolerate anything that reminds them of the dead. 'When a member of the tribe dies, all words having any affinity with the names of the deceased are immediately dropped from the vocabulary. This parallels a process of scotomisation in patients who deny persecutors in the external world by narrowing their interests.' 'Scotomisation' means 'denying the existence of': the *Penguin Dictionary of Psychology* says: 'a term used by some psychoanalysts for a process of depreciating or denying everything conflicting with the valuation of the ego'. From *Scotoma*, the blind spot in the retina.

stages of acutest anxiety about the consequences of phantasy attacks on the subject, since phantasy and reality are as yet undifferentiated.

At this early stage, however, denial can be achieved by splitting, so that 'bad' internal objects may be identified with parts of the external world and either denied existence (as by scotomisation) or annihilated by equation. There would seem to be two important relevant features of this stage of symbol formation. One is that *objects are still split*, and so can only be dealt with by primitive hate – annihilated or denied. The other is that this mode of dealing with the world belongs to the stage of capacity to deal with 'partial objects': the stage is the oral stage, everything is approached in terms of the mouth in relation to the breast, and the characteristic impulse is *taking*, eating up, by primitive hate. The self is split in a split world, and the only relation with the world is a direct incorporative attack on it. One achievement of the capacity to symbolise is at one with the achievement of a higher stage of being human.

Thus the 'undifferentiated equation' belongs to a stage in which the complexities of relationship with reality are dealt with by primitive methods – by splitting, and by hate. Such direct 'equation' acts in reality, of course, might be psychopathological. This 'equation' stage is pre-symbolic: yet reversion to this stage (as in 'happenings') is a manifest aspect of our cultural scene, and in many ways we may see in tendencies of our *avant-garde* culture an impulse to regress to more primitive and pre-symbolic modes of expression. Whether or not this is offered in the name of 'human freedom' we need to consider whether the forfeiture of achievement of symbolism does not involve the forfeiture of humanness too.

The next state in normal growth in the infant is both the discovery of the object as a whole object, the parallel acceptance of the self as a whole, in the dawn of the capacity to wrestle with the problems of life by creativity and love, as a whole person engaged with a real world and with other whole persons.

> When the depressive position has been reached, the main characteristic of object relation is that the object is felt as a whole object. In connexion with this there is a greater degree of awareness and differentiation of the separateness between the ego and the object. At the same time, since the object is recognised as a whole, ambivalence is more experienced. The ego in this phase is struggling with its ambivalence guilt, fear of loss, or actual experience of loss and mourning and a striving to recreate the object.

The problem is now for the infant, by loving and giving, to make the object 'whole', by discovering the object as a real person (good and bad combined), without splitting, and to develop this integrative process by making reparation by creative activity of all kinds. Winnicott also makes the important relevant point that the parents when discovered as real persons are far less savage than the parent imagos of talion fear: *'meeting'* humanises the savagery of primitive phantasy.

By this activity of creative phantasy and love we establish 'a good object in the ego': that is, we become more whole or integrated – able to accept good and bad, love and hate, in ourselves, and so gain 'a growing sense of reality both internal and external'.

> The internal world becomes differentiated from the external world. Omnipotent thinking, characteristic of the earlier phase, gradually gives way to more realistic thinking. Simultaneously, and as part of the same process, there is a certain modification of the primary instinctual aims. Earlier on the aim was to possess the object totally if felt as bad. With the recognition that the good and the bad objects are one, both these instinctual aims are gradually modified. The ego is increasingly concerned with saving the object from its aggression and possessiveness.

Another consequence of the increased coming to terms with ambivalence is a lessening of the intensity of projection, that is of the defence mechanism by which the object is made to contain parts of the self. This problem we encounter when we attack a partner in a love relationship who seems to be 'getting at us' because we have projected our destructiveness into them, or turn our aggression against one of another colour or race over whom we have projected our own hate. We know it also from the equation symbolism of morbid fears in which internal 'bad' objects are thrown in to the external world and regarded as persecutors, as when a child fears a spider will attack him. As we learn to symbolise we escape from such 'equation' problems. The growth of the capacity to symbolise is thus at one with the capacity to accept one's ego-weakness and ambivalence – one's humanness.

This later stage of growth brings a new meaning and function to symbolism. In the first stage the symbol, as equation, *was* a split-off part of the self, or the world, and the relationship with it was undifferentiated, direct, and primitive: *the primary impulse in dealing with it often being that of hate* (as in murder which can be an equation act). At such a stage the subject merely employs a savage incorporating mouth, on a substitute object not even recognised as a substitute for the object – not recognised as a symbol. The realities behind the symbolic act are not even engaged, because the three-term relationship cannot be recognised. At the depressive position, however,

> The symbol is needed to displace aggression from the original object, and in that way to lessen the guilt and fear of loss. The symbol is here not an equivalent of the original object, and the guilt experienced in relation to it is far less than that due to an attack on the original object. The symbols are also created in the *internal* world as a means of restoring, recreating, recapturing and owning again the original object. But in keeping with the increased reality sense, they are now felt as created by the ego and *therefore never completely equated with the original object.*

To the patient quoted above the pencil *was* Melanie Klein. At the first stage the undifferentiated equation is not a tool, is not created by the self, to create with: it stands in direct relationship to the (un-whole) self as (partial or split, also un-whole) object: the essential impulse is to incorporate or attack the equated-article-as-object, both forms of hate. The first 'equation' object is primarily needed in the role of serving the needs to relieve the pangs of growth, by splitting, projecting, dividing: it is a focus of forms of primitive hate. As with schizophrenics, symbols, such as words, at this stage cannot be used for purposes of communication.

Communication by symbols *is* possible later. But communication is but one aspect of the whole complex role of symbols: for the three-term relationship involves a relationship between symbol and the objects within the self. The modern concept of 'communications' which sometimes expresses itself in a belief that all human problems could be solved if only we could 'communicate clearly', leaves too much out of account the fact that the ability to communicate outwardly, man to man, is in complex with our ability to communicate with our inward selves – in the world of internalised objects – and with integration. On this inner relationship symbolism itself depends:

> Symbols are needed not only in communication with the external world, but also in internal communication. Indeed, it could be asked what is meant when we speak of people being well in touch with their unconscious. It is not that they have consciously primitive phantasies, like those which become evident in their analyses, but merely that they have some awareness of their own impulses and feelings. However, I think that we mean more than this; we mean that they have actual *communication* with their unconscious phantasies. And this, like any other form of communication, can only be done with the help of symbols. So that in people who are 'well in touch with themselves' there is a constant free symbol-formation, whereby they can be consciously aware and in control of *symbolic expressions* of the underlying primitive phantasies. The difficulty of dealing with schizophrenic and

schizoid patients lies not only in that they cannot communicate with us, but even more in that they cannot communicate with themselves. Any part of their ego may split off from any other part with no communication available between them.

An important aspect of internal communication is in the integration of earlier desires, anxieties, and phantasies into the later stages of development by symbolization. For instance, in the fully developed genital function, all the earlier aims, – anal, urethral, oral – may be symbolically expressed and fulfilled, a point beautifully described in Ferenczi's *Thalassa*.*

Thus it is futile to seek to improve human wellbeing, as many seek to do, by merely 'improving communications', or promoting rational understanding and insight. We must pay attention to inward communication and creative work, as a process of establishing identity: the need to 'come to terms' which is primary.

The symbolic exploration of experience is thus a fundamental necessity for man. Here we need to recognise, of course, that many 'outward' pursuits have themselves a cultural value, while some cannot be distinguished from relational modes (like giving a woman flowers). There are immense symbolic satisfactions to be found in 'male doing' or 'thinking' activities, like sports, or mathematics, science, and technology. In such forms of creative living as making a home, or cooking and sharing a meal, there are symbolic meanings – the latter, for instance, being a form of enrichment of the inner world in two senses. But here I am especially concerned with that symbolic creativity which is engaged with 'inner reality' and the core of identity. It must be emphasised that the symbols employed in all creative engagement with experience are themselves '*created in the internal world* as a means of restoring . . . and . . . re-creating'.

The concept of 'reparation' from Melanie Klein, and her attitude to art as a form of reparation seems, however, to belong to the 'depressive diagnosis'. The 'schizoid diagnosis' further draws attention to those elements in our cultural activity by which we not only 'restore the object' but develop our own sense of 'real', of the I AM, and of 'confirmation' in 'meeting'.

According to Hannah Segal, the development of metaphorical capacities at the depressive position yields creative powers we may employ to work on our earlier schizoid problems: we can now symbolise, and so seek to exert creativity and love over, by 'finding', 'giving' and 'making' over the deeper problems of primitive hate. We can work on the 'backlog' of schizoid problems of identity:

> I think that one of the important tasks performed by the ego in the depressive position is that of dealing not with depressive anxieties alone, but also with unresolved earlier conflicts. A new achievement belonging to the depressive position, the capacity to symbolize and in that way to lessen anxiety and resolve conflict, is used in order to deal with the *earlier* unresolved conflicts by symbolizing them. Anxieties, which could not be dealt with earlier on, because of the extreme concreteness of the experience with the object and the object-substitutes in symbolic equations, can gradually be dealt with by the more integrated ego by symbolization, and in that way they can be integrated. In the depressive position and later, symbols are formed not only of the whole destroyed and re-created object characteristic of the depressive position, but also of the split object – extremely good and extremely bad – and not only of the whole object but also of part-objects. Some of the paranoid and ideal object relations and anxieties may be symbolized as part of the integrative process in the depressive position.

Hannah Segal here gives fairy tales as examples of using powers of symbolism derived

* Ferenczi's *Thalassa* is *Versuch Einer Genitaltheorie, Thalassa, A Theory of Genitality*, published by the Psychoanalytical Quarterly Inc., U.S.A., 1938. Scientifically, it seems to be erroneous, based as it is on out-of-date biological notions that the organism re-enacts its primeval history in its interuterine growth. To Ferenczi, the womb was a moist environment 'provided' by evolution when animals left the sea and moved on to land. In coition we are seeking to return to Thalassa, our mother, the sea. Poetically speaking, and taken as symbolism, the phantasy is fascinating and often beautiful: but it would seem to have little value in terms of psychological truth or rational exploration of the ontogenesis of psychic disorder.

from developments at the depressive stage, to deal with schizoid problems. I have come to similar conclusions in my examination of children's nursery rhymes and their own poetry: these can be a 'highly integrated product, an artistic creation which fully symbolises the child's early anxieties and wishes . . . '.

Hannah Segal's conclusion is worth quoting, since it emphasises, from the clinical observation of patients struggling to be whole, the integral role of creative symbolism in the development of sanity, maturity and continuing wholeness:

> The way in which the maturing ego, in the process of working through the depressive position, deals with the early object relations, is of paramount importance. Some integration and whole object relations can be achieved in the depressive position, accompanied by the splitting off of earlier ego experiences. In this situation, something like a pocket of schizophrenia exists isolated in the ego, and is a constant threat to stability. At worst, a mental breakdown occurs and earlier anxieties and split-off symbolic equations invade the ego. At best, a relatively mature but restricted ego can develop and function.
>
> However, if the ego in the depressive position is strong enough and capable of dealing with anxieties, much more of the earlier situations can be integrated into the ego and dealt with by way of symbolization, enriching the ego with the whole wealth of the earlier experiences.
>
> The word 'symbol' comes from the Greek term for throwing together, bringing together, integrating. The process of symbol formation is, I think, a continuous process of bringing together and integrating the internal with the external, the subject with the object, and the earlier experiences with the later ones. (Segal [121], p. 391.)

Conversely, to misuse symbolism, or to undermine the viability of symbolic processes, is to undermine our capacities for integration. This should bring us to reflect carefully on the exploitation of symbolism in our culture for other than creative purposes.

Creative symbolism, then, is thus something far more complex than mere 'self-expression' or 'release'. Here we may find it useful to return to Suzanne Langer, and her recognition of symbolism as a primary need, while we can also infer from what object-relations psychology tells us about the role of symbolism that our attitude to culture needs to be both more confident and more serious and responsible than much of what passes for criticism and comment, in the 'Arts' pages of journals and newspapers. To a pragmatic utilitarian society, of course, art is merely a form of relaxation, between episodes of activity and doing. Our concern is with creative symbolism as it belongs to the realm of being – in which we discover *what it is to be*. This relates art to the 'whole being' and our total existence. The dramatisation of endopsychic situations by the symbolism of art which relates to actual felt experiences, is felt as a living process in the body, because the structures of the endopsychic life are felt as if they were bodily. This disposes of the aesthete who takes 'mere architecture in sound' or 'pure music', and of the mere intellectual approach to art. As Cooke says of music:

> The widespread view of music as 'purely music' limits the listener's understanding of the great masterpieces of their purely aural beauty – i.e. to their surface attraction – and to their purely technical construction. The latter is no more (and no less) than the magnificent craftsmanship *whereby composers express their emotions coherently*: it is forever unintelligible to a layman, except to almost anyone but a potential composer. Music, is, in fact, 'extra-verbal', since notes, like words, have emotional connotations; it is, let us repeat, the supreme expression of universal emotions, in an entirely personal way, by the great composers. (Cooke [16], p. 33.)

Cooke's conclusion is that music has a moral effect: 'we need not feel ashamed that music should have a moral effect only by placing emotional moods in a significant order: psychology has shown that our whole life is propelled by these instinctive urges, and that it is by balancing and ordering them that we achieve a valuable, creative attitude to life' (Cooke [16], p. 271).

'Instinctive' is a word I would challenge here. By 'instinctive urges', perhaps, we can take Cooke to mean all those intrapsychic dynamics explored above by Hannah Segal. But Cooke's most valuable emphasis is that music is a means of man's ultimate quest to 'discover the truth about himself', and his painstaking book is an attempt to show how he may properly speak of music as a 'language of the emotions', by which inward truth may be explored and ordered.

One must applaud the emphasis – that music is *about* something. Suzanne Langer takes the same point of view, rejecting the concept of music as pure form:

> The most vehement critics of the emotive-content theory seem to have caught a germ from the doctrine they attacked: in denying the very possibility of any content of music, they have fallen into the way of thinking about it in form and content. . . . And while they fiercely repudiate the proposition that music is a semantic, they cannot assert that it is meaningless . . . they try to eat their cake and have it too, by a logical trick that is usually accepted only among mathematicians – by a statement which has the form of an answer to a question in hand, and really commits them to nothing. Musical form, they reply, is its own content; it means itself. This evasion was suggested by Hanslick when he said: 'The theme of a musical composition is its essential content.' He knew that this was an evasion; but his successors have found it harder and harder to revisit the *question* of content, and the silly fiction of self-significance has been raised to the dignity of a doctrine. (Langer [55], p. 237.)

There is no philosophical justification for the position of the aesthete, or the individual who wants art to be 'pure', and to have no bearing on 'life' – or who seeks art for art's sake, or, worse, 'art for artists' sake' (Edward Lucie Smith).

There is, of course, much more to explore here, about form content, sign, and meaning. But it will do here to take account of Suzanne Langer's term 'insight' and Cooke's phrase 'know thyself' – and the references in both authors to 'ordering' and 'exploring'.

What is the area of 'universal emotion' to which an art such as music contributes 'insight'? What is it, since it is not merely outward sounds in the world (like cuckoos and thunderstorms), that is being 'explored'? And what is it that is being 'ordered'? If the answer is 'emotion', then what area and dimension of experience are being referred to when we speak of the 'ordering' of emotions?

We may answer in some such terms as the effect 'harmony' or 'peace' in the 'nervous system': but does this merely mean in terms of tension and relaxation of organic elements of the body? Such an answer hardly seems adequate since, for instance, a work like the *St. Matthew Passion* involves complex feelings and attitudes to oneself and the universe, and aspects of human relationship. Where does music touch on 'sentiment responsive life' and how?

Suzanne Langer finds that the meanings of music operate 'probably below the threshold of consciousness, certainly outside the pale of discursive thinking' (p. 244).

> The imagination that reponds to music is personal and associative and logical, tinged with affect, tinged with bodily rhythm, tinged with dream, but concerned with a wealth of formulations for its wealth of wordless knowledge, its whole knowledge of emotional and organic experience, of vital impulse, conflict, the *ways* of living and dying, and feeling. . . . The lasting effect is, like the first effect of speech on the mind, to *make things conceivable* . . . not communication but insight is the gift of music, in very naïve phrase, a knowledge of 'how feelings go'. (Langer [55], p. 244.)

It is most refreshing to have a philosopher writing so in terms of whole being, who also refuses to break down the complex processes of artistic meaning as if seeking to explain them away. Art, she tells us, deals with 'something much deeper than any intellectual experience': it symbolises: 'the life-rhythms we share with all gnawing, hungering, moving and fearing creatures: the ultimate realities themselves, the central facts of our brief, sentient existence . . . ' (Langer [55], p. 260).

However, we need to ask – since they are not to be intellectually experienced, but 'wholly' experienced, what are the 'ultimate realities' and the 'central facts'? They cannot be mere bodily sensations and tensions. Where are they, then, since they are not merely organic, but 'ways of living', i.e. aware and psychic elements? Is the effect of music ultimately 'making things conceivable'? Or conveying 'how feelings go'?

Suzanne Langer emphasises in an important way the necessary complexity of artistic statement:

> Artistic symbols . . . are untranslatable; their sense is bound to the particular form which it has taken. It is always *implicit*, and cannot be explicated by any interpretation. This is true even of poetry, for though the *material* of poetry is verbal, its impact is not the literal assertion made in the words, *but the way the assertion is made*, and this involves the sound, the tempo, the aura of associations of the words, the long or short sequence of ideas, the wealth or poverty of transient imagery that contains them, the sudden arrest of fantasy by pure fact or of familiar fact by sudden fantasy, the suspense of literal meaning by a sustained ambiguity resolved in a long-awaited key-word, and the unifying, all embracing artifice of rhythm. . . . The poem as a whole is the bearer of artistic import. (Langer [55], p. 261.)

Only in the local context of the work does symbolism have the 'life' given it by 'the way the assertion is made'. This 'life' surely belongs to that area of 'being', which cannot be expressed wholly in the 'male element' terms of conception and explicit meaning. These belong to structure. But the essential content of art surely belongs to the realm of 'female element being', by which there is 'communication', though of a very deep kind, but whose essence is the communication with oneself, and that 'at-one-ness' which belongs to the unspoken, and has also a 'silent incommunicable core'. When one learns 'insight' from music one is not learning that insight from a real experience, as Suzanne Langer indicates, when she refers to 'The notion that certain effects of music are so much *like* feelings that we mistake them for the latter . . . ', and goes on 'until symbolic forms are consciously abstracted, they are regularly confused with things they symbolise . . . ' (Langer [55], p. 245).

This confusion belongs to the inexplicitness of the realm of being. For what the symbolism of genuine art fosters is the creative energies of the 'female element' of being itself. So, if we examine what we mean by insight, it is not only 'understanding ourselves', though this is one obvious gain from art. It is true that culture brings us at best to an awareness of possible and other kinds of human experience through 'as-if' symbolism, and an understanding of our own make-up. 'Insight' in this sense is what we gain every time we respond to a work of art – a deeper sense of how we share our problems with other human beings. There is a gain in 'knowing how feelings go'.

But there is a more dynamic satisfaction, a greater gain: an enrichment of 'structure' and 'content' in the inner world. There is also a meeting with the whole human world at the deepest level, where consciousness is rooted in bodily existence. We take from the work of art – from its dynamics of symbolism – the benefit of work already done in 'as-if' terms on problems which, since they are universal, are also *ours*, and belong to the realm of being inapproachable in any other way. They are as universal as the deepest patterns of inner reality at the core of being, where internal objects, feelings of emptiness and division, are felt in the 'psychic tissue' which cannot separate itself from bodily tissue and the phantasies that arise from bodily feelings.

The artist has thrown open an inner contest in terms of the symbolic dramatisation of endopsychic energies and structures. We experience not only the degree of order he has achieved, but are able to share through his symbolism the achievements won along his arduous quest to 'preserve his existence'. What is achieved is *reparation*: the modifying of hate and the consequent achievement of a sense of structure and content in the identity. This may involve us in the artist's depression or dissociation – consequent upon his very discovery and exploration of his own destructiveness and hate and his struggle for ego-maintenance. This explains why there is often so much resentment over new works of creativity, and so much resistance to them. We may have to share schizoid insights into weakness at the heart of identity which are almost intolerable. But in experiencing the symbolic contest with the artist's life-problems, it is as if we learn how someone else has grappled with them, in terms of how he felt the conflict embodied. We have not been through his hell: but we follow his torment there in its symbolic issues, in 'as if' terms, and we see, among other things, both that it *is* possible to come through such conflicts, and *how* it is possible to come through towards integration. What we may have to encounter is the possibility of being overcome by our own weakness and the hate turned on this, and yet surviving. We are also made aware of what kind of torments others, and thus we ourselves, *may have to go through*, especially the torments of feeling the identity itself threatened by loss and hate. And we also see, by what creative effort we can engage with our own hate, in order to 'repair the object', become whole, and survive.

After responding to a deeply disturbing work one can feel 'I have imagined and felt the worst that I fear to be possible, but my life still has meaning'. How structure and content link here is obvious: the content is in the deeper feelings of richness, security and wholeness gained by the achievement of a sense of being 'good enough to survive', even when the worst destructiveness has been recognised and admitted. The sense of structure comes by the experience gained symbolically by the metaphorical record of how the contest of love and hate felt in the individual psyche and soma. This can result in the feeling: 'although I know hate in myself and the world, and have brought myself face to face with it, I survive, I am invulnerable.'* Creativity is our primary means of 'confronting the problem of existence', and of asking What is it to be human?

If this is so, then this triumphant primary reality of our culture is one which Freud never found. Here one of the most revolutionary of Winnicott's papers is that given in 1966 to the British Psychoanalytical Society on 'The Location of Culture' (Winnicott [130]). In this paper Winnicott picks up a remark he made in an earlier speech:

> Freud did not have a place in his topography of the mind for the experience of things cultural. He gave new value to inner psychic reality, and from this came a new value for things that are actual and truly external. Freud used the word 'sublimation' to point the way to a place where cultural experience is meaningful, but perhaps he did not get so far as to tell us where in the mind cultural experience is.

Winnicott seeks to extend some ideas first put forward in an earlier paper on 'Transitional Objects and Transitional Phenomena' (Winnicott [90], p. 229). This paper was about the first cultural artefacts of the child – his rudimentary songs or rhymes, his piece of cloth, his cuddly toy. These Winnicott saw as the child's first symbols. The child hugs the piece of cloth rather than his mother, and it is an 'object' in the philosophical-psychological sense. He devotes to it the affections which he would otherwise devote to his mother, but the cuddly cloth belongs not to his union with her, but with separateness. It is his first step on the way to a relationship with culture in the world, and with objects in the world.

---

* The artist may even feel that there is a risk involved to others in experiencing his work. Bruno Walter records how Mahler said to him, when he gave him *Das Lied Von Der Erde*. 'What do you think? Is it at all bearable? Will it drive people to make an end of themselves?' See my analysis in *Gustav Mahler and Peace Without God*.

> If we study any one infant . . . there may emerge some thing or some phenomenon – perhaps a bundle of wool, or the corner of a blanket or eiderdown, or a word or tune, or a mannerism, which becomes vitally important to the infant for use at the time of going to sleep, and is a defence against anxiety, especially anxiety of a depressive type. Perhaps some soft object or cot cover has been found and used by the infant, and this then becomes what I am calling a *transitional object*. This object goes on being important. The parents get to know its value and carry it around when travelling. The mother lets it get dirty and even smelly, knowing that by washing it she introduces a break in the continuity in the infant's experience, a break that may destroy the meaning and value of the object to the infant. (Winnicott [90], p. 232.)

Later, as the individual 'puts away childish things', 'It loses meaning, and this is because the transitional phenomena have become diffused, have become spread out over the whole intermediate territory between "inner psychic reality" and "the external world as perceived by two persons in common", that is to say, over the whole cultural field.'

So important, however, can this transitional object be that it can influence adult interests: Winnicott cites the case of a man whose transitional object as an infant was a piece of cloth with brightly coloured threads (as emerged in his analysis): in adult life he came to be a textiles expert, and the feeling for the early plaything was an important influence in choosing the adult métier.

Winnicott ponders a quotation from Tagore, on which he found himself often returning: 'On the seashore of endless worlds, children play.' As a Freudian he thought he knew what it meant:

> The sea and the shore represented endless intercourse between man and woman, and the child emerged from this union to have a brief moment before becoming in turn an adult or parent. Then, as a student of unconscious symbolism, I *knew* (one always *knows*) that the sea is the mother, and on to the sea-shore the child is born. Babies come up out of the sea and are spewed out upon the land, like Jonah from the whale. So now the sea-shore was the mother's body, after the child is born, and the mother and the now viable baby are getting to know one another. (Winnicott [130], p. 368.)

But this, says Winnicott, implies a sophisticated concept of the relationship between mother and child. There could be another point of view – that of the infant itself. Here we need to penetrate into regions of objects and phenomena located 'in the personal psychic reality, felt to be inside', and the mental mechanisms of projection and introjection. And yet, in struggling to find a place for that play on the sea-shore, we may find that *'play is in fact neither a matter of internal psychic reality nor a matter of external reality'*.

This leaves us with the question: If play is neither inside nor outside, where is it? Winnicott has used the phrase 'building bridges between subjective and objective': but this still leaves the question open, where, then, is the bridge, and what is happening across it?

Winnicott, with characteristic humility, says that his patients have taught him where play is.

> I have claimed that when we witness an infant's employment of a transitional object, the first not-me possession, we are witnessing both the child's first use of a symbol, and also the first experience of play. An essential part of my formulation of transitional phenomena is that . . . we agree never to make the challenge to the baby: did you create this object, or did you find it conveniently lying around? In fact the object is a symbol of the union of the baby and the mother (or part of the mother). This symbol can be located. It is at the place in space and time where and when the mother is in transition from being (in the baby's mind) merged in with the infant and being experienced as an object to be perceived rather than conceived of. The use of an object symbolises the union of two now separate things, baby and mother, *at the point of the initiation of their state of separateness*. (Winnicott [130], p. 369.)

The symbol relates to an image of the mother in the child's mind, and this is in complex with the actual experience of the mother's handling and care. Both contribute to a sense of continuing existence and to a sense of being in the same body. Here Winnicott also refers to Middlemore's *The Nursing Couple* [61] in which there is delineated 'infinite richness in the intertwined techniques of the nursing couple' – as a positive source of a feeling of being real and whole. By using its symbol to build up a sense of the existence of its union with the mother, while she, of course, comes and goes in space and time, the baby comes to benefit from separation. 'This is the place that I have set out to examine: *the separation that is not a separation but a form of union*' (Winnicott [130], p. 369).

This kind of experience differs in that it has no climax: it is not orgiastic, and does not bring that kind of satisfaction of relaxation. It is thus not of the kind of psychosomatic functioning to which Freud devoted his attention, or which can be regarded, whether erroneously or not, as 'instinctual'. 'But these phenomena that have reality in the area whose existence I am postulating belong to *the experience of relating to objects*. One can think of the "electricity" that seems to generate in meaningful or intimate contact, and that is a feature when people are in love. . . . '

In this way, obviously, psychoanalysis is recognising that here are primary human 'realities' which Freud could not find because he had concentrated on orgiastic experience: 'Psychoanalysts who have rightly emphasised the significance of instinctual experience and of reactions to frustration *have failed to state with comparable clearness or conviction the tremendous intensity of these non-climactic experiences that are called playing*' (Winnicott [30], p. 370; my italics).

We see here Winnicott's thought emerging from his own Freudian background. Lomas says that 'certain elements in Winnicott's terminology remain unsatisfactory, for he has tried to retain Freudian "metapsychology" in parts of his description' – as by his use of the word 'instinctual' which we have seen can be challenged as valid. Yet, as Lomas also says, 'he conveys, even more vividly than Laing, the picture of a self that remains its own agent'. Winnicott here sees that psychoanalysis has patently remained blind, like sexology, to the fact that love is far more important than climax, because it has to do with the *point of life*. Psychoanalysis tends, says Winnicott, to think of ego-defences and the anxiety that arises from the instinctual life: 'we tend to think of health in terms of the state of ego-defences – we say it is more healthy when these defences are not rigid, etc.' But 'You may cure your patient and not know what it is that makes him or her go on living . . . we have not yet started to describe what life is like apart from illness or the absence of illness' (Winnicott [130], p. 370).

As Farber points out, we often have a tendency in psychoanalysis to generate a picture of a normal man in terms of the absence of illness with some kind of healthy perfectibility in the background. Winnicott says: 'That is to say, we have yet to tackle the question of *what life is about*. Our psychotic patients force us to give attention to this sort of basic problem . . . it is not instinctual satisfaction that makes a baby begin to be, to feel that life is real, to find life worth living.' (Winnicott [130], p. 370.)

Obviously, what a baby takes in from its mother, in terms of 'female element being', is something more than mere milk and comfort: it is a capacity to perceive the world, to love, and to develop symbols, and a sense of richness in union – that which is meant by all the paintings in the world of Virgin and Child. It is also the capacity to be and to be alone, relying on inner resources. By contrast, as Winnicott says, mere functioning is mere seduction unless there is a personal meaning:

Instinctual satisfactions start off as mere part-functions and they become *seductions* unless based on a well-established capacity in the individual person for total experience, and for experience in the area of transitional phenomena. *It is the self which must precede the self's use of instinct*; the rider must ride the horse, not be run away with . . . '*Le style c'est l'homme même*'. When one speaks of a man one speaks of him *along with* the summation of his cultural experiences. The whole forms a unit. (Winnicott [130], p. 370.)

Here, indeed, we have a very different view of man from that of Freud's. Winnicott is invoking culture, not as 'sublimation' of instinctual drives, but as a source of meaning in life. He is uncertain about whether he can define the word 'culture', but 'The accent indeed is on experience. In using the word culture I am thinking of the inherited tradition. I am thinking of something that is in the common pool of humanity and into which individuals and groups of people may contribute, and a source from which we may all draw *if we have somewhere to put what we find*.' (Winnicott [130], p. 370.)

This involves some kind of 'recording method' – in which, obviously, Winnicott includes the language. This brings poetry, obviously, to a central place in personal development in a way that was impossible to Freud. What also interests Winnicott is how: 'in any cultural field it is not possible to be original except on a basis of tradition. . . . The interplay between originality and the acceptance of tradition as a basis for inventiveness seems to me to be just one more example, and a very exciting one, of the interplay between separateness and union.' (Winnicott [130], p. 370.)

Thus in the origins of our humanness in the interplay between union and separateness of the baby in his mother's care we may find the origins of that interplay between union and separateness, between the individual and the culture he inherits. Unless he can take possession of that culture he cannot begin to be human. For too long has psychoanalysis implied that to be truly human is to merely *function* as an organism.

It is of first importance for us to acknowledge openly that absence of psychoneurotic illness may be health but it is not life. Psychotic patients who are hovering all the time between living and not living force us to look at this problem, one which really belongs not to psychoneurotics but to all human beings. I am claiming that these same phenomena that are life or death to our schizoid or 'borderline' patients appear in our cultural experiences. It is these cultural experiences that provide the continuity in the human race which transcends personal existence. I am assuming that cultural experiences are in direct continuity with play, the play of those who have not yet heard of games. (Winnicott [130], p. 370.)

Culture then arises out of 'the potential space between the subjective object and the object objectively perceived, between *me*-extensions and the *not-me*', and cultural development is thus at one with the discovery of actuality – 'there being objects and phenomena outside omnipotent control'. It is thus hand in hand with what Winnicott calls 'disillusion' – the gradual natural relinquishment, on the way to maturity, of the sense of omnipotence, magical powers, and monism which are necessary to the baby at the beginning, but which could only impede his capacities to live if they were not relinquished as he grows.

In cultural growth an important concept for Winnicott is 'trust' – the capacity to have confidence here based on primary experience. Trust in culture is based in a mutual respect between one human being and another. As we have seen there are areas in our culture where this mutual trust is replaced by contempt, and the impulse to exploit. Freudian theory can even be taken to vindicate this. But in the cultural field at large, and in education, if we apply Winnicott's insights here we shall find it most alarming to see the degree to which this area of trust is neglected and abused. Is the content of our education helping to create that 'trust'? Does our culture at large foster that 'confidence in the environmental factor' by which we can go on trying to find the 'point of life'? Or is our trust in cultural relationship not 'sometimes gravely abused' – indeed, does not a great deal of our commercial and *avant-garde* culture take advantage of this trust to rape us, even at the heart of being?

PART V

Psychoanalysis and Existentialism

CHAPTER 20

Psychoanalysis and Existentialism

AT FIRST sight, Laing, the chief exponent of existential psychoanalysis in England, seems to be on the side of the angels against the traditions in psychology derived from natural science:

> The theoretical and descriptive idiom of much research in social science adopts a stance of apparent 'objective' neutrality. . . . But . . . the choice of syntax and vocabulary are political acts that define and circumscribe the manner in which the 'facts' are to be experienced. Indeed, they go further and even create the facts that are studied. . . .
> Natural Scientific investigations are conducted on objects, or things, or the patterns of relations between things or on systems of events. Persons are distinguished from thing in that persons experience the world, whereas things behave in the world. Thing events do not experience. Personal events are experiential. (Laing [53], p. 53.)

Here Laing is attacking a whole tradition of 'non-psychological psychology', as from an existential concern with the I–Thou and 'man in his totality'. He seems to be saying what Guntrip has also said: 'Science is the emotionally detached study of the properties of "objects" . . . ' (Guntrip [37], p. 16).

'Scientific' psychology takes little or no account of the truth that 'personal events are experiential':

> the struggle to equate 'scientific explanation' with the 'elimination of individuality' goes on, aiming to produce theories which are still in principle materialistic and mechanistic, even though the earlier crude materialism and mechanism are outmoded. This has been the standard around which the modern battle rages for the capture and possession of the truth about man himself. (Guntrip [37], p. 16.)

Laing seems at first to be concerned with the pursuit of the same kind of truth: 'The requirement of the present, the failure of the past, is the same: to provide a thoroughly self-conscious and self-critical human account of man' (Laing [53], p. 11).

Laing's most important contribution was to explore the nature of what he called 'ontological insecurity' in schizoid individuals by a phenomenological approach as in *The Divided Self*. This exploration of the 'strategies of survival' belongs to the pursuit of a sense of man's 'totality' by listening to *meanings* and relating them to the problem of existence. From his investigations Laing shows clearly (as we need to bear in mind) that there are those who feel secure and real, and those who do not. From this he went on to explore theories which seek to explain why this should be so, and also to suggest kinds of programme for tackling this problem, in social terms. Laing says that in normal life 'A man may have a sense of his presence in the world as real, alive, whole, and, in a temporal sense, continuous person' (Laing [52], p. 40).

His particular interest is the situation in which 'there is the partial or almost complete absence of the assurances derived from an existential position' in those 'whose experiences may be utterly lacking in any unquestionable self-validating certainties. . . . '

He compares the characters of Shakespeare with those of Kafka: Shakespeare's characters 'evidently experience themselves as real and alive and complete however riddled with doubts or torn by conflicts they may be . . .' (Laing [52], p. 42).

By contrast with those of Kafka 'this is not so': 'the effort to communicate what being alive is like in the absence of such assurances seems to characterise the work of a number of writers and artists of our time. Life, without feeling alive. . . . '

Laing here cites Beckett and Francis Bacon, artists who are schizoid individuals, struggling to feel real. The difference between feeling real and not feeling real Laing expresses thus:

> The individual, then, may experience his own being as real, alive, whole; as differentiated from the rest of the world in ordinary circumstances so clearly that his identity and autonomy are never in question; as a continuum in time; as having an inner consistency, substantiality, genuineness and worth; as spatially co-existent with the body; and, usually, as having begun in or around birth and liable to extinction with death. He thus has a firm core of ontological security.

Other individuals do not have this security:

> The individual in the ordinary circumstances of life may feel more unreal than real; in a literal sense more dead than alive, precariously differentiated from the rest of the world, so that his identity and autonomy are always in question. He may lack the experience of his own temporal continuity. He may not possess an over-riding sense of personal consistency or cohesiveness. He may feel more insubstantial than substantial, and unable to assume that the stuff he is made of is genuine, good valuable. And he may feel his self as partially divorced from his body. (Laing [52], p. 43.)

A little further on in this chapter Laing quotes a patient as crying out in an analytic group debate, saying 'I can't go on. We are arguing in order to have the pleasure of triumphing over me. At best you win an argument. At most you lose an argument. *I am arguing in order to preserve my existence*' (Laing [52], p. 45).

A dilemma arises when an individual needs to 'argue' to preserve his existence, but lacks the symbolising capacity to 'argue', or create, in the realm of being. In such creative workers as Sartre, Beckett, and Francis Bacon we have the schizoid individual seeking to discover an ontological security he does not know as a person, in what he exhibits. Reflected in his work perhaps he hopes to feel real. But because of the schizoid condition itself there is a deficiency of the capacity to symbolise. This raises considerable problems to do with the relationship between the artist and the public – and the individual and society. Winnicott says of the painting of Francis Bacon: 'the exasperating and skilful and challenging artist of our time who goes on and on painting the human face distorted significantly. From the standpoint of this paper this Francis Bacon is seeing himself in his mother's face, but with some twist in him or her that maddens both him and us.' (Winnicott [96], p. 29.)

Is such art 'insurrection'? Or is it an anguished plea to be 'confirmed'? What of our relationship to 'society'? Must we find ourselves by attacking 'society' or seeking to find ourselves reflected in it?

In the light of our examination of object-relations psychology and philosophical anthropology, and of the implications of these for our relationship with society, we would surely expect an existentialist to find society a context for 'meeting'.

Laing's view, however, is very different. His view seems to be that society conditions and inhibits a 'natural' individual, so that the family and the community are instruments of coercion, 'violence', and alienation: 'We are born into a world in which alienation awaits us. We are potentially men, but we are in an alienated state, and this state is not simply a natural system. Alienation as our present destiny is achieved only by outrageous violence perpetuated by human beings on human beings.' (Laing [53], p. 12.)

While it is impossible to deny that there is much violence in our world, and that there are many forms of hate behaviour which are dissociated, even while we accept them as sane and normal, can we see these as forms of 'alienation' which are forced on us by 'the family' and 'society', as Laing does? In the family – is the *mother* – an 'instrument of coercion'?

Laing's attitudes to love also seem radically different from that of, say, Winnicott: 'Love (as in education) is the path through permissiveness to discipline: and through discipline, only too often, to betrayal of self . . . ' (Laing [53], p. 62).

Laing's view of the relationship between the individual and society is that the 'family' and 'society' conspire to coerce those individuals who do not 'conform'. Of schizophrenia he says: 'There is no such "condition" as "schizophrenia", but the label is a social fact and the social fact a *political event*. This political event, occurring in the civic order of society, imposes definitions and consequences on the labelled person.' (Laing [53], p. 57.)

Laing attacks even psychiatric diagnosis:

> Lidz calls schizophrenia a failure of human adaptation. In that case, this too is a value judgement. Or is anyone going to say that this is an objective fact? Very well, let us call schizophrenia a successful attempt not to adapt to pseudo social realities. Is this also an objective fact? Schizophrenia is a failure of ego functioning. Is this a neutralist definition? But what is, or who is, the 'ego'? In order to get back to what the ego is, to what actual reality it most nearly relates to, we have to desegregate it, de-personalize it, de-reify, and we get back to you and me, to our particular idioms or styles of relating to each other in social context. The ego is by definition an instrument of adaptation, so we are back to all the questions this apparent neutralism is begging. Schizophrenia is a successful avoidance of ego-type adaptation. Schizophrenia is a label affixed by some people to others in situations where an interpersonal disjunction of a particular kind is occurring. This is the nearest one can get at the moment to something like an objective statement, so called.

This 'labelling' begins in the family:

> The family is, in the first place, the usual instrument for what is called socialization, that is, getting each new recruit to the human race to behave and experience in substantially the same way as those who have already got here. We are all fallen Sons of Prophecy, who have learned to die in the Spirit and be reborn in the flesh.
> This is known as selling one's birthright for a mess of pottage. (Laing [53], p. 58.)

Examined more closely, Laing's attitude to society and the family surely belongs not to interpersonal psychoanalysis but rather, still, to Freudian theory, by which civilisation is inevitably inimical to individual fulfilment.

> The schizophrenic may simply be someone who has been unable to *suppress his normal instincts* and *conform* to an abnormal society. The Family's function is to *repress* Eros. . . . The ego is by definition an *instrument of adaptation* (and so can be seen as belonging to the family as an instrument of socialization). The family, is in the first place, the usual *instrument* for what is called socialization. . . .
> From the moment of birth . . . the baby is subjected to those *forms of violence* called love . . . mainly *concerned with destroying* most of its potentialities. . . .
> Thus, while creativity is an act of insurrection. True sanity entails in one way or another the *dissolution of the normal ego*, that false self competently adjusted to our alienated social reality. . . . (Laing [53], *passim*; my italics.)

Laing's picture of the normal adult personality seems to be one of the human being having *lost* something, having been destroyed by nurture, losing potentialities in the process of maturation: 'We are all fallen Sons of Prophecy, who have learned to die in the Spirit and be reborn in the flesh' (Laing [53], p. 57).

According to Laing, Freud's value was in showing how much we lost by being socialized: 'The relevance of Freud to our time is largely his insight, and, to a very considerable extent, his *demonstration* that the *ordinary* person is a shrivelled, desiccated fragment of what a person can be' (Laing [53], p. 22; Laing's italics).

'What we call normal is a product of repression . . . ' and 'This state of affairs represents an almost unbelievable devastation of our experience'. Psychotherapy is 'a search, constantly reasserted and reconstituted for what we have all *lost*'.

In the light of object-relations theory, if psychotherapy is a search for something we have 'lost', it could be that what is being sought is what should have been the patient's by right but what he has never had. Winnicott, for instance, makes this interpretation of the symbolism of stealing in children. What has been lost is that primary experience of the capacity *to be* in the mother's nurture: what is 'lost' is not a 'natural' self but the experience of at-one-ness in which the True Self should have grown. The True Self waits to be born psychically. It isn't that it is 'lost' but that it has never been found or created by 'reflection', rather.

As we have seen, however, to the schizoid individual, whose loss of this primary nurture has been disastrous, yet nothing is more threatening than nurture. This was made clear by Fairbairn: the schizoid must preserve 'alienation'. From Laing's work in *The Divided Self*, too, we can understand how it is that the schizoid person feels so hollow at the core of being that he fears implosion in the least experience of sympathy, love, or contact.

From Fairbairn's work we can also understand that what is feared is what Winnicott calls 'female element being'. That is, the vulnerable core of the self, and the very female element in others, the experience of which has originally been so disastrous. By *false male doing*, 'bad thinking', and False Self activity, the schizoid individual must preserve his alienation – even from 'what he has lost': as the patient of Guntrip's said: 'You must never love me.'

Laing is one of those in present-day psychiatry who resists mechanical treatments in favour of person-to-person therapy. In his work he seeks, alongside those seeking to develop object-relations theory, to arrive at a true psychology, which recognises, as we have seen (p. 37 above), that 'A human being can only be known as a living and highly individual, unique "person" '.

Any 'thoroughly self-conscious and self-critical human account of man' needs to include subjective experience as human truth. This seems acceptable if we remind ourselves that medical diagnosis and care – like teaching – have always worked substantially through intuition, imagination, and the 'female element' modes of dealing with experience.

But how can we reconcile this emphasis on the 'female way of knowing' in a doctor with the intemperate hostility which Laing demonstrates towards society? It surely only requires a short step in our thinking to see Laing's dogmatic insistence on 'alienation' as itself a form of pseudo-male or 'bad' thinking?

Guntrip's distinction between male and female ways of knowing is most relevant when we are considering Laing's claim to represent existentialist psychology. As we have seen, Buber's kind of concern with man's 'totality' is rooted in his recognition of the origin of human identity in the primary 'togetherness' between mother and child. His kind of existentialism finds the root of being *in* the 'female element'. By contrast, I believe that Laing has not been able to find this area as, say, Winnicott delineates it. Laing's problem, I believe, is that he attempts to fuse the search for 'female element being' from existentialism of one kind (Kierkegaard, Buber) with the 'pseudo-male' 'thinking as doing' of the very different kind of existentialism developed by Heidegger and Sartre – with Freudian 'hate theory' in the background.

Laing thus stands very much at a parting of the ways: but while he seems to be pointing towards the subjective disciplines, he is actually marching firmly along the same path as Freud and those who follow metapsychology and 'instinct' theory – towards pessimism, the death instinct, and the rejection of civilisation.

Here I believe we need to remind ourselves of Guntrip's theory of knowledge. He sees the different kinds of knowledge as rooted in primary experience:

> At first the infant knows no difference between himself and the breast, but feels that he 'is' because the breast 'is'. Here is the origin of all knowing by identification. Thus there are two ways of knowing. The male way of knowing in its highest development is objective analytical scientific investigation. The female way of knowing in the completest sense is the mother's intuitive knowledge of her baby. (Guntrip [38], p. 26.)

Thinking and 'objective analytical investigation' are aspects of doing, and a way of dealing with the world. But where there is ego-weakness, these can become an aspect of 'false male doing' in the absence of an adequate sense of being. Where there is integration, 'doing' and 'being' can go side by side, in human experience. So can intuition and reason, synthesis and analysis, poet and scientist.

But where there is a pathological lack of integration, thinking can be an activity of false male doing which, since it belongs to the False Self, needs to deny and exclude both the female way of knowing and the female element of experience. Guntrip says: 'the male element [can be seen as] the need to be able to take practical action in an often dangerous world', while the female element is 'the need to be emotionally susceptible, the capacity for sensitiveness to what others are feeling.'

But the trouble arises because 'The female element is the emotionally sensitive self that can be more easily hurt, and then can be felt as a weakness to be resisted, resented, and hidden beneath a tough exterior.'

There can thus be in the very energy of intellectual 'doing' a hatred and denial of the vulnerable female elements in us. This accounts for many of the difficulties we encounter in obtaining recognition of 'inner reality'.

From this tendency to deny our inner vulnerability also arises a clash in philosophy. Can the philosopher accept the basis of all thought in 'being' – in intuition, phantasy, symbol, dream, and the bodily life underlying these? Suzanne Langer, who admits heresy, recognises the primary need for symbolism, which she sees as 'an act essential to thought and prior to it'. Symbolism emerges from feminine knowing and precedes Sartre's *cogito*: it belongs to 'other' ways of knowing (see Polanyi and Marjorie Grene).

Melanie Klein has emphasised the importance of unconscious phantasy and its psychosomatic origins, underlying all effort – scientific or otherwise. In Suzanne Langer's recognition of symbolism we have a recognition of those basic processes of phantasy, dream, and metaphor by which we develop and employ human understanding. As we have seen, perception, in the view of Winnicott and Marion Milner, itself depends upon delusion, and the hidden processes of ego-maintenance.

In looking at philosophy in this way I believe we can invoke two further relevant observations of Winnicott's. One is that the origin of over-intense intellectual activity (such as a philosophical system) may be itself in a failure of early mothering. 'As a more common result of the lesser degrees of tantalising infant care in the early stages we find *mental functioning becoming a thing in itself* practically replacing the good mother and making her unnecessary' (Winnicott [90], p. 246).

The philosopher may be one who needs to 'replace the good mother' by an intellectual system: obviously then, as Fairbairn indicates, there will be an intense libidinal attachment to the system.

The other is that the sense of being depends upon the child being given a 'female element breast'. The converse (as Guntrip points out) is disastrous:

> By contrast, the not very maternal, busy, bustling, organising, dominating mother, who is determined that her baby shall 'get on with his feed' at the rate the timetable dictates, will present him with a 'pseudo-male-element breast' which seeks to 'do things' to him. The maternal mother, who understands her baby's emotional needs, especially in the earliest stages, can let him feed and enjoy it at his own pace, and can then (most important) let him go to sleep peacefully and restfully at the breast. She gives him a 'female element breast' par excellence, at which he can experience utter peace of tranquil existence, simple 'being'. This must represent the most complete experience of security possible in human life. If it is sufficiently adequate and repeated for long enough, it can lay the psychic foundations of basic inner strength of ego-development as that proceeds and proliferates. It is an experience that we could only express in sophisticated verbal form by the simple statement I am', or possibly 'I am because I *feel* secure and real.' (Not 'I do' or even 'I think' *for thinking is only a psychic form of 'doing'*.) (Guntrip [38], p. 250. My italics.)

'*I am* because I feel secure and real' is the basis of Buber's kind of existentialism. My contention will be that it could not be Sartre's and cannot be Laing's – because what is missing from their existentialism is both the mother and the 'female element'.

From these psychoanalytical insights I believe we may begin to explore in a significant way the nature of knowledge itself.

The psychoanalytical philosopher Money-Kyrle suggests that the classical philosopher was one who could not tolerate splits – a predicament which drove him to seek harmony. The modern epistemological philosopher by contrast may well be one who seeks to preserve splits. He cannot feel the harmony of I AM, and so must seek to live in an intellectual system which he idealises, and this, in a system like Marxism, may become a horrifyingly callous and inhuman 'pseudo-male' system to which any being must be forfeit. Such a schizoid intellectual energy has an impulse to construct an intellectual world as a 'substitute for the good mother' while trying to make her unnecessary by denying the whole area of being, and that of the female element. In this there may be implicit a denial of the intuitive, creative, and bodily, of the emotional life, and of the area of phantasy and metaphorical symbol. *There may be a callous denial of being human.**

To return to Laing's social theory, we can ask, I believe, from this point of view: could we, for instance, ever imagine Buber endorsing a public advertisement advocating the relaxation of controls on hallucinogens pronounced by international human agencies to be dangerous? Could we imagine Buber saying, 'let me drive you out of your wretched mind'? Can we imagine a Buber advocating the use of LSD as a means of 'release'? Or writing intemperately against 'them' – 'the Establishment' – while seeming to recommend the 'derangement of the senses' as Laing does in *The Politics of Experience*? May we not see in the contrast between these men a contrast between one motivated by

* See D. H. Lawrence and L. H. Myers on Bertrand Russell, discussed by G. H. Bantock (Bantock [4]). Also *Personal Knowledge*, Michael Polanyi; *The Knower and the Known*, Marjorie Grene.

the 'female element' and the other motivated by what looks 'like 'pseudo-male doing' – and moral inversion?

This problem in culture we can link with the whole question of interpreting the schizoid predicament, and making deductions for social policy – including policy for the arts, education, and political action. In my view the 'schizoid diagnosis' – the Fairbairnian analysis of the consequences of problems of identity and ego-weakness made by Guntrip – does not endorse Laing's approach, but rather exposes it as itself based on a false diagnosis and false solutions.

This is not to deny the urgent need for social change. As will be obvious from everything I have written here and elsewhere, I believe that in our society we need much greater provision for creativity, and many more opportunities for people to enrich their sense of 'being' – though it seems futile to try to legislate for any such thing. We may, however, make these things possible through education, child care and cultural work. As will also be obvious, I share Laing's antipathy to a 'senescent capitalism', if without much conviction that bringing about a new system would bring us any immediate transformation of the human situation (Where is the 'new Soviet man'? Isn't Socialism showing itself more Philistine still? How do we avoid the 'fanatical cult of power'?)

But in seeking change I cannot find 'society' inevitably inimical, as Laing seems to do, nor do I believe that society is 'insane'. Nor, from experience of creativity in education can I believe with Laing that art must necessarily be 'insurrection'. I want a more human society, but I can only see the violence and hostility vindicated by Sartre's 'endless hostility' in the pursuit of his kind of 'freedom' as likely to lead to something less human. Indeed, I believe this kind of action is likely to promote a kind of disruption to which the eventual reaction will be authoritarian or fascist. It is inimical to democracy and true solutions. If anything it is likely to provoke further forfeiture of our humanness and greater neglect of our needs to 'confront the problem of existence', as, perhaps, by helmeted students fighting in the streets, rather than arguing and winning battles by argument and insistence on subjective human needs and their primacy.

I believe that there are many elements in Laing's advocacy which, because they are based on false assumptions, are likely to lead to such destructive and nihilistic forms of social action, and, for many, to personal disaster. This is hardly a service to existentialism, philosophical anthropology or therapy. In order to see this, I believe we need to re-examine some of the aspects of European existentialism, by which Laing has been influenced.

CHAPTER 21

Thought in Existence

S<small>OME</small> of the European existentialists, while they are compelled to 'Confront the problem of existence' can be seen in the light of the 'schizoid diagnosis' to be confronting it in a certain state of blindness. In rejecting traditional assurances of meaning in life and declaring that we have nothing within us nor outside us on which to rely, they were blind to human facts such as Winnicott, for example, has made clear to us the 'healthy moral sense' and culture as a point of meeting 'between union and separateness'. While this tradition is existentialist, it has not fully explored the pronouncement of Kierkegaard, endorsed by Buber, that 'thought does not authorise itself, but is authorised by the existence of the thinking individual'.

Kierkegaard, of course, was a Christian philosopher, and was concerned with faith. Faith for him needed to be based on 'a constant willingness to accept what can neither be fully known or proved in any logical or material way. . . . (Roubiczek [120]).

His approach to spiritual experience demanded the 'leap into the unknown' or 'jump into the abyss', because

> anything absolute or transcendental cannot be used and tried out as a kind of scientific hypothesis, because it cannot be understood unless we commit ourselves to it and are involved in it; our experience must first open us to the impact by which alone it can become real. We have to surrender to it with nothing tangible to grasp, merely in the hope that the ensuing experience will prove us right.

Buber's way of developing this is obvious. But, also, Sartre has obviously extended this Christian concern with the leap into 'committed' faith into a humanistic philosophy. We do not fall into the arms of God: we commit ourselves on behalf of mankind. Man for Sartre defines himself by an authentic impulse to action.

> Man makes himself; he is not found ready-made; he makes himself by the choice of his own morality. To begin with he is nothing . . . he is what he wills. . . . Man will only attain existence when he is what he purposes to be. . . . Man is condemned at every instant to invent man . . . he is . . . nothing else but the sum of his actions, nothing else but what his life is. . . .
> What is at the heart and centre of existentialism is the absolute character of the free commitment by which every man realizes himself is realizing a type of humanity. . . . (Sartre [73], p. 304.)

In this, as in the philosophy of Kierkegaard, 'we give up all the certainties on which we customarily rely without knowing beforehand whether the risk is worth taking' (Roubiczek). But, characteristically, Sartre's realisation is in action (or doing) – at least in *choice*.

If, by contrast, we are to rely on 'being', the problem is to know if one is to rely on inner experience, how 'this kind of evidence can be made reliable . . . (how can we) ensure that

250

inner experience becomes sufficiently profound to awaken the desire for faith' (Roubiczek [120]).

If we are not to rely on science, how can we be sure that 'inner experience' is not mere wishful thinking or misleading feelings? 'Subjective' after all, as Roubiczek points out, nowadays tends to mean 'giving way to bias and prejudice', and the opposite of 'objective' – implying a discipline in which the observer is excluded as far as is humanly possible. But as Farber shows, the belief that the observer can be excluded in the observation of human experience is fallacious. What we have to do, as existentialism implies, is to have faith in subjective disciplines – in collocations and reconsiderations of our whole experience of ourselves and man. Kierkegaard's impulse was to seek to establish these subjective disciplines:

> He tries to solve the first problem by developing what he calls the 'subjective method' . . . this knowledge should be based on what his inner participation discloses. Vast spheres of experience cannot be grasped in any other way . . . (such problems as morality or faith) will be meaningful only if we approach them from within (and only) if we ourselves decide what is to be accepted. . . . (Roubiczek [120]).

Kierkegaard believed that we could avoid error here, and that we could achieve a degree of detachment 'which allows us to differentiate methodically between purely individual or wrong inclinations and the common human nature within us, embodied in the "ethical self" ' (Roubiczek [132]).

This 'ethical self' of Kierkegaard's is perhaps a recognition of the reparative impulse, and the 'healthy moral sense' registered by Melanie Klein and Winnicott. This inward ethical flame is the basis of Buber's ethics. But to what degree is it recognised in the existentialism of Laing?

Presumably it is this ethical self, with all its history in each person, that Sartre denies when he proclaims that 'we have nothing to rely upon within us'. Moreover, when Sartre denies that there is a human nature which precedes man's existence, does he also deny that there can be a truth of 'common human nature' established by the collocation of explorations by 'ethical selves'? If any group of individuals exchange their deductions from their own ethical living, values, and concepts of human nature will inevitably arise as cultural realities with an objective existence (as real, shall we say, as the values embodied in a Shakespeare tragedy). *Since not all individuals are schizoid*, these cultural realities will embody those creative meanings by which healthy human beings feel real, alive, and 'confirmed'. They will embody those 'cultural experiences' which provide a 'continuity' that 'transcends personal existence', and on which each individual can draw, as by the meeting 'between union and separateness'. This is a positive aspect of social life which Laing implicitly denies and to which Sartre, like Freud, is blind.

A useful discussion of how this process of the creation of values happens is given by Professor John Wisdom in his *Philosophy and Psychoanalysis* [97], where he is reviewing Waddington's *Ethics*.

Wisdom is there discussing ethics in terms of the difference between ethics which depends upon 'essence' and that which is 'living ethics' based on experience. (He also invokes aesthetics, in such a way as to indicate how we can apply his findings to the cultural sphere.)

Professor Wisdom says:

> Just as in deciding whether a picture is good, and even in deciding whether a show is funny we don't merely look at the picture and sift *our* reaction to it but *also* count the reactions of *others*, especially

Clive Bell, so in deciding whether it would be right to do so and so we count the reactions of others. If, say what we will and say what they will, they differ from us still, then we say either that they use words differently or, in different circumstances, that though it is funny to us, or lovely to us, it isn't to them, and but for the extra regularity of nature in the matter of sweetness and redness and hotness and roundness we should do the same for them and say, 'It's red to us but not to the others', or 'It's sweet to children but not to adults.' And just as the redness, the real objective redness, of a red flag is a matter of its redness to nearly everybody today and also tomorrow unless it's been dipped in ink, so is the beauty of a face, the niceness of a person, and the rightness of an act, a matter of not only of how they seem to oneself but also of how they seem to others, and not only now but also when the band stops playing. (Wisdom [97], p. 106.)

In our account from experience of the properties of things we must recognise first that there is nothing to discuss but our subjective impressions. But this is not all, nor are we confined (as Sartre suggests) to the recognition of other subjective experience in inter-subjectivity. Each child 're-creates civilisation within himself' in being reflected by the mother. Between separateness and by being in touch with others, we together establish values in the collocation of 'Naturalistic descriptions'. Aesthetic and ethical values are therefore as valid as scientific truths (since these too are now recognised to be of the 'order of the colour red'):

To sum up in jargon: Real redness is constructed from redness to A and redness to B and redness to C. etc., etc. And redness to A is constructed from seeming now red to A, still seeming, e.g. on closer inspection, red to A. Likewise satisfactoriness is constructed from satisfactoriness to A, to B, to C, and really satisfactory to A is constructed from seems satisfactory to A after listening to it again, or even now that he is sober, or etc. Likewise rightness is constructed from really seems right to A, to B, etc., and really seems right to A is constructed from seems right to A at first blush, still seems right to A after review, comparison, etc. It is with the business of the transition from 'seems for the moment acceptable and right to A' to 'seems really right and acceptable to A' that one is concerned. (Wisdom [97], p. 106.)

Wisdom records how after going to an analyst for about a month he suddenly said: 'Why, this *is* ethics.'

What I had been doing struck me as being just more of the sort of thing I should call thinking a thing over to see whether it seems right to me, whether I can 'accept myself' as I do it. And yet what I had been doing could also be described as going into how I felt towards doing this with those consequences, or that with those other consequences. (Wisdom [97], p. 106.)

But just as out of this process, between the inner conscience and the critical conscious-ness of the problems of conscience, tangible values emerge, so they do from our response to symbolism. Wisdom calls his process a *metaphysic* of ethics:

To say that right is a matter of what at infinity still seems right to everybody and that what seems right to so and so is a matter of what he finally feels, is not to make right more subjective than red or round – (though it *is* more subjective). But it is a naturalistic and anti-transcendental *metaphysic* of ethics, i.e. ultimate description of ethical activity. It is opposed to the type of talk, e.g. in *Principia Ethica*, which suggests that goodness is related to those natural characters which make a thing good and our feelings to them like the power of a horse is related to those structural characters which cause that power and our feelings to them. The naturalistic type of talk suggests that on the contrary goodness is related to stopping on the way from Damascus and cups of water and so on, and our reactions to these, like the grace of a dancer to her movements and our feelings for these. Her grace *is* a matter of the patterns she gives to her eyes and the lift she gives to our hearts. So there is no problem of how we know she's graceful. (Wisdom [97], p. 107.)

Wisdom also says, of another way in which psychoanalysis is connected with ethics as we have seen: 'analysis isn't concerned only with what one really approves really accepts in oneself, but also with what one really wants, fears, loves, hates.' That is, it involved a recognition of one's nature, and so of human nature, as we know it by the collocation of subjective facts, by dialogic rather than logic.

So the collocation of what one seeks to hold 'good' in life (or culture) has to be achieved in relation to what one believes one knows human beings including oneself to want, fear, love, and hate. That is, there will inevitably be implicit *a collocation of attitudes to human nature*, in which a description of human nature exists, and truths about it, as well as a collocation of 'senses of rightness'. But both can only be processes of experiencing and commenting on human experience – yet never through processes of elaborating theoretical abstractions alone. 'Female knowledge' needs to be present in such a perception of human truth, and the process Wisdom is discussing is at one with the quest for the True Self.

Here, I believe we shall become able to see certain significant limitations in Sartre's approach to the same problems. How much does Sartre recognise 'common human nature'? How much is he aware of an ethical self? Sartre sees man as making himself in choice and action: but what about intention and inclination – the propensities which exist before action, and in men's motives? Here the significant historical fact is that enormous contributions have been made to these questions by psychotherapeutic workers such as Farber and Winnicott, but without their implications being fully seen at large. Here, I believe, we shall be led to the question, Though he claims to be an existentialist, *how much does Sartre really trust inner experience at all*? How much confidence does he have in *being*? The answers here, I believe, help us to see significant differences between Laing's kind of existential psychoanalysis in England, and that represented by, say, Farber in America or by Rollo May, who invokes Husserl's concept of 'intentionality (see *Love and Will*).

In America the influence of Martin Buber has drawn attention to the need for despair. Here 'despair' is used in a special sense. It does not mean that one has a sense of futility about man's future or the possibilities of his ever being able to solve his problems or find a meaning in his life – which can be anti-human. It is rather a true recognition of the tragic conditions of our existence – a recognition of humanness. As Roubiczek points out, Kierkegaard put much emphasis on dread and despair.

> He believes that despair, if only experienced deeply enough, makes us aware within ourselves of that reality with which religion claims to deal; thus we know that, in the last resort, everything must be good and right; this enables us to make the leap and thereby our trust is confirmed, for we then recognise this reality also outside ourselves. . . .

Kierkegaard, of course, believed that if we took the 'leap', we should 'fall into the open arms of God', and this aim Sartre is not prepared to accept, for his existentialism is an atheistic philosophy.

But surely the problem of despair need not be confined to the Christian. We can, I believe, interpret the experience explored by Kierkegaard in terms which require neither the existence of God nor of a transcendental reality. Despair can lead to the discovery of the True Self and of the sources of confirmation: as in a poetic tragedy such as *King Lear* the experience of despair can bring us to an engagement with the question – What is man?, or, as Lear puts it, 'Who is it that can tell me who I am?' – truly 'confronting the problem of existence.' Farber gives an account of the anguish that must be gone through if a therapist is genuinely to enter into a relationship with a schizophrenic patient, by which the patient can begin to find a sense of identity, an answer to the problem of what it is to be human. This cannot be achieved without despair, and the despair has a therapeutic significance, since only once the therapist has achieved despair can he draw out from his patient a pity for his own condition that in itself, since it is a human feeling, conveys to the patient that he himself is human.

As Farber says, concluding a chapter on the treatment of schizophrenics:

> It is when we stand stripped of every artifice and prop, every technical support of our profession, that we are closest to reality. And if it is only then, in the moment of extremity, that we approach genuine dialogue, genuine confirmation – the lack of which has driven us to this despair – so we may find the remedy concealed in the disease. It may be that only in such moments do we approach reality at all. It may be that at such moments the patient, too, is obeying such deep and elementary needs that it would be gratuitous to speak of pity and despair. But however that may be, it is only when the therapist has exhausted every conceivable device for reaching his patient that he may, from the very heart of his despair, cry out with his entire being, as if to his Maker. Such a cry is as far from dialogue or confirmation as it is from love or sympathy. Any response awakened by it will be a response to pain and loneliness. (Farber [20], p. 182.)

Here Farber quotes Kierkegaard:

> One must really have suffered very much in the world, and have been very unfortunate before there can be any talk of beginning to love one's neighbour. It is only in dying to the joys and happiness of the world in self-denial that the neighbour comes into existence. One cannot therefore accuse the immediate person of not loving his neighbour, because he is too happy for the neighbour to exist for him. No one who clings to earthly love loves his neighbour, that is to say his neighbour does not exist for him. (Kierkegaard [44], p. 219, quoted by Farber [20], p. 183.)

The kind of experience in which this kind of despair can be found, as a way to come close to the reality of others, experiencing at the same time the reality of oneself, is found not only in psychotherapy but certainly in education (see, for instance, Herbert Kohl, *Thirty-six Children*, Gollancz, 1968, an account of teaching children in a Harlem school). And it could, I believe, be linked with problems of literature and literary criticism. That literature is most valuable in which we find the despair that arises from experiences in which the writer 'cries out with his whole being', and goes beyond dialogue, confirmation, love, and sympathy, to ask 'What is it to be human?' and 'What is the point of life?'

CHAPTER 22

Sartre and 'Freedom'

FOR us to get the best from Freud we have to exorcise the ghost of the death instinct in order to make full use of his 'poetic' insights. A similar effort seems necessary with Sartre. While Freud tended to obscure human truth by the chimera of a universal predator, which he had to believe in in order to survive, Sartre's dogma requires, with cunning intensity, that *we do not see certain conspicuous human facts at all*. His ghosts are the vacancies where love and reparation should be: to Sartre these are the most terrible threat of all. His strategy of survival is constructed on a form of thinking which belongs to 'false male doing', and 'bad thinking' as a form of this. His philosophy, I believe we can say, is all False Self activity: while Sartre's greatest enemy, which he prefers never to allow himself to see, is 'female element being'.

These are, of course, very rash statements for a layman to make in an area in which so much work has been done by acute and prominent minds. But others have noticed the essentially schizoid nature of Sartre's approach to human experience. Since the schizoid is both one who desperately seeks the point of living, a sense of identity, and who wants to be loved, there are positive and significant elements in a schizoid philosophy as well as negative ones. When he was an existentialist, Sartre was driven by that need to confront the problem of existence. But in the negative elements of his intellectual efforts we shall find those characteristic inversions of normal values diagnosed as elements of the schizoid syndrome by Fairbairn. Instead of hope and a sense of meaning in life we have a preoccupation with futility; instead of love, hate; instead of inner security of being, an anguished sense of the need to sustain an identity by active 'doing' and 'bad thinking' – much of it around alienation and violent contact. This has coloured our whole culture, as Professor Bantock notes: yet the preoccupation is not with 'passion' but rather with false ways of feeling that we exist at all: modes of hate.

Guntrip says:

> These thinkers, from Kierkegaard to Heidegger and Sartre, find human existence to be rooted in anxiety and insecurity, a fundamental dread that ultimately we have no certainties and the only thing we can affirm is 'nothingness', 'unreality', a final sense of triviality and meaninglessness. This surely is schizoid despair and loss of contact with the verities of emotional reality, rationalized into a philosophy: yet Existentialist thinkers, unlike the Logical Positivists, are calling us to face and deal with the real problems of our human situation. It is a sign of the mental state of our age. (Guntrip [110], p. 103.)

In this chapter I hope to try to suggest that we can find the same origins both for Freud's concept of the death instinct and Sartre's failure to find resources within us in the schizoid denial of 'female element being'. I have tried to suggest above that we can link Freud's fear and denial of the female elements in human nature with his astonishing feeling about the kind of moment at which 'Eros could do its deadly work', as if any relaxation of the external crust of 'male element doing' would lead to some terrible impingement or implosion of the identity. The only way he could explain this deep feeling of being threatened with annihilation by collapse was to postulate an instinct whereby all life sought from within to return to a state of inanition which was disturbed by the arrival of life: a paranoic model of the cosmos. If we see his concept of the 'arrival of life' as a symbol derived from his personal experience of birth, his theory can be taken to mean, 'this problem arose when I was born'. That is, the 'arrival of life' for Freud is associated with the very start of identity: at the heart of being for him lurks the emptiness which is there because experience of togetherness with the mother was not good enough, at the beginning. In consequence, so great was Freud's fear of his weak female element that he must deny it and suppress it, as by his devoted attachment to rational intellectual 'scientific' analysis, and his distrust of poetry and religion.

In Sartre the fear of emptiness at the heart of identity associated with the same problems arising at the beginning of life leads him to a denial of all the experience which an individual takes into himself from the experience of the mother. 'There is no reality except in action': the denial of the sphere of being is absolute, and the implication of his theory is that we begin when we begin to *act* or *think*. There is no predetermining of a man's moral character: 'Man makes himself; he is not found ready-made; he makes himself by the choice of his morality, and he cannot choose a morality, such is the pressure of circumstances upon him . . .' (Sartre [73], p. 306).

As we have seen, there are many implications in the work of Melanie Klein, Fairbairn, and Winnicott which expose this view as false. Man does not have to make himself. He emerges out of a subtle complex, between his own potentialities and the environment which his mother is able to supply him. Thus, as he emerges, he develops the I AM feeling and a healthy moral sense (or not, according to how things go). His early environment does not predetermine his actions, but it does determine whether or not he is equipped to cope with situations as they arise, by capacities in which 'being comes first' and 'doing later'.

Sartre emphasises the 'pressures of circumstances': but a healthy child is already equipped from the beginning to deal with these, and is, indeed, already engaged in complex with them. His essential capacity for ethical living emerges from his experience of *being* as the centre of the True Self. He does not form his morality in response to a pressure of circumstances which impel him to devise a morality. His morality has already become part of his rich living from moment to moment, and at the centre of this healthy moral impulse is a powerful creative urge, by which he feels I AM, and, from this, 'What can I be?' – 'What can I make of experience?' The relationship is not merely between the man and the pressure of circumstances, but between the man, – his 'pristine unitary ego', his internalisation of culture, his experience of togetherness with the mother as object – and the world as object. There is a special significance, as we shall see, in the way Sartre reduces this to something as oversimplified direct and passive as action and reaction and fails to find true 'intentionality'.

From the account given by Melanie Klein, Fairbairn, and Winnicott, it is obvious that there could be a 'cowardly temperament', which would arise from a weak ego-structure, unable to deal with the world from a position of strength and security. Sartre says that 'the existentialist, when he portrays a coward, shows him as responsible for his cowardice': 'he is like that because he has made himself a coward by his actions'. 'A coward is defined by the deed that he has done.' In this attitude Sartre resolutely defies any explanation which smacks of predetermination by early environment. He rejects the view that 'the behaviour of [such] characters was caused by their heredity, or by the action of their environment upon them, or by determining factors, psychic or organic'. People would be reassured, they would say: 'You see, that is what we are like, no one can do anything about it.'

Sartre wants us to take the responsibility to define and make ourselves, and this sounds heroic. He does not want us to explain our bad faith away by causality. But he still fails to indicate the most subtle and challenging human problem which is that of exercising what freedom of thought and imagination one can achieve to exert on those areas of one's make-up which are inescapably conditioned by the nature of one's psychic tissue.

Sartre's heroism is the heroism of False Self solutions. This view involves Sartre in denying that there is something which can be called Human Nature (such as could be established by naturalistic description) because even this concept would be for him too predetermining: it would indicate too clearly the problem of our 'psychic tissue'. We may see it as philosophically valuable to resist Human Nature as a concept in so far as it was taken over by philosophical atheism from the Christian philosophers. To the latter, God had a concept of man before he invented him, and so man must seek to conform to this ideal concept, and this should be the basis of his morality. In atheistical philosophy this ideal concept still remained, and so a postulated ideal remained as the basis of morality – man must always strive to realise an essence which exists before his existence. Existentialism puts existence before this essence. As Sartre puts it. 'Atheistic existentialism – declares with greater consistency that if God does not exist there is at least one being whose existence comes before its essence, a being which exists before it can be defined by any conception of it. That being is man.' (Sartre [73], p. 290.)

In the world of 'inter-subjectivity' 'man has to decide what he is and what others are'. But where he starts from, according to Sartre, is from the need to make himself from scratch, by *action*, but without, it appears, any essentially reliable gifts, such as moral health, inherent in human nature and creative resources in 'intentionality' in the realm of being.

Beside action, there is knowledge. But for Sartre even my knowledge of myself is to be gained from others, by thinking as a form of doing. Sartre cannot see the feminine mode of knowing, the sense of I AM created by togetherness: he can only conceive of making oneself by opposition and reaction. He cannot recognise knowing by identifying, as by allowing the object to become the subjective object:

> I cannot obtain any truth whatsoever about myself, except through the mediation of another. The other is indispensable to my existence, and equally so to any knowledge I have of myself. Under these conditions, the ultimate discovery of myself is at the same time the revelation of the other as a freedom which confronts mine, and which cannot think or will without doing so either for or against me. (Sartre [73], p. 303.)

From Sartre's point of view it seems that we confront the world without anything within us which we can call human nature; 'it is impossible to find in each and every man a universal essence that can be called human nature. . . . ' But there is 'nevertheless a human universality of *condition*'. These are all the '*limitations* which *a priori* define man's fundamental situation in the universe'. Every human purpose 'presents itself as an attempt to surpass these limitations, or to widen them or to accommodate oneself to them'.

K

In every purpose there is universality, in this sense that every purpose is comprehensible to every man. Not that this or that purpose defines man for ever, but that it may be entertained again and again. There is always some way of understanding an idiot, a child, a primitive man, or foreigner if one has sufficient information. In this sense we may say that there is a human universality, but *it is not something given; it is being perpetually made.* I make this universality in choosing myself; I also make it by understanding the purpose of any other man, of whatever epoch. This absoluteness of the act of choice does not alter the relativity of each epoch.

What is at the very heart and centre of existentialism, is the absolute character of the free commitment, by which every man realizes himself in realizing a type of humanity – a commitment always understandable, to no matter whom in no matter what epoch – and its bearing upon the realativity of the cultural pattern which may result from such absolute commitment. (Sartre [73], p. 304.)*

Reading Sartre, one cannot escape the feeling 'There is something missing'. Is it true that 'To begin with he [man] is nothing'? 'He is what he *wills*': 'Man will only attain existence when he is what he *purposes to be*.' Here, we need to consider the infant who obviously feels I AM, even though he has not yet had any opportunity to 'purpose to be', and has certainly not reached the stage of being able to feel *cogito ergo sum*.

In his conditions Sartre is willing to recognise the difference between an 'idiot' and a 'foreigner' – but not the difference between an individual who can feel I AM and a schizoid individual who cannot. He can only see human 'universality' as being made by choosing: he cannot see it as having a basis in the unalterable facts of early life in the complex between 'the maturational processes and the facilitating environment'.

From such insights, though we can hardly aspire to demolish Sartre's philosophical structure, we can, I am sure, reject many of its pessimistic implications. Man is not 'condemned at every instant to invent man' because he is not condemned at every instant to invent himself: his sense of identity does not have to be sustained and continually pieced together by the activity of thought – unless he is a schizoid person – because he is defined by his I AM feeling from infancy. Of Sartre it may be true that he has to continually invent himself: it is not true of those who had a mother rather than a wet nurse and a grandfather. It may be true of those who can only exist by False Self activity. But it is not true of those who are in touch with the True Self. Of course, there is a great gain in Sartre's rejection of the adherence of previous philosophies to concepts of human nature to which, by their ethical systems, man must aspire. If there is no God, and no transcendental source of values, then these concepts must have been spun from the human mind and its capacities for reification or idealism, from which to elaborate intellectual structures to use in browbeating normal experience – as theology depletes creativity. But there is something still missing from Sartre's view when he says: 'he is nothing else but the sum of his actions, *nothing else but what his life is* . . . ' and 'there is no love apart from the deeds of love; no potentiality of love other than that which is manifest in loving . . . ' (Sartre [73], p. 300).

It would be interesting to ask Sartre at what stage does a man's life begin? And, how is love manifest? How can we say of a very young infant, 'he is nothing else but the sum of his actions'? A very young infant has a quite definite identity, and as everyone in the house responds to him, delights in him, loves him, worries about him, is enriched by his 'gifts' – he is very definitely a human being with a moral existence. Yet he does not exist in the world of action because he does not have to make choices or act in the world of men. He simply *is* as he sleeps and feeds: he is possessed of his own sense of being human.

* It is of course true that Sartre has since disowned *Existentialism is a Humanism*, but we must hold him responsible for it still.

Neither does he express his love in terms of the 'deeds of love'. The love between himself and his mother very definitely exists, but it is manifest essentially in quietness and an inexplicit togetherness. It is love in being. There is as yet hardly any play: only 'at oneness' at first. The potentialities of love in the infant are not only manifest in any visible experienced living: they are inseparable from certain profound preoccupations of the mother and infant with aspects of *identity*. The mother and the infant are exploring the nature of being in the world: in this sense the mother is conveying to the infant, at the core, his knowledge of himself in terms of I AM. As we have seen, in this the mother's function is that of a creative mirror: she gives back what the infant brings. But this involves her in being able to allow the infant to make use of her as subjective object: that is, she allows him to imagine (though this is not quite the right word) that she is him: or, rather, she allows him to be her, and loses herself in becoming him. This kind of psychic parturition was understood by Martin Buber. It is *not* understood by Sartre, because he had no experience of it, and so must remain forever blind to it.

Let me return to the quotation above about how we obtain the 'truth about ourselves'. To find the truth about ourselves, we obviously require some kind of mirror. But this can be either a creative mirror or a mere environment to react to as with a mother who cannot forfeit her self-interest and enter into the state of Primary Maternal Preoccupation. A mother who cannot be for her child cannot return to him, by creative reflection, the truth about himself. Thus while it is true, as Sartre says, 'I cannot obtain any truth about myself, except through the mediation of another,' I believe he cannot have confidence in the normal way in which being is confirmed in this way. It is also true that 'The other is indispensable to my eixistence' – though, having read Winnicott we may see in this another meaning, which is that we cannot ever become able to say I AM except through the capacity of the mother (or foster mother) to forfeit her self-interest (and to suspend her concern with the I AM feeling) sufficiently to enable us to make use of her.

Sartre goes on however: 'the ultimate discovery of myself is at the same time the revelation of the other as a *freedom which confronts mine.*' Obviously Sartre is not thinking of the mother as creative mirror. He can only think of the process of the formation of the identity, and the discovery of the self, as a desperate process in which doing and knowing confront doing and knowing and the whole experience is imbued with the schizoid terror *of being taken over.* His experience of discovering the self is not one of being confirming being, but of will and thought engaged in impingement with will and thought, to no certain outcome. The indispensableness of the other is conceived in terms of *impingement.* His whole philosophy emerges out of this concept of confrontation in a conflict of wills (or hate) and many of the forms of violent confrontation in our world fostered by Sartre's influence, such as student riots, can be seen not only as 'protest', but also as ways of feeling real by 'false male doing', promoted by those to whom there is no other way.

This way of feeling confirmed by 'confrontation' is, of course, characteristically schizoid. Here we may, I believe, usefully return to Guntrip's account of primary formation, based on Winnicott's theories of male element and female element, in the bisexual roots of human identity. The basic permanent experience of ego-relatedness has the sense of 'being' at the core, and without this sense of being the psyche loses all sense of its own reality as an ego. 'One cannot "be" anything in a vacuum. Having developed this capacity to "be" by experiencing the primary relationship with a good enough mother, this will lead spontaneously to the arising of a healthy unforced capacity to "do". . . . The experience of "being" would be stultified if it did not lead on to the practical experience of "doing".' (Guntrip [38], p. 254.)

Sartre sees the need for doing, in the positive sense, as a means to realise the sense of who one is, to define one's humanness by action. He is very careful to resist any suggestion of quietism, and emphasises that 'Life is nothing until it is lived'. But, we may ask, when he talks about life and how it is lived, *when does the living begin*, and what are the consequences of the first steps in living? Here we may recall Winnicott's remark 'We take for granted a great deal that had a beginning and a condition out of which it arose.' Sartre's living does not begin with being.

One of Sartre's most perverse insistences is 'Dostoevsky once wrote, "If God did not exist, everything would be permitted," and that for existentialists, is the starting point. Everything is indeed permitted if God does not exist, and man is in consequence forlorn, for he cannot find anything to depend upon either inside or outside himself. He discovers further that he is without excuse.' (Sartre [73], p. 294.)

In *Crime and Punishment* Doestoevsky set out to discover whether or not it was true that man had nothing to rely upon inside himself. What he found was that whether God exists or not has nothing to do with the problem. What Dostoevsky discovered, through identifying with Raskolnikov, was the capacity for reparation within himself, and from that discovery he found the capacity to love. The 'false solution' heroism of Raskolnikov's murder is acceptable only as creative symbolism, not as a primer for action in the world. In the symbolism, Dostoevsky is seeking to discover 'what it is to be human' and to find touch with the True Self.

In the light of Winnicott's picture of the origins of morality, I believe we can revise Sartre's view thus: where the inward moral sense is healthy the intervention of God is not needed: God, for those for whom He exists, confirms the existence of the 'inner light' in the individual. Where the moral sense is 'unhealthy', then there may be a great struggle in the wrestle with God involving the kinds of problems of splitting Winnicott discusses. That is, all the split-off goodness may be thrust by an individual into God, to keep it pure, and all the badness into the Devil, or evil spirits and the consequence will be the impoverishment of the individual's moral sense.

But the individual who does not believe in God can still find within himself his own healthy moral sense. He can find a great deal within himself at the heart of being where one discovers what it is one really wants, upon which he can rely. 'Everything is not permitted' because some acts will be an insult to the True Self. Moreover, to take Winnicott's attitude to the location of culture, this healthy moral sense is also linked by his possession of the mother with that personal culture in which he meets the culture of human civilisation. In this culture exists the collocation of naturalistic descriptions which establish ethical truths. A child who grows up in a good environment, therefore, can find a great deal both within and without, on which he can rely: ultimately his culture is the link between his separateness and his union with the whole human race and its values. He may not need God at all, or may see Him as a human concept, embodying all the goodness which has emerged from the countless healthy moral energies of all the human beings who have ever lived. Such an individual does not feel 'abandoned' either: a point which we shall return to in a moment. But first we need to note here that Sartre denies both the inward and outward resources. What happens where the earliest environment is not good enough? Then, indeed, the individual cannot find anything to rely upon within himself nor can he find the interaction of union and separateness. His lack of moral health is indivisible from his need to hold his identity together by a false form of doing: 'The experience of "doing" in the absence of a secure sense of "being" degenerates into a meaningless succession of mere activities, as in the obsessional's meaningless repetition of the same thought, word, or act, not performed for their own proper purpose, but as futile effort to "keep oneself in being," to manufacture a sense of "being" one does not possess' (Guntrip [38], p. 254).

Of Sartre I believe we can say this is how much human activity seems – futile and meaningless. And yet this futile activity to him is the only way of establishing one's identity – by action. Inevitably, 'doing' without a sense of being is an aggressive form of self-assertion and so feels that it must inevitably come into conflict with other forms of doing, which it is felt must be the same. In this there is considerable danger when there is no other kind of inner substantiality to fall back upon. If the world appears to one as a world in which no one has any inner resources of being and love to fall back on, and everyone's identity must be based on (pseudo-male) 'doing' and hate, then one has a world in which there can only be 'endless hostility' – which is Sartre's world. As a model it thus resembles Freud's which he could only conceive of as being an endless defensive reaction against impingement from a hostile universe. As Guntrip says of schizoid individuals, 'Patients realise that they have been working hard all their lives busily "doing" not in a natural but in a forced way, to create an illusory sense of reality as a person, a substitute for the experience of "inbeingness" in a solid and self-assured way that is the only basis of the self-confidence nearly all patients complain of lacking' (Guntrip [38], p. 254).

It is this 'self-confidence' which Sartre says we can never have – because he has never known it himself. He thus rationalises this state of finding nothing to rely upon within ourselves into a philosophy – by which no one can achieve security. Yet for the majority there is no such problem of lack of self-confidence and of the I AM feeling, God or no God.

Where there is no such sense of the world being reliable, all 'doing' takes on a forced emphasis, and this I believe we see in Sartre's emphasis on action. 'Being' never begins before 'action' in his philosophy, and the area from which we bring so much to our action, to condition it, is scotomized. As Guntrip says: 'If it ("being") is not there, "doing" in (the) natural sense does not occur. Activity is forced, tense, strained, an attempt to compel an insecure personality to carry on as a "going concern". This may become a manic or compulsive activity, for the "mind" cannot stop, relax, or rest because of a secret fear of collapsing into non-existence.' (Guntrip [38], p. 255.)

This virtually explains Sartre's paragraph above about the inevitable clash of will and action with the 'other'. If the identity is based on 'doing' and 'thinking' as an aspect of doing, then there is inherent in this activity a compulsiveness and will, compelling the personality to go on as a going concern. The fear is naturally that this will may be crossed by the will emanating from another identity – since to Sartre all identities are kept going by this compulsive activity. Then, if one's 'freedom' clashes with another, as it is inevitably bound to do, the danger is defeat and a collapse into non-existence. From Laing's account of schizoid individuals we can recognise this as a paranoid-schizoid fear of contact with others altogether. The very energy by which the identity is sustained seems to Sartre a universal threat – just as, in Freud, the very energy by which life is sustained must at the same time be seen as having an essential destructive quality of 'bringing about the end of life'. The two pictures of human make-up are essentially based on the reliance of 'false male doing' in the form of compulsive thinking. Just as in Freud's death-instinct theory we have the origins of his negative and destructive social theory, leading him into the arms of Schopenhaur's belief that the purpose of life is death, so in Sartre's belief that we claim our freedom in endless hostility we have a social theory based on schizoid inversion and the need to feel real by hating.

There is no confirmation in object-relations psychology of a need to clash inevitably with the freedom of others in the realisation of ourselves. In the processes of mutal confirmation between men there need not be the threat of implosion that the schizoid person inevitably feels, and social theory need not be based on the continual need to exert one's hate and to promote alienation. If we have ego-strength we do not need to exert ourselves at the expense of others: it is only the weak who must.

Sartre's social theory, in fact, is based upon the view of a minority suffering from extreme 'ontological insecurity', on the compulsive needs of the schizoid who must sustain his identity by false male doing and thinking. As Guntrip says, this also goes with a hatred and denial of female elements and female ways of knowing human experience:

> In such patients one sees clearly the conflict between opposed pseudo-male and pseudo-female attitudes, always involving them in hatred of the supposedly female characteristics (located in the weak parent, irrespective of sex). The pseudo-female side in these cases is not dissociated but rejected and if possible repressed, both in men and women, in favour of a pseudo-male role. The true female potentiality remains dissociated. Here are the pathological versions of 'being and doing', 'female and male' in the forms of passivity (weakness, submissiveness, helplessness, nonentity) and 'forced activity' – toughness, strenuousness, aggressiveness, destructiveness, compulsive over-activity. (Guntrip [38], p. 257.)

In Sartre's exercise in existential psychoanalysis, in his study of Genet, we can see him valuing, as the basis of identity and a valid way of dealing with the problem of existence, these essentially pseudo-male and pseudo-female forms of false doing.

What I believe we can conclude here is that while Sartre's philosophy is the expression of the ruthless need of the schizoid person to ask the essential questions about humanness, his answers are essentially based on the schizoid reversal of values, and point towards solutions which belong to the False Self rather than those which require us to discover the True Self. In fact his answers do not begin to be genuine to answers in the discovery of the human at all. We should ask urgently, not least at the universities, whether his influence, in promoting forms of action essentially based on hate, is not threateningly destructive, even where there are genuine grievances and to genuine needs to reform the basis of society. He promotes fanatical moral inversion, but diverts us from true intentionality.

Sartre's philosophy is one in which there always has to be 'invention' as the basis of identity: 'The content is always concrete, and therefore unpredictable. It has always to be invented. The one thing that counts, is to know whether the invention is made in the name of freedom.' (Sartre [73], p. 308.)

As we have seen, this 'freedom' seems to be based on the refusal to acknowledge any other sources of validity than the will and action of the moment. Existentialism to Sartre is a doctrine of action, and the 'invention' of values as if we began with none.

Interestingly enough here, while, in his essay on 'Existentialism as a Humanism', Sartre rejects the criticism that existentialism only shows the evil side of human life, he does not really come to grips with the question at all. 'Pseudo-male doing' as we have seen, includes 'thinking' – as Guntrip says, it 'centres round the intellectual processes'. Guntrip also reports patients who needed to hold themselves together by compulsive 'bad' thinking. In this, I believe, we can see the origins of all the preoccupation of Sartre as a writer and the literary movement he has influenced, with violence, sex, 'inner contents', physical nausea and depersonalisation, evil and futility. These are not 'realism' but an attempt to hold the identity together by 'false male thinking'. If we can think 'bad' thoughts, at least we are someone, and alive. This preoccupation with evil can be seen as a false way to solve the identity problem, rather than a preoccupation with truth. But Sartre fails completely in his essay to justify this preoccupation: all he says is that existentialism is concerned with what is 'real' – and, he implies, evil is real. He fails entirely to admit that there are other (positive) human realities – and, indeed, we feel that he is totally blind to these, as when he proclaims that the only possible outcome of a love affair is sadism, masochism, or indifference. To him the female elements of being, and the female ways of knowing and experiencing, and all such aspects of being in life must remain obliterated and denied, because they are too dangerous.

As a consequence, despite his position as an existentialist concerned with 'inner experience' Sartre, like Freud in the end, because of his inability to believe in the reality of those moral values and energies created between mother and child, comes to believe in 'instincts' as what is essentially real about man: 'If values are uncertain, if they are still too abstract to determine the particular, concrete case under consideration, nothing remains but to trust in our instincts . . .' (Sartre [73], pp. 296–7).

As we shall see, Laing follows this lead, and it brings him to a position as lacking in essential belief in human nature as that of Freud. Here we have the crux of the difference between existentialist psychoanalysis in America and England.

There is a positive value in Sartre's rejection of causality, because it forces us to accept responsibility for our actions. But the work of Melanie Klein and others has shown that our responsibility as more extensive and complex than it is in Sartre's scheme of things because it involves responsibility to the True Self within us. We arrive at adult life with capacities for good and bad 'woven in the weakness of the changing body'. If we are impelled (for instance) to maltreat a woman because of some unconscious form of hate derived from a fear which remains with us from our experience of the mother, then at least we also have the reparative urge to overcome this hate and treat the woman in ways which belong to love, which also is derived from our experience of the mother, and we have the cultural sources of values. Sartre's view excludes both these positive sources of moral energy.

He recognises 'conditions', but even in this recognition we can find further weaknesses in Sartre's view. I have said that his action and will belong to pseudo-male self doing, as a false way of feeling real. Such false male doing requires an object, and Sartre finds this is the 'others' who are always Hell, and whose freedom imposes its limitations on ours. In Freud the necessary paranoia of false male doing found its ultimate object in the death instinct. In Sartre the object of this hate becomes 'them' – les autres, 'les bourgeois salauds': so long as we can hate 'them' we can feel we exist, and are claiming our 'freedom'. The confirmation 'they' give to our identities by conflict of will and action, seems to guarantee against the collapse of identity from within. Thus it is logical for Sartre to become a Marxist, since this places him in an ideological setting in which he can always rely upon a contentious paranoic stance as a source of compulsive support for a weak identity and vindication for a philosophy of hate. 'They' now stand for the parents, from whom love and meaning are demanded, because they failed to give these in the first place. He is claiming something he feels he should have had by rights, like the 'wicked' child.

Here Laing, with his revolutionary social theory, follows Sartre. As I believe, he follows

Sartre into a schizoid delusion of which his brand of existentialism is a rationalisation. How is it that existentialism has come to contribute to forms of violent protest against 'them'? These surely can only be seen by the lights of philosophical anthropology as the false solutions of the weak and ontologically insecure (Take, for instance, Sartre's support of Maoism, even though he does not 'believe' in it, because it is 'violent'. Spring, 1970).

From this diagnosis we can turn to ask what Sartre means when he says that the writer 'has only one subject – freedom'. Explaining one of Sartre's theses is 'What is Literature?' Iris Murdoch says:

> Since the creation and enjoyment of literature demand a disciplined purging of the mind on the part of the writer and on similar 'free' response from the reader, the literary man has a special interest in a 'free' society; he desires a certain harmony of wills between himself and his readers, and cannot but be concerned about the promotion and preservation of the possibility of a similar free response throughout society at large. (Murdoch [63], p. 71.)

What is this 'free response' in the reader's mind, which Sartre seeks to promote without taking responsibility for the similar free response at large? If we follow the Sartrean existentialists, what do we need to face experience 'nakedly' *for*? Or to 'what *end* should we seek to *épater les salauds*? Undoubtedly Sartre had a purpose for which we must hold him responsible, despite his rejection of existentialism, not least in the realm of psychology.

Here we may consider Iris Murdoch's account of his relationship to psychoanalysis. Sartre, she says, as we have seen, is 'an amateur psychoanalyst' and has as a moral teacher, 'a driving force in all his writing' which is to 'change the life of his reader'.

To seek to 'change the life of the reader' is a moral impulse, but I believe that with Sartre, because of the manifest schizoid nature of his approach to experience, we must see it in the light of Fairbairn's account of the 'amazing reversal of moral values' which is a consequence of the inversion of love and hate in the schizoid individual. If love is harmful, then it is beneficial to hate others, to thrust harm into them, to involve them in hate. Yet in this positive False Self role we can find confirmation of Fairbairn's reminder that 'deep down' the schizoid individual wants to love and be loved.

Sartre can therefore set out to link his philosophy with psychoanalysis, and hope to change the lives of his readers by his work. But he can only attempt these positive roles so long as the schizoid logic concerned to avoid love and the recognition of 'being' at all costs is maintained. This means that his concern with healing, with solutions to problems of identity, and his influence on ethics must always be in False Self terms: *there must never be any possibility of the discovery of the feminine element or the reality of the True Self.*

The implications for Sartre's influence on psychoanalytical theory through Laing's advocacy, are surely alarming. Iris Murdoch says:

> Sartre is undoubtedly a connoisseur of the abnormal: yet his interest therein is not necessarily a morbid one. Sartre, like Freud, finds in the abnormal the exaggerated forms of normality. His more lurid characters are to show us, either by direct analysis (Daniel) or half-symbolically (Charles), something of the *malaise* of the human spirit in face of its freedom. (Murdoch [63], p. 20.)

Thus for Sartre, abnormality is no indication of deviation from a norm but a larger-than-life strategy of survival. The heroism may be recognised by the therapist: but it should not imply acceptance of false solutions. As Guntrip says of 'the Central Ego':

> It perhaps deserves a better Label than Winnicott's 'False Self'. It is the result of an often heroic struggle to stay alive and discover a *modus vivendi*, and in this process the individual has to make use of his actual abilities and has often achieved important results. The Central Ego possesses knowledge and has developed skills that must remain a part of the whole matured self. Yet it is a False Self in so far as it is a Conformist self in which creativity and originality have had to be sacrificed to safety and the

need for external support. The pattern that is conformed to will vary with the cultural environment and may be tough, hard, competitive, submissive to authority, self-sacrificing, intellectual, obsessively moral, and so on. But it is not really the patient's true and proper self for it finds no room for his uniqueness and originality. (Guntrip [38], p. 190.)

The whole of Sartre's philosophy would surely endorse these heroic false solutions at the expense of human originality and uniqueness which he cannot find.

The effects of such endorsement, however, is to contribute to the taboo on weakness and to anti-human solutions.

While Sartre draws our attention valuably to the meaning and heroism of abnormal behaviour, he has also promoted the elevation of abnormalities to a high significance by which normal life seems 'pallid'. The problem here is that such adulatory regard for the abnormal is liable to lead to an overvaluation of false solutions to problems of identity – Sartre's own canonisation of Genet being a case in point. Sartre only recognises the *malaise* of the discomfort we feel about our experience of impulses to keep the identity together, by False Self activity, in order to imply that such discomfort is unnecessary. His moral urge is to eradicate this discomfort by persuading us it is moral cowardice. Why should we feel discomfort, he implies, over our 'freedom'? Cannot we accept responsibility for such actions – and for making ourselves by such actions. That is, should we not 'give ourselves over to the joys of hate'?

But the diagnosis of Fairbairn and Winnicott makes it plain that the discomfort we feel when we base our dealings with the world by pseudo-male doing, by schizoid hate, is that of knowing, from our primary urges towards integration, that there is a True Self which still lurks in the darkness waiting to be born, and which False Self activity merely leaves in the darkness. Sartre wants us to deny this discomfort, although it is the voice of hope, and to deny the origins of it – which are in the formative experience of 'female element being'. To achieve this denial he must deny causality, as we have seen.

In his early 'Essay on the Emotions' Sartre writes:

> 'The deep contradiction in all psychoanalysis is to present at once a relation of causality and a relation of comprehension between the phenomena it studies.' 'What occurs in the consciousness,' he says, can receive its explanation only from the consciousness. Psychological abnormality must be understood in terms of the subject's own choice of a 'mode' of appropriating the world, and the subject's own purposefully sustained symbolism.
>
> So where a Freudian might say that Daniel's guilt feelings at his homosexuality *cause* him to punish himself, Sartre puts the matter in terms of Daniel's semi-deliberate projection, his chosen mode of life. . . . The subject is the final arbiter, Sartre argues, and this the practising psychoanalyst well knows, although he tends to forget it when he enters his study to theorise. Sartre thus rejects the idea of the unconscious mind, but has his own substitute for it in the notion of the half-conscious, unreflective self-deception which he calls 'bad faith' (*mauvaise foi*). As a metaphysician, as moralist, and as psychoanalyst Sartre works with the same tools; a single picture of the mind serves him in all his fields. Since freedom is fundamental there is no clash between psychoanalysis and morality. (Murdoch [63], p. 20–21.)

There has been a value in the existential phenomenological attention to the 'relation of comprehension' between phenomena: what a patient's madness means in the here and *now*. But Sartre's account of consciousness here is confined to *thinking*. To him Daniel's 'chosen mode of life' is a 'conscious choice', and Sartre is unwilling to 'explain' it in any other terms than explanations which can come from the consciousness, explaining consciousness. He is only willing to encounter the sphere of doing.

Daniel's homosexuality and his guilt can be understood better by insights which are not intellectual. For instance, when Winnicott heard the 'girl' talking to him from a man's body he had to 'live through a real personal experience' to gain his uncanny

insights into the meanings of human bisexuality. From this arises theory which is not at
odds with the recognition that the 'subject is the final arbiter'. It is not at odds with it
because Winnicott knew by the female intuition in himself as a man that the 'girl' who
spoke was a split-off feminine element who stood in the way of integration and the
discovery of the True Self. Daniel's homosexuality and his guilt at his homosexuality
could derive from such a split. The homosexuality could be seen as a mark of an inability
to accept his female element of being. His guilt could derive from his discomfort at being
barred from integration and his True Self: his discomfort could be the voice of hope and
the need to 'be'.

Insights into the existence of such entities as True Self and False Self cannot merely
come from intellectual consciousness: they can only come from the female way of
knowing, which is at first unconscious. Thus Winnicott, when he said 'It is not you who is
mad. It is I who am mad, for I am looking at a man and listening to a girl', was virtually
living through the experience of the patient's mother when she held a boy baby and treated him as a girl.
Can one imagine Sartre's feelings at being involved in such an experience? The truth
is that it is just this kind of experience which is meaningless to him. Sartre's is a strange
existentialism, for his subjective disciplines and his world of inter-subjectivity eludes the
unconscious and he distrusts emotion His subjectivity must exclude feminine intuition
and the female way of knowing.

Of course, Sartre must reject the idea of the unconscious mind, since it belongs,
together with dreams, phantasies, insights, telepathy, 'togetherness', the electricity
between lovers and Primary Maternal Preoccupation, to female element being. His
substitute is *mauvaise foi*: and this I believe can be defined from the schizoid diagnosis as
being *'untrue to one's False Self'*. That is, by mirror-inversion of normal values Sartre sees
as 'unreflective self-deception' any glimpse of the True Self, and any flinching departure
from the purity of the false solutions of hate. Where there is the most utter hate, as in
Genet, there is the highest and most saint-like morality: yet, from Winnicott's point of
view, such 'false success' is 'morality at its lowest ebb' and from Polanyi's 'pathological'.

Sartre's morality is thus Satanic, and he manages to bring psychoanalysis and morality
together, not by relinquishing demoralisation as an aim but by building his moral theory
on the need to make oneself by will, by action, and choice, without any regard for or
recognition of the life-patterns embodied in one's psychic tissue or the ego-weakness at
one's core of being. His metaphysic, morality, and psychoanalysis are constructed on a
pure freedom to hate, which can only be achieved by leaving out the essential meaning
of life. For him our ultimate freedom is to feel our identity confirmed by the hate of
others, as the Nazi identity depended upon collective international and racial paranoia.
His answer to the point of life is only a negative one, which is in terms of the purity of
avoiding any recognition of one's ego-weakness – and one's humanity. No wonder
Sartre's influence in the world has been so sterile and degrading to the human image.

There is another way to 'freedom' and to the sense of meaning in life. It is not one
which Sartre can see: and it is one to which his work is concerned to blind us, not only
in the sphere of theory, but also in the cultural sphere, where Sartre has managed to
establish an ethos in which that which is not schizoid is not art, and that which is not
based on hate is not creative.

In the therapeutic practice, in effect, it is true, as Sartre argues, that 'the subject is
the final arbiter' – but only within a situation which (as Winnicott implies) there is a
'belief in human nature', a *'belief in the developmental process'* – and a recognition of the

power of love to grow, and to heal – a concept essentially of normality as a goal of integration. It is therefore not possible to allow the subject to be final arbiter in an absolutely relative sense, but only in so far as his inner creative and organising impulses are enabled to become aware of the inner need to love and to be loved, to find feminine element being and the True Self. But it is Sartre's concern as a psychoanalyst to prevent the subject finding these needs at all.

Sartre's objection to the 'deep contradiction' in Freudian psychoanalysis is understandable. The presence at once of a 'relational causality and a relation of comprehension' seemed to leave no room for creative self-assertion, for the recognition of integrative dynamics, nor for reference to values established by collocation. It seemed to lead merely to a situation of accepting determinism, and of *tout comprendre, c'est tout pardonner* – and so to moral stagnation. There was an ethical dilemma, which obviously troubled many concerned with social problems of crime and morality – in which it seemed that since the causes of an aberrant nature could be understood, no blame should be attached to an individual because he was a victim of environmental failure which predetermined his actions. His chosen role was his way to survive as a person at all: his choice of freedom. Yet some individuals were obviously culpable. But with some the law seemed but an expression of the community's punitive denial of its own hate and guilt. What value has punishment to a 'bad' individual who is not to 'blame'? Shall we disapprove of those who cannot lead moral lives because their 'instinctual drives' are less governable than others? Sartre wishes to establish a view which is a corrective in its radical insistence on responsibility for our every act in terms of commitment. Our acts inevitably involve the rest of mankind, and what is better for one is unacceptable unless it is better for all. What is better for all is 'freedom': this is applied to the cultural as well as the social and moral sphere.

But Sartre's responsibility seems too much to ignore certain major sources of morality to which we must be responsible, namely our moral health as a source of insight into 'what we really want' and the collocation of insights into 'what we really want' which includes, of course, all established human values. Without reference to these he seems not to be able to encounter the essential ethical problem, which is that of the degree to which we are entitled to claim our 'freedom', or solve our problems of identity, at the expense of others.

On this point, as one exponent of Sartre says, existentialism is 'curiously silent'. Yet this problem surely needs urgently to be explored by existential psychoanalysis? As Mary Warnock says:

> ethics must be defined as the theory of how people should live together . . . it would be generally agreed that the desires and wishes of others, their interests and liberties, constitute a limit to the morally desirable exersise of our own freedom to satisfy *our* desires. This moral platitude, which, though platitudinous, is the very foundation of morality, must have particular importance for the existentialists, who preach the doctrine of absolute and total human freedom. (Warnock [86], p. 38.)

The truth is, as Mary Warnock indicates, that Sartre's answer to 'How ought I to treat people?' and 'What is that which should be valued above all else?' is 'endless hostility'.

> In *Being and Nothingness* other people are the enemy, 'the original scandal of our existence'. We are committed to endless hostility, and our freedom must often be won at the expense of sacrificing the wil of another, who seeks to ensnare us. . . . It is thus the *freedom* of the other people which is an outrage to us, and we try to overcome it by pretending it does not exist.

Do we not hear this echoed in Laing's attitude to the family? Sartre says:

While I attempt to free myself from the hold of the other, the other is trying to free himself from mine; while I seek to enslave the other the other seeks to enslave me. We are by no means dealing with unilateral relations with an object-in-itself, but with reciprocal and moving relations . . . descriptions of concrete behaviour must therefore be envisaged within the perspective of *conflict*. Conflict is the original meaning of being-for-others. (Warnock [86], p. 45.)

Thus, for Sartre, there are no alternatives in love to indifference, masochism (i.e. aiming to become a thing ourselves, to be used and controlled by the other) or sadism (trying to possess the other by violence). As we have seen, this pessimism is echoed in Laing's negative attitude to love.

The only safeguard for the schizoid who fears contact is to alienate everyone who might come to love him. So this schizoid point of view underlies the attitudes of Laing – who quotes with approval a passage of Sartre depicting the way a child is horrifyingly forced into the patterns of his family – as he is forced to become 'absurd'. *Normal child care feels to Sartre and Laing like a coercive threat.* For them there can never be any reconciliation between 'man' and 'society': the only way to feel real is by conflict with society. The only possible relationship between persons is one of 'conflict'.

How can this point of view be reconciled with that of the psychotherapist?

Such existentialists offer themselves as pursuing the 'nakedness' of experience and the real nature of man. But the results of their exploration seem often in the end of doubtful value. As Iris Murdoch says, discussing *La Nausée*, such a novel 'does not offer a clear answer to the ethical problems it raises . . . it reads more like a corrective, a sort of hate poem, whose negative moral is "only the *salauds* think they win" and its positive moral, "If you want to understand something you must face it naked".' The end of the exploration is but a schizoid egocentric aggressiveness, which is mistaken for 'freedom': yet involves the strange inversion of values and the denial of those 'female being' sources and energies by which most of us achieve sanity. How can this approach to experience be taken into psychoanalytical theory? How can it be called 'existentialist'?

In Laing's existentialist psychoanalysis we have a strange mixture of emphasis at best, on the uniqueness of each human being and his 'Journey', combined with vestiges of instinct theory which would seem to be irreconcilable with the experience he records by his insights into the meaning of schizoid madness.

CHAPTER 23

Is R. D. Laing an Existentialist?

LAING objects to the syntax and vocabulary of social science and the way psychiatry tends to label individuals, so that 'me' and 'you' become submerged under 'objective' categories – 'its' and 'things' rather than persons. But Laing himself has his own syntax and vocabulary derived from Sartre and others which itself predetermines his approach and the way man is seen by him. He accuses social science of 'defining and circumscribing the manner in which "facts" are to be experienced . . . ' and even of *creating* the facts that are studied. But he himself does something of the same. He himself has his own terminology, and uses terms such as 'violence' in a particular way, borrowed from existentialism and used in his polemic to prejudge issues. He himself tries to persuade us to approach a subject in a way strictly determined by his own presentation and a use of various dogmas in a hybrid way, which is, nonetheless, dogmatic.

The result is a theory which has its own politics. His may be politics of 'insurrection' – but his use of this word is highly coloured with emotional conviction. Insurrection, *ipso facto*, is a good thing. (We expose this if we ask whether Laing would have approved of General Franco's 'insurrection' against the Spanish Socialist Government.) Thus while we can endorse the insistence in Laing's existentialism on the need to pay attention to things human, to potentialities of being, and to begin from whole experience, we do need, I believe, to question coolly many of his generalisations. Moreover, I believe we can question whether these are existentialist at all.

Is society 'insane'? It is a thought so terrible that one can hardly confront it that men have killed perhaps 100,000,000 of their own species in this century by violence, as Laing points out. From this we can see how horrible it is that there can be huge manifestations of group psychopathology, and we cannot escape recognition of a death impulse. But there were perhaps 2,300,000,000 other human beings who were not slain, many of whom did not wish the deaths to happen. Were these *all* insane *because of their socialisation*? Is it permissible to deduce, as Laing does, that all men seek death and destruction *as much as* life and happiness, that the violence expressed in the death impulse is a *product of the violence* we do ourselves in 'violating' ourselves by adjusting to society, that the way out is to *accept our violence* and that if we do not accept our violence we are displaying a 'fear to live'? Perhaps the problem is that we need to accept our weakness rather than our violence.

Laing seeks to carry his case (as do many pacifists) by hurling at us the incontrovertible facts of the figure of so many dead, the hydrogen bomb, and the Vietnam war. But these do not prove he is correct in his explanations for these hideous truths as he seems to think. And here his explanations do not differ from the pessimistic view of Freud, surely, that man has to be unwillingly coerced into civilisation, that in the process a forfeiture of potentialities is involved, and that man's animal hate is the most real thing about him.

Laing's account of Freud's attitude is that 'the *ordinary* person is a shrivelled, desiccated fragment of what a person can be . . .' Would not Fairbairn see this view of normality as schizoid itself?

The problem could surely have been better expressed as 'everyone's potentialities are unpredictable and rich but inevitably become limited and frustrated by a society which does not provide adequately for their enrichment and development'. But Laing could not put it thus because his adherence to schizoid dogma would not allow him to. In Laing's work, strangely enough, we feel affection for the schizoid individual – but by contrast contempt for the 'ordinary man' and the 'ordinary good home' – a manifestation of a deprecation of normal existence strange in a therapist.

Moreover, it seems characteristic of Laing's approach by contrast with Buber's or Winnicott's, that there is such a degree of hopelessness about education. Laing endorses the Freudian view of Professor Jules Henry:

> Children do not give up their innate imagination, curiosity, dreaminess easily. You have to love them to do that. Love is the path through permissiveness to discipline: and through discipline, only too often, to betrayal of self.
> What school must do is to induce children the way school wants them to think. . . . (Laing [53], p. 60.)

To Laing 'love' as experienced in the family and school is the most deadly 'instrument of violence' – bringing a threat of annihilation to the True Self. 'The double act of destroying ourselves with one hand, and calling this love with the other, is a sleight of hand one can marvel at. . . . '

Laing's 'love' is the force which compels 'adaptation'. He quotes that characteristic passage from Sartre about sewing a child up in a dead man's skin: 'he will stifle in such senile childhood with no occupation save to reproduce the avuncular gestures, with no hope save to poison future childhoods after his own death' (Sartre, quoted in Laing [53], p. 56).

The normal nurturing processes of the 'ordinary good home' – processes which Winnicott sees as, at best, those which enable the child to become himself – Laing sees as 'maiming and mutilating'.

The creative work of thousands of teachers who devote themselves to helping children to develop their potentialities Laing sees (with Jules Henry) as 'the pathetic surrender of babes.' He sees everywhere 'violence masquerading as love'.

Laing has observed violence in the schizophrenic family. But he makes the mistake of seeking to apply conclusions based on a hundred families of schizophrenics to all families. What he cannot take into account are the creative processes which create identity in non-schizophrenic families. In this he manifests a surprising lack of confidence in human nature and even blindness to what is lacking in the schizophrenic himself.

One of the problems indicated by Peter Lomas over the Sartrean existential position is that these thinkers tend to neglect the implications of Melanie Klein's exploration of the bodily origins of psychic phantasies and capacities to relate to objects, then tend to ignore Fairbairn's dictum 'The child's ego is a mouth ego' and its implications. This can be linked with Sartre's denial of the unconscious and of female modes of being and knowing. Lomas says:

> If the schizoid person is encouraged – as he is by Laing – to formulate his anxieties in non-bodily, non-infantile language, may this not facilitate the idealization of conceptual thinking at the expense

of bodily experience to which the schizoid person is rather prone? Is there not a danger of forgetting that the original deprivations, even if best formulated in terms of 'self', 'identity' and so on, were to a large extent physical? However misguided was Freud's biological theory of human development it enabled him to remain aware at all times that we have bodies. (Lomas, in Rycroft [22], pp. 129–30.)

Indirectly, Lomas indicates another aspect of Laing's position in which there is so little of that 'simple passionate openness' which Winnicott establishes as necessary, nor is there much preoccupation with 'togetherness' in a bodily self human way.

Laing's own blindness to depressive processes, to 'the stage of concern', and thus to reparative modes of establishing a sense of inner richness, is apparent in the way in which he gives a confused and inaccurate account of theories such as those of Winnicott. Though Laing appears to show great respect for the object-relations school and seeks to believe that there is 'no sharp delineation' between one school of thought and another, he seems not to have really possessed the implications and meanings of some of the basic tenets of their psychodynamics.

He admits that there are differences:

> What help are the prevailing theories of psychotherapy to us? Here it would be misleading to delineate too sharply one school of thought from another. Within the mainstream of orthodox psycho-analysis and even between the different theories of object-relations in the U.K. – Fairbairn, Winnicott, Melainie Klein, Bion – there are differences of more than emphasis. (Laing [53], p. 41.)

But has Laing grasped the essential differences? He says, for instance, on a previous page:

> The first intimations of non-being may have been the breast or mother as absent. This seems to have been Freud's suggestion. Winnicott writes of the 'hole', the creation of nothing by devouring the breast. Bion relates the origin of thought to the experience of no-breast. The human being, in Sartre's idiom, does not create being, but rather injects non-being into the world, into an original plenitude of being. (Laing [53], p. 32.)

It is surely very misleading to make it seem as if Winnicott is saying much the same thing as Sartre: nothing could be further from the truth.

Take the reference above to the 'hole' in Winnicott's theory. This refers to an extremely complex essay by Winnicott called 'The Depressive Position in Normal Emotional Development (1954–5) (Winnicott [90], p. 268). Laing is trying to tell us that 'Nothing, as experience, arises as absence of someone or something'. Winnicott, however, emphasises that the word 'normal' in his title is important, and that he is dealing not with the schizoid feeling of emptiness at the core of being but with the inevitable consequences of certain aspects of the mother–child relationship when mothering is adequate and the processes of maturation are proceeding *normally*. What is happening here is happening before concepts of absence or separation are really meaningful. Moreover, Winnicott looks at these processes positively: he wants to call Melanie Klein's 'depressive position' (i.e. the origin of depressive illnesses) 'the stage of concern' (i.e. the dawn of ruth). He emphasises the developments that take place at this stage as achievements, and sees them as ways by which the very young infant builds a sense of continuity of being: 'The mother is holding the situation and the day proceeds, and the infant realises that the "quiet" mother was involved in the full tide of instinctual experience, and has survived. This is repeated day after day, and adds up eventually to the baby's dawning recognition of the difference between what is called fact and fantasy, or outer and inner reality' (Winnicott [90], p. 268).

Winnicott sees this process of finding, and building, as the positive basis of identity. It belongs to reparation. Laing, by contrast, with Sartre, can only see what goes on between family and child as a violent subjugation of a natural creature as if it existed before nurture. To Winnicott the 'instinctual experience' was the expression of 'biologically driven' love: from his hunger and need the baby launches a 'cannibalistic attack' which 'partly shows in the baby's physical behaviour, and which partly is a matter of the infant's own imaginative elaboration of the physical function': 'If we like we can use words to describe what the infant feels and say: there is a hole, where previously there was a full body of richness' (Winnicott [90], p. 267).

This 'hole' does not arise from 'absence', but from presence, from surges of hunger and the phantasy associated with it. It is created by life, however terrifying it may be to see this, and it is associated with the problem of ambivalence: 'the human infant cannot accept that his mother who is so valued in the quiet phases is the mother who has been and will be ruthlessly attacked in the excited phases.' It does not arise from the failure to find the mother at all in terms of 'subjective object' and 'later objective object': that produces another kind of 'hole', and belongs to earlier stages. Negative elements of the kind Winnicott is discussing in our experience do not arise from separation anxiety since the concepts of the distinction between *me* and *not-me* are too rudimentary. Nor does Winnicott's account imply that the 'first intimations of not-being' arise from the 'creation of nothing by devouring the breast'. Moreover, there is a very great difference between Winnicott's account of the problems of the dangers felt by the infant to be in the give and take with the mother and Sartre's schizoid inversion of the whole process. To Winnicott the mother and infant *create being* between them. Sartre's position is remote from this because, having never experienced it, he cannot conceive of this process. To him the depressive position and all its achievement is largely meaningless, and can only conceive of genesis in terms of the *injection of not-being into an original plenitude*. In the differences here we can perhaps begin to see two radical distinctions between attitudes to negative experience. These Laing seems likely to confuse.

Perhaps Laing cannot grasp Winnicott, or give an adequate account of object-relations theory, because depressive achievement does not mean very much to him. Winnicott's picture is of the anguish and achievement which come from our primitive dawn of concern when we begin to apprehend the dangers in the mother–child relationship. Laing's value has been in his depiction of the agony of the schizoid whose problem is the earlier one, which is the dangers felt to be *in any form of relationship at all*: that is, the dangers of love, where there is an agony of not being able to feel a 'full body of richness' at all. The schizoid *begins* with a feeling that there is only a hole: his is the utter environmental deprivation. Winnicott's point is that a *normal* baby who has completed the 'schizoid position' or first phase of integration, inevitably comes to feel that a hole can *come* in the place of a full body of richness, as by the moment of satisfaction which brings 'flop' or by the phantasies of the hunger to live.

His neglect of intrapsychic dynamics, from fear of 'inner contents' and relationship, leads Laing to underestimate and even to deny the part played in problems of identity by the earliest childhood experiences. Thus his theories seek to attribute schizophrenia, for instance, to social causes, the violence of the family, and such influences which obviously only impinge on a subject at later stages.

Lomas says:

> In their recent book *Sanity, Madness and the Family* . . . Laing and Esterson describe a study of families, one of whose members had been diagnosed by psychiatrists as schizophrenic. . . . Contrary to the expectations of current psychiatric thought, the authors found that the 'patient' presented a view

of events which, in their estimation, was often nearer the truth than the rest of the family. . . . Her identity was being crushed because the family colluded, in cruel and subtle ways, in invalidating her experience of life, causing her to doubt the evidence of her senses. We are made to feel how, if we had been put in the same position as the 'victim', we would have been hard pressed to find a better solution than she did.

These findings suggest to the authors that schizophrenia is not, as is commonly thought, a disease process, but the label attached to a type of behaviour shown by certain people who, having been subjected to strange experiences by their families, come, understandably, to behave in a strange way themselves. (Lomas, in Rycroft [72], p. 143.)

This, says Lomas, challenges the psychoanalytical assumption that schizophrenia originates in a faulty mother–infant set-up. Whatever one thinks of the conclusions, certainly the study helps to develop a conception of personality that helps us, as Lomas says, 'to explore very fruitfully the schizophrenic's search for identity and the truth in his apparently mad perceptions.' This capacity in Laing makes *The Divided Self* such a valuable book.

But Lomas has some significant objections:

One criticism which a psychoanalyst would make of their formulations, however favourable he might be to their work, is that the events are being described *as* though the 'patient' *were contributing nothing to the disaster*. The psychoanalysis of schizophrenia has shown that the pathological distortions of love and hate characteristic of this illness, engendered by whatever original causes, are self-destructive and involve a masochistic manipulation of others to behave badly towards the self. It is difficult to believe that this tendency does not in some measure contribute to the clinical, picture described by Laing and Esterson. (Lomas, in Rycroft [72], p. 143.)

In 'coming to the aid of someone whose vioce has been unheard for too long' says Peter Lomas, Laing and Esterson have shown a bias. '. . .a more likely assumption to make is that an early parent-child failure has been followed by a vicious circle in which both family and victim play their unhappy parts . . . ' (Lomas, in Rycroft [92], p. 144).

Lomas also points to a deeper problem: 'perhaps the existentialists, although usefully emphasising the agency of the person, may, paradoxically – by denying the validity of what psychoanalysts refer to as 'unconscious motivation' or 'repressed drive', fail to see the agency of the person in certain pathological techniques.'

I would add, that from Fairbairn's analysis of schizoid inversions, that perhaps such 'existentialists', who are following a schizoid philosophy, have reasons of their own to ignore these agencies in pathological techniques because they have fallen for the appeal of what Polanyi calls the 'logically stabler state of complete moral inversion.'

Here I believe a great deal of light is cast on the origins of such social and cultural theories of Laing, based as they are on work with schizophrenics, by the acute perceptions of Farber, in his chapter 'Schizophrenia and the Mad Psychotherapist'. Farber is writing of the experience of himself and of colleagues who have treated schizophrenics. Farber has been stressing the value in therapy of the experience of despair. He quotes T. S. Eliot's lines 'our only health is the disease' and ' . . . to be restored, our sickness must grow worse', and says:

In this earthly 'hospital' I have spoken of the patient's need to recover from his treatment. But there is a deeper sense in which the cure may be implicit in the disease. As Freud taught long ago, there is some health in every symptom; or, 'to be restored, our sickness must grow worse'. And this holds true, not only for the patient, but for that therapeutic despair that is, after all, a collaboration between two people. If there are moments when it seems that 'our only health is the disease', and we must 'obey the dying nurse whose constant care is not to please but to remind of our, and Adam's curse', these are not inauthentic moments. (Farber [20], p. 182.)

He then writes the passage quoted above, about how out of despair, in the treatment of schizophrenics, the therapist may find the remedy inherent in the disease.

Farber is concerned, however, in the chapter under discussion, to examine what happens when this despair is 'not acknowledged, not contended with'. When he discussed the subject of despair with colleagues, he found that some felt his picture of the suffering involved was 'overdrawn'. And he also found that some were giving up work with schizophrenics not because they might 'catch' schizophrenia – but because, in subtle ways, 'they wondered to what degree they were becoming what they were not, or – with equal relevance – to what degree they were not becoming what they were'. After twenty years' experience of treating schizophrenics himself, and having had experience of those treating them, Farber concludes that there are special hazards which are indeed serious for those who choose to devote their lives to the treatment of schizophrenia.

Farber notes that an outsider's impression of the manner of therapists in a ward of schizophrenics would be of a particular style: an extraordinary manner: 'He would have to consider that, for reasons mysterious to himself, these therapists had apparently abandoned what must have been their more usual habits of expression in favour of some more florid and declamatory style – a style that appeared to transcend style, elevating mere form or manner to substance itself' (Farber [20], p. 187).

After giving account of some manifestations of this kind of histrionic manner, Farber speaks of 'overblown therapeutic encounters' which become inevitable in such work. These come to seem especially real to the analyst. By contrast his own life, outside the hospital, may come to appear 'artificial and pallid'. 'It is not unusual for the therapist, as he settles into his work with schizophrenics, to begin to prefer the company of schizophrenics, even those that are mute.'

Some analysts tend to fill more and more of their waking hours with such therapeutic work, and 'to feel quite bereft and impotent and lonely' when deprived of their company.

Do we not begin to detect a description of the Laing of *The Politics of Experience* – the florid tone, the histrionic manner, the sense conveyed of being in love with schizophrenics? – And the Laing of 'The Dialectics of Liberation' and the 'Anti-University'?

The incidents Farber has recorded have a 'quality of being larger than life'.

> But it is not merely the therapeutic encounter which is habitually writ large in this way; something of this quality passes over from the event to the man, and not infrequently the gifted therapists themselves come to be writ large. They begin to resemble certain spectacular personalities . . . in that they no sooner enter a room than they fill it . . . how they accomplish this . . . must to some extent remain a mystery . . . a quality that seems to unfold to full-flower – quite a *large* flower usually . . . filling a room is not merely – and sometimes not all – a matter of talking long and loud; even silence may, on occasion, produce a unique resonance, affecting an entire scene. (Farber [20], p. 194.)

What is peculiar about this effect is that it is not the content of what the analyst has to say, but since 'his province is relation' what is exerted all around him is 'the spell of relation, wilfully exploiting whatever personal expedients come to mind'.

This arises, Farber believes, out of the experience of treating schizophrenics, and especially out of the experience of refusing to acknowledge despair. For instance, 'knowing that the wrong approach is better than none', the therapist, in desperation to 'get through' may 'soliloquise'. The patient the therapist believes 'hungers for relation', even if he is unresponsive. The patient fears many things about contact, and one of them is that if he ventures an overture he might, owing to his gross deficiency in the capacity for relationship, only reveal himself as more unacceptable than he already appears. 'Given the schizophrenic's incapacities, not to mention his experience in hypocrisy and betrayal, the overtures of others will seem to him more dubious than this own.'

There is an inequality: the patient is confined, the doctor is free; the doctor is sane, the patient mad. What shall the therapist talk about? From what point of view? In what manner? Most topics will remind the patient of his predicament – such as, for instance, any reference to the family relationships by which the doctor as a person finds himself confirmed and enrichened.

If he speaks of his own friends and relatives at all it will be 'to emphasise whatever estrangement exists or has existed, seeking an appeal to his patient at the level of a fellow-sufferer':

> The danger here . . . is that often to the patient such talk about estrangement will serve to invoke inimations of those times when estrangements is (or was) either overcome or absent altogether. To forestall this danger, the therapist, almost without realising it, may overstate and generalise his case, he may invertively overextend and exaggerate the oppressiveness of the situation he describes . . . he may persuade himself that he has discovered patterns of pathology in himself and in his private life. . . .

In thus seeking to establish kinship with his patient, the therapist discovers his own *schizophrenic possibilities*, and then deterministic causes by which he arrived at them. As Farber says:

> regardless of the school . . . to which he belongs, the therapist comes to regard himself as victim *acted upon by the forces of nature, society, or family, in such a manner or at such an early age as to render him powerless* . . . 'I am this way because' he announces to his patient as casually as possible . . . implying that it is possible to live this life in spite of devastating victimisation. . . . (Farber [20], p. 198; my italics.)

Here we hear an echo surely of Laing's 'society brings about a devastation of our powers'. Do we not have here the whole basis, in a professional manifestation based in the experience of such therapy, of the theories of Laing and Esterson, about the origins of schizophrenia itself? Have they not, from the subtle 'double binds' of their attempts to enable their patients to find them acceptable, come to believe these imaginings, and then to erect them into a psychological theory which must inevitably deny both the normal satisfactions and confirmations found by normal people in family life and relationship, and also deny the origins of schizophrenia itself in early deprivation and the consequent intrapsychic patterns?

What the 'mad' therapists are virtually saying, says Farber, is something like, 'My failure to hear you has always been provoked by withdrawal, whether yours or my mother's'. What is characteristic of these statements, says Farber, is their clarity: 'in vain will we seek here for a hint of mystery, ambiguity, paradox, surprise, or uncertainty.' Such 'countertransference' explanations seem like brutal confessions: but is confession the word, asks Farber, for such remarks as 'I am this way because'? What his imagined visitor to a sanitorium of therapists who treat schizophrenics finds is: 'a chamber of distorting mirrors, such as one finds in amusement parks, in which all that may be seen are reflections of reflections of reflections – of the psyches of the therapists.'

Most of the responsibility for this absorption with countertransference, says Farber, lies 'in the nature of schizophrenia itself, which is a disorder consisting of a double failure in areas that might loosely be called meaning and relation'. 'Such civilised qualities as discretion, reticence, humour, judgement, and logic are poorly developed. While all these characteristics belong to the patient, they are also transmitted to the therapist, as he seeks to make up for the effect upon himself of the patient's inability to relate or mean.' And so all these characteristics become part of the therapist's public advocacy, as they have become part of Laing's – of which *The Politics of Experience* is evidence enough.

But there are further hazards, too. Laing's value has been in enabling us to find meaning the utterance of schizophrenics. At the same time, as Farber says, there develops in such a therapist an impulse to find within the schizophrenic a non-schizophrenic poet who is really in his own head. The therapist inevitably attributes meaning to the verbal or gestural productions of the schizophrenic patient, even when there is no meaning there. This is valuable in therapy, because 'not only does the patient need such imaginative assistance, if he is to recover, but such an exalted view of his capacities also incites an enthusiasm for this work on both sides that urges its continuance in the teeth of the discouragements that are intrinsic to the therapeutic situation.' But if the therapist forgets how much *he* supplies to complete the schizophrenic utterance *he may come to regard the schizophrenic as a sort of oracle with whom he sits all day,* 'who has the rare power to cut through the usual hypocrisies and pretensions of ordinary life, thereby arriving at some purely human meaning'.

This fallacy certainly pervades the work of Laing, who seeks to 'drive you out of your wretched mind' so that, like his patients, we can come into touch with some 'purely human meaning'.

Nor does the hazard stop there, for the next stage, as this writer indicates, is that in the course of supplying meanings to his patient, the therapist,

> partly because the work itself has required him to assert meanings with an assurance he himself did not at first possess, and partly because his audience was both captive and unresponsive, the therapist, by virtue of the prolonged apprenticeship he has served in the most self-indulgent kind of self-expression, may gradually be led toward both the posture and, ultimately, the belief, *that he, too, is an oracle* – well-dressed rather than ragged, affluent rather than impoverished, legally sane rather than clinically schizophrenic, and yet possessed of the same charismatic power to grasp the real truth in any situation. (Farber [20], p. 204; my italics.)

It was Laing who claimed in a television interview that he was a 'prophet'. But, as Farber is trying to say, this pattern is part of an essential self-indulgence, and this would be in accord with my own contention that the attribution of blame to 'society' for our faults, in Laing's social theory, is a false kind of comfort. Its origins, too, are in that recourse to causality, 'I am this way because' which is a way of avoiding true despair, and thus of avoiding rather than confronting one's own humanness.

A philosopher recently examining the arguments given by Laing in the psychoanalytical field as the basis of this application of Sartre's existential thought to psychotherapy, found many inconsistencies. First it seems doubtful whether Laing really follows Sartre's philosophy to the letter at all.

> ... Laing and his co-workers have been greatly influenced by Sartre and acknowledge their indebtedness to him. But the sense in which Sartre explains and defends existential psychoanalysis is very different indeed from the point of view that Laing and others are advocating.
>
> For Sartre rejects the whole notion of the unconscious; he maintains that anything in consciousness can only be explained by reference to consciousness itself ... and he argues that the aim of existential psychoanalysis, in his sense, is to enable the person to arrive at a knowledge – through necessary, self-evident intuitions – of her own free conscious choices that make herself a person. Moreover, Laing *et al.* do not appear to adopt any of Sartre's characteristic theses (for example, that Bad Faith is a very familiar and important human trait). Nor is it evident which of his concepts they adopt.

But it would seem that what Laing and his colleagues have taken over from Sartre is less his philosophical concepts than a mode of approach to experience. This critic is able to indicate not only the confusion of thought and terminology in Laing's position, but also the dogma of attitudes to society that is mingled with Sartre's influence. Here the use of the word 'violence' is crucial:

In *Views* Cooper uses the word 'violence' in what he says is Sartre's sense – it is 'the corrosive action of the freedom of a person on the freedom of another.' But this use does not help him either. For a psychiatrist could argue that ECT, for example, has been shown to be very helpful, and it is therefore not 'corrosive' at all.

If Cooper accepts this as an appropriate reply, he will then have to show empirically that ECT does 'corrode' *before* he can characterise it correctly as 'violent' – which is something he does not appear to have done.

The writer of the article under discussion was also concerned to indicate aspects of Laing's approach to schizophrenics which resemble those diagnosed in the 'mad thera-pist' by Farber: 'They would also help themselves if they could avoid giving the impres-sion that they had fallen in love with their schizophrenic patients and their schizo-phrenia...' – and he also speaks of Laing's 'intemperate language and abusive caricature of the Establishment'.

This 'intemperate abuse' is surely a way of escaping the essential problem, which is not that of 'violence' at all. From the point of view of the 'schizoid diagnosis', violence is an attempt to feel real, when ego-weakness threatens. When we feel unreal, empty and dead, we also feel a tremendous inner hunger from the Regressed Libidinal Ego, which threatens in consequence to 'eat' all objects and the whole world as object. Against the hunger of this weakness we turn our own Anti-libidinal Ego. Our way of dealing with this problem surely cannot be seen as a way of preserving ourselves against the 'family', or 'society', or against the coercive 'violence' of conventional psychiatry. Where individuals resort to violence, that is a defence mechanism against *their own needs to love and be loved*. Individuals who commit suicide, for instance, for schizoid reasons, prefer actual self-destruction to the horror of the nameless threat from the immense hunger of their own inner unborn psychic embryo. The False Self organises the suicide to 'protect the True Self from insult', as Winnicott puts it. Can we not see the kind of attack on society advocated by Sartre and Laing as itself a way of escaping the True Self problem by resort to False Self activity and a spurious mode of confrontation by hate?

Here surely is the real danger to the world: that man is capable of splitting, projecting, and denial – thus thrusting his own hate into the world in order to escape the jaws of his own ego-weakness. The only true solution to such splitting and hate is to find ways in which, in 'togetherness' men can bear to accept their weakness and take the painful path of self-discovery and re-growth, but not through 'insurrection', so much as real repara-tion, through creative reflection – between 'union' and 'separateness' and their sym-bolism in culture and values.

By contrast, Laing's concept of therapeutic or cultural re-discovery seems strangely lacking in what Suttie called 'feeling-interest responsiveness'. Here, of course, we are in great difficulties because we are seeking to resist Laing's social and cultural theories without being able to counter his clinical experience with any of our own. But Laing's influence (even on our own students) means we must examine the theories available, and then we may have doubts when Laing insists that the patient must go back to an inner place *where he has been before*. Where is this? He goes through a mirror, like Alice. 'Sometimes, having gone through the looking glass, through the eye of the needle, the territory is recognised as one's *lost home*, but most people now in inner space and time are, to begin with, in unfamiliar territory and are frightened and confused. They are lost. *They have forgotten that they have been there before.*' (Laing [53], p. 104; my italics.)

Laing resists attitudes which might regard such regression or withdrawal as anti-social or a departure from 'sanity'. He seeks to remove all doubts, about giving way to a process which involves giving oneself up to a 'journey' in which one forfeits all one's human bearings.

> They clutch at chimeras. They try to retain their bearings by compounding their confusion, by projection . . . and introjection. . . . They do not know what is happening, and no one is likely to enlighten them. . . . There is nothing intrinsically pathological in the experience of ego-loss, but it may be very difficult to find a living context for the journey one may be embarked upon. (Laing [53], p. 104).

It seems to involve even a rejection of that relatedness to others on which true personal autonomy depends. Behind Laing's view there seems to be even a dread of mutality, leading to an idolisation of incommunicable isolation. The terms I am using now are not mine, but come from a private communication from an analyst: 'the extreme . . . celebration of a state of shut-in-ness, in an amorphous, unmind stance, where sensation is the sole experiential attribute of life . . . is little more than . . . nihilism.'

In this, says this critic, Laing has adopted 'Sartre's dismay about life' and its 'contempt for all value systems that are the achievement of some two thousand years of individual creativity and cultural process in the West.' Laing's 'journey' sounds like a kind of flight from life, out of contact even with one's own 'intentionality' and hope.

So for social health, says Laing, individuals must be 'allowed to experience' this 'journey': and Laing puts this in such a way as to lay his work open to the charge made by the philosophical writer above that he and his followers write 'romantic moonshine' ('. . . if they could attempt to make their case, clearly and cogently, without pretentiousness, in ordinary humdrum English') : 'This journey is experienced as going further "in", as going back through one's personal life, in and back and through and beyond into the experience of all mankind, of the primal man, of Adam and perhaps even further into the being of animals, vegetables and minerals . . . (Laing [53], p. 104).

How can one speak of 'going back through the experience of all mankind'? It is true that Jung does speak in this way, and discusses archetypal experience. But this is, surely, as in dreams, a symbolism of going 'back' through one's own inner experience, of which human history is a *metaphor*? The aim of such regression is surely to come back?

Here we need to remind ourselves of the view held by Fairbairn and Guntrip that there is a pristine ego from the beginning, and that each individual's journey in normal circumstances is the creation of a self by a complex interchange between what the neonate has to offer and what the mother (and father) can provide.

Thus:

> A secure sense of being, shared with a stable mother both before and after birth, must remain as a permanent foundation in the unconscious, on the basis of which a separate ego-identity can develop stably and elaborate into a highly individual personality. . . . The conscious ego is the ego of separation, of 'doing', of acting and being acted on, and in that sense is the location of the male element in the personality. It must derive its strength from the deepest unconscious care of the self that has never lost the feeling of 'being at one' with the maternal source of its life. (Guntrip [38], p. 266.)

Any 'journey' to make good elements which have failed in this process of growth requires a complex in which there can be found (1) a source of being, the female element – a lap (2) opportunities to experience growth processes for the first time in a relation of 'simple, passionate openness'. Forms of therapy such as drugs or ECT may dismally fail to provide anything of the kind. But Laing's alternative, by his own account, seems also a defence against recognising the essential identity problem, a way of avoiding our own fear, guilt, hate, and responsibility for ego-weakness by blaming our problems on the 'violence' of the family and 'society' while 'going back' and 'dissolving'.

What Laing offers here is surely false hope. He says of his 'journeys': 'one cannot clearly distinguish active from passive here . . .' – the individual merely gives himself over to an extrapersonal mystical flux. So mystical, indeed, that Laing even suggests we shall even re-enter the experience of *minerals*. How can one take this seriously? Laing recommends to us the re-experiencing of 'primal man' and 'the being of animals'. But surely these can only be experienced symbolically? Is he asking us to believe in the trans-migration of souls?

Winnicott's view is that we need to give more attention to 'inner space'. But of what does this 'inner space' consist? It is, surely, the dynamics and structure of the present living human being, and his relationship to himself which he can only approach by symbolism? It is the complexity of internalised objects in their dynamic life as the basis of his identity – the structure of which is maintained by the continual creative effort of as-if symbolism.

While he insists on the human uniqueness of individuals, Laing, despite himself, writes as if the territory of 'inner space' was a non-personal desert – a desert of the collective unconscious outside individuals. He writes as if we need somehow to enter a realm outside our existence – which is no doubt felt to be possible by those who take hallucinogens: and who then may be temporarily experiencing a schizoid confusion of the *me* and the *not-me*. This flowing into an extra-personal territory seems in quite another direction from that indicated by Fairbairn who says of the therapeutic relationship:

> What the patient seeks above all is salvation from his past, from bondage to his (internal) bad objects, from the burden of guilt, and from spiritual death . . . I am convinced that it is the patient's relationship to the analyst that mediates the 'curing' or 'saving' effect of psychotherapy. Where long-term psycho-analytical treatment is concerned, what *mediates* the 'curing' or 'saving' process more specifically is the development of the patient's relationship to the analyst, through a phase in which earlier pathogenic relationships are repeated under the influence of transference into a new kind of relationship which is at once satisfying and adapted to the circumstances of outer reality. (Guntrip [37], p. 414).

The essence of Laing's 'journey' by contrast is its solitariness.

Winnicott, too, as we have seen, emphasises that psychotherapy is a reflective human collaboration in which there is expressed a belief in human nature and a quest for a True Self. From his experience of schizoid patients Winnicott links the capacity to feel real with the discovery of the True Self as the operational centre: 'While the individual's operational centre is the false self there is a sense of futility, and in practice we find the change to the feeling that life is worth while coming at the moment of the shift to the operational centre from the false to the true self . . . that which proceeds from the true self feels real' (Guntrip [37], p. 411).

Winnicott divides patients into three categories, corresponding roughly to Laing's division of individuals who feel 'ontologically secure' and those who don't:

> *First*, there are those patients who operate as whole persons and whose difficulties are in the realm of interpersonal relationships. The technique for the treatment of those patients belongs to psycho-analysis as it developed in the hands of Freud at the beginning of the century. Then *secondly* there come the patients in whom the wholeness of the personality can only just be something that can be taken for granted; in fact one can say that analysis has to do with the first events that belong to and inherently and immediately follow not only the achievement of wholeness but also the coming together of love and hate and the dawning recognition of dependence. (Winnicott, quoted by Guntrip [37], p. 409.)

These patients are depressive patients: the second group have reached 'the stage of concern' – that is the stage of becoming concerned for the destructive effects of their own hate. The third group are concerned with deeper and earlier schizoid problems:

> In the *third* grouping I place all those patients whose analyses must deal with the early stages of emotional development before and up to the establishment of the personality as an entity, before the achievement of space-time unity status. The personal structure is not yet securely founded. In regard to this third grouping, the accent is surely on management, and sometimes over long periods with these patients ordinary analytical work has to be in abeyance, management being the whole thing. (Guntrip [37], p. 409.)

Management is a special problem: but for all groups therapy means the attempt to provide for the patient what the mother has failed to provide at the earliest stages – by 'being' for the infant by her care and handling. The True Self is frozen and hidden away. '*Until some time when it is hoped that a chance may once more arise of bringing it out under more favourable circumstances.*' Winnicott regards the existence of this hidden and secret hope as decisive for the prospects of therapy. 'The analyst has to reach and help this hidden self with its secret hope.'

As Guntrip says, Winnicott discovered this 'At obviously high cost in personal strains' – and 'his work must have far-reaching consequences'. He was able to achieve this because of his marvellous humility:

> Our patients teach us these things, and it is distressing to me that I must give these views as if they were my own . . . everything we say has been truly taught us yesterday. . . . In our work, especially in working on the schizoid rather than the psycho-neurotic aspects of the personality, we do in fact wait, if we feel we know, until the patients tell us. . . . An anorexia patient is teaching me the substance of what I am saying now as I write it down. (Winnicott [94], p. 182.)

We may compare Winnicott's tone with Laing's here:

> I am a specialist, God help me, in events in inner space, in experiences called thoughts, images, reveries . . . refractions of refractions of refractions of that original Alpha and Omega of experience and reality, that Reality on whose repression, denial, splitting, projection falsification, and general desecration and profanation our civilisation as much as anything is based. (Winnicott [94], p. 50.)

I make the comparison to suggest that there is something coercive – or 'violent', to use his own term – in Laing's approach to therapy itself. Although he seeks to resist objectifying in psychological theory, his approach to psychic rebirth seems to recommend something almost petrifying – certainly depersonalised. We feel, as we read him, that he is seeking to browbeat 'ordinary' 'shrivelled' individuals, urging them towards a transcendental 'realm' which is larger than life. (This is not to disparage or deny what Eliot called 'the higher dream' or religious ecstasy.)

But Laing's point of view he expresses by the quotation 'L'enfant abdique son extase' (Mallarmé) in order to adapt to this world. To believe this is surely to become involved in the schizoid individual's view that maturity brings a loss of freedom?

Laing's way of putting the goal of our quest for self-fulfilment, as a search for something we have lost, seems to imply that it is a natural Rousseauistic self that civilisation has thwarted. This, combined with the impersonality of his Voyage, and the implication that this is to be larger than life, seems likely to militate against what Guntrip calls 'the . . . acceptance of need for "healing in a state of passive recuperation" '. It could contribute to a deepening of the 'taboo on weakness', and thus indirectly to a further flight from psychoanalytical ideas, which depend upon a recognition of our deepest human needs. As Fairbairn says about psychotherapy:

> The question that will be raised is that the patient *wants* to be treated as a baby, with the implication

that he should not be indulged in this. I believe this to be a grave misrepresentation of the case. There is an infant in the patient who actually *needs* to be accepted for what he is, by being helped to whatever degree of 'therapeutic regression' proves to be necessary. But there is also a 'forced antilibidinal adult' in the patient who hates this . . . we witness the intensity of the patient's resistance to treatment as a struggle not to depend upon the analyst for help. . . . We need to know more about the processes of rebirth and regrowth of the profoundly withdrawn infant self hidden in the schizoid citadel. . . . One patient said simply, 'If I could feel loved, I'm sure I'd grow. Can I be sure you genuinely care for the baby in me?' – a statement which makes it clear that fundamentally what the patient is seeking and needing is a relationship of a parental order which is sufficiently reliable and understanding to nullify the results of any environmental failure. (Guntrip [115], p. 161.)

Realistic recognition of this 'baby' is missing from Laing's work, as it is not from that of Winnicott and Guntrip.

Besides, Laing would seem to seek to subject everyone (as I have suggested before) to procedures suitable only to Winnicott's third type. His comments on society, culture, and morality, on the 'ordinary' man and his 'shrivelled' condition, are based on his dealings with the small minority of schizoid individuals. He fails to take into account that for most people the problem of life is dealt with by forms of ego-maintenance belonging to those reparative impulses whose origin is the stage of concern. It is valuable to indicate the deeper schizoid problems of discovering 'what is human' that underlie these. But his acceptance of Sartrean dogma involves too much the denial of the validity of reparation on the one hand, while insisting on the exclusive value of false solutions of hate on the other.

Winnicott says: 'for the whole manic-depressive group that comprises the majority of so-called normal people the subject of the depressive position (stage of concern) in normal development is one that cannot be left aside; it is and it remains the *problem of life*. . . . The child, having reached the depressive position, can get on with . . . intra-personal relationships.'

To schizoid individuals 'it is not the thing that matters'.

The schizoid persons of Winnicott's third group Laing knows well, and he has remarkable insights into their condition. He sees how they lack entity and the 'achievement of space-time unity status'.

But there is a sharp contrast between Laing's approach to their problems and that of Winnicott. Winnicott discovered at 'great personal risk' that he had to take on the role of the mother – that of manifesting the female element. In doing so he discovered by feminine knowing the poignant truth that in these patients there is an unborn psychic neonate – the regressed ego, hiding *'until some time when it is hoped that a chance may once more arise of bringing it out'*.

What does Laing offer this neonate?

In this particular type of journey, the direction we have to take is *back* and *in*, because it was way back that we started to go down and out. They will say that we are regressed and withdrawn and out of contact with them. True, enough, we have a long, long way to go back to contact the reality we have all lost contact with. And because they are humane, and concerned, and even love us, and are very frightened, they will try to cure us. They may succeed. But there is still hope that they will fail. . . .* (Laing [53], p. 137.)

Normality is 'alienation': Laing is rigid in his adherence to the dogma of alienation: 'Can we not see that this voyage is not what we need to be cured of, but that it is a natural

---

* It is interesting to note that Freud came across a medical nihilist, Schweninger, Bismarck's doctor, in 1898, who said 'The world belongs to the brave, including the brave sick' – a statement akin to some of Laing's. Freud pronounced Schweninger a 'disgrace.' (See *Letters to Fliess*.)

way of healing our own appalling state of alienation called normality?' (Laing [53], p. 136).

Laing can see that 'The schizophrenic is one who is broken-hearted, and even broken hearts have been known to mend, if we have the heart to let them'. But Laing's mending involves, as I believe, the preservation of a closed circuit which is the system of the False Self. Moreover, in the light of certain of Guntrip's insights into schizoid suicide, some of Laing's advocacy looks disturbingly like the false beliefs of a schizoid individual that death can be a pathway to rebirth. The 'chance' Laing offers is a *trip*: and a trip is circular. We may contrast the approach to therapy of Winnicott and Fairbairn, who emphasise the potentialities of finding integration, realisation, and coherence, fulfilment of the secret hope to be 'brought out' as a whole self through confirmation in a relationship, with Laing's emphasis on a going 'in and back', regression, into the being of animals and even the minerals.

Laing's outline of the necessary journey runs thus:

>   (i) a voyage from outer to inner;
>   (ii) from life to a kind of death;
>   (iii) from going forward to a going back;
>   (iv) from temporal movement to temporal standstill;
>   (v) from mundane time to cosmic time;*
>   (vi) from the ego to the self;
>   (vii) from being outside (post-birth) back to the womb of all things (pre-birth);

and then subsequently a return voyage from:

>   (1) inner to outer;
>   (2) from death to life;
>   (3) from the movement back to a movement once more forward;
>   (4) from immortality back to mortality;
>   (5) from eternity back to time;
>   (6) from self to a new ego;
>   (7) from a cosmic foetalization to an existential rebirth. (Laing [53], p. 106.)

We need to accept our 'violence', apparently, but characteristically, *not* our need for dependence – that which needs confirmation in meeting. Laing speaks of an 'initiation' ceremony which shall replace the 'degradation ceremonial' of psychiatric examination, diagnosis, and prognostication: and he speaks of 'guidance', but by *'expatients helping future patients to go mad'*. He demands the 'dissolution of the ego': 'let me drive you out of your wretched mind'. The only concession to togetherness in *The Politics of Experience* is the remark that there will be an 'ex-patient' to 'sort of look after you'.

From the point of view of object-relations psychology it is necessary to ask Laing – How is it possible to have a 'new ego'? What can from 'ego to self' and 'self to a new ego' mean, when identity depends upon a complex of internalised elements for which from the beginning there is an ego as an integrating dynamic? We are the same self in the same body from birth to death. It is surely not possible to plant a new ego like a new kidney. What is 'cosmic foetilisation' to the True Self waiting in the darkness, woven in the structure of the changing body, for a chance to be?

Surely the terms of Laing's Voyage as expressed above are too inhuman: they belong to what Sylvia Plath called 'the light of the mind, cold and planetary'. By contrast with the insightfulness of his concern with human meaning in *The Divided Self*, the 'visionary' passage *The Bird of Paradise* at the end of Laing's Penguin is also strangely inhuman, too,

---

* Amniotic time?

in its obsession with inner contents, its chaos, its visceral sensationalism, and its pre-occupation with feelings of repulsiveness at physical contact – at being human. Laing seeks 'the emergence of the 'inner' archetypal mediators of divine power, and through this death a rebirth, and the eventual establishment of a new kind of ego-functioning, the ego now being the servant of the divine, no longer its betrayer' (Laing [53], p. 119).

The normal ego has to 'be dissolved' and the False Self has to 'die'. By 'ego' and 'self' we mean those organising and integrative factors which are the individual, and which begin with his pristine being. Laing's attitude implies a break in ego continuity. This implicitly denies that we are dealing with living human individuals whose existence depends upon maintaining a structure of personality formed of two forms of 'together-ness'. His approach seems unlikely to help anyone escape from what Guntrip calls the 'inner contradiction of the schizoid condition.'

> The weak schizoid ego is in urgent need of a relationship, a therapeutic relationship capable of filling the gap left by inadequate mothering. Only that can rescue the patient from succumbing to the terrors of ultimate isolation. Yet when it comes to it, the weak ego is afraid of the very relationship that it needs . . . at the very moment when 'rescue' seems imminent it will rush away again into the wastes of isolation. (Guntrip [114], reprinted in [38] p. 288 ff.)

Guntrip says:

> The deepest thing in human nature is 'togetherness'. From that starting-point the psyche passes through the separation of birth into 'aloneness' which would be unsupportable unless beneath it, as its foundation, there still persisted that oneness of the child with the mother, and through her 'mother-nature', in the sense in which Buber quotes "the mythical saying of the Jews, 'In the mother's body man knows the universe, in birth he forgets it,' " but he never forgets it at bottom. It remains the secret foundation of the stillness, security and peace . . . a foundation which must be preserved and developed in post-natal growth through identification to object-relationship.
> . . . in the deepest unconscious it is never lost, and human beings struggle to return to it when their 'ego' is most desperately menaced. . . . (Guntrip [38], p. 269.)

Moreover, Guntrip insists, 'There needs to be an ability to defend against "male element" impingement at a conscious level without losing "female element" relationship in depth. He concludes: 'Grave questions are raised by psychiatric attempts to bypass the conscious ego and contact the unconscious direct.'

But is this not what Laing desires, when he recommends the 'dissolving' of the ego? Here I believe we must invoke an important paper by Winnicott *On Communication* (Winnicott [94]). He commends in this essay many of Laing's observations in his earlier books. But Winnicott emphasises that 'while healthy persons communicate and enjoy communicating . . . *each individual is an isolate, permanently non-communicating, permanently unknown, in fact unfound*' (p. 187). This unfound self is 'Sacred and most worthy of preser-vation':

This fear of being 'found' presents the deepest of all problems in psychotherapy. Laing's approach seems likely to thrust those who seek true rebirth further and further into those 'wastes'. For Laing says:

> True sanity entails in one way or another the dissolution of the normal ego, that false self competently adjusted to our alienated society.

The dangers of this view may perhaps be discussed in the light of this passage:

> In health there is a core to the personality that corresponds to the true self of the split personality: I suggest that this core never communicates with the world of perceived objects, and that the individual person knows that it must never be communicated with or be influenced by external reality. . . . Rape, and being eaten by cannibals, these are mere bagatelles as compared with the violation of the self's

core, the alteration of the self's central elements by communication seeping through the defences . . .
we are dangerous because we are too nearly in communication with the central still and silent spot of
the patient's ego-organization. (Winnicott [94], p. 189.)

Yet Laing wants to 'dissolve the normal ego . . . that false self' – and release 'archetypal mediators' within us, as though these were impersonal forces, like Freud's Id. He
seeks to *do* something to us: 'If I could turn you on, if I could drive you out of your
wretched mind . . . ' What does he mean when he seeks a 'natural way of healing our
own appalling state of alienation called normality'? What I believe he means among other
things is a way of 'contacting the unconscious direct' as through the use of LSD, which is
a violation of that 'still and silent spot' of the ego-organisation: a rape of the true self.

The core of being is the only hope as the foundation of ego-growth. It is to this basic
'being in relationship' in the unconscious depths that the schizoid individual in schizoid
suicide seeks to take flight. With him the failure of the earliest stages of maturation has left
this self's core dissociated, cut off and felt to be unavailable (it cannot be destroyed).
This is the ultimate meaning of "ego-weakness" and "loss of identity". 'For health, the
female and male elements need to be released from dissociation and integrated. This is
possible because it is the essence of the female element that it can relate, know and
communicate in a fundamental way by feeling, than the more external relating, knowing
and communicating of the male element' (Guntrip [38], p. 270).

What is needed for psychic health, according to Guntrip, then, is a new relationship
between the ego and the core of being, between the 'male element' relating and organising
ego, and the 'female element' of being at the core.

But what happens if we put this theory beside Laing's?

By contrast with the tone of the writing of Winnicott and Guntrip, Laing's 'intemperate' and defiant attitude echoes rather the tone of a patient clinging to his own
defences against his deepest needs. Here we can compare the voice of Fairbairn's patient
'Ivy' – who seemed to Fairbairn to exemplify that death impulse in a patient the
experience of which led Freud to postulate a death instinct to explain the phenomenon.
Here is the 'subject as final arbiter' – choosing death, and defending negation as her
norm.

> In this case [says Fairbairn] the particular phenomenon in question is an obstinate tendency on the
> part of the patient undergoing psycho-analytical treatment to keep his aggression localized within the
> confined closed system of the inner world. The operation of such a particular tendency, as well as
> of the general tendency to maintain the inner world as a closed system is well illustrated in the case of
> 'a patient whom I have previously designated 'Ivy', and who, in a sequence of sessions, provided
> associative material of which the nature may be gathered from the quotations which follow. It should
> be added that the insights registered in this material were only achieved after prolonged and painstaking
> analysis.'
>
>> I have no words to describe how I hate you. But why can't I just hate you and get on with it?
>> The only reason I can think of is that I need my hate for some other purpose. It's too precious to
>> waste on you. It is vital to my internal economy not to waste hate on you. I feel I need the hate for
>> myself. I need the hate to run myself on. . . . Now I feel sleepy. I've grown indifferent and couldn't
>> care less. . . . That shows that I want my hate to keep me short-circuited. Instead of running myself
>> on outside people and things, my sex-object is myself and I get gratification from self-things. . . . Every
>> bit of hate has to be accounted for. Every bit of autoeroticism has to be economized. I hate you for
>> trying to make me stop doing this. I need to hate you to get energy for my inner persecution. I'm
>> breathing it. I'm in a orgy of destruction. I can't wait to get my hands on myself to destroy myself.
>> That is my life – a drawn out ecstasy of slowly killing myself. That is wicked: and it's the only wicked-
>> ness I can do. I want to be evil in other ways, but I can't. I've sold myself to the Devil; and this is
>> the only way I can do it. I'm a willing Isaac. The greater the frustration outside, the greater the
>> ecstasies inside. I want to have no inhibitions in bringing about my own destruction.

I dedicate my life to my bowels. I used to think I wanted to get on with life, and my bowels were a nuisance; but now I think my bowels are my real life, and ordinary life is a nuisance. My inner economy is different from that of ordinary people. . . . If an ordinary person is cross, they're cross and that's an end of it; but I hoard my anger to use for inner purposes. That is like my bowels. The ordinary analytical idea seems to be 'Let out your temper, and you'll be better': but that does not apply to me. I need my temper for inner purposes; and I'm not interested in life outside. . . . That's different from wanting to let it out and being stopped. I suppose this state of affairs has been with me all the time; but it is better to become aware of it.

My aim is to sail as near the wind as I can to killing myself. My aim is to carry out Mother's and Father's wishes. . . . I do it partly to please them . . . and partly to annoy them. I'm going as near the wind as I dare to killing myself. I don't confine it to sexual things. . . . I extend it to my whole life. . . . I feel my life is interfering with my neurosis, instead of *vice-versa*. When I began to be afraid of gas-ovens, I knew it was me that was wrong; but I did not want to be changed. Instead, I wanted all gas-ovens removed. This is queer, but it fits in with my attitude that my ordinary life is an interference with my neurosis. . . . I feel my unconscious life is my true life; and it is a life of frustrated excitement, which I seem to regard as bliss. I feel I really have a strong urge to destroy myself. . . . I want to see how near I can get to the edge of the cliff. There is a bit of me that keeps me alive; but my real purpose is directed to killing myself and frustration. I have trouble over you; for I don't want to tell you things. *If I have a relationship with you, it interferes with my death-circuit.* . . . You interfere with my neurosis and my desire to destroy myself. You are just a nuisance. It is daft to have a relationship with you, because it just weakens my inner purpose. . . . The worse I get the better I'm pleased because that is what I want – which is a negation of all that is right. . . . I want to devote myself to working myself up to a state of need and not having it satisfied. This is involved in my desire for self-destruction. I must accept that I frustrate myself. I expect that originally I was frustrated from outside; but now I impose frustration on myself; and that is to be my satisfaction. . . . It is a terrible perversion. (Fairbairn [108], pp. 374 ff.)

Can we not hear a tone here which Laing's voice significantly echoes?

Surely we must conclude that Laing's social theory is a death circuit in itself like Ivy's described above. He wants '*the gas-stoves removed*'. That is to say, he attacks 'society' as the cause of our self-destructive ills, when in fact the gas-stove problem is within ourselves.

While we may all have schizoid problems (in the sense of needing to find a new centre for assurance as to the validity of our identity in the absence of the old cosmological assurances), it is not true that we are all schizoid individuals. As Guntrip says:

We may finally summarise the emotional dilemma of the schizoid thus: he feels a deep dread of entering into a personal relationship, i.e. one into which genuine feeling enters. . . . The schizoid feels faced with utter loss, and the destruction of both ego and object, whether in a relationship or out of it. In a relationship, identification involves loss of the ego, and incorporation involves a hungry devouring and losing of the object. In breaking away into independence, the object is destroyed as you break away out to freedom, or lost by separation, and the ego is destroyed or emptied by the loss of the object with whom it is identified. The only real solution is the dissolving of identification and the maturing of the personality: the differentiation of ego and object and the growth of a capacity for cooperative independence and mutuality. (Guntrip [38], p. 48.)

Laing's problem, I believe, is that he sees that what is necessary is 'dissolution of identification'. He misinterprets this, however, as dissolution of the ego. Moreover, he is so hopeless of relationship in which genuine feeling is involved, that the later stages (of maturation, of the growth of independence) appear largely meaningless to him. Laing understands disintegration, but seems less to believe in integration. Thus he cannot emphasise growth in relational therapy; nor can he see any hope in 'contributing in' to the family and social order. The 'rebirth' he offers is an extra-personal, cosmic affair; it is, above all, not 'weak', in the recognition that we may after all be no more than human.

According to Guntrip by contrast, what is needed is an atmosphere in which, instead of seeking a Wagnerian territory of transcendental mysticism, we accept our ego-weakness – and begin from there, in our needs for one another and our needs *to be*.

Laing's mysticism is surely a further contribution to the prevalent most dangerous tendency to pretences that we are Big and Strong. Projection, splitting, and other self-deceptive processes are not (as Laing sees them) 'defences' against society's 'violence': but against our own inward weakness. This can, however, be used to attach and project hate on to others: and isn't this what Laing does by his abuse of the 'Establishment'?

Laing's earlier insights are valuable and full of human sympathy. But in *The Politics of Experience* he departs strangely from being human. The meticulous work of Melanie Klein, Bowlby, Winnicott, and others has established a new perspective in psychoanalysis in which those of us in education find vindicated the processes of love and creativity – in the formation of identity, in the natural development of a moral sense and social altruism. They see in reparation and the creative quest for integration the sources of strength of a civilised democracy, and in this they provide a platform for social change, in the needs of each of us to realise our human potentials. How is it that Laing can find himself in another camp?

Speaking of the 'uncanny insights' of the schizoid individual, Fairbairn says that this kind of person when 'he has not regressed too far' is 'capable of greater psychological insight than any other class of person'. This is because such persons are 'able to be familiar with their own deeper psychological processes' – 'processes which, although not absent in individuals who ordinarily would be classified as 'psychoneurotic', are nevertheless exluded from the consciousness of such individuals by the most obstinate defences and stubborn resistances'. Because of such insights, Laing has been able to open our eyes to aspects of experience to which we were blind because of such defences and resistances.

To become involved in the schizoid ethos involves one in its characteristic blindnesses. To the schizoid individual reparative effort, concern, the capacity to be depressed, love, altruism, creativity, the consequent individual moral growth, and the existence of moral values in the collocation of naturalistic ethical descriptions are meaningless. He must fall back on the inversions of hate, futility, violence, insurrection, alienation, and nihilism.

The popular figure in English psychoanalysis today appears to be Laing as existentialist. He has taken over Sartre's schizoid and love-denying philosophy, and seeks to involve us in the destruction of personality, the logic of death, and an ultimately ineffective protest against all of 'them' – over whom we may comfortably project our hate. He endorses that depreciation of human value so prevalent in the schizoid ethos of the followers of Sartre. This is a strange and sinister development at a moment when there seemed to be hope for greater recognition of the inner life and subjective disciplines as through other existentialist influences*. But, since his use of Sartre is so confused, while he seems to have learnt less from Buber than Guntrip and Winnicott, how can Laing really claim to be an existentialist at all?

---

* e.g. Rollo May's remarkable work, *Love and Will* (1969).

PART VI

Conclusions

CHAPTER 24

Society and Inner Needs

PERHAPS what we need to rediscover is something like the ideological aim of classical Chinese philosophy: 'The chief key to the mystery of the universe, and man in it, is personality, and personality at liberty through obedience to the Given in life, and to the Eternal; and this is the key to ethical achievement and the achievement of the good life in society' (E. R. Hughes, *Chinese Philosophy in Classical Times*, Dent, 1942, p. xl).

It is possible to interpret the terms of the above in ways which need not conflict with the insights of psychoanalysis and philosophical anthropology. From what we learn from those who have worked with psychotic patients, we shall perhaps feel that the problem of identity is what matters rather than 'personality': the problem of feeling real, whole, continuous and confirmed, at a deeper level than that of how we present ourselves to the world. This feeling of being real involves inevitably the capacity to discover and come to terms with 'the Given' – both within and without – by such a process of coming to terms with the conditions of life such as are explored in the Book of Job. 'The Eternal' perhaps we can interpret as those elements in human nature which do not change, and the human situation in the world which we cannot alter. If we confront these, we confront them with despair: but this despair can be positive – a way of recognising truths. And since what is involved is a subjective change in us, we need perhaps to admit that the 'Given' requires the feminine way of knowing. To find 'liberty through obedience' requires the apprehension of inner truth through subjective disciplines and the collocation of naturalistic descriptions of experience. In such disciplines of a creative kind lie a whole range of human potentialities which at the moment we have tended to neglect, or have even failed to find. Yet in the light of the recognition of such human facts many pronouncements of political organisations, governments, sociologists, educationists, industrialists, and planners seem nonsense.

A great deal could be said here from a literary point of view, invoking the one major voice in our twentieth-century literature who has invoked the realm of 'being' – D. H. Lawrence. Lawrence's self-inquiry was 'terrifyingly honest': his continual cry was 'Worse, let me not deceive myself . . .'.

It was the cry of the genuine artist in the quest for the truth of being and to seek the point of life. Lawrence saw that this was at one with the pursuit of the True Self. Perhaps his most succinct record of his quest is his poem *Manifesto*:

> To be, or not to be is still the question.
> This ache for being is the ultimate hunger.

Being is found by relinquishing, and going beyond, the 'male knowing', merely intellectual, sense of the self that limits identity:

> I have come, as it were, not to know . . .
> . . . ceased from knowing; surpassed myself.

It is almost unspeakable because it is a penetration to the silent core of oneself: yet it is
found in *meeting*:

> How can one speak, where there is a dumbness on one's mouth?
> I suppose, ultimately she is all beyond me,
> She is all not-me, ultimately . . .
> . . . It is the major part of being, this having surpassed oneself. . . .

Lawrence was using Winnicott's language thirty years before the psychologist: and
everything object-relations psychology says confirms Lawrence's insight, his recognition
that the capacity to feel I AM involves entering into another mode of being in the realm
of togetherness, of I–Thou experience. He is also aware of the fears inevitable in giving
oneself in relationship, and records the feeling of relief at having given in relationship,
only to find that the phantasy threats were not justified: 'having touched the edge of
beyond, and perished, yet not perished.' Confirmation of one's being is inseparable from
giving in a relationship, with all the dangers we fear from the 'schizoid position'. Confirmation is only to be found in relationship between two beings who recognise one
another as separate identities.

> Then, we shall be two and distinct,
>   we shall have each our separate being.
> Two of us, unutterably distinguished, and
>   in unutterable conjunction . . .
> Then we shall be free, freer than angels, oh, perfect.

If this sense of one's whole separate being, independent, but in the recognition of
dependence, could be achieved by all of us, then it might come about that:

> Having no laws but the laws of our own being . . .
> Every human being will then be like a flower, untrammelled
> Every man himself, and therefore, a surpassing singleness of mankind . . .
>   (D. H. Lawrence *Manifesto*.)

Such an ideal of perfection is impossible. But what we could hope for is a development
of self-realisation in a majority to such a degree that they could feel strong enough to
forgo those false solutions which alienate men from one another because they cannot
tolerate their own psychic weaknesses. The problem is how to promote this consciously.

Lawrence emphasised in an important way the need for us to pay attention to 'inner
needs', and to the 'female element'. Unfortunately, however, this best creative insistence
is mingled with a great deal that is full of False Self will and mentality, in Lawrence
himself. There was an underlying 'model' in Lawrence's thinking which he could not
throw off for unconscious reasons – hence his belief in 'blood' and his strange celebration
at times of death as a goal – the symbolism of which could be related to Freud's attachment to the death instinct.

Before we can achieve any advance in the fostering of our essential being, we need to
throw off the burden of such destructive chimeras about man's fundamental brutishness
and his innate urge towards death. Strangely enough, despite his positive humanness,
Lawrence was at times very close to Freud when he lost hope in the human future (as

at times in *Lady Chatterley's Lover*). He, too, was ambivalent about the reality of instinct and the reality of intuition: 'We are *afraid* of the instincts. We are *afraid* of the intuitions within us. We suppress the instincts, and we cut off our intuitional awareness from one another and the world.'

Lawrence's 'We suppress the instincts' reveals to what degree he shared Freud's traditional model of the structure of the personality, as a contest between reason and nature. Yet 'We cut off our intuitional awareness from one another and the world' by contrast, however, is the kind of observation Fairbairn and Winnicott might endorse. It is what Birkin and Ursula learn in *Women in Love*, or the protagonists in *Look! We Have Come Through!* They did not learn to 'free' their 'instincts'. On the other hand, to 'release' instincts may be what Lady Chatterley is supposed by Lawrence to have done: but the very failure of that novel reveals how false a solution is offered with such 'impulse release' theory. Lawrence's worst novel has contributed to the falsity and decadence of modern attitudes to the sexual life, which have proved so degrading to human dignity and the concepts we hold of ourselves.

Lawrence largely invented his own psychology and so continued to wrestle with inconsistent conjectures unqualified by his own best insights. He explored his own experience, however, with courage and intelligence, and this makes him an illuminating, if uncertain —and sometimes destructive—guide. But at worst his account of human nature is embroiled in his own guilt and fear, and tends therefore to become as misanthropic as Freud in his hate theory. In his theory Lawrence often offers what seems to be a primitivism that sees 'instinct' as the primary reality: '*Think* with your *blood*' rather than '*be* with your own *femininity*'. So he sometimes sought to promote freedom by demoralisation, while confusing intuition, instinct, and procreation – and championing all these against 'consciousness': 'Let us never forget that modern morality has its roots in hatred, a deep, evil hate of the instinctive, intuitional, procreative body. This hatred is made more virulent by fear, and an extra poison is added by unconscious fear of syphilis. And so we come to modern bourgeois consciousness. . . . '

So, many of us in the humanities and education have found Lawrence a disastrous guide to 'living', despite the powerful advocacy of Leavis. In truth, while we need to follow Lawrence's better insights, we need also to pay more attention to what is emerging from the dispassionate work of those whose major concern is to help others to find their humanity. In the light of this, many of Lawrence's conclusions were themselves false solutions. For instance, if in the above paragraph we suppose Lawrence is talking about 'intellectual hate', we can assent; but not if he is abusing consciousness itself.

The fresh view of man being developed by philosophical anthropology ought surely to help those concerned with the humanities and the study of man in society to be more hopeful about our future – more hopeful even than Lawrence was, in the end – for he lost hope. Yet perhaps not as idealistic as he is at the end of *Manifesto*. Certainly, we need have no lack of confidence in the function of the humanities themselves. In philosophical anthropology we find a secure vindication of the positive role of culture in each individual. The primacy of personal culture, and its role in ego-maintenance as the basis of a sociable identity, makes any creative contribution to the community a gift to the possibilities for peace and a truly richer human life at large. Such contributions are likely to be far more revolutionary than mere 'insurrection' against 'bourgeois ideology' or against 'them'. And if there is to be change, it needs governing by a deeper sense of the nature of being human, and a responsibility to this.

While we need to be realistic in the recognition of a death impulse in man, we need not, however, feel that this is ineradicable and unchangeable. Where we find pessimism and misanthropy we need to trace this to the subjective origins behind social theories. For example, in *Culture Against Man* Jules Henry comes to the conclusion that 'the capacity to use culture against himself may overtake man and destroy him while he works on his ultimate problem – learning to live with himself' (Henry [40], p. 11).

Professor Henry sees American society so preoccupied with physical survival that, in neglecting inner needs, it is suffering 'emotional death'. '. . . man is deprived of inborn ways to interpersonal satisfaction and thus is compelled to search for them, evolving along the resultant pathways of dissatisfaction and intrapsychic conflict . . . ' (Henry [40], p. 11).

Professor Henry's view is perhaps Freud modified by Karen Horney and Erich Fromm: personality is a product of environment. But since he does not know the work of Melanie Klein, Winnicott, and Fairbairn he cannot achieve their kind of confidence in inner creative energies. His thinking is still influenced by Freud's negative way of looking at our psychic energies as defence measures and adaptations – while he could not find a place for man's positive cultural energies and achievements. Behind Professor Henry's cultural theory lurks Freud's belief that man in unwillingly socialised, and his word 'inborn' reveals that his thinking is based on Freud's instint theory. Professor Henry's view of culture therefore can only be the dismal concepts of 'release and sublimation': 'The root of life is impulse and its release in the right amount . . . is a primary concern of culture' (p. 305).

To Professor Henry intrapsychic conflict results from the difficulties man has in *adjusting* to social life rather in the imperfections in the complex between maturational processes and the environment. He says: 'society has been established primarily for the purpose of guaranteeing food and protection . . .' – all kinds of evils, he says, spring from this necessity. Might it not be that there is an even more primary need, which impels man to live in society, which is *the need of* men to live together, because they find fulfilment by relationship to one another in a group ? That is, cannot we accept society as the expression of being human and the way in which identity is confirmed, rather than as a necessity forced on us in self-defence by a harsh environment?

Professor Henry's point of view seems to be that man has been so busy seeing to social needs of the material kind, of food and protection, that 'inner needs have scarcely been considered'. I agree with him profoundly that 'inner needs' are too little taken into account by modern American and British society. But must we not first see that a primary inner need is to live socially – a need for society itself? And that creative living itself, as a means to sustain identity, is the purpose and advantage of social life, in the family and the community? It is true, as Professor Henry says, that 'within its formal legal institutions, no organised society has stipulated the procedures and guarantees for *emotional* gratifications between husband and wife and between parents and children, but all societies stipulated the relationship of protection and support.'

But is it correct to conclude as he does thus?

> The very efficiency of human beings in ordering relationships for the satisfaction of these external needs has resulted in the slighting of plans for the satisfaction of complex psychic needs; everywhere man has literally had to force from an otherwise efficient society the gratification of many of his inner needs . . . the orientation of man towards survival, to the exclusion of other considerations, has made society a grim place to live in, and for the most part human society has been a place where, though man has survived physically he has died emotionally. (Henry [40], p. 12.)

Professor Henry begins his book from the concern that 'unthinking subjection to the primordial impulse to survive is simply producing new varieties of destruction'. But is it *efficiency* that so threatens to kill our emotional life? We have attached identity to externals – but our failure surely is that we have not provided for our deepest primary needs which are for *psychic* survival? Our emotional death is not an inevitable consequence of our socialisation, but of a failure to be socialised *enough* – that is, enough to express in the social organisation our primary inner needs.

Is society a 'grim' place because we have become so devoted to the need for 'food' and 'protection'? Is the material activity with which American society is so preoccupied, really in the same human tradition as the organisation of food-getting and protection in primitive societies?

By his own demonstration Professor Henry makes it clear that many of the 'external' activities of our society have a culturally symbolic purpose, which has very little to do with the purpose for which he believes society to have developed. Much of the material activity of American society is delusional:

> Enormous numbers of Americans participate in . . . delusions. In a society where people work at what they have to do rather than at what they want to do, work is denied and even home becomes a kind of delusional reality – not in the sense that it does not exist, but rather in the sense that it becomes magnified into the *only* reality, while work becomes a kind of phantasm. The fairy-book way in which many American homes are furnished, so that every inch of space is elaborated into some kind of moonshine – figured and filmy draperies, strange-looking little animals, weird shapes on the walls, exotically tapestried and convoluted lamps – is an expression of the somewhat delusional nature of the American home, halfway between reality and fantasy. Even the home machinery is fey. The function of the American home is to deny the existence of factory and office: it is a concrete expression of the logic of nonexistence wrapped up in delusional extrication. (Henry [40], p. 384.)

By 'extrication' Professor Henry means the attempt to symbolically extricate oneself from an intolerable situation by creating a phantasy about it.

He reveals the attempt to deny, by symbolism, that we belong to a real human society at all: we pretend to live in fairyland, while our actual lives are so unrewarding that our sense of identity is threatened. The decorations at home mentioned, are 'moonshine': they are deficient in *creative* symbolism related to inner needs. Work is 'denied' because it provides too little symbolic meaning. Home is delusional except for the realms of actual relationship and family life, which remain one fundamental basis of confirmation and for many the only source of creative satisfaction.

From the point of view of the human truth explored by object-relations psychology I believe we can say that the material preoccupations of our society and much of its activity divert energy which might otherwise be given to inner needs and the problem of existence. Such preoccupations have largely become a substitute for symbolic work on our inner needs itself. They belong to that impulse to substitute the pursuit of 'external goodness' for that of 'inner goodness' to which Joan Rivière and Melanie Klein drew attention long ago. They represent attempts to deny inner needs, by pretending that inner needs can be satisfied by 'outer' preoccupations.

The incorporative features of our era, of course, were explored by Tawney, who condemned our society for its obsession with 'its *own digestion*':

> The burden of our civilisation is not merely, as many suppose, that the product of industry is ill-distributed, or its conduct tyrannical, or its operation interrupted by embittered disagreements. It is that industry itself has come to hold a position of exclusive predominance among human interests, which no single interest, and least of all the provision of the material means of existence is fit to occupy. Like a hypochondriac who is so absorbed in the processes of his own digestion that he goes

to the grave before he has begun to live, industrialised communities neglect the very objects for which it is worth while to acquire riches in their feverish preoccupation with the means by which riches can be acquired. (Tawney [79], p. 140.)

The solution, according to Professor Tawney, is that society must learn to 'see industry in the right perspective':

> . . . it must regard economic interests as one element in life, not the whole of life. It must persuade its members to renounce the opportunity of gains which accrue without any corresponding service, because the struggle for them keeps the whole community in a fever. It must so organize its industry that the instrumental character of economic activity is emphasized by its subordination to the social purpose for which it is carried on. (Tawney, [79], p. 191.)

As Tawney says, economic effort and expansion have become ends in themselves – more important than their social purpose. We may apply this to the cultural sphere and link it with individual feelings of emptiness in the identity. In cultural symbolism, too, ingestion has become a predominant mode. Ingestion is all, because it is the means by which we sustain our identity. In our culture, for instance, an individual may lower standards and debase human value – so long as he is successful. Acquisitiveness in our world is the mark of success in living, even if others are 'eaten' in the process, even if the sensibility at large is coarsened as the price paid for this.

The problem of alternatives, however, is one of confidence: could we bear to be human? For in a more genuine culture the pains of creativity would have to be borne. That is, we would have to face the kind of 'despair', sense of mortality, sense of human weakness, and awareness of life's difficulties, that are expressed in folk culture, and the greatest art. But here doubts arise, because of the deadness of our external environment, and the 'existential vacuum' at the heart of our life. One may be doubtful of the capacities of those whose quality of life and work has been so trivialised and dehumanised by the industrial-commercial environment to be able to endure their own cultural starvation, if it were exposed to them, by the withdrawal of the manic false-solution symbolism of popular culture, for instance. At school, it is true, their children dare 'confront the problem of existence', in their creative work and their pursuit of the humanities. But much gained here is destroyed by the kind of patterns for identification offered to the adolescent today. To offer continuity, the development of a creative culture would have to go hand in hand with a humanisation of the whole environment of work and living space, and a fundamental change in the ethos of society as a whole. Such a development would require great confidence in human civilisation and culture – a confidence which, of course, theories which emphasise our 'animal' reality or which attribute our problems to an ineradicable death instinct, tend to undermine, as they undermine responsibility.

In considering how to radically change our environment we need to ask: What is it that reassures us we are not dead, assures us that we are human and alive, that life has a point? This problem becomes apparent if we look at areas where individuals have either never felt alive (like Laing's patients in *The Divided Self*) or where they have lost such assurance. Here there is a most valuable account by Professor Jules Henry of how 'humanness is ebbing' in the public hospitals of America. There, human beings are allowed to become obsolecent: those in charge even stop referring to the weather, without realising the implications: 'Weather is important to the aged, as well as to prisoners, lunatics, and others confined against their will. It is not merely a subject for value-free chit-chat, but is a veritable *actualizer of existence*: if one can be moved by the weather one is not yet dead.' (Henry [40], p. 448).)

At worst, where contact in the community breaks down, there is a horrifying degree of dehumanisation. In some of the worst hospitals observed by Professor Henry the attendants had ceased to use patients' names: 'The aides worked silently, speaking to the patients only to make requests such as "turn over", "sit down". . . . '

Symbolism as an energy of preserving a sense of identity sinks to a nadir. Some patients preserve a false hope – about recovery, about relations trying to get them out – which is but a 'delusion' whose 'inner function is to prevent the patient thinking he is dead'. The overall effect is discussed by Professor Henry in these terms:

> If in every human contact something is communicated, something learned, and something felt, it follows that where nothing is communicated, learned or felt there is nothing human either. The vast hospital silences . . . tell us that humanness is ebbing there. The very quietness, however, informs the inmates – not so much because they think it, but rather because they feel it – that they are not human beings. (Henry [40], p. 404.)

The weather reports, the use of personality, and such elements in our mass media also serve a related purpose. But to restore the tide of humanness we need much more than they can give. It is not enough for us merely to be provided with just sufficient culture to provide an 'inner function' which is barely enough to prevent us feeling dead!

Professor Henry was surprised, in his investigation of hospitals by the tenacity of a sense of identity: it is as if

> *culture outlasts body and mind*, for even as the body remains barely alive and the mind declines into senile rigidity, beset by hallucinations, the cultural configuration remains . . . long after she can no longer move she . . . woman is concerned with appearance and status, and her capacity to hate . . . she retains the lesson that she learned when she was strong, that it is easier to be hostile than compassionate. (Henry [40], p. 473.)

Professor Henry does see that 'Man in our culture wants to retain his "mind" until he dies, for to lose it is to be despised, as if one were poor'. As a Freudian, he is naturally startled when presented with evidence that a personal culture, for which Freud was unable to find a place, is more important than anything else to a human being. Object-relations psychology makes it clear that since 'the ultimate goal of the libido is the object' loss of identity is far more terrible than physical death (or to put it in a more meaningful way, it *is loss of identity which we fear in death*). The philosophical anthropology with which we have been dealing alters the whole perspective of our thinking about cultural and social issues by placing the major emphasis squarely on the *problem of identity*: the key question for all of us is Lear's 'Who is it that can tell me who I am?' – while the answer lies in finding touch with one's True Self, as well as the True Selves of others.

In conclusion to a book like this one is drawn to utter some kind of manifesto. Yet, surely, the book itself indicates well enough, I trust, that to do so would only show up in its own light as yet another delusion. No intellectual theory is going to solve the kind of problems indicated by our exploration of this realm of human experience, and, as we have seen with Sartre and Laing, to erect a dogma from a psychology can become itself a false form of strength that weighs down the potentialities of fresh insights.

If there is any conclusion, it can surely only be that we need to pay more attention to, and to trust, the 'female element' way of knowing and experiencing, without disparaging the male element. Then we are left confronting the question – can the solutions of the True Self triumph in the human world? Our problems can only be solved if there are sufficient adults able to draw on the resources of the True Self, and to be strong enough to try to avoid false solutions. This means that there must be a majority who are both able to feel a secure sense of identity, and are able to learn from the schizoid minority, while yet resisting their particular capacity to involve others in the False Solutions of hate.

One problem here, however, haunts me. We may agree with Guntrip that 'It is the weak who hate: only the strong can love'. But the schizoid inversion of this has its own fascinating appeal. A community can be composed largely of individuals who have profound ego-strength, and a rich life informed by 'female element being'. Ancient Greece, perhaps, had such a predominance of strength of Being.

But the neighbours of such a community may be tormented, for whatever reason, by inner weakness and by envy. Basing their solutions on hate ('we will have no weakness or tenderness in our youth') they may decide to strengthen their collective identity by paranoia and march on their psychically more secure neighbours. These in turn must now resort to 'pseudo male doing' in order to defend themselves. In any case, their own true security has been disturbed, and it could be that they might be destroyed simply because the female element was predominant in their psychic patterns. The interhuman problem then presents itself in these terms – can human beings ever become inwardly secure enough everywhere, so that communities can dare to choose peace? Could we ever relinquish our atomic rockets – and be sure we would not be overrun by those (like the Communist countries) who are hypnotised by their false solutions and collective psychopathology, based on adherence to intellectual systems to which humanness must needs be sacrificed? Fortunately, the hideous power of the hydrogen bomb, as the ultimate manifestation of the false solutions of hate, is now itself driving us back to the painful human solutions of negotiation, disarmament, and world co-operation – despite lapses. The ultimate logic of false solution is exposed for ever, as 'endless hostility' is seen to mean 'eventual annihiliation'. We can survive if only we can learn to bear the agonies of finding ourselves no more than human and life no larger than life.

CHAPTER 25

The Humanist Conscience

THERE is, however, one important immediate and urgent conclusion to be drawn from object-relations psychology and the philosophical anthropology with which it may be associated. This is that both individual viability in the psychic sense, and the survival of civilisation, depend upon the activity of conscience – on that 'healthy moral sense' that Winnicott finds, which is bound up with a personal culture as the meeting point between 'separateness and union'.

Here, the tendency of thought at the moment follows 'enlightened' concepts based on belief in 'release' and 'relaxation' – the origins of which are in 'instinct' theory. As we have seen, the implications of this approach are fundamentally pessimistic – the best we can do is to tolerate the brute in us as far as possible. Also in this there is an inherent irresponsibility, a characteristic which Towers and Lewis associate with the belief that man is 'really' nothing but an ape – so that it can be a relief to us to be told that our impulse to live at the expense of others is, after all, only natural – innate and ineradicable. In its turn this suits the ethos of a ruthlessly acquisitive society which has attached identity to pseudo-male 'doing' – while even 'protest' becomes the inverse of this, in 'endless hostility'. All these contribute to the 'taboo on weakness' and to yet further flight from the essentially human. As Suttie pointed out, mere demoralising tolerance, meanwhile, 'leaves the (individual) more isolated then before', while the attribution of guilt to 'society' is, as Money-Kyrle implies, a mere evasion of an inner problem.

What we need to foster in such a situation is a kind of conscience that ruthlessly pursues the question *What is it to be human?* – and resists developments which reduce or attack humanness. In *Love, Hate and Reparation* Melanie Klein and Joan Rivière wrote of how 'the standards of conscience and morality that sprang from our guilt . . . suffer from neglect' when 'the inner life of man' comes 'into contempt'. The present ethos of 'permissiveness' and 'frankness' is based on no scientific or philosophical realism. Of course it is encouraged by the cynical philosophies of commerce and the manic hedonism on which it depends. But essentially it is a complement to the neglect by our philistine society of inner needs, rather than a claim for humanness arising from within it. The attitudes of modish 'enlightenment' are not based on recognition of the processes of love and creative symbolism such as we find recognised in therapeutic practice, child care, education, and normal family life. Many such attitudes, both 'humanist' and Christian, are, in fact, based upon the 'demoralising' and 'disillusionment' theories which Suttie rejected thirty years ago – with their promise of 'quick solutions' and basis in a futile 'mitigation of the severity of the super-ego'. To a psychoanalyst such as Winnicott a 'healthy moral sense' is at one with the development of an adequate 'super-ego organisation' – i.e. a positive guilt-sense. This sense requires development rather than 'mitigation': we need more conscience, not less.

Money-Kyrle discusses the origins of conscience, first according to Freud:

> Everyone is by now familiar with Freud's explanation of conscience: that it begins with the child's fear of displeasing his parents and reaches its final form when he 'introjects' them or rather his ideas of them, as far stricter and 'better' than they really were. But because this idea of an internal authority, or super-ego to give it Freud's term, is largely unconscious, it is to this extent unalterable, so that the conscious ego, which does develop and mature, may become increasingly in conflict with it. The initial impulse to ethical inquiry may well come from conflicts of this kind, and end in one of two ways: either the authority of the super-ego is bolstered up by the construction of systems that purport to be absolute, or undermined by a scepticism designed to rob it of its terrors. Kant's ethics, with its stress on the categorical imperative, would seem a good example of the first alternative: that of the Epicureans, who attacked superstition as the cause of fear, a good example of the second. (Money-Kyrle, on 'Psychoanalysis and Philosophy', in Sutherland [77], p. 109.)

Money-Kyrle goes on to discuss deeper conflicts of conscience as they seem to psycho-analytical theory after the work of Melanie Klein: ' . . . below such ego-super-ego conflicts is another which is, I think, more fundamental . . . '.

Even if we cannot share Money-Kyrle's belief in the death instinct, we can surely agree with him that there are destructive impulses 'which necessarily hate the, at first solipsistic, self as their primary object, and so give rise to the fear of death.'

We may, with Winnicott, Suttie, and Fairbairn, see hate and destructiveness as consequences (or inversions) of frustrated love. But since everyone is frustrated in some way at some time, everyone has a 'hate problem' which at times seems to bring a threat of loss of identity from the hungry mouth of the regressed libidinal ego.

From this diagnosis, the ethical discussion becomes a discussion not of the 'ego' in conflict with 'restraints' (or a child against parents, or the individual against 'society') – but of the *problems of establishing, discovering, and maintaining a True Self* by achieving integration, so that we do not fall into what Melanie Klein calls the cycles of hate which export these problems in the form of attacks on others, which can solve nothing, but only spread disruption, and provoke further anxieties of identity at large. Money-Kyrle says: 'The underlying problem of how to thrive without feeling guilty at doing so at the expense of others is primarily internal. . . .'

The problem can be avoided by denying the problem altogether – as is done by some philosophers: 'Rousseau, for example, blamed society for all our faults . . . he substituted, as it were, a myth of primal innocence for that of original sin. Thus his system was achieved at the cost of leaving something out – namely, the whole problem of the individual's sense of guilt which is rooted in ambivalence.'

Among 'enlightened' commentators today there are many adherents of the Rousseauistic myth of a golden natural innocence. It is only possible to believe in this natural man who does not experience guilt and hate by denying the problems of incorporation and aggression inevitably bound up with love, felt in our bodily needs and associated with our phantasy life. Money-Kyrle links this kind of denial with the capacity for the most terrible abrogations of conscience.

> Rousseau has inspired many progressive impulses: we can give him credit for helping to inspire those liberal movements which really reduced some social tensions and so lessened one cause of internal conflict. But the consistent development of his denial of the individual's unconscious sense of responsibility for predatory aggression led in the end, not to the emancipation of individuals from their sense of guilt, but to the mass projection of conscience, in its most ferocious form, into totalitarian states, which sought to control even the thoughts of individuals (Money-Kyrle [77], p. 111.)

Money-Kyrle does not wish to suggest that all effort to improve the external world is futile: but he questions the gains we have made over aggressiveness, greed, and envy by tackling their '*apparent external cause*': 'the unconscious guilt they arouse (i.e. greed and envy) remains a secret motive for a demand for scapegoats . . . '.

The only answer is a better understanding of ourselves – yet this requires inevitable pain and even what Money-Kyrle calls 'self-sacrifice'. It requires the pains of love and creativity. The intellectual world of fashionable 'amorality' contributes to an atmosphere in which individuals find it hard to resort to the resources of 'True Self being' because these have become discredited (and taboo as 'weak'). It inhibits the exploration of our true human nature, and the quest for what the True Self wants: 'What is really desired is what is desired when *all* our inclinations toward it are faced and not some ignored, including desires not to have a desire for such a thing . . . ' (Wisdom [97], p. 106).

The problems involved here are not recognised by the fashionable intellectual ethos nor by popular theories of man nor by much psychology and social science. Yet from philosophical anthropology they are all too clear. Here we may turn to another valuable paper by Money-Kyrle on 'Ethics'. Money-Kyrle is speaking from clinical experience, and points out that, through the work of Melanie Klein, analysts have been able to distinguish two types of guilt. The first is that with which we are familiar, as the butt of the demoralisers:

> Unlike psychopathic delinquents and some psychotics, who often give the (incorrect) impression of having no capacity for guilt at all, most neurotics and especially obsessionals are extremely conscientious. And it was with neurotics that analysis was at first concerned. Their guilt seemed to have been first aroused in early childhood by certain primitive wishes and to have subsequently become attached to, and so interfered with, many non-sexual sublimations. The result was a crippling and often progressive inhibition of whatever activities they tried. They seemed to be suffering from an excess of guilt, so that the diminution of this guilt appeared to be the ultimate aim of their analyses. (Money-Kyrle on 'Psycho-analysis and Ethics' in Klein [48], p. 128.)

This has led to the problems Suttie discusses of how psychoanalytical theory has given rise to the attempt to reject or undermine a 'crippling, self-defeating' morality.

The assumptions of much 'enlightened' permissiveness are based on the (false) supposition that psychoanalysis effected a 'liquidation of a morality based on an irrational anxiety'. But here, as Suttie indicates, there was always a division between theory and experience. Freudian theory did not seem to explain the facts observed by sociology such as human altruism. Freud implied that human beings only behave morally under coercion, and this is evidently not true. Psychoanalytical theory therefore needed to become aware of some inner integrative spring which prompted moral impulses: 'No special analytic knowledge is required to convince us that there must be another aspect of morality based not on fear but love' (Klein [48], p. 431).

The bases of this proved difficult to unravel. The newly discovered basis of morality seemed first to 'consist of unintegrated phantasy objects, by which the infant believes himself to be persecuted from within [but which have not] yet acquired [their] final character of an integrated internal mentor' (Klein [48], p. 431).

Melanie Klein's theory seeks to explain how, after the paranoid–schizoid position, the sense of persecution diminishes and depressive feelings begin to appear. As these were analysed they were found to express grief and remorse '*for injuries to a loved object for which the patient feels himself to be responsible*'. This grief and remorse constitute the other element in guilt which we may describe as 'depressive as distinct from persecutory'.

This guilt arises from the complex dynamics in the intellectual and emotional development of the newborn baby. Kleinian object-relations psychology finds here the bases of
all moral and philosophical problems: 'That these ideally "good" and ideally "bad"
objects are different aspects of the same one (and the same child both loves and hates
them) is a discovery which is delayed because it is so intensely painful' (Klein [48],
p. 432).

Money-Kyrle here means 'delayed' in analysis: but the discovery is also painful and
'delayed' in life – it is the kind of discovery we have to go on making all our lives, endur-
ing in the discovery the pain of recognition of our true nature – but with consequent
satisfaction too.

Indeed, combining all our capacities to accept our whole nature, and becoming
capable of relating to a world recognised in all its wholeness and complexity, through
creative culture and living *is the problem of life*. Ethical problems are essentially problems
of splits in object relations, and so of identity. These are poetic-philosophical problems,
and their solution is found in the creative dynamics of ego-maintenance, not in removing
fear and guilt merely.

As we have seen, if we approach morality from the point of view of such object-
relations psychology, we find ourselves dealing not with the pressures of libidinal impulse,
unwillingly restrained to recognise the obligations of reality, but rather a complexity of
intropsychic processes whose goals are integration of being, in relationship, the individual
seeking to feel confirmed and to become integrated against the terrors of inner vacancy,
the threat of 'being nobody', and loss of meaning in life. These goals are sought through
'meeting', love, and culture: our society inhibits each.

The effect of Melanie Klein's work was to indicate a positive kind of guilt in human
nature: a natural guilt whose solution was *reparation* – reparation which is only possible
through give-and-take and creative culture. This is the source of all altruistic and creative
satisfactions: to make the 'object' whole is to be whole, and to discover one's gratitude for
having existed in the world. From Winnicott's point of view cultural symbolism develops
from the interplay between union and separateness – and this is a 'sacred area' of 'creative living'. From May's it is the source of psychic potency.

As we have seen, 'enlightened' arguments are often based on the assumption that
rational explanation (as in some forms of early analysis) reduces guilt, and 'frees inhibition'. This may be true, as Money-Kyrle says, for the 'persecutory' patient, and may have
the effect of helping him to a condition in which he comes to fear only real dangers in
the external world – and one in which he ceases to fear because he has ceased to believe in
those existing only in unconscious phantasy. (This process, as Money-Kyrle says, is
never achieved in practice.) But, as Money-Kyrle says, psychoanalysis in fact *increases*
the other kind of guilt:

> In the case of depressive guilt, however, the effects of analysis is somewhat different. Since much of
> this guilt arises from acts performed in unconscious phantasy, the exposure of the phantasy as distinct
> from fact certainly relieves it. *But phantasied acts imply a desire to commit them.* That the patient has wished
> to destroy, to injure, to desert or to betray his loved objects is itself a fact, which analysis cannot disprove
> but rather exposes to the light of day. Thus a substantial reduction in this kind of guilt cannot be
> achieved merely by showing that the destructive impulses have not in reality achieved their aim. . . . It
> also helps to free the reparative response to the irreducible destructiveness that still remains . . . it
> diminishes the capacity to feel guilt of a depressive kind whenever a 'good' object is in any way injured
> or betrayed. (Klein [48], pp. 433–4.)

Philosophical anthropology therefore indicates that there is no escape from fear and guilt we feel in our psychic tissue, related to deep problems of identity, as by sudden abreaction, 'education', or 'rational exploration'. We simply have to live with a continual need for ego-maintenance. Our conclusions in the sphere of the social regulation of culture should surely be that this 'sacred' area of symbolic creativity should never be violated, exploited, or laid waste. Yet this is exactly what our culture is doing at both popular and *avant-garde* levels. Meanwhile the 'enlightenment' of demoralisation reduces our responsibility for dealing with our own hate and undermines the impulses of that inner morality on which we base our sense of identity. Much of our cultural symbolism and popular thought encourages us to abandon our creative attempts to come to terms with those elements in ourselves, to split these off and project them, and to promote persecutory anxiety and the cycles of hate. When sign and meaning are corrupted, all those processes by which we are human and know ourselves to be human are corrupted also.

Not least does this affect in its turn the very springs of our ethical capacities. As Buber sees it, these are to be found in our sense of our potentialities:

> . . . What really matters is 'that the critical flame shoot up ever again out of the depths' and the truest source for this critical flame is 'the individual's awareness of what he 'really' is, of what in his unique and non-repeatable created existence he is intended to be'. One foundation of this definition of ethics . . . is his philosophical anthropology with its emphasis on the potentiality which only man has and on the direction which each man must take to become what only he can become. (Friedman, in Buber [10], p. 172.)

Thus any assault on our ethical capacity and its sources is also an assault on our potentialities and our discovery of ourselves.

There is thus an urgent need to protect symbolism against that abuse which corrupts the deepest sources of our sense of our potentialities. There is also a need to insist on our primary human 'inner' needs in social and political spheres. But nothing can be achieved until we have devised a new kind of conscience. This kind of conscience will need both to recognise hate and to be capable of 'incidental hate' itself in the rejection of abuse – yet be neither authoritarian nor hypomanic.

Money-Kyrle makes the valuable distinction between the authoritarian and the hypomanic conscience. We are in possession of a body of truth, he insists, 'a certain kind of wisdom', and we have it because 'we know from the records of many past analyses a good deal about the various types of unconscious belief or phantasy we are likely to meet, and experience is continually adding to the list'.

It is this kind of wisdom of human truth learnt from subjective disciplines that is embodied in that 'philosophical anthropology' which emerges from psychoanalytical work. The conscience we need (Money-Kyrle says) is itself tending to emerge from such humanist studies.

Money-Kyrle distinguishes four types of attitudes to morality (admitting that things are, however, never quite as simple as this):

> In it the first group are those who do not appear to have any morality at all. They do not consciously experience either form of guilt themselves, and regard those who claim to be influenced by moral obligations and scruples as hypocrites and weaklings. But this is because they deny their unconscious guilt, not because they do not have any to deny. They pride themselves on being super-normal; but in reality they are hypomanic, for their freedom from anxiety and depression is achieved at the cost of the capacity to understand themselves. (Klein [48], p. 434.)

At the extreme this is the position of the psychopathic murderer, who has no conscience to a terrifying extent and whose crimes are the attempt to feel guilt, to feel conscience –

and to feel real. This hypomanic attitude underlies the position of much 'enlightened' moral opinion that has, in denying problems of hate and guilt, in consequence 'forfeited the capacity to understand itself' – and therefore of generating anything genuinely creative, or morally revolutionary.

The second category is the authoritarian whose guilt is 'for export only' – those who live in a state of moral indignation with the scapegoats for their own offences. These 'believe themselves to be normal people, who indeed excel others in virtue; but they are really hypo-paranoid and live in terror of discovering the truth about themselves.'

The two remaining groups are represented by those who are self-disciplined but are living under a tyrannical super-ego; and lastly those who 'less afraid of disobedience' but who are 'distressed by any disloyalty to the values or persons who symbolise their good internal objects'. The latter are less law-abiding but 'more ready to take up arms in defence of other people's wrongs'. They have more freedom within themselves and more responsibility towards their neighbours.

The latter group, Money-Kyrle claims, represents the humanist conscience – those who surpass the other groups in the insight which, on the one hand, diminishes their irrational persecutory anxieties and, on the other, enables them to feel grief 'if they injure or abandon what they have'. The humanist conscience is based on being 'capable of feeling' on 'that kind of wisdom which consists in insight and self-knowledge' and on 'love rather than fear'.

If insight is the basis of such conscience, then it can be fostered by a truly creative culture which takes account of and provides for the whole range of being, and provides insight through subjective disciplines into human truth of the 'inner kind'. This we must foster.

The effect of much in our prevalent intellectual fashions because of their anti-human and nihilistic tendencies is to leave us feeling yet more 'isolated' and 'distressed' by disloyalty to the 'values . . . which symbolise our good internal objects'. Its influence is often to bring the efforts we have made in the search for a sense of meaning in life into contempt, and to deepen our 'existential frustration', while diverting us more and more from the pursuit of humanness. It seems urgently necessary that we should foster where we can the development of a truly humanist conscience which can bear the pain of accepting our nature, and which dares to accept the responsibility of being human.

Bibliography

BOOKS

1. ARDREY, R., *The Territorial Imperative*, Collins, 1967.
2. BALINT, M., *Primary Love and Psychoanalytical Technique*, Hogarth, 1952.
3. BANTOCK, G. H., *Education, Culture, and the Emotions*, Faber, 1968.
4. BANTOCK, G. H., *L. H. Myers – A Critical Study*, Cape, 1956.
5. BETTLEHEIM, B., *The Informed Heart*, Thames & Hudson, 1960.
6. BOWLBY, J., *Child Care and the Growth of Love*, Penguin, 1953.
7. BREWER, J., *A Dictionary of Psychology*, Penguin, 1952.
8. BRIERLEY, M., *Trends in Psychoanalysis*, Hogarth, 1951.
9. BUBER, M., *I and Thou*, Clark, Edinburgh, 1937.
10. BUBER, M., *The Philosophy of Martin Buber* (edited by Paul Arthur Schillp and Maurice Friedman), Open Court, Illinois, 1967; published in England by Cambridge University Press, 1968.
11. BUTLER, J. A. V., *The Life of The Cell*, Allen & Unwin, 1964.
12. CASSIRER, E., *An Essay on Man*, Yale University Press, 1944.
13. CHALONER, L., *Feeling and Perception in Young Children*, Tavistock, 1963.
14. COATE, M., *Beyond All Reason*, Constable, 1964.
15. COHEN, J., *Human Nature, War and Society*, Watts, 1946.
16. COOKE, D., *The Language of Music*, Oxford, 1959.
17. ERIKSON, E., *Insight and Responsibility*, Faber, 1966.
18. ERIKSON, E., *Childhood and Society*, Penguin, 1965.
19. FAIRBAIRN, W. R. D., *Psychoanalytical Studies of the Personality*, Tavistock, 1952.
20. FARBER, L. H., *The Ways of the Will*, Constable, 1966.
21. FENICHEL, O., *The Psychoanalytical Theory of Neurosis*, Kegan Paul, 1945.
22. FERENCZI, S., *First Contributions to Psychoanalysis*, Hogarth, 1952.
23. FERENCZI, S., *Further Contributions to Psychoanalysis*, Hogarth, 1926.
24. FERENCZI, S., *Final Contributions to Psychoanalysis*, Hogarth, 1955.
25. FERENCZI, S., *Thalassa: Versuch Einer Genitaltheorie, A Theory of Genitality*, Psychoanalytical Quarterly Incorporated, U.S.A., 1938.
26. FREUD, A., *The Ego and Mechanisms of Defence*, Hogarth, 1936.
27. FREUD, S., *Collected Papers*, Hogarth, 1928.
28. FREUD, S., *The Interpretation of Dreams*, Hogarth, 1953.
29. FREUD, S., *Beyond the Pleasure Principle*, Hogarth, 1920.
30. FREUD, S., *The Ego and the Id*, Hogarth, 1923.
31. FREUD, S., *Civilisation and Its Discontents*, Hogarth, 1930.
32. FREUD, S., *Outline of Psychoanalysis*, Hogarth, 1938.
33. FREUD, S., *The Origins of Psychoanalysis, Letters to Fliess*, Hogarth, 1954.
34. FREUD, S., *The Future of an Illusion*, Hogarth, 1928.
35. FROMM, E., *The Fear of Freedom*, Kegan Paul, 1942.
36. GREGORY, R. L. and WALLACE, J., *Recovery from Early Blindness*, Experimental Psychology Monograph No. 2, 1963.
37. GUNTRIP, H., *Personality Structure and Human Interaction*, Hogarth, 1961.
38. GUNTRIP, H., *Schizoid Phenomena, Object-relations, and the Self*, Hogarth, 1968.
39. HAYMAN, R., *Harold Pinter*, Heinemann, 1968.
40. HENRY, J., *Culture Against Man*, Tavistock, 1966.
41. HORNEY, K., *Our Inner Conflicts, a Constructive Theory of Neurosis*, Kegan Paul, 1946.
42. JONES, E., *Sigmund Freud, His Life and Work*, Vols. I–III, 1954, 1955, 1957.
43. KACSER, H., The Kinetic Structure of Organisms, in *Biological Organisation of the Cellular and Supercellular level* (ed. R. J. C. Harris), Academic Press, 1963.

44. KIERKEGAARD, S., *The Journals of S. Kierkegaard* (edited and translated by Alexander Dru), Oxford, 1938.
45. KLEIN, M., *The Psychoanalysis of Children*, Hogarth, 1932.
46. KLEIN, M., *Contributions to Psychoanalysis*, Hogarth, 1948.
47. KLEIN, M., *Developments in Psychoanalysis*, Hogarth, 1952.
48. KLEIN, M., *New Directions in Psychoanalysis*, Tavistock, 1955.
49. KLEIN, M., *Envy and Gratitude*, Tavistock, 1957.
50. KLEIN, M., *Our Adult Society and its Roots in Infancy*, Tavistock 1963.
51. KLEIN, M. with RIVIÈRE, J., *Love, Hate and Reparation*, Hogarth, 1938.
52. LAING, R. D., *The Divided Self*, Tavistock, 1960.
53. LAING, R. D., *The Politics of Experience*, Penguin, 1967.
54. LAING, R. D. with ESTERSON, *Sanity, Madness and the Family*, Tavistock, 1964.
55. LANGER, S., *Philosophy in a New Key*, Harvard, 1942.
56. LEVY, D. M., *Maternal Overprotection*, Columbia, 1943.
57. LOMAS, P. (ed.), *The Predicament of the Family*, Hogarth, 1967.
58. LOMAS, P. Psychoanalysis – Freudian or Existential?, in *Psychoanalysis Observed* [ed. C. Rycroft] Constable, 1966.
59. LOVELL, Sir BERNARD, *Our Present Knowledge of the Universe*, Manchester, 1966.
60. MAY, ROLLO, *Existence – a New Dimension in Psychiatry*, New York, 1960. Also *Love and Will*, Souvenir, 1970.
61. MIDDLEMORE, M. P. *The Nursing Couple*, Hamish Hamilton, 1941.
62. MILNER, M., *On Not Being Able to Paint*, Heinemann, 1950.
63. MURDOCH, I., *Sartre*, Bowes & Bowes, 1953.
64. MONEY-KYRLE, R. E., *Man's Picture of His World*, Duckworth, 1961.
65. MONEY-KYRLE, R. E., Psychoanalysis and Philosophy, in *Psychoanalysis and Contemporary Thought* (ed. J. D. Sutherland), Hogarth, 1958.
66. MORRIS, D., *The Naked Ape*, Cape, 1967.
67. NIBLETT, W. R., *Moral Education in a Changing Society*, Faber, 1963.
68. PICKEN, L. E. R., Molecular Biology and the Future of Zoology, in *The Cell and the Organism*, Ramsey & Wigglesworth, Cambridge, 1961.
69. PUMPHREY, R. J., Concerning Vision, in *The Cell and the Organism* (ed. Ramsey & Wigglesworth), Cambridge, 1961.
70. RAMSAY, I. T., *Biology and Personality*, Oxford, 1966.
71. ROUBICZEK, P., *Existentialism*, Cambridge, 1964.
72. RYCROFT, C., *Psychoanalysis Observed*, Constable, 1966.
73. SARTRE, J.-P., Existentialism is a Humanism, in *Existentialism* (ed. W. Kaufmann), Meridian, 1956.
74. SARTRE, J.-P., *What is Literature?*, Paris, 1964
75. SEGAL, H., *Introduction to the Work of Melanie Klein*, Tavistock, 1964.
76. STORR, A., *Human Aggression*, Penguin, 1968.
77. SUTHERLAND, J. D., *Psychoanalysis and Contemporary Thought*, Hogarth, 1958.
78. SUTTIE, I. D., *The Origins of Love and Hate*, Penguin, 1960.
79. TAWNEY, R. H., *The Acquisitive Society*, Fontana Books, 1921.
80. TEILHARD DE CHARDIN, P., *The Phenomenon of Man*, Collins, 1959.
81. THOULESS, R. H., *General and Social Psychology*, University Tutorial Press, 1935.
82. TILLICH, P., *The Courage to Be*, Nisbet, 1952.
83. TOWERS, B. and LEWIS, J., *Naked Ape or Homo Sapiens?*, Garnstone Press, 1969.
84. TRILLING, L., *The Liberal Imagination*.
85. WARREN, J. W., *The Teaching of Physics*, Butterworths, 1965.
86. WARNOCK, M., *Existentialist Ethics*, Macmillan, 1967.
87. WELLS, G. P. How Lugworms Move, in *The Cell and the Organism* (ed. I. T. Ramsey), 2 Vols., 1969.
88. WESTMAN, H. *The Springs of Creativity*, Kegan Paul, 1961.
89. WILLIAMS, R., *Communications*, Chatto & Windus, 1950.
90. WINNICOTT, D. W., *Collected Papers, Through Paediatrics to Psychoanalysis*, Tavistock, 1958.
91. WINNICOTT, D. W., *The Child and the Outside World*, Tavistock, 1957.
92. WINNICOTT, D. W., *The Child and the Family*, Tavistock, 1957.
93. WINNICOTT, D. W., *The Family and Individual Development*, Tavistock, 1965.
94. WINNICOTT, D. W., *The Maturational Processes and the Facilitating Environment*, Hogarth, 1966.
95. WINNICOTT, D. W., *The Child, the Family, and the Outside World*, Penguin, 1964.
96. WINNICOTT, D. W., Mirror Role of Mother and Family, in *The Predicament of the Family* (ed. Lomas), Hogarth, 1967.
97. WISDOM, J., *Philosophy and Psychoanalysis*, Oxford, 1957.
98. ZILBOORG, G., *The Psychology of the Criminal Act and Punishment*, Hogarth, 1955.

PAPERS

99. BALINT, M., Pleasure, Object and Libido: Some Reflections on Fairbairn's Modifications of Psycho-analytical Theory, *British Journal of Medical Psychology* **29** (2), 162–7 (1956).
100. BALINT, M., Criticism of Fairbairn's Generalization about Object-relations, *British Journal of the Philosophy of Science* **7** (28), 323 (1957).
101. BUBER, M., Distance and Relation, *Psychiatry (USA)* **20** (97–104) 102 (1957).
102. BUBER, M., Theory of Knowledge, *Review of Metaphysics, London*, 1954.
103. ERIKSON, E., Identity and the Life Cycle, *Psychological Issues*, vol. 1, no. 1, monograph 1, New York, International University Press.
104. FAIRBAIRN, W. R. D., Prolegomena to a Psychology of Art, *British Journal of Psychology* (General Section) **28** (3) (1938).
105. FAIRBAIRN, W. R. D., The Ultimate Basis of Aesthetic Experience, *British Journal of Psychology* (General Section) **29** (2) (1938).
106. FAIRBAIRN, W. R. D., Observations on the Nature of Hysterical States, *British Journal of Medical Psychology*, **27** (3) (1959).
107. FAIRBAIRN, W. R. D., Observations in Defence of the Object-relations Theory of the Personality, *British Journal of Medical Psychology* **28** (2 and 3), 144–56 (1955).
108. FAIRBAIRN, W. R. D., On the Nature and Aims of Psychoanalytical Treatment, *International Journal of Psychoanalysis* **29** (5), 374–85 (1958).
109. FARRELL, B. A., The Logic of Existential Psychoanalysis, *New Society*, 21 October 1965, p. 9.
110. GUNTRIP, H., A Study of Fairbairn's Theory of Schizoid Reactions, *British Journal of Medical Psychology*, **25** (2 and 3), 36–103 (1952).
111. GUNTRIP, H., Recent Developments in Psychoanalytical Theory, *British Journal of Medical Psychology* **29** (2), 82–99 (1956).
112. GUNTRIP, H., Ego-weakness and the Hard Core of the Problem of Psychotherapy, *British Journal of Medical Psychology* **33** (3), 163–84 (1960).
113. GUNTRIP, H., Review of *Introduction to the Work of Melanie Klein* by Hannah Segal, *British Journal of Medical Psychology*, 0000 .
114. GUNTRIP, H., The Schizoid Compromise and Psychotherapeutic Stalemate, *British Journal of Medical Psychology* **35**, 273 ff. (1962).
115. GUNTRIP, H., Psychodynamic Theory and the problem of Psychotherapy, *British Journal of Medical Psychology* **36**, 161 (1963).
116. GUNTRIP, H., The Manic-depressive Problem in the Light of the Schizoid Process', *International Journal of Psychoanalysis* **43**, 98 ff. (1962).
117. HARTMANN, K. and LOEWENSTEIN, Comments on the Formation of Psychic Structure, *The Psycho-analytic Study of the Child*, vol. 2, Hogarth, 1946.
118. HOME, H. J., The Concept of Mind, paper read to the British Psychoanalytical Society, 15 April 1964; discussed in C. Rycroft (see Ref. 72).
119. HUNTER D., Analysis of a Fetishist, *International Journal of Psychoanalysis* **35**, 303.
120. ROUBICZEK, P., Søren Kierkegaard, in 'Makers of Modern Theology' series, *The Times*, May 1968.
121. SEGAL, H., Notes on Symbol Formation, *International Journal of Psychoanalysis* **38**, 391.
122. SHARPE, E., An Examination of Metaphor, 1944, in *Collected Papers on Psychoanalysis*, 1950.
123. SOLOMON, J. C., Alice and the Red King: A Psychoanalytical View of Existence, *International Journal of Psychoanalysis*, 196?.
124. SZASZ, T. S., On the Theory of Psycho-analytical Treatment, *International Journal of Psychoanalysis* **38** (3 and 4), 166–82 (1957).
125. SZASZ, T. S., On the Psychoanalytical Theory of Instincts, Summary in the *International Journal of Psychoanalysis*,
126. TAYLOR, L., Monkeys and their Mothers, in *Parents in Playgroups*, 1968.
127. WINNICOTT, D. W. and CLAIR, Homeless Children, *Journal of Human Relations*, **50**, 84, (1947).
128. WINNICOTT, D. W., The Split-off Male and Female Elements to be Found Clinically in Men and Women: *Theoretical Inferences* (not yet published).
129. WINNICOTT, D. W. with KAHN, M., Review of Fairbairn, *International Journal of Psychoanalysis* **34** (4), 329 (1953).
130. WINNICOTT, D. W., The Location of Culture, *International Journal of Psychoanalysis*, **48**, 368 (1966).
131. WISDOM, J. O., *The Unconscious Origins of Berkeley's Philosophy*, Tavistock Press.

Index